Pacifism, Just War, and Tyrannicide

Pacifism, Just War, and Tyrannicide
Bonhoeffer's Church-World Theology and His Changing Forms of Political Thinking and Involvement

DAVID M. GIDES

◆PICKWICK *Publications* • Eugene, Oregon

PACIFISM, JUST WAR, AND TYRANNICIDE
Bonhoeffer's Church-World Theology and His Changing Forms
of Political Thinking and Involvement

Copyright © 2011 David M. Gides. All rights reserved. Except for brief quotations in critical publications or reviews, no part of this book may be reproduced in any manner without prior written permission from the publisher. Write: Permissions, Wipf and Stock Publishers, 199 W. 8th Ave., Suite 3, Eugene, OR 97401.

Pickwick Publications
An Imprint of Wipf and Stock Publishers
199 W. 8th Ave., Suite 3
Eugene, OR 97401

www.wipfandstock.com

ISBN 13: 978-1-60608-702-2

Cataloguing-in-Publication data:

Gides, David M.

    Pacifism, just war, and tyrannicide : Bonhoeffer's church-world theology and his changing forms of political thinking and involvement / David M. Gides.

    xviii + 404 pp. ; 23 cm. Includes bibliographical references and index.

    ISBN 13: 978-1-60608-702-2

    1. Bonhoeffer, Dietrich, 1906–1945. 2. Christian ethics. 3. Anti-Nazi movement—Germany. 4. Germany—Church history—1933–1945. I. Title.

BX4827 B57 G46 2011

Manufactured in the U.S.A.

To
Jacinda Thedders Townsend
Rhianna Folasade Gides
Fadzai Iman Gides
MaryAnn Gides
Robert T. Cornelison

Contents

Preface / ix
Abbreviations / xv

1. Introduction / 1
2. Bonhoeffer's Early Life: His Theological, Political, Ecclesial, and Family Contexts / 41
3. Phase 1: Church and World in Mild Tension / 76
4. Phase 2: Church and World in Heightened Tension / 137
5. Phase 3: Church against or apart from World / 208
6. Phase 4: Church as World / 280
7. Conclusion / 341

Bibliography / 377
Index / 389

Preface

THIS BOOK, LIKE MANY other dissertations I would imagine, is born out of curiosity, the desire to study a troubling phenomenon, and a degree of dissatisfaction with approaches and answers available in existing scholarship. Some facets of the "phenomenon" are "troubling" for obvious reasons. That is, no further exploration is necessary to show or explain why they disturb. The merciless, irrational, and unjustified slaughter of millions of Jewish persons, the elderly, and others is one such component. The mostly unchecked drive for absolute power resulting in inevitable worldwide warfare, seemingly aided and abetted by other nations and their leaders at points, is another such component. Finally, we might wonder how or why the vast majority of German citizens offered their robot-like albeit enthusiastic support for Hitler and his project. Yet, one need not look too far to find many legitimate and convincing scholarly answers to these problematic features of German socio-political history during Hitler's rise and the Nazi regime.[1]

Other components or questions may not be so glaring or prominent in the popular imagination. This is the case most likely because they do not put on display the macabre theater of brutal weaponry, gory warfare, shady public international politics, and the gross machinery of mass execution and death. They are nonetheless arguably a bit more upsetting than the ones listed above. We might wonder, for example, how it is that the vast majority of church persons and organized churches fell under Hitler's spell (there was some notable church resistance but not widespread and obviously not very effective politically or religiously). Here, the disturbing part is not so much that church members fell in line with Nazi ideology. After all, all of these churches were made up of a German citizenry who basically supported Hitler. Rather, the troubling part is how readily, easily, and smoothly Christianity and Nazism mixed for church leadership; a church leadership who often relied on

1. See, for example, Gellately, *Backing Hitler*.

the overtly nationalistic War Theology of Germany's most famed and celebrated theologians. Yet, and like the first set of questions, scholars can fairly easily locate the historical roots of War Theology and have provided innumerable convincing answers as to why church leadership and church members followed Hitler.[2]

What is really the most "troubling" part of the Hitler "phenomenon" is even more chilling than any of the above; it strikes much deeper and at the very heart of Christianity, Christian doctrine, Christian theology, or Christian behavior. Namely, the Hitler phenomenon and the churches' response actually call into question the continued viability of Christianity itself. That is, what good is the Christian enterprise at all if it cannot offer any adequate resistance to that degree of evil? One might also wonder, with an even greater sense of horror, if there is something intrinsically deficient about, or wrong with, the entire Christian enterprise if there is anything about it that makes it either actually or potentially amenable to the gruesome whims of vicious dictators and their regimes.

Robert P. Ericksen's *Theologians under Hitler: Gerhard Kittel, Paul Althaus and Emanuel Hirsch* captures well why the phenomenon unsettles. It is true that there were a small number of radical Nazi-supporting theologians who can be easily dismissed as extremists. However, Ericksen deftly shows how mainstream theologians such as Kittel, Althaus, and Hirsch were "well-meaning, intelligent and respectable individuals" who nonetheless supported Hitler. They also had "intellectually defensible" rationales for their political positions. He also argues that the differences between their political positions and those of people like Barth, Tillich, and Bonhoeffer are not attributable to "superior or inferior intelligence or insight."[3]

Ericksen's conclusions shock. They shock because we want to hear that all Nazi-supporting theologians (not just the radicals) were insane extremists who were not well informed and not well meaning. We want to hear that important theologians like Kittel, Althaus, and Hirsch could find no support for their positions anywhere in Christian theology or in any other facet of Christianity. We want to hear that Kittel, Althaus, and Hirsch's political positions rested on faulty logic. We want to hear that

---

2. See Bergen *Twisted Cross*; or Ericksen and Heschel, *Betrayal*, as two examples.
3. Ericksen, *Theologians Under Hitler*, 26.

Barth, Bonhoeffer, and Tillich's political positions rested on stronger and more rational foundations.

We do not hear these things. Instead, what we hear draws us into a process of elimination in the blame game leading to an undesirable conclusion. It was not the leading theologians in Germany for Ericksen assures us that they were well-meaning and legitimate theologians. He even tells us that their political positions were rationally defensible. In addition, earlier in his first chapter Ericksen discounts the relationship between the theologies of the resisting theologians and their resistance stances mostly by reminding us that some of the Nazi-supporting theologians would have agreed with their theologies. For example, Ericksen notes that Bonhoeffer's predominant stance, that "no ethical questions are really complex, for each is answered simply by listening for direction from Christ," would be something "that all Christians would endorse."[4] In addition, Ericksen explodes the notion that dialectical and Christocentric theologians like Barth and Bonhoeffer might be immune to the draw of Nazism by pointing out three things. First, some dialectical theologians supported Hitler. Second, some resisters would agree with the Nazi-supporting theologians that God favors some "historical moments and political systems" over others. Finally, many pro-Nazi theologians "carefully defended their Christocentric concern and their respect for the true Christian values."[5] So presumably we cannot blame the bad theology of the Nazi-supporting theologians, as we are assured that there are significant points of continuity or agreement between them and the Nazi-rejecters. With nothing left to blame, we are left with the horrible impression that there might be something about Christianity itself that we can point to as the source of the problem.

Ericksen's concluding chapter articulates more clearly the scary implications of his look into the Nazi phenomenon and the churches. He writes,

> The role of Christianity in history is also called into question by this study. These three theologians saw themselves and were seen by others as genuine Christians acting upon Christian impulses. Even in retrospect a Christian basis for each of their individual positions can be discerned; Christianity has strains which are both anti-Jewish and anti-Modern. In light of the German ex-

4. Ibid., 25.
5. Ibid.

perience, a Christian which stresses these strains, in which, for example, the love of Christ cannot be readily perceived, should arouse our suspicion . . . A second warning in the German church experience lies in the failure to distinguish adequately between Christian values and German values, between inherently Christian concerns and patriotic concerns. Finally, there is a question of whether Christianity can face the modern world, the 'world come of age,' without turning to protection to an Adolf Hitler. That is the ironic position in which Kittel, Althaus and Hirsch found themselves, and they were not alone.[6]

All of Ericksen's insights are related to this current study in one way or another. There are two that are especially important and relevant to this current study; one explicit and one implicit. Moreover, in light of the results of my study, these two insights strongly suggest that Bonhoeffer was undoubtedly the most important of the resisters. In terms of the explicit insight, Ericksen wonders whether Christianity can face the "world come of age." I argue that there is a direct relationship between Bonhoeffer's church-world theology and his political activities. In the last years of his life Bonhoeffer coins the "world come of age" phrase while actively planning to kill Hitler. Bonhoeffer thus provides a resounding yes to Ericksen's question about Christianity's ability to face the modern world without relying on a dictator like Hitler. Ericksen's implicit insight concerns the relationship between Christian theology and the ability to resist political tyranny. My study shows a Bonhoeffer whose church-world theology can provide the ammunition for resisting or killing a tyrant.

The other impetus for this study involves a dissatisfying facet of existing Bonhoeffer scholarship. The contribution of those who study and write about Bonhoeffer is, of course, impressive and invaluable and all current Bonhoeffer scholars truly stand on the shoulders of giants. So what follows here is not meant to disparage the entirety of any particular Bonhoeffer project. Rather, my dissatisfaction concerns the all too apparent tendency in approaches to Bonhoeffer's forms of political involvement which is really just a manifestation of what I see as a larger difficulty with Bonhoeffer studies in general. Namely, many who write on Bonhoeffer often use original quotes from differing writings of vastly differing genres and from different times in his career to defend or sup-

---

6. Ibid., 199.

port whatever argument they may be making. So for example, a scholar might quote or reference Bonhoeffer from both 1929 and his *Ethics* in the very same paragraph to support an argument about his thinking on church-state relations, and not an argument about continuities or discontinuity. In other words, some scholars pretend like these different works were written at the very same time and thereby entirely ignore any sense of difference that may exist between them or, maybe more importantly, questions about how the conditions under which they were written help to account for any differences.

Using quotes from different points in his career is appropriate when the express and very clearly stated aim is to consider either how Bonhoeffer's earlier ideas or works lay the foundation for later ones or how the later ones significantly diverge from earlier ones. There are several scholarly articles that make these types of arguments about developments in various facets of Bonhoeffer's career. Yet, if that aim is not stated clearly, then the uncritical use of Bonhoeffer quotes from different phases in his career seems irresponsible. Moreover, this way of using original texts is particularly problematic when applied to the specific issue of examining Bonhoeffer's changing political activity and especially if one posits a direct or positive relationship between theological category and form of political action (thought and life). For example, if one was to hold the 1929 and the 1941 Bonhoeffer as the same on the church-state relations, then one would have to hold that the possibility for tyrannicide existed at that early date. This proposition is patently unacceptable.

This current work intends to directly combat any tendency to quote Bonhoeffer out of context. My aim is to show how Bonhoeffer's thinking on the church-world relationship and his actual actions in the political sphere are mutually conditioning with respect only to the multi-dimensional contexts in which this drama played out at each significant juncture in his life. By not placing Bonhoeffer quotes from vastly different points in his career side by side (and by my singular concentration on what those quotes mean solely within their own multi-faceted contexts), I actually allow for a more responsible analysis of what any difference between them might mean for understanding Bonhoeffer's development. That is, once all of the parts of Bonhoeffer's writings relevant for examining his church-world and political thinking are examined in terms of the contexts in which they were produced, we stand in a more favorable position to judge how earlier works and later works are related to each other.

Finally, a project of this scope would not have been possible without various forms of support from several parties. I am indebted first and foremost to those at Fordham University who patiently helped me shape my thinking and writing into a form that allowed me to ask and offer an answer to the difficult questions surrounding Bonhoeffer's political behavior: Dr. Elizabeth A. Johnson, CSJ; Dr. Leo D. Lefebure; Dr. Daniel P. Thompson; and the late Dr. Robert T. Cornelison. Dr. Cornelison was instrumental in awakening an interest in the development of contemporary Protestant theology and ultimately in Bonhoeffer. I owe a special thanks to Dr. Thompson, who took over for Dr. Cornelison as my dissertation mentor upon his untimely passing. Thanks, too, to Father Mark S. Massa, SJ, PhD; and Dr. Christophe Chalamet for serving as respondents at my dissertation defense. The library staffs at various institutions that helped me get materials also deserve a thank you. I have also presented parts of this book at national and regional conferences in the American Academy of Religion and other places. So I thank those who responded to these papers and offered helpful feedback, especially those members of the International Bonhoeffer Society. Thanks also to Terry Feye and Vicky Maloy for helping me prepare the manuscript.

There are a few more acknowledgements of a more personal nature. Many of my colleagues throughout the years have been helpful in responding to my ideas for this book. I also thank Jacinda T. Townsend for graciously and valiantly allowing me the time to work. Finally, I would like to thank my two beautiful and precious daughters, Rhianna Folasade and Fadzai Iman, who teach me what love means.

Abbreviations[1]

PRIMARY LITERATURE
(WORKS BY DIETRICH BONHOEFFER)

AB   *Act and Being: Transcendental Philosophy and Ontology in Systematic Theology.* Edited by Hans-Richard Reuter. Translated by H. Martin Rumscheidt. Dietrich Bonhoeffer Works 2. Minneapolis: Fortress, 1996.

DBW   *Dietrich Bonhoeffer Werke*, Volumes 1–17. Munich: Kaiser, 1986–1999.

DBWE-6   *Ethics.* Edited by Clifford J. Green. Translated by Reinhard Krauss et al. Dietrich Bonhoeffer Works 6. Minneapolis: Fortress Press, 2005.

DBWE-8   *Letters and Papers from Prison.* Edited by John W. de Gruchy. Translated by Isabel Best et al. Dietrich Bonhoeffer Works 8. Minneapolis: Fortress, 2009.

DBWE-9   *The Young Bonhoeffer: 1918–1927.* Edited by Clifford J. Green. Translated by Mary C. Nebelsick and Douglas W. Stott. Dietrich Bonhoeffer Works 9. Minneapolis: Fortress, 2003.

DBWE-10   *Barcelona, Berlin, New York: 1928–1931.* Edited by Clifford J. Green. Translated by Douglas W. Stott. Dietrich Bonhoeffer Works 10. Minneapolis: Fortress, 2008.

DBWE-12   *Berlin: 1932–1933.* Edited by Larry L. Rasmussen. Translated by Isabel Best and David Higgins.

---

1. These abbreviations have been used in the footnotes.

	Dietrich Bonhoeffer Works 12. Minneapolis: Fortress 2009.
DBWE-13	*London: 1933–1935*. Edited by Keith Clements. Translated by Isabel Best. Dietrich Bonhoeffer Works 13. Minneapolis: Fortress, 2007.
DBWE-16	*Conspiracy and Imprisonment: 1940–1945*. Edited by Mark. S. Brocker. Translated by Lisa E. Dahill. Dietrich Bonhoeffer Works 16. Minneapolis: Fortress, 2006.
LPP	*Letters and Papers from Prison*. Edited by Eberhard Bethge. New York: Macmillan, 1972.
NRS	*No Rusty Swords: Letters, Lectures and Notes 1928–1936*. Edited by Edwin H. Robertson. Translated by Edwin H. Robertson and John Bowden. New York: Harper & Row, 1965.
SC-E	*Sanctorum Communio: A Theological Study of the Sociology of the Church*. Edited by Joachim von Soosten. Translated by Reinhard Krauss and Nancy Lukens. Dietrich Bonhoeffer Works 1. Minneapolis: Fortress, 1996.
TF	*A Testament to Freedom: The Essential Writings of Dietrich Bonhoeffer*. Rev. ed. Edited by Geffrey B. Kelly and F. Burton Nelson. San Francisco: HarperSanFrancisco, 1995.

SECONDARY LITERATURE

ADOB	Hopper, David. *A Dissent on Bonhoeffer*. Philadelphia: Westminster, 1975.
ATS	Green, Clifford J. *Bonhoeffer: A Theology of Sociality*. Rev. ed. Grand Rapids: Eerdmans, 1999.
CCUH	Cochrane, Arthur C. *The Church's Confession under Hitler*. Philadelphia: Westminster, 1962.

DB	Bethge, Eberhard. *Dietrich Bonhoeffer: A Biography*. Revised and edited by Victoria J. Barnett. Minneapolis: Fortress, 2000.
HNG	Spielvogel, Jackson J. *Hitler and Nazi Germany: A History*. 2nd ed. Engelwood Cliffs, NJ: Prentice Hall, 1992.
NPC	Conway, J. S. *The Nazi Persecution of the Churches: 1933–45*. New York: Basic, 1968.
RR	*Dietrich Bonhoeffer: Reality and Resistance*. Studies in Christian Ethics. Nashville: Abingdon, 1972.

1

Introduction

INTRODUCTION TO THE PROBLEM

DIETRICH BONHOEFFER CLAIMED TO be a pacifist relatively early in his writing and ministerial career.¹ Even after years of active resistance to Hitler's regime (steadily progressing in intensity from 1933 to 1943), Bonhoeffer designated himself a pacifist as late as 1939.² Around that very time his resistance activity, which had primarily consisted of preaching against Hitler, helping in the formation of a Confessing church and heading up a clandestine seminary to provide leaders for that church, took the form of participation in an organization of conspirators against Hitler.³ His actions as part of this group initially con-

---

1. Eberhard Bethge, *Dietrich Bonhoeffer: A Biography*, 204. (Hereafter abbreviated as *DB*). Bonhoeffer, in a January 27, 1936, letter from Finkenwalde to a female friend, referring to his change of mind following upon "the crisis of 1933," writes, "I suddenly saw the Christian pacifism that I had recently passionately opposed as self-evident."

2. Rasmussen, *Dietrich Bonhoeffer: Reality and Resistance*, 58. (Hereafter abbreviated as *RR*). On March 13, 1968, Larry Rasmussen conducted an interview with Paul Lehmann, Bonhoeffer's close Union Theological Seminary friend from his first trip to America in 1930–31. According to Rasmussen, in 1939, during Bonhoeffer's second visit to America, Lehmann and Bonhoeffer were discussing Hermann Rausching's *The Revolution of Nihilism: Warning to the West*. Bonhoeffer's statement that the book "actually confirmed his pacifism" leads Rasmussen to state, "Bonhoeffer was a self-proclaimed pacifist as late as mid-1939."

3. *DB*. Various sermons and teachings with either implicit or explicit critiques of Hitler are described between pp. 222 and 417. The most notable are the mysteriously cut-off March 1, 1933, radio address on "The Younger Generation's Altered View of the Concept of *Führer*" (259–60), his essay on the nature and theological dangers of the Aryan Clauses, "Die Kirche vor der Judenfrage" (263–76) and his contribution to the Barmen Declaration (366–72). See pp. 419–586 for an extensive account of Bonhoeffer's

sisted of making international contacts and discussing arrangements for negotiating with a post-Hitler Germany.[4] In 1940, however, the group decided an assassination attempt would best serve the German church and German people. Bonhoeffer was not directly involved in the attempted act of violence. He did, however, support this particular form of political involvement.[5] Bonhoeffer was arrested and imprisoned for his *Abwehr* activities on April 5, 1943.[6] He was tried and sentenced to death at the infamous Flossenbürg concentration camp on April 8, 1945. The 39 year old Dietrich Bonhoeffer was hanged there the following day.[7]

Bonhoeffer's actions raise a significant question for both his academic and non-academic admirers. He was a theologian and churchman self-admittedly committed to peace in his middle writings. Bonhoeffer made strong statements about his peace positions in 1931[8] and 1932.[9] He made perhaps his most notable peace statement at the 1934 Universal Christian Council for Life and Work at Fanø, Denmark.[10] Bonhoeffer also planned trips to India to meet Gandhi.[11] Finally, his

work in the seminaries. See pp. 620–797 for an extensive treatment of Bonhoeffer's conspiratorial activities.

4. *DB*, 681–799.

5. *DB*, 722–24; 755. See also Dramm, *Dietrich Bonhoeffer and the Resistance*.

6. *DB*, 780–85.

7. *DB*, 921–33.

8. Robertson, *The Shame and the Sacrifice*, 66. Robertson writes of Bonhoeffer and his pacifist friend Jean Lasserre's Mexico trip in the summer of 1931, "What Jean Lasserre remembered most about the Mexican visit was the platform he and Dietrich shared with a Quaker called Herberto. It was a peace meeting and the audience of several hundred were impressed by the German and the Frenchman, both speaking earnestly about the Christian's responsibility to work for peace. It served to reinforce Herberto's witness for peace. Bonhoeffer spoke forcefully and, according to Jean Lasserre, the convinced pacifist, made a statement stronger than his own."

9. *DB*, 210. At the World Alliance Youth conference on peace at Ciernohorské Kúpele in July 1932 Bonhoeffer said, "the next war must be outlawed not from the fanatical imposition of one commandment—the sixth for instance—but from obedience towards the commandment of God which is directed towards us today, namely that there shall be no more war, because it prevents us from seeing revelation. Nor shall we be afraid of the world pacifism today."

10. *DB*, 372–92. Bethge explains: "never before had he stated so decisively that, for the disciple, the renunciation of force meant the renunciation of defense" (388). See also, *RR*, 103. Rasmussen refers to his position at Fanø as "Bonhoeffer's most unqualifiedly pacifist one. He is very close to absolute pacifism."

11. *DB*, 409. Bonhoeffer had a sustained interest in visiting India beginning in 1928. His interest in 1928 was motivated by desire for "a wider experience of the world." His

1937 *Discipleship* has been described "as pure a pacifist statement as one can find anywhere in theological literature."¹² How could a theologian and churchman so clearly committed to peace involve himself in a plot to assassinate his German leader?

In their approaches to these seemingly contradictory forms of political thinking and involvement some scholars focus on an intriguing April 11, 1944, Bonhoeffer letter from Tegel prison. Part of the letter reads, "Nor have I ever regretted my decision in the summer of 1939, for I am firmly convinced—however strange it may seem—that my life has followed a straight and unbroken course, at any rate in its outward conduct."¹³ For these scholars, the full articulation of the problem reads: how can one reconcile Bonhoeffer's move from admitted pacifism to tyrannicide with his own "straight and unbroken course" continuity claim? They have thus, in effect, made the changing forms of political involvement a Bonhoeffer versus Bonhoeffer enterprise. Scholars can successfully defend Bonhoeffer against himself if he either never was a pacifist or the type of pacifist where tyrannicide is acceptable in extreme cases. If, however, he was an absolute pacifist, for whom tyrannicide is

---

1931 desire was motivated by "his skepticism about the western form of Christianity." His 1934 desire, however, "was motivated by the desire to witness Gandhi's exemplification of the Sermon on the Mount—in the spiritual exercises aimed toward a certain goal, and the Indian ways of resistance against tyrannical power." Bonhoeffer devised a study project and even procured an invitation from Gandhi for a 1935 trip to India. Reinhold Niebuhr discouraged Bonhoeffer from going on the journey but he was not dissuaded. The plans never materialized. See also *RR*, "Appendix A: Bonhoeffer, Gandhi, Resistance," 213–17, for further discussion of Bonhoeffer's interest in Gandhi and India.

12. Brown, "Bonhoeffer and Pacifism," 32–43. Brown's full quote reads, "most pacifist interpreters see little reason to qualify Bonhoeffer's pacifism of the thirties. I have talked to many who regard *The Cost of Discipleship* to be as pure a pacifist statement as one can find anywhere in theological literature" (39).

13. Bonhoeffer, *Letters and Papers from Prison: The Enlarged Edition*, 272. (Hereafter abbreviated as *LPP*). It is clear from pp. 653–62 in Bethge's *Biography* and from a footnote in the text itself that the "decision" refers to the decision to return back to Germany from America in June of 1939—not explicitly the decision to enter the conspiracy. (The footnote on p. 363 reads, "To return home from the USA.") Scholars, however, seem to use this quote as if the "decision" refers to the decision for tyrannicide. Regardless, in April of 1944 Bonhoeffer does assert a continuity while reflecting on his whole life, thus including the move from admitted pacifism to tyrannicide See also the newer translation, *Letters and Papers from Prison, DBWE-8*, 352. The footnote in the new English edition also indicates that the "decision" refers to the decision to return to Germany from the United States. But "Outward conduct" reads "how I led it," thus making it a bit more general. This text will be abbreviated as *DBWE-8*.

never acceptable, then Bonhoeffer clearly did not understand himself or the course of his life correctly.

While acknowledging both that Bonhoeffer's move from admitted pacifism to tyrannicide is an important shift and that the "straight and unbroken course" continuity claim stands as an important instance of a particular type of data, this project presupposes or holds that: 1) his move from admitted pacifism to tyrannicide is striking enough to be worthy of in-depth scholarly analysis with or without the "straight and unbroken course" continuity claim; 2) this most famous move is one of two other extremely significant shifts; 3) there is a way of framing the problem, organizing the sources, and, finally, providing a plausible explanation for Bonhoeffer's changes, which relies on all existing forms of data (Bonhoeffer's letters, his theological literature and even secondary sources as well as any explicit statements about self-understanding); and 4) this other way of both stating and solving the problem can arguably approach an accurate vision of Bonhoeffer's self-understanding. I will look at the changing forms of political involvement in terms of their relationship with an illuminating theological category throughout the various phases of Bonhoeffer's career. My approach shifts the perspective primarily from Bonhoeffer's self-understanding (and judging his actions against his self-understanding) to a broader-based perspective that attempts to embrace all kinds of data, explain all significant shifts in Bonhoeffer's forms of political thinking and involvement and solve certain problems that other approaches present.[14] Ultimately, my articulation of the problem reads simply, "what is the most comprehensive and effective way to approach and explain all of Bonhoeffer's changes in forms of political thinking and involvement?"

My answer to this question forms the thesis of this study in four interrelated arguments or parts: 1) a look at Bonhoeffer's theology throughout his entire life reveals four distinct understandings of the church-world relationship in four distinct phases of his career;[15]

14. I will, though, address Bonhoeffer's "straight and unbroken course" continuity claim sometimes explicitly, and most times implicitly, throughout the work as it is an important piece of data and in some ways overlaps with my concern with Bonhoeffer's changing forms of political involvement. Moreover, I will treat more extensively and explicitly in my final chapter the merits of my way of approaching the problem relative to the shortcomings of focusing on the claim in the particular ways that some scholars have.

15. A three-part division of Bonhoeffer's life and work is not unprecedented. A four-part division is unique. Bethge's *Biography*, for example, is subtitled *Theologian*,

Introduction 5

2) Bonhoeffer's thinking on the church-world relationship is a consistent indicator of his forms of political thinking and involvement in each of these four phases in his career. That is, Bonhoeffer's thinking is "consistently consistent" with his actions and vice versa in each of the four phases; 3) his response to life circumstances manifests in discontinuities in his understanding of the church-world relationship as these phases progress and, therefore, corresponding discontinuities in his forms of political involvement (or, his response to life circumstances manifests in discontinuities in his forms of political involvement as these phases progress and, therefore, corresponding discontinuities in his understanding of the church-world relationship); and 4) my way of approaching and offering a solution to the problem using the church-world relationship both maximizes the benefits of certain existing approaches and minimizes their weaknesses, thus maximizing its own effectiveness as a framework for interpreting Bonhoeffer's shifting forms of political involvement.

The resulting vision, while emphasizing discontinuity in four distinct phases of Bonhoeffer's life, respects and preserves the integrity of each of his varied positions and therefore the sometimes drastic differences in his forms of political involvement and his church-world thinking from one phase to the next. For example, with this method there is no reason or need to temper or mitigate the intensity of his commitment to some variety of pacifism during his Fanø and *Discipleship* phase and seminary work. Moreover, there is no reason or need to qualify or question his self-assured sense of mission during his commitment to tyrannicide. Ultimately, exposing the discontinuities in the church-world/

Christian, Contemporary. David Hopper argues that these three titles, "represent progressive stages in Bonhoeffer's life" (*A Dissent on Bonhoeffer*, 30. (Hereafter this title will be abbreviated as *ADOB*). Bethge himself, in his essay, "The Challenge of Dietrich Bonhoeffer's Life and Theology," in *World Come of Age*, 22–92, explicitly breaks Bonhoeffer's life and work into three stages: "Foundations" (1927–33), "Concentration" (1933–40) and "Liberation" (1940–45). He writes, "Theologically, these same periods might be called the dogmatic, the exegetical, and the ethical; or, again, the theoretical period in which he learned and taught at Berlin University, the pastoral period in which he served the Confessing Church in a preachers' seminary, and the political period in which his life first became ambiguous," 25. See also, John Godsey, *The Theology of Dietrich Bonhoeffer*, 266. Godsey writes of three phases of Bonhoeffer's theological development, "During the first period his thought centered on *Jesus Christ as the revelational reality of the church*. During the second period his emphasis was on *Jesus Christ as Lord over the church*. In the third period Bonhoeffer concentrated his attention upon *Jesus Christ as the Lord over the world*."

political action dyad helps paint a vivid portrait of a visionary thinker and a bold and dynamic political actor who was way ahead of his contemporaries for most of his career. It is precisely the discontinuities in the church-world/political action dyad that show a theologian whose acute sensitivity to his life contexts and his ability to respond meaningfully to them in both theology and action made him a unique and exemplary figure.

In order to fully understand and appreciate the nature of this four-part claim in all of its ramifications, it is first necessary to frame it within the context of other significant scholarly approaches to the problem of Bonhoeffer's changing forms of political involvement. These approaches are the "Definition of Pacifism Approach" and the "Theological Categories in Context Approach."[16] Further, these two approaches are types of a larger more general approach, the "Continuity/Discontinuity Approach."[17]

THE CONTINUITY/DISCONTINUITY APPROACH

Since the late 1950s, Bonhoeffer scholars have approached his theology and career in terms of tracing continuities and discontinuities. More specifically, scholars focus on the relationship between changes in one or a cluster of related theological categories and the changing life contexts in which Bonhoeffer found himself. They can make theology the driving force (the changing theology influenced the way Bonhoeffer confronted changing life circumstances) or give priority to the life circumstances (Bonhoeffer's theology changed in response to the differing situations in which he found himself). In both cases, theology and life contexts are in some form of relationship. Scholars look at the progression of Bonhoeffer's career as an interaction between life and thinking and they judge continuities or discontinuities in any number of designated categories. This Continuity/Discontinuity Approach has become the standard and responsible way to appreciate Bonhoeffer.

---

16. These categories are my own. They have not been used explicitly by other scholars to describe their own work or to organize Bonhoeffer's life and thinking.

17. This designation is also my own.

The Development of the Continuity/Discontinuity Approach

Scholars' realistic attention to both continuities and discontinuities in Bonhoeffer's theology was motivated by two factors. First, some early Bonhoeffer commentators overstated the influence of life circumstances on his theology. Second, later scholars took certain quotes and ideas out of the context of their relation to ideas in previous works. Both approaches tended to highlight discontinuities.

Eckhard Minthe represents a scholarly approach that puts an overemphasis on the influence of life circumstances. For Minthe, Bonhoeffer's thinking is so determined by the changing life circumstances that theological continuity is not possible. He stated,

> The attempt to systematize Bonhoeffer's thought and then to work out its application is doomed from the start to failure, for his ideas were impulsive reactions to a peculiar set of circumstances. They are so impetuous and so conditioned by the situation in which Bonhoeffer found himself that one could almost speak of them as prophetic oracles.[18]

Harvey Cox captures the spirit of the second problem, "picking and choosing" any useful Bonhoeffer idea out of context. He writes,

> Psychologists rejoice at Bonhoeffer's emphasis on maturity, secular sociologists at his pungent opposition to clericalism. Barthians see his work, despite a few pot shots at "revelation positivism," as an application of the master's critique of religion begun in *Epistle to the Romans*. Tillichians find the "world come of age" another symbol for the truly "theonomous culture." Deciphering Bonhoeffer has become a wide-open pastime, for he wrote just enough, but not too much, to make room for everyone in the gambol.[19]

The more specific and well-known instance of scholars taking ideas out of context was the use of statements from Bonhoeffer's *Letters and Papers from Prison* to justify various radical theological positions in the

---

18. *ADOB*, 26. Hopper also notes Karl Barth's 1952 description of Bonhoeffer: "As always with Bonhoeffer, one is faced by a peculiar difficulty. He was—how should I put it?—an impulsive visionary thinker who was suddenly seized by an idea to which he gave lively form, and after a time he called a halt (one never knew whether it was final or temporary) with some provisional last point or other" (27). Hopper takes the quotation from p. 251 of John A. Phillps's *Christ for Us*.

19. Cox, "Using and Misusing Bonhoeffer," 195–99. This quotation is from p. 195.

1960s. Bonhoeffer phrases such as "religionless Christianity," "the non-religious interpretation of biblical concepts," "a world come of age," and "Before God, we have to live today without God," for example, became important in the "death of God" movement. William Hamilton was especially forceful in arguing, "My Protestant [Bonhoeffer] has no God, no faith in God, and affirms the death of God and all forms of theism."[20] This second use of Bonhoeffer also emphasizes discontinuity. The earlier Bonhoeffer was a theist, the later Bonhoeffer an atheist.

Scholars responded to the overemphasis on discontinuities with attempts to establish some systematic theological coherence throughout Bonhoeffer's writing career.[21] Works by Dumas, Feil, Godsey, Müller, Ott, and others all in some way or another echoed Moltmann's 1959 judgment that there was a "pattern of continuous development in Bonhoeffer's thought."[22] Scholars also confronted the "death of God"

---

20. Altizer and Hamilton, *Radical Theology and the Death of God*, 36.

21. *ADOB*, 28. Hopper describes the situation as follows: "In point of fact, the more positive and now dominant appraisal of Bonhoeffer was beginning to take shape about the time of Bethge's 1961 Chicago lectures. This alternate appraisal was built around the assertion that Bonhoeffer's thought was *not* impulsive as Barth had suggested, but rather that it was grounded in some basic unifying themes and concerns discernible throughout the course of his theological career. It is clear that Bethge himself was long associated with this estimate of Bonhoeffer's work, but support from other quarters was needed to give currency to the argument. This support began to emerge in the middle and late 1950's."

22. *ADOB*, 28. This is Hopper's assessment of Moltmann's work. These scholars are the classic or major interpreters of Bonhoeffer. While not all of them asserted a perfect or flawless continuity without certain shifts or developments in a given theological theme or theological category, they did establish that Bonhoeffer's sporadic ideas could be organized into some sort of system centered around that given theological theme or theological category. André Dumas, in his *Dietrich Bonhoeffer: Theologian of Reality*, argued that "Bonhoeffer's central conviction remained unchanged throughout [his career]: in Jesus Christ God is present in the midst of the reality of the world," 167. Ernst Feil, in his *The Theology of Dietrich Bonhoeffer*, argued that Bonhoeffer's understanding of the world is an organizing theme and that, "In our examination of Bonhoeffer it has become more and more apparent that his theology does represent a sustained unity," xx. John D. Godsey, in *The Theology of Dietrich Bonhoeffer*, wrote, "The cohesive and elucidative element in the theology of Dietrich Bonhoeffer is his steadfast concentration on the revelation of God in Jesus Christ," 264. Heinrich Ott, in his *Reality and Faith: The Theological Legacy*, argues for two central themes in Bonhoeffer's theology, Christology and "reality." He is attentive to movements in Bonhoeffer's thought but asserts these two categories as organizing themes. These are just a few examples of important works that assert some systematic stability in Bonhoeffer's works. See Hopper's chapter, "The Questions of Stature and Continuity of Thought," 25–39 and his chapter "Interpretative

theologians with attempts to understand the seemingly radical concepts from the latest production in the *Letters* in terms of their relationship to the earlier thought.[23] The general thrust was an attempt to look for some theological continuity in the Bonhoeffer corpus.

Scholars' acknowledgment of the continuities, as well as discontinuities, in Bonhoeffer's thought was ultimately born from a more accurate and sober recognition of how his life experiences may have conditioned his thinking and vice versa. More specifically, scholars realized that theology and life experience had equally legitimate roles in determining the overall texture of Bonhoeffer's contribution. They exist in some type of mutually-informing relationship. So, although they might look different at different phases in his career, Bonhoeffer brought some consistent theological themes into each life circumstance. If the radically changing life circumstances are given too much priority, they can eclipse any theological concerns that may be consistent throughout the whole of his thinking. Bonhoeffer's theology then looks impetuous and discontinuous.

The "death of God" theologians, for their part, did not adequately recognize that Bonhoeffer's seemingly radical statements make sense only in relationship both with some theological concerns which are arguably continuous throughout his whole writing career and his life circumstances. The completion and availability of Eberhard Bethge's 1967 exhaustive and definitive biography greatly enhanced scholars' ability to adequately connect theology with life circumstances and thus

---

Points of Difference," 40–70, for a more extensive and detailed examination of how major works argue for a unifying theological theme throughout Bonhoeffer's works and how shifts or modifications are explained.

23. Godsey, *The Theology of Dietrich Bonhoeffer*, 260. Godsey captures perfectly the essence of the problem: "The problem of Bonhoeffer's theology lies in its development in the final period, especially during the time of his imprisonment, and in the relation of the thought of this period to that of the two preceding periods. Are the fragmentary insights of the third period continuous or discontinuous with the development of his theology up to that time? The connection between the concentration on the sociological phenomenon of the church during the initial period and the stress on the ethical demands of discipleship during the second is obvious, but how do these relate to the emphasis on the world come of age and the nonreligious character of the Christian faith during the third? Does the third period represent a break with the former periods, or is it possible to discover a fundamental unifying element that provides continuity to Bonhoeffer's theology from beginning to end?"

judge realistically both continuities and discontinuities.[24] Today, responsible scholars do not work without Bethge's *Biography* in one hand and Bonhoeffer's writings in the other.[25]

The Continuity/Discontinuity Approach is the fairest to Bonhoeffer and most responsible way to approach him for another and perhaps more obvious reason, the varied genres in his writings. His major works include two doctoral dissertations written as a Barth-influenced academic reacting to Protestant liberalism. There are a few lecture series turned into books based on students' notes produced in between pastorates. The spiritual treatises, *Life Together* and *Discipleship*, were written while he was heading up clandestine (and eventually illegal) seminaries. There are essays compiled posthumously and titled *Ethics* written during varying forms of resistance activity and while in prison. Finally, there are the posthumously compiled letters written while in prison. Circumstances were simply not favorable for producing a systematic theology.[26] The very make-up of the corpus itself raises the concern about continuity and discontinuity.

Finally, in terms of evaluating continuities and discontinuities in Bonhoeffer's life and writings, different Bonhoeffer scholars have used similar terminology. There are three basic possibilities. Scholars still could, even with the appreciation of the mutually-informing relation-

24. *ADOB*, 49. Hopper affirms, "Those studies of Bonhoeffer's thought which come after the publication of Bethge's biography generally reveal major indebtedness to that work, and, with the qualified exception of Dumas's analysis, recognize the impact of events upon Bonhoeffer's thought. This is not to say that Bethge's biography has brought or will bring about extensive agreement in fundamental matters of interpretation but only that, methodologically, it has become increasingly difficult to avoid dealing with Bonhoeffer's life experiences as an important dimension of any discussion of his thought."

25. *DB*, xi. Green, for instance, in the Foreword to the 2000 edition of Bethge's *Biography*, writes, "Now that volumes of the English edition of Dietrich Bonhoeffer Works are appearing regularly, this biography is their indispensable companion for studying the life and theology of Dietrich Bonhoeffer."

26. Dumas, *Dietrich Bonhoeffer: Theologian of Reality*, vii. Dumas, comparing Bonhoeffer to Kierkegaard, writes, "Kierkegaard's entire literary production was carefully conceived and meticulously carried out, each book thought out in relation to the others, the whole orchestrated with incredible artistic as well as theological foresight and ingenuity. Not so with Bonhoeffer, whom circumstances denied the life of careful and scholarly output that might otherwise have been his. Save for his first two books, both of which were university dissertations done in typically thorough pattern of solid German theological research, Bonhoeffer's literary output was sporadic, hasty and frequently incomplete."

ship between life and theology, assert total discontinuity in Bonhoeffer's life and work. Most scholars do not, however, like Eckhard Minthe did, assert radical discontinuity throughout. Scholars could also argue for total continuity throughout the works. Dumas, for instance, holds that "the later Bonhoeffer thought in perfect continuity with all of his preceding work although in a much more radically confined context."[27] This position is somewhat more common than the judgment of radical discontinuity throughout, but is also somewhat rare. A second position is a nuanced or mixed one where scholars assert discontinuities in one area of his life or theological category and continuities in others. The term "discontinuity" or "break" constitutes a real separation from what was there prior. One might argue, for example, that Bonhoeffer has two entirely different Christologies in different phases of his career.[28] Or, in terms of political involvement, one might argue that the change from admitted pacifism to tyrannicide is a discontinuity or a break.

The third position, where scholars argue for "development," is the most common. Commentators argue that what was in seed form in early works reaches its fruition in later years through interaction with life circumstances. The later development is in organic continuity with the original form of whatever category in question. One might argue, for example, that Bonhoeffer's later Christology, while evolved, is not a fundamentally different Christology. Bonhoeffer presents what is essentially the same theological position in different ways to meet differing conditions, with respect to varying life contexts, or in terms of the genre in which he is writing.

TWO FORMS OF THE CONTINUITY/DISCONTINUITY APPROACH IN THE SPECIFIC QUESTION OF BONHOEFFER'S CHANGING FORMS OF POLITICAL INVOLVEMENT

Scholarship on the matter of Bonhoeffer's shifting forms of political involvement has tended to focus on the supposed move away from some

---

27. Dumas, *Dietrich Bonhoeffer: Theologian of Reality*, 165.

28. *RR*, 92–93. This is Rasmussen's assessment of John Phillips's position in *Christ for Us in the Theology of Dietrich Bonhoeffer*. He writes, "The difficulty is when Phillips fails to hold carefully enough to his own guide and proceeds to argue Christolog*ies*, two of them, as the guides. The insistence of this dissertation [Rasmussen's work] is that there is one, not two."

form of pacifism in the later phase of his life. The move has been the topic of several German and English articles in the 1970s, 1980s and 1990s all the way up to the present. The problem has also received attention in chapters from a few important books. Scholars all judge continuities and discontinuities in theology, form of political involvement (action), or some combination of theology and action, all in response to Bonhoeffer's changing life circumstances. When the Continuity/Discontinuity Approach is applied to the problem of Bonhoeffer's changed form of political involvement it has two forms, the "Definition of Pacifism Approach" and the "Theological Categories in Context Approach." These two approaches each offer positive contributions toward a comprehensive solution to the problem. Their inherent weaknesses, however, render them insufficient if taken exclusively or by themselves.

The Definition of Pacifism Approach

Scholars who employ the Definition of Pacifism Approach choose or construct a definition of pacifism and use it to judge whether or not Bonhoeffer ever was a pacifist. Or, after establishing that he was a pacifist, they use this definition to judge whether he remained one during his conspiracy activities. They also tend to give special attention to Bonhoeffer's "straight and unbroken course" continuity claim and thus engage in the project of defending Bonhoeffer against himself.

Mark K. Nation, for example, concludes that Bonhoeffer never was a pacifist.[29] He borrows Rasmussen's definition, "the pacifist is one who always views the use of violent coercion as an evil and who rules out war even as a necessary evil."[30] Nation views pacifism as an absolute position.[31] Nation does admit that there are certain writings and personal statements throughout Bonhoeffer's career that place him very close to Rasmussen's definition. Yet, Bonhoeffer simply does not meet the criteria established by the Rasmussen definition or any other definition of absolute pacifism. Nation gives a few reasons for his conclusion.

---

29. Nation, "Pacifist and Enemy of the State," 61–77. Nation writes, "I believe the evidence points to the conclusion that he probably never was a pacifist," 74.

30. *RR*, 95.

31. Nation, "Pacifist and Enemy of the State," 76. Nation admits he is tempted to condition pacifism with terms like "provisional" or "conditional" but resists, as these terms are "tantamount to saying a woman is partly pregnant."

First, Bonhoeffer basically ascribed to situation ethics. Acting out the potentially changing "concrete command of God for now" characterizes Bonhoeffer's fairly consistent ethical stance.[32] Pacifism, according to Nation's accepted definition, is an absolute moral norm good for all times and situations. Second, when Bonhoeffer does use absolute language about pacifism, it is usually in sermons rather than in any "carefully nuanced lecture." The dramatic language is simply consistent with the medium rather than descriptive of any absolute position. Finally, when Bonhoeffer seems to hold to absolute pacifist positions in writings that are not sermons, it is because of "the urgency of the political situation as well as the passion he held for the subject."[33] Bonhoeffer never was a pacifist so, according to Nation, there was no shift and thus no discontinuities.

Dena Davis, on the other hand, goes about defending the "straight and unbroken course" continuity claim in a different manner. Her perspective is unique as she "take[s] Bonhoeffer's interest in Gandhi to be central to his thinking and [tries to] see if a Gandhian perspective of pacifism will provide a perspective of pacifism from which Bonhoeffer's own categorization of the 'straight course' becomes more understandable."[34] Davis agrees with Rasmussen's claim that "all the twisting possible cannot make the author of *The Cost of Discipleship* a volunteer for assassinating even Adolf Hitler. Somewhere some modifications have taken place."[35] Yet, she tries to soften the seemingly vast differences between the *Discipleship* author and the conspirator by pointing to three similarities between Bonhoeffer and Gandhi on nonviolence.

According to Davis, Gandhi and Bonhoeffer both saw nonviolence as "an active force in pursuing justice" rather than trying to fight injustice while remaining "untainted." They both perceived violence or injustice as "inherent in the status quo of their situation." Thus, if one does not act against injustice, even with the possible use of violence, one is participating in the violence existing in the status quo.[36] Second,

---

32. See, for instance, Richard Weikart's chapter "Ethics" in his *The Myth of Dietrich Bonhoeffer*, 101–17. See especially p. 105 where he indicates that Joseph Fletcher considers Bonhoeffer a fellow situationist.

33. Nation, "Pacifist and Enemy of the State," 75–77.

34. Davis, "Gandhi and Bonhoeffer," 44–49. This quotation is from 44.

35. Ibid., 49. The Rasmussen quote is from *RR*, 120.

36. Davis, "Gandhi and Bonhoeffer," 46.

they both understood faith as necessarily making them available for others. Finally, they both equated suffering and sacrifice with discipleship.[37] She then offers a definition of pacifism applicable to both men. It reads, "nonviolence as inseparable from active resistance," with, however, "violence [being] better than not to resist at all."[38] With this Bonhoefferian-Gandhian definition in place,[39] Davis can conclude that the move from Bonhoeffer's earlier pacifism to his involvement in the conspiracy does "follow a reasonably straight line" (with, however, the thinking in *Discipleship* still being somewhat problematic).[40] Thus, Bonhoeffer's life is basically consistent with his own "straight and unbroken course" continuity claim.

Dale Brown's article, "Bonhoeffer and Pacifism," is a bit more complicated. Brown is a pacifist who wants to bring this pacifist perspective to bear on all of the existing data.[41] He briefly traces Bonhoeffer's writings and positions on war and peace throughout the various phases of his career. Brown argues against the

> nonpacifist interpreters of Bonhoeffer [who] are reluctant to accept his own self-identification as a pacifist during the decade of the thirties. Rather than taking Bonhoeffer at his word, Bethge, Lehmann, Rasmussen have tended to qualify Bonhoeffer's self-assessment by placing adjectives like relative, conditional, and provisional before the word *pacifism* as well as pointing out how Bonhoeffer's life-time contextualism would not have allowed him to ever have become a "principled pacifist."[42]

Brown, against Rasmussen's above-quoted definition, "prefer[s] a more refined and positive definition."[43] This definition tries to lessen the gap between "provisional" pacifism and a "pacifism of principle" in Bonhoeffer. Brown also critiques Rasmussen's use of the terms "asceti-

---

37. Ibid., 45–47.

38. Ibid., 49.

39. Ibid. Davis does not explicitly label this a definition. However, it does function as a definition in her argument.

40. Ibid.

41. Brown, "Bonhoeffer and Pacifism," 32. Brown claims that Rasmussen's *Reality and Resistance*, especially part 2, "Pacifism and Tyrannicide," provides the most thorough "data" on the subject of Bonhoeffer's pacifism.

42. Ibid., 39.

43. Ibid.

Introduction 15

cism" and "parasitism" as they apply to Bonhoeffer's pacifism.[44] Brown does not offer an explicit definition of pacifism. However, he does open the door for a definition of pacifism that could help in defense of Bonhoeffer's "straight and unbroken course" continuity claim with his critiques of Rasmussen's definition and extensive treatment of the difficulties in defining pacifism. His lengthy treatment of, and concern with, Rasmussen's definition allows us to place Brown loosely with those who employ the definition approach.

STRENGTH OF THE DEFINITION OF PACIFISM APPROACH

The Definition of Pacifism Approach has one very important strong point. Definitions of pacifism are clearly necessary when the problem concerns understanding Bonhoeffer's changing forms of political involvement, specifically his seeming move away from pacifism in particular. Scholars clearly need some parameters or fixed standards in order to make judgments about continuities or discontinuities in Bonhoeffer's forms of political involvement or thinking over a period of time. There has to be some form of designation of what his position was or something that at least acts like a definition in order to make an argument about what Bonhoeffer is shifting away from or shifting toward. Some scholars have even provided analysis of Bonhoeffer's explicit writings and statements concerning war and peace in the various stages of his career. Nation and Brown, for example have divided the developments in Bonhoeffer's thinking on war, peace and resistance on the way to conspiracy into roughly five phases: traditional Lutheranism, Selective Conscientious Objection, Pacifist (Qualified), Selective Conscientious Participation, and Agonized Participation.[45]

This careful attention to Bonhoeffer's exact form of political thinking or involvement in the various phases of his career may have in some instances had the express purpose of determining his consistency or inconsistency with a certain definition of pacifism throughout his career. Regardless of the motivation, the categorization is useful as it at least hints at the complexity of Bonhoeffer's thinking on war and peace in relation to changing life situations. While still concerned with placing

---

44. Ibid., 39–41.
45. See Brown, "Bonhoeffer and Pacifism," 38, for Rasmussen's categorization of Bonhoeffer's various positions. Rasmussen summarizes Bonhoeffer's positions on p. 125 of his *Reality and Resistance*.

Bonhoeffer in categories tied to certain definitions of positions on war and peace, this scholarship at least suggests that context is an important consideration when judging Bonhoeffer's differing forms of political involvement.

Weaknesses of the Definition of Pacifism Approach

There are some very significant weaknesses associated with the Definition of Pacifism Approach. First, it tends to be useful only in terms of the shift away from some form of pacifism in Bonhoeffer's later life. If scholars focus only on the change from some form of pacifism (a position he arguably held beginning in 1930/31) to tyrannicide in late 1939, they are ignoring a whole segment of his pre–1930/31 career where he definitely did not meet even a minimum definition of pacifism. This represents a form of lack of attention to context. In this case there is ignorance of what the change from pacifism to tyrannicide looks like in terms of the context of his whole writing career.

Second, there are problems involved in any attempt to treat pacifism as having a stable, universally recognized definition. Pacifism, of course, can and has been defined in a variety of ways. The famed theologian John Howard Yoder's 1992 *Nevertheless,* for example, describes no less than 28 different types or definitions of pacifism.[46] Moreover, the history of Christian pacifism is a history of formulations or definitions conditioned by circumstances.[47] There is almost certainly a definition of pacifism somewhere that would cover tyrannicide, essentially nullifying the seemingly radical difference between these two positions.[48] How can one effectively gauge the nature of Bonhoeffer's changing forms of political involvement with a definition so broad that it has lost the power to really define?

---

46. Yoder, *Nevertheless: The Varieties and Shortcomings of Religious Pacifism.* See also Chapman, "What Would Bonhoeffer Say to Christian Peacemakers Today?" 167–75. Chapman uses the fact of Yoder's twenty-eight definitions to argue that the question of "whether and to what extent Bonhoeffer should be called a 'pacifist' is unresolvable" (169).

47. Roland H. Bainton's *Christian Attitudes toward War and Peace* and Geoffrey F. Nuttall's *Christian Pacifism in History* are two notable works (of many) that clearly show how Christian pacifism's meaning varies with respect to the historical context in which it manifests itself.

48. Dena Davis, for example, with her use of a "Gandhi-Bonhoefferian" definition of pacifism, implies that pacifism and tyrannicide can be continuous.

Third, these examples rely either explicitly or implicitly on definitions of pacifism that are partially, if not wholly, derived from sources other than Bonhoeffer himself. That is, while they do refer to Bonhoeffer's thinking on pacifism, they oftentimes represent the imposition of a definition from the outside onto his thinking and actions. Thus, another form of the Definition of Pacifism Approach might rely on Bonhoeffer's own understanding of his behavior in terms of his own definition of pacifism. However, Bonhoeffer's writings and personal statements simply do not yield a consistent or stable definition of pacifism. He did not write in a comprehensive, lengthy or sustained way about pacifism in theory or about his own perspective in particular. The evidence and materials consist of personal statements recounted in Bethge's authoritative biography, a few reports of Bonhoeffer's avid interest in pacifism based on interviews with acquaintances (including the desire to study with Gandhi) and a few lectures (1932's "Christ and Peace," for example). It is true that his 1937 *Discipleship* offers a fairly lengthy treatment of nonviolent themes. However, Bonhoeffer certainly did not offer any definitive answer to the seeming inconsistency between his pacifism and his agreement with the attempted elimination of Hitler based on a definition of his pacifism. Bonhoeffer's treatment of pacifism, and second-hand testimonies to his personal pacifism, are simply not weighty or exact enough to construct a consistent or reliable definition to be used as a measuring stick apart from the conditions that surrounded their formulations.

A final weakness may look like a strong point. The Definition of Pacifism Approach seems like the best approach if the goal is defending Bonhoeffer's "straight and unbroken course" continuity claim. Scholars simply establish a definition and see if he stuck to it throughout his career. Yet, even when so applied, this approach is problematic because two conflicting conclusions (each with their own problems and controversies) can result from the same method. The method can be used to prove both that Bonhoeffer did, and did not, remain true to his claim. The results depend on the chosen definition. If one adopts a strict definition of pacifism, where tyrannicide is not a possibility, Bonhoeffer's continuity claim is clearly indefensible and he appears inconsistent with himself. This conclusion is, however, an unacceptable one for some Bonhoeffer scholars.[49] We arrive at the opposite conclusion if we apply a different

---

49. Bethge, "Bonhoeffer's Pacifism," 6–7. Bethge argues, "What I'm pointing to is this kind of thinking: the man of *Cost of Discipleship* may be a pacifist, and he becomes

and wider definition where pacifists can engage in tyrannicide. We can successfully defend Bonhoeffer's continuity claim because pacifism and tyrannicide are not mutually exclusive positions (one could be a pacifist and attempt tyrannicide). Some scholars would, however, question a definition of pacifism that allows for any form of attempted or actual killing, even in special circumstances.

Conclusion

It is certainly important to determine whether Bonhoeffer ever was a pacifist, or fit in any other of a number of possible categories, when examining his changing forms of political involvement. It would be impossible to evaluate the nature of his shifts or changes without developing definitions or some measuring sticks that at least function as definitions. The problems associated with this approach are ultimately twofold. They revolve around the derivation of the definition and how the definition is applied. Definitions of Bonhoeffer's political positions at any given juncture must derive from an in depth analysis of the complex matrix of his theology, life circumstances, personal convictions, the German church situation, and the German political scene. Indeed, even the casual observer of Bonhoeffer's life would have to admit to its extraordinarily complex and tumultuous nature. Thus, the meanings of these categories (pacifism, just-war, tyrannicide, etc.) when applied to Bonhoeffer are highly contextualized. It would seem, then, rather unfair to judge this man's continuities or discontinuities using an ahistorical or detached definition of pacifism, especially one with which he himself might not have even agreed. Moreover, any constructed definition of pacifism would seem relevant mostly to judging the nature of his final shift, thus discounting what that final move looks like with respect to his entire career. An approach is needed that takes into account Bonhoeffer's forms of political involvement throughout his entire career and really takes seriously and reflects explicitly in its methodology (including the formulation of any definitions) how his thinking and political involvement were influenced by differing life contexts.

---

a volunteer for assassinating Adolf Hitler—for me this is a wrong way of speaking of the whole problem, as if Dietrich had moved from a conviction of non-violence to a conviction of using violence; for me this does not at all express what was going on" (6).

Introduction

The Theological Categories in Context Approach

The Theological Categories in Context Approach comprises three moves. First, scholars presuppose a relationship between theology and actions.[50] Next, they choose an area of Bonhoeffer's thought or some other stable category and trace continuities and discontinuities in that area throughout his career with consideration of his life contexts. Finally, since there is a relationship between thinking and actions, scholars can correlate the continuities, developments, or discontinuities in the theology with continuities, developments, or discontinuities in the forms of worldly involvement as Bonhoeffer's life progresses.

William Kuhns's chapter, "From Pacifism to Resistance," from his *In Pursuit of Dietrich Bonhoeffer*, represents a version of the approach. However, Kuhns does not really trace the continuities or discontinuities in a specific theological category. Rather, the category he uses is more of a stance. Kuhns points to the idea of acting responsibly "in the present" or responding to one's circumstances "in the present" out of Christian motives as the standard. He clearly thinks that Bonhoeffer held to some variety of pacifism from the early thirties to 1938/39. He writes, "Bonhoeffer's pacifism was a profound belief, an important aspect of his psychological and moral life."[51] Kuhns explores five factors from Bonhoeffer's life experiences and historical situation that influenced the meaning of pacifism for him in this phase.[52] Kuhns then acknowledges

---

50. Simply stated, there is a relationship between Bonhoeffer's thinking and his activity. Again, scholars, especially with the availability of Bethge's *DB* and its demand that continuity and discontinuity issues be examined, have to ask the question of how Bonhoeffer's political or other activity influenced his theology or how his theology provided the justification or framework for the type of activity he undertakes. The tricky part, of course, is determining whether it is the actions that influence the theology or the theology that influences the actions at every or any point in Bonhoeffer's career. This enterprise is unavoidably speculative on some level as Bonhoeffer did not explicitly or extensively comment on this mutually informing relationship between thinking and activity at all points in his career.

51. Kuhns, *In Pursuit of Dietrich Bonhoeffer*, 222. Kuhns continues, "He abhorred violence and admired Gandhi precisely for his ability to achieve important political goals through the moral use of nonviolent techniques. During the 'thirties Bonhoeffer came to loathe Hitler, to see in him and his disfigured government a capacity for evil which could destroy Germany. But the thought of murdering Hitler to check his atrocities cut across the grain of Bonhoeffer's beliefs. As much as he sensed a responsibility to the German people, he instinctively withdrew from whatever means would involve violence or a form of destruction."

52. Kuhns, *In Pursuit of Dietrich Bonhoeffer*. The five are: 1) Bonhoeffer's friendship with the French pacifist Jean Lasserre while at Union Theological Seminary (223–24);

the obvious change in the nature of Bonhoeffer's political involvement from pacifism to resistance and ultimately the plot to take Hitler's life.[53] He lists four possible motivations from Bonhoeffer's life experiences and historical situation that may have influenced that changed form of political involvement.[54]

In his description of the fifth influence on Bonhoeffer's "pacifism," Kuhns notes the theoretical "split" between pacifism out of political motives and pacifism out of Christian motives. He then foreshadows the judgment he will later make at the end of the chapter. Kuhns writes, "Only later would it become evident that for Bonhoeffer the distinction [between pacifism out of political motives and pacifism out of Christian motives] could never really exist: as a purpose for pacifism, or for active resistance to Hitler's regime."[55] Kuhns thus holds that a look at Bonhoeffer's whole career shows that the motives for both forms of political involvement (pacifism and active resistance) are the same, Christian motives. In terms of continuity and discontinuity, then, Kuhns argues that Bonhoeffer's "stance" of manifesting Christ in the present situation is continuous throughout his career. Kuhns accounts for the discontinuity between pacifism and resistance by exploring how Bonhoeffer applies that stance in response to his particular life situation. From the early thirties to 1938/39, pacifism was the appropriate way to relate Christ to the present situation. In 1938 and beyond, the appropriate way to relate Christ to the present was actively resisting Hitler, even to the point of tyrannicide. Kuhns thus holds that the move from pacifism to tyrannicide is not a "total reorientation," just a change in his

---

2) the witness of Mahatma Gandhi (224); 3) Christ's admonitions on peace—"Bonhoeffer found Christ's statement in the Sermon on the Mount the most relevant statement of the Gospels for the present," (225–26); 4) Bonhoeffer's participation in the ecumenical movement from 1932 to 1938 (226); and 5) Bonhoeffer's knowledge that he would be called into military service (227).

53. Ibid., 222. Kuhns writes, "The thought of taking part in a plot to assassinate the Führer would have been totally alien to him," and "Bonhoeffer's movement from a state of pacifism to an outright effort to participate in a necessarily violent overthrow of his government marks a personal reversal of major dimensions."

54. Ibid., 222. The four are: 1) a disillusionment with pacifism (229); 2) Bonhoeffer's "growing disillusionment with the Confessing Church"(230); 3) his sense—out of "his profound love for Germany and the German people"—that he must do something more drastic (230–31); and 4) his understanding of resistance action as an act of repentance (231).

55. Ibid., 227.

Introduction

form of political involvement based on the proper way to relate Christ to a changed historical situation.[56]

The obvious theological category by which to approach Bonhoeffer's political involvement is Ethics. Clifford Green, for example, looks at Bonhoeffer's understanding of "his role in the conspiracy from the perspective of ethics" in his paper, "Bonhoeffer's Christian Ethics in Resistance to Tyranny and Genocide."[57] Green begins his essay with a clear statement of the classic problem. He writes, "Bonhoeffer's story appears to present us with two opposite poles, pacifism and violence, which repel each other like the negative and positive poles of a magnet."[58] Green does not explicitly state his concern with defending Bonhoeffer's "straight and unbroken course" continuity claim.

Green describes Bonhoeffer's rationale for participation in the conspiracy. He argues for two different contexts in Bonhoeffer's *Ethics*. First, there is his ethics of resistance or "ethics *in extremis*" ("ethics in an extreme and abnormal situation"). The second is "the ethics of everyday life, ethics concerned with a future post-war Germany and Europe at peace."[59] He deals with the ethics *in extremis* and lists a few facets of that type of ethics which make participation in the conspiracy a reasonable course of action. He begins with Bonhoeffer's critiques of traditional approaches to ethics.[60] An answer to deficiencies of traditional approaches is "responsible action" or "free responsibility."[61] Moreover, he argues that the "ethical impulses that support this course of action (free or responsible action)" are Bonhoeffer's Christology and his discussion of "The Structure of Responsible Life." Green shows how the latter category provides specific or detailed reflection on how tyrannicide can be "responsible action" in accordance with God's will. He describes Bonhoeffer's four sections there as themes (vicarious representative action, correspondence with reality, readiness to take on guilt, and free-

---

56. Ibid.

57. Dr. Green delivered this paper at the Conference on "Bonhoeffer's Dilemma: The Ethics of Violence" at Pennsylvania State University, October 28-31, 1999. This quotation is from p. 4.

58. Green, "Bonhoeffer's Christian Ethics in Resistance to Tyranny and Genocide," 3.

59. Ibid., 5.

60. Ibid., 6-8.

61. Ibid., 9-11.

dom). Green ultimately shows how Bonhoeffer's thinking in these four categories supports his decision for tyrannicide.[62]

Green's paper does not fit perfectly into the Theological Categories in Context Approach as I have described it. He does not really look at Bonhoeffer's changing actions with respect to continuities or discontinuities in the theological category Ethics in all of the various phases of Bonhoeffer's career. Rather, he concentrates on evidence from a work near the end of Bonhoeffer's career and shows how a decision for tyrannicide is justified given the thinking in that work. Yet, Green's work does belong in this approach simply because he chooses a theological category and seeks to understand Bonhoeffer's actions in terms of that theological category. Green also presupposes the relationship between Bonhoeffer's thinking and actions and his life situation in that later phase. Green explicitly states that Bonhoeffer formulates that particular type of Ethics partially in response to his experience of resistance.

Larry Rasmussen's *Dietrich Bonhoeffer: Reality and Resistance* provides the most comprehensive and informed treatment of the problem.[63] His method also fits most properly into the Theological Categories in Context Approach. Like many Bonhoeffer scholars, Rasmussen considers Christology as Bonhoeffer's central theological category.[64] His thesis reads,

---

62. Ibid., 11–23. Green concludes, "In extreme situations where life itself is at stake, the killing of a tyrant may be wagered. This is a particular act, not the enactment of a general principle; it occurs only in a specific case of extreme necessity. The act is one of vicarious responsibility, and its purpose is the healing and peace of the human community. It is not justified by any principle of human ethics, but is a wager, with its risk, about the will of God. It is done in freedom, with appropriate analysis of the situation, and with a willingness to take on guilt. This free, responsible action is an act of faith" (23).

63. This text is widely quoted and held as the most thorough treatment of Bonhoeffer's political involvement. See, for example, Brown, "Bonhoeffer and Pacifism," 32. Brown describes Rasmussen's work as "masterful."

64. *ADOB*, 53. David Hopper writes, "all of the major interpreters mentioned in our survey agree on the basic Christological focus of Bonhoeffer's work." The major interpreters mentioned in Hopper's survey would be the major interpreters of Bonhoeffer in any survey. Even when these interpreters choose some other facet of Bonhoeffer's thought as their focus, they generally assert the centrality of the Christology. See, for example, Dumas, *Dietrich Bonhoeffer: Theologian of Reality*, 276. Dumas focuses on "ontology." However, he argues that "Bonhoeffer's central purpose [is to] understand and follow the structuring presence of God in reality by means of the Christology of the incarnation and to overcome the dualism of metaphysics and inwardness by an ontology of presence and openness." See also, Feil, *The Theology of Dietrich Bonhoeffer*,

Bonhoeffer's resistance activity was his Christology enacted with utter seriousness. Bonhoeffer's resistance was the existential playing out of christological themes. Changes and shifts in his Christology are at the same time changes and shifts in the character of his resistance. In the other direction, changes in his resistance activity had an impact upon his Christology.[65]

The first two elements of the Theological Categories in Context Approach are in his thesis statement (a presupposed relationship between theology and political involvement and choice of Christology as the theological category Christology). Rasmussen treats the third element, gauging developments in his political involvement in terms of developments in the chosen theological category, throughout the text.

Bonhoeffer's Ethics and Christology are inextricably linked for Rasmussen. More specifically, Bonhoeffer's *Gestalt Christi* is related to reality "because reality itself has a christocratic structure." Moreover, the "cosmic" reality of Christ seeks to become "concretized" in reality. Finally, Ethics is the field of theological discourse where we see or inquire about how it is that "the cosmic reality given in Christ" manifests itself in this world.[66] Thus, in even more specific terms, the main theme in Bonhoeffer's "christological ethics" is his concern with answering the question "Who is Christ for us today?" or, in other words, how to relate Christ to the present situation.[67] Rasmussen writes, "With this methodology moral action is action that conforms to Christ's form in the world (that accords with reality); immoral action is action that deviates from Christ's form in the world (from reality)."[68]

For Rasmussen, Bonhoeffer's methodology implies a tension between this "form" of Christ and the relevance of that form to any

---

59. Feil, while concentrating on Bonhoeffer's understanding of the world, nevertheless asserts that "One cannot present Bonhoeffer's view of the world adequately without including his Christology." See also, Godsey, *The Theology of Dietrich Bonhoeffer*, 264. Godsey, while concentrating on ecclesiology, nevertheless plainly states, "For Bonhoeffer theology was essentially Christology, but because Christ is not without his body, Christology includes ecclesiology within itself." See also, Phillips, *Christ for Us*. Phillips focuses explicitly on Bonhoeffer's Christology throughout this work.

65. *RR*, 15.
66. Ibid., 88.
67. Ibid., 89.
68. Ibid., 23.

present situation (or any present "today"). Rasmussen thus considers Bonhoeffer's Ethics to be "contextual." He writes,

> Bonhoeffer's ethic is therefore contextual in a double sense. On the one hand, the Christian should make his decisions in a particular *theological* context, namely within a Christo-universal understanding of the world, a world reconciled in Christ, the ontological center of existence. On the other hand, the Christian's decisions are also made in a particular *historical* context, the knowledge of which is indispensable for discerning Christ's peculiar *Gestalt* in this time and place, for uncovering the concrete command of God that will bring reality to expression here and now.[69]

Any particular decision does not derive its rightness or wrongness from an absolute moral standard outside of history. The way reality should conform to the *Gestalt Christi* varies with respect to historical circumstance. Rasmussen writes, "Thus, 'who Christ is for us today' may not be who Christ was for us yesterday."[70]

The foregoing methodology, and most of Rasmussen's work here, is relevant in some way to this current study. The most pertinent part, however, is his chapter titled "The Character of Bonhoeffer's Pacifism." Here, Rasmussen deals specifically with the relationship between developments in Bonhoeffer's "christological ethics" and pacifism as a particular form of resistance activity or political involvement (the previous chapters deal with the relationship between developments in his "christological ethics" and resistance activity in general). Rasmussen very clearly articulates the differences in conspiracy and pacifism. These are two distinct types of political involvement. He thus cautions against "unnuanced" defenses of the "straight and unbroken" continuity claim.[71] He writes, "All the twisting possible cannot make the author of *The Cost of Discipleship* a volunteer for assassinating even Adolf Hitler. Somewhere some modifications have taken place."[72] There are two modifications (developments) in Bonhoeffer's Christology (in the dynamics between Bonhoeffer's theology and historical situation) responsible for the decision for tyrannicide: 1) the "guilt bearing, freely responsible Jesus

69. Ibid., 25.
70. Ibid., 24.
71. Ibid., 117–19.
72. Ibid., 120.

Introduction 25

amidst the new claims of resistance effected the end of asceticism that surfaced as 'pacifism,'" and 2) abandonment of "two-sphere" thinking or the acceptance of one reality or world as "the only place where Christ *is* Christ."[73]

Even with these modifications in Christology, Rasmussen ultimately wants to defend Bonhoeffer's "straight and unbroken course" continuity claim. He is very careful to designate the changes as "modifications" in Christology rather than "new" Christologies. Christology is the base *cantus firmus* that manifests itself differently in different phases of Bonhoeffer's resistance activity. Sometimes it manifests as some variety of pacifism and other times it provides the legitimate possibility of tyrannicide. In other words, the different forms of political involvement are all manifestations of a Christology that was, in form, continuous throughout Bonhoeffer's career. Rasmussen thus declares, "There are modifications, as we have seen, and they are significant; but the search for Jesus Christ among new claims can still be said to show continuities strong enough as to merit the judgment that his life had been without major breaks."[74]

Strengths of the Theological Categories in Context Approach

The strengths of this approach emerge against the backdrop of the weaknesses in the Definition of Pacifism Approach. In terms of the first weakness treated above (the inability to address all phases of Bonhoeffer's life), this approach, because it connects political action with an area of theology, can be used to trace development all throughout Bonhoeffer's career and thus cover all significant shifts and changes. Second (in response to the weakness associated with having to choose and apply a single definition of pacifism out of several possible options), this approach does not require the scholar to choose one single definition from outside the complex matrix of factors determining any of Bonhoeffer's positions. Rather, while still formulating definitions or at least things that function as definitions in order to judge continuities and discontinuities, these definitions emerge strictly from an analysis of the complex interaction between Bonhoeffer's theology and life circumstances. While they incorporate much of what is associated with traditional

73. Ibid., 120–24.
74. Ibid., 126.

definitions of pacifism, just war or tyrannicide, these "definitions" are specific to Bonhoeffer and broader, encompassing the complex factors which helped produce whatever theo-political stances Bonhoeffer takes at any given juncture in his life.

Third, in terms of the weakness associated with the fact that Bonhoeffer did not offer a definitive definition of pacifism, this approach makes more sense than the Definition of Pacifism Approach given both Bonhoeffer's complicated life and the available materials. If Bonhoeffer's position on his own personal pacifism or pacifism as prescriptive for all Christians or all people were so clear, well-defined or consistent in his writings, there would be no scholarly disagreement over the nature of his pacifism or over whether he remained one throughout his life. The available materials (dissertations, sermons, posthumously published fragments, lecture series turned into books, spiritual treatises, prayers, letters, addresses, and essays all born of the tumultuousness of a life marked by significant changes in historical and political circumstances and ministries) simply do not lend themselves to choosing a single definition, either Bonhoeffer's own or an ahistorical definition imposed from the outside, and judging Bonhoeffer's life against it. Rather, these materials, and an honest appraisal of the life situations in which they were produced, lend themselves to contextualizing Bonhoeffer's thinking and actions and looking at continuities and discontinuities.

Weaknesses of the Theological Categories in Context Approach

There is one seeming weakness in this approach from the perspective of those who want to defend Bonhoeffer's "straight and unbroken course" continuity claim. It does not *require* the scholar to provide a standard definition of pacifism by which to judge whether Bonhoeffer ever was a pacifist or remained one. Thus, there is also no absolute standard by which to judge whether Bonhoeffer remained true to his "straight and unbroken course" continuity claim. This weakness, however, is offset by the fact that a look at Bonhoeffer's thinking on war and peace in terms of his historical, theological, and personal life contexts at each phase of his career actually paints a more authentic picture of exactly whatever type of pacifism Bonhoeffer adhered to at each phase (or just-war theory, etc.). Thus, this approach is actually better suited than the Definition of Pacifism Approach for judging whether Bonhoeffer remained faithful to

Introduction

his "straight and unbroken course" continuity claim. Rasmussen, for example, does address the "straight and unbroken course" continuity claim in his work. Indeed, the Theological Categories in Context Approach is eminently valuable in that it is simultaneously "phenomenological" and "historical." When scholars "bracket out" questions about whether or not Bonhoeffer remains true to his claim they allow a more complete, sophisticated and unbiased account of the historical evidence to simply appear. There is no imposed standard or judging device.[75]

There are no formal weaknesses in this method. That is, there is nothing structurally or logically deficient in the approach if one accepts the relationship between a given theological category and form of political involvement for Bonhoeffer. We can thus speak of weaknesses only in terms of the judgments reached as a result of this method's application by certain scholars. Rasmussen and Kuhns, for example, come to similar conclusions. They both want to stress the continuities in Bonhoeffer's forms of political involvement based on continuous Christologies (for Kuhns Bonhoeffer is concerned throughout his career with the appropriate way to "make Christ present" to any historical situation and for Rasmussen Bonhoeffer is consistently concerned with making the cosmic Christ conform to present reality). Kuhns judges that the seeming discontinuity in the type of political involvement is not a "total" reorientation.[76] Rasmussen, for his part, concludes that there are no major breaks in Bonhoeffer's life.[77]

Their conclusions, though, raise a significant question. Is Bonhoeffer's Christology really the most accurate indicator of his forms of political involvement? Or, more specifically, is Christology the category most sensitive to changes in form of political involvement (or, is the form of political involvement the most sensitive to changes in Christology)? Rasmussen and Kuhns both admit that pacifism and tyrannicide are two forms of political involvement different from each other (or at the very least, pacifism and tyrannicide would have been very differ-

---

75. Green, *Bonhoeffer: A Theology of Sociality*, 11. Green implies the importance of avoiding imposing outside frameworks onto Bonhoeffer's life and theology. He writes, "'Historical' points to the examination of Bonhoeffer's writings which takes each work in its own right, and builds up the coherent development of his thought by analyzing continuities, innovations and revisions as his thinking proceeds." Hereafter this title will be abbreviated as *ATS*.

76. Kuhns, *In Pursuit of Dietrich Bonhoeffer*, 227.

77. *RR*, 126.

ent from each other for Bonhoeffer himself).[78] If their presupposition is that Christology informs or influences Bonhoeffer's form of political involvement, one might expect two different types of Christology informing these two different forms of political involvement. Or, if Bonhoeffer's form of political involvement is placed temporally prior in the dynamic (that is, if it is the form of political involvement that affects the Christology), then one would expect two different Christologies resulting from these two different forms of political involvement.[79] Yet, they both argue for a continuous Christology or at least a Christology that only "develops," but does not have "breaks," along with these very different or even totally separate forms of political involvement. Perhaps, then, two very different, or even directly opposing, forms of political involvement (some form of pacifism and tyrannicide) can be connected to what is essentially the same Bonhoefferian Christology. This, however, suggests that Christology is not the most accurate or reliable predictor or determiner of Bonhoeffer's forms of political involvement. Thus, it might not be the best theological category for gauging the developments in his forms of political involvement.

Green's treatment of Bonhoeffer's *Ethics* seems like the more direct, responsive, or appropriate theological category when asking about differing forms of political involvement. After all, any study of pacifism, just-war, and tyrannicide falls properly under the rubric of Ethics. Yet, there are two reasons (I will develop these more extensively in my final chapter) for why Ethics is not the most useful or responsive category in an analysis such as this one. The first one is practical. Green does masterfully show how the thinking in Bonhoeffer's *Ethics* justifies his decision to enter into the conspiracy and agree to tyrannicide. However, Bonhoeffer did not start to write a formal Ethics until 1940. Concentration on one later work does not provide an adequate basis for

78. Kuhns, *In Pursuit of Dietrich Bonhoeffer*, 222. Kuhns writes, "The thought of taking part in a plot to assassinate the Führer would have been totally alien to him." See also, *RR*, 117–20. Rasmussen writes, "Bonhoeffer's movement from a state of pacifism to an outright effort to participate in a necessarily violent overthrow of his government marks a personal reversal of major dimensions."

79. *RR*, 15. Rasmussen implies that the dynamic can work in either direction. He states, "The thesis of this study is that Dietrich Bonhoeffer's resistance activity was his Christology enacted with utter seriousness. Bonhoeffer's resistance was the existential playing out of christological themes. Changes and shifts in his Christology were at the same time changes and shifts in the character of his resistance. In the other direction, changes in his resistance activity had an impact upon his Christology."

Introduction

following developments or breaks in his thinking and actions throughout a whole career, thus concentration on this category does not allow for the type of analysis that can make sense out of the nature of the shift from pacifism to conspiracy in terms of the broadest possible context.[80] The second reason is theological and thus perhaps more weighty and it concerns primarily the nature of Bonhoeffer's Ethics itself. Bonhoeffer's prevailing ethical position is arguably a situational one that can legitimately accommodate a variety of political positions depending on an innumerable variety of factors. Ethics cannot therefore serve as a reliable predictor of responses in the political sphere in a longitudinal study such as this one.

CONCLUSION

The Theological Categories in Context Approach is a methodology tailor-made for understanding Bonhoeffer's thinking, actions, and life. If one wants to understand Bonhoeffer's writings, one has to ask certain questions. What is the genre of the work? What was happening to him personally when he wrote? Where was he when he wrote? What existing church or political situation may have influenced his thinking? His remarkable and dynamic life necessitates this contextualization and any judgment of continuity of discontinuity is simply not fair without very careful attention to this contextualization.[81] One has to be prepared for

---

80. Understanding the change from admitted pacifism to tyrannicide within the context of Bonhoeffer's whole life is not Green's primary aim. Still, I would argue that the category Ethics is too specific for such an analysis—as Bonhoeffer did not make Ethics the explicit subject of a major work until the last phase of his career—thus making an early-phase vs. a later-phase Ethics somewhat difficult. Along these lines it is interesting to note that although Geffrey Kelly or F. Burton Nelson argue in their introduction to Bonhoeffer's writings on Ethics in *A Testament to Freedom*, 343–44, that "the formation of a Christian ethic was something that engaged Bonhoeffer throughout his life," the only writings they chose ("What Is a Christian Ethic?" and a fragment from *Ethics*) were written in 1929 and 1940–43, respectively. While Ethics is a topic Bonhoeffer touches upon in writings throughout his career, the lack any explicit treatment of Ethics in the years between the two writings makes it difficult to accurately trace his thinking on the category throughout all phases of his career. (Hereafter *A Testament to Freedom* will be abbreviated as *TF*).

81. *ATS*, 11. Green writes, "A final comment on the meaning of the word 'contextual' in a 'historical-contextual' method is necessary . . . 'Contextual' points to the personal and social matrix in which his [Bonhoeffer's] thinking was done. Almost all interpreters of Bonhoeffer's theology have repeatedly emphasized the close connection between Bonhoeffer's theology and his life experience."

the fact that the very same concept, word, or theological category may mean something totally different in different parts of his career when one takes context into account. One also has to ask how his thinking may have been either affected by, or a determining factor in, his actions throughout his career.

ELABORATION OF THESIS AND OUTLINE OF PROJECT

The Theological Categories in Context Approach is comprehensive, fair to Bonhoeffer, and, thus, the best approach to his changing forms of political involvement. A careful look at the weaknesses in the instances where this method has been applied, however, shows the importance of the operative theological category. Scholars must find the category that most accurately and reliably illuminates the relationship between his theology and his forms of political involvement. As noted at the onset, I will argue that this theological category is his understanding of the relationship between the church and the world (the church-world relationship). I will also address why it is that the church-world relationship is a more effective category for gauging Bonhoeffer's changing forms of political involvement than Christology and Ethics implicitly throughout the text and explicitly and at length in the concluding chapter.

Chapter 2 explores familial, political, and educational influences from Bonhoeffer's early life and thereby sets the foundations for understanding his thinking and political behavior in his later life. It treats the prevailing ecclesial structure and mindset in pre-Weimar and Weimar Germany, the general German theological backdrop (including implications for political positions and especially prevailing notions of Luther's Two Kingdoms doctrine), the influence of Bonhoeffer's theological mentors, the German political scene, and influences from his early family experience. In particular, this chapter highlights the tension between Bonhoeffer's Lutheran heritage (including an intense love of his country) and his desire to respond to the call of Christ to act for the benefit of others in spite of the dictates of the status quo.

Chapter 3 begins the analysis of the church-world relationship/political position dyad. Bonhoeffer's first phase (1927–1930) comprises writings wherein the relationship between the church and world is characterized by a mild tension. In terms of a comprehensive definition of the thought-action dyad in this phase, the political thinking and behavior consistent with this church-world vision is a "traditional German

Lutheranism" associated with political passivity and support of the status quo. In this vision, citizens and church members do not engage in state-critical behavior and are expected to participate fully in state directives like war. "Tension" indicates a relationship where neither the church nor the world is allowed to take precedence to the point where one or the other becomes rejected or loses its identity or importance. The church offers a message and plays a role (it preaches the Word and dispenses the sacrament) in a somewhat recalcitrant outside world. The church's presence and message does not, though, in any way imply a disavowal of the world. Engaging in the world's concerns does not imply a disavowal of the church. The Christian as church member can and should engage in both the church and the world.

Bonhoeffer holds to a variety of theological positions that support a vision where the church and the world coexist as equally legitimate entities. He, for example, understands transcendence as "this-worldly," social, or ethical in this phase. The experience of transcendence requires contact with the concrete other in time-bound reality. Transcendence is not some specifically religious sphere other than the one available concrete reality in sin-ridden history. Church and state share equally in the world's historical reality as mediated by Christ and thus have equally legitimate and non-interfering roles and jurisdictions. Being part of the church does not place the Christian in another world, reality, or sphere and thus does not interfere with a person's duty to the state. Again, Bonhoeffer's positions on church and state and war and peace were typically Lutheran and German. More specifically, he appears to have adhered to a more conservative interpretation of Luther's Two Kingdoms doctrine, an interpretation requiring political action only in the form of carrying out state directives uncritically. That is, political engagement with and in the world is definitely allowable and expected for the church member. That political engagement, though, means fulfilling expected obligations to the state (like fighting in wars) rather than challenging the state. He was not a pacifist. He had, in fact, espoused an even more radical notion of aggressive war as a necessary instrument for the unfolding of God's purposes in history.[82] Further, in line with his conservative

---

82. Weikart, *The Myth of Dietrich Bonhoeffer*, 120. Weikart writes, "It will probably surprise many to learn that in 1929 Bonhoeffer followed Nietzsche in his adulation of strength and fighting. He blended together Nietzsche's cult of power with Friedrich Naumann's nationalist expansionism, a volatile mixture indeed. He thought that God,

thinking, he was not a political agitator or anti-state political activist in this first phase. He was both a pastor and an academic, fulfilling his role as church teacher and German citizen within the German state.

Chapter 4 addresses Bonhoeffer's second phase (1930–1934) wherein his writings are marked by a vision of the church and world in a "heightened" or "strong" tension. Here, the mutual limits of both entities are more clearly and sharply defined. In terms of political thinking and behavior, he moves from his phase 1 "traditional German Lutheranism" to what can be defined as a "militant, worldly, or political form of pacifism," a position that stands in significant discontinuity relative to his phase-1 vision. His stay in America for one year, wherein he forged a strong relationship with the committed pacifist Jean Lasserre and performed social work as a pastor in Harlem and in classes at Union Theological Seminary, influenced him to construct a new theological vision. He fleshed out the highly theoretical or academic appreciation of church-world and church-state issues from the first phase. Bonhoeffer became more specific about the exact message the church has to offer the world, including primarily designation of the Sermon on the Mount as a world-challenging component of the Word that might call Christians to act according to its dictates. He began to break out of the status quo and react against elements of the oncoming Nazi takeover that he found abhorrent. Bonhoeffer became attentive to what political word the church might say to the state, attending conferences and giving speeches challenging Nazi policies. Thus, along with this sharpening in the church-world relationship came adherence to a more liberal interpretation of Luther's Two Kingdoms doctrine, where the church can criticize the state if it infringes upon the church's ability to preach the gospel.

Some of the themes he sounded in this phase were pacifistic in nature. Bonhoeffer did not, however, set the church against the world so starkly as to advocate for withdrawal from the world. The pacifism was provisional or political, based in both the church's message to a more negatively-construed world and a sense of brotherhood or sisterhood with all humanity. The pacifism took the form of a call for peace within the context of Bonhoeffer's work with the international ecumenical movement. There was an active, this-worldly, or political component to

---

in guiding history, calls on peoples and nations to expand, and this leads inevitably to fighting."

his pacifism from this phase. While commanding obedience and more clearly counter-world, the church's message was not drawn so anti-worldly as to require a church member to disengage from the world. Bonhoeffer's other political behaviors were also consistent with his changed theological vision.

Chapter 5 describes Bonhoeffer's move into the third phase (1934–1939). In this phase his church-world vision can be defined as a "church against world" or "church apart from world" vision, where his writings indicate something close to a sectarian church set against a very negatively construed world. The prevailing political position accompanying this church-world vision for Bonhoeffer was a world-withdrawn or apolitical pacifism. Bonhoeffer reacted to what he and others saw as the increasingly dangerous implications of the oncoming Nazi program. He moved from a worldly or political form of pacifism to a position approaching absolute pacifism. While the church and world existed in some form of tension in phases 1 and 2, in phase 3 Bonhoeffer presented a church-world relationship where the tension was effectively released. Choosing to be a church member meant disavowal of the world and choosing to be part of the world meant disavowal of the church. Bonhoeffer expressed his negative understanding of the world in a variety of ways. The result was a type of "two-sphered" thinking where there was a worldly sphere and an otherworldly sphere. Response to Christ's call to discipleship necessarily put the Christian in the otherworldly sphere. It put the Christian in opposition to the structures or immediacies of life or the world.

Bonhoeffer's "church against world" (or "church apart from world") stance, after a few years of active resistance, became a prescription for passivity. The Christian's radical disengagement from the world meant that he or she relinquished responsibility for its course. The church could only stand by as the world moved on in whatever political or other direction it moved. In fact, the church's non-involvement and inactivity in worldly affairs served only as a way to highlight the negativity of the world. If Christians were to engage in the world, it would not be done for the sake of the integrity of the world's structures but only to suffer for being Christ's disciples. In this way, the release of the tension between church and world placed Bonhoeffer outside of the Lutheran Two Kingdoms thinking. Two Kingdoms thinking presupposes some form of tension between church and world such that engagement in the world for the sake of the legitimacy of its structures is required of the Christian. Along with his most negative understanding of the world (and the corresponding prescription for church passivity) came Bonhoeffer's most strongly pacifistic statements and positions, positions not typically associated with Luther or the two kingdoms thinking. In terms of the connection between thought and action, Bonhoeffer, although initially involved in the Church struggle in a more visible way, eventually engaged from a withdrawn position.[83] He spent time away from Germany in London, directed a clandestine seminary, and even contemplated escaping permanently to the United States in 1939.

Chapter 6 treats Bonhoeffer's fourth phase (1939–1945). In the final phase his understanding of the church-world relationship took a radical turn. Reacting to perceived failures in the actions of the Confessing Church and the ecumenical movement and the atrocities of Hitler's regime, Bonhoeffer related the church and world in this phase such that the difference between the two was seemingly eclipsed. Bonhoeffer's changed church-world vision moved him from something close to absolute pacifism to a position that can be defined as "just war thinking including the possibility of tyrannicide." His changed church-world understanding found its most radical expression in his *Letters and Papers from Prison* where the distinction between Christian as church member and Christian as citizen in the world faded. As in phase 3, because the tension between the church and the world experiences a release (although in the opposite direction), political positions not typically associated with Luther or the Lutheran Two Kingdoms doctrine (like tyrannicide, for instance) become acceptable. Indeed, Bonhoeffer decided that action in the world in the form of direct involvement in the secular or political sphere was again acceptable. Although he had the opportunity, he did not escape to the United States during the war. Instead, he returned to Germany to share in the struggle against Nazism in a new way and entered into the conspiracy.

The final chapter re-visits the scholarly positions and the framework laid out in the first chapter. In light of the church-world/political action connection developed in the body of the text, this chapter shows how using the church-world category in the context of the Theological

---

83. See Karl Barth's scathing November 20, 1933, letter attacking Bonhoeffer for this withdrawal in *No Rusty Swords*. From Robinson, *Collected Works of Dietrich Bonhoeffer* 1:237–40. Hereafter this title will be abbreviated as *NRS*.

Categories in Context Approach both maximizes the strengths and minimizes the weaknesses of the Definition of Pacifism Approach and the Theological Categories in Context Approach (as it has been used by other scholars). In terms of the Theological Categories in Context Approach, this chapter also shows how use of church-world rather than Christology and Ethics is more effective in tracing and understanding the continuities and mostly the discontinuities in Bonhoeffer's career. Indeed, the results of my work indicate somewhat strong discontinuities in Bonhoeffer's thinking and political behavior rather than continuities or developments, thus making this work subject to criticism by scholars who argue for stronger continuities in his life. This chapter will also present some scholarship from outside of Bonhoeffer and Bonhoeffer studies indicating that the church-world relationship is a reasonable choice in terms of understanding how the church and its members engage politically in the world. The final part of the chapter will address the controversial concern with continuity in general and especially in light of Bonhoeffer's "straight and unbroken course" continuity claim made near the end of his life.

METHODOLOGICAL ISSUES AND CONCERNS

My way of looking at the relationship between Bonhoeffer's church-world thinking and his political involvement raises a few methodological concerns. First, it should be clear that the application of the Theological Categories in Context Approach does not represent an attempt to impose a framework from the outside onto Bonhoeffer's career or to fit his theology or actions into a construct. Rather, as stated earlier this way of approaching the problem is historical or even phenomenological in the truest sense. It attempts to understand the relationship between Bonhoeffer's thinking and activity as they appear only within the context of his life as that life progressed. Simply stated, a look at Bonhoeffer's career reveals that his phases as someone who accepts war, a political or qualified pacifist, a more intense pacifist, and a conspirator are accompanied by four different understandings of the church-world relationship. I will, however, point to scholarship from outside Bonhoeffer's life and theology in my concluding chapter and argue that certain conceptions of the church-world relationship logically or theoretically support certain forms of political thinking and involvement. However, I do this as a way to buttress my argument. I do it to explain on a theoretical level why it makes sense that Bonhoeffer was some form of pacifist during the time in his career where he had a certain conception of the church-world relationship. This scholarship does not try to establish "why" or "that" he thought or acted in a certain manner. The historical evidence from Bonhoeffer's life and writings is self-corroborating and stands on its own. In other words, history reveals that Bonhoeffer's understanding of the church-world relationship changes in unison with his form of political involvement (or vice versa) with or without any explanation of why a certain conception of the church-world relationship makes sense in relation to a certain form of political involvement.

Another important methodological issue concerns the connection between continuities and discontinuities in the church-world relationship and other related theological categories like Ethics or Christology. As Charles Marsh points out, there is a danger of misinterpreting Bonhoeffer if scholars separate out some portions of his theology.[84] This is especially the case here as Bonhoeffer's church-world theology and his Ethics and Christology are all closely connected. A full examination of these relationships could be the focus of other similarly lengthy works. In short, the argument in this work presupposes that the church-world relationship, while obviously connected to Christology and Ethics, can be isolated as the more effective determiner of forms of political behavior without having to entirely sever their relationships. Christology and Ethics will appear in circumscribed roles in my work. I will treat Christology in two ways. First, I will examine Bonhoeffer's Christology where its overlap with the church-world relationship is significant enough to help illuminate or further explain the nature of the connection between the church-world relationship and Bonhoeffer's political positions. Second, in the concluding chapter I will treat in a thorough and detailed way why focusing on the church-world relationship, rather than Christology, is a more effective way to approach the stated problem. It is a bit more difficult to separate Ethics from the church-world relationship in this particular study as positions like pacifism, just-war, and tyrannicide technically fall under the jurisdiction of Ethics. Ethics will thus be an implicit and mostly explicit overlapping category with church-world at points. I will, though, just like in the case of Christology, highlight Bonhoeffer's Ethics explicitly where its overlap with the church-world

---

84. Marsh, *Reclaiming Bonhoeffer*, viii–ix. Marsh's argument centers on resetting Bonhoeffer's Christology into its Trinitarian grounding.

relationship is significant enough to help illuminate or further explain the nature of the connection between the church-world relationship and Bonhoeffer's political positions. Second, in the concluding chapter I will treat in a thorough and detailed way why focusing on the church-world relationship, rather than Ethics, is a more effective way to approach the stated problem. Specifically, I will show how the church-world relationship actually determines Bonhoeffer's ethical thinking and action.

A third methodological question emerges in relation to how to use the broad, well-informed, and comprehensive definitions of Bonhoeffer's political thinking and forms of political involvement that arise from careful analysis of his church-world theology in its context. Because the source of these definitions is the cluster of interrelated factors at moments from within Bonhoeffer's life, judgments about continuity and discontinuity must also come strictly from within the flow of Bonhoeffer's life itself. Thus, rather than using a definition from outside of his life to make one judgment about one shift at one point in his life (from some form of pacifism to tyrannicide in 1939), judgments about continuities and discontinuities are made as Bonhoeffer moved from one phase to the next. More specifically, the observer can only look at the shifts from the perspective of one step ahead (looking backwards from the standpoint of the succeeding phase) or look at them from one step behind (how does the succeeding phase look from the standpoint of the preceding phase). The only acceptable judgments made from outside of Bonhoeffer's developing life come from an overall assessment of all of the shifts and changes made from the standpoint of the very end. However, in that instance the observer would simply be reiterating the evaluations made concerning any individual shifts. The important methodological concern is avoiding as much as possible making judgments about discontinuities or continuities with definitions that come from outside of Bonhoeffer himself or from outside of the flow of his life as it developed. Another way to look at this method is to try to see it as a process of following Bonhoeffer's development along with him, discovering his shifts as he made them rather than holding him to a framework from outside of his developing life.

Another methodological issue concerns this very problem of using materials from outside of Bonhoeffer himself. While there obviously are ample secondary sources providing definitions of pacifism, just war thinking, or tyrannicide, the focus here will be developing definitions from Bonhoeffer's life and writings themselves. Again, the concern here is with avoiding unfair judgments of Bonhoeffer. This does not mean that the positions Bonhoeffer takes do not fall to some degree into certain categories (like pacifism and just war thinking) as those positions have been generally defined. In addition, and as noted above, there is ample scholarship from outside Bonhoeffer's thinking and experience to suggest that certain understandings of the church-world relationship are consistent with certain political positions. Again, though, scholarship of these sorts do not actually establish what type of pacifist Bonhoeffer may have been, for example, or establish any existential connection between his church-world thinking and his political positions.

Another issue related to methodology concerns the usefulness of this study like this current one. It should be made clear from the outset that the main purpose of my work is not to show how Bonhoeffer's thinking or political action either is, or somehow could be, directly relevant or applicable to any similar specific situation we may be encountering currently. Further, this work is not directly concerned with the general problem of violence, war, or tyrannical dictatorships in the modern world. There are many articles and some important books on Bonhoeffer's relevance for today in various ways. Rather, this work falls under the category of historical theology. In this version of historical theology the goal is to understand a theologian's life, writings, and behavior strictly within his or her own historical context. In particular, this work stands as another voice in the conversation about how to understand the largely historical, multi-faceted, and seemingly intractable problem of Bonhoeffer's shifting behavior in the political sphere with respect to his theology and life contexts.

There are of course insights about Bonhoeffer's theological and political responses to his situation that might be useful for any seemingly relevant contemporary situation today. Yet, as Stephen Haynes strongly implies in his section "Harlem and Berlin" in his *The Bonhoeffer Legacy: Post-Holocaust Perspectives*, scholars have to take great care even when trying to apply dynamics from one historical moment in Bonhoeffer's life to a later one. Haynes sharply gives reason for pause when considering the transferability of Bonhoeffer's concern for ethnic minorities in Harlem in his early years to his later actions on behalf of the Jews on the basis of anti-racist sensibilities. His argument rests on both a distinction for Bonhoeffer between class and racial oppression and an unsophisticated understanding of the differences between the ideological foundations for anti-black and anti-Jewish thinking. Haynes goes on to make a further distinction between acting on behalf of the oppressed out of theological motives and out of a concern for "violated human rights."[85] If the connection between, or applicability of, Bonhoeffer's theology and actions from one event or situation to another one just a few years later in his life is fraught with such potential thorny contextual difficulty, then how much more care must scholars take when connecting or applying Bonhoeffer's thinking or behavior to situations years beyond or geographical worlds apart from his own?

Perhaps the most controversial issue has to do with the questions of political and theological continuity or discontinuity in Bonhoeffer. As I noted above, there are several other examples of scholars insisting on continuity in thought or action besides the ones cited in above sections. One need only look at Heinz Eduard Tödt's "contradiction" of his teacher, Karl Barth. Tödt insists, "Bonhoeffer's theological outline does have a strong continuity in it, from its beginnings to the end."[86] Or one could look at a more recent 2005 article, "Pacifism and Tyrannicide: Bonhoeffer's Christian Peace Ethic," wherein Clifford Green ultimately wants to preserve some continuity between Bonhoeffer's pre- and post-conspiratorial theology and activities. He does so by arguing that for Bonhoeffer the standard definition of pacifism (a definition equated primarily with a principle of non-violence) can be broadened into the concept "peace ethic" (a category which is more consistent with Bonhoeffer's disavowal of ethical systems rooted in principles). This broadening allows Green to dissolve Bonhoeffer's commitment to peace throughout several aspects of his theology. He argues that Bonhoeffer's peace ethic "cannot be separated from his Christology, his understanding of discipleship and the Sermon on the Mount, his way of reading the Bible, and his understanding of the gospel and of the church."[87] Green can thus argue that Bonhoeffer does not relinquish his "peace ethic" during the plans for violence as there is enough theological continuity between themes in *Ethics* and *Letters* and previous works. In addition, there is some historical evidence to suggest that Bonhoeffer was still committed to peace during the conspiratorial activities.[88]

85. Haynes, *The Bonhoeffer Legacy*, 8–9.
86. Tödt, *Authentic Faith: Bonhoeffer's Theological Ethics in Context*, 7.
87. Green, "Pacifism and Tyrannicide," 31–47. This quotation is from p. 45.
88. Ibid., 45–47.

The concern for establishing continuity in thought and action is understandable for a few reasons, all of which have been addressed above in various ways. To summarize, first there is Bonhoeffer's own "straight and unbroken course" continuity claim. In addition, there is a legitimate concern for guarding the integrity of Bonhoeffer's theology from those who would use it to espouse novel and arguably unfounded positions like the "death of God" theologians. Lastly, there do appear to be general strains of significant continuity in various theological categories throughout Bonhoeffer's career (Christology provides the prime example). While understandable, this scholarly concern for establishing continuity runs the risk of robbing Bonhoeffer the freedom or spontaneity to creatively respond to extreme challenges in both his theologizing and his activity in the political sphere; to not let him go beyond the constraints imposed by holding him to his initial ideas or even later variations on them. In addition, as noted above, if there is some kind of consistency between thought and action, and the type of pacifism described in *Discipleship* is decisively inconsistent with tyrannicide as many scholars admit or even common sense would dictate, then it is only logical to assume discontinuities in theology. For these reasons, and for reasons much more intricate and complicated to be addressed more explicitly throughout this study and in a section in the concluding chapter, highlighting discontinuities in Bonhoeffer's thinking and action would seem unproblematic.

Finally, my way of organizing the material and approaching the problem is designed to understand and explain the problem of Bonhoeffer's changing forms of political involvement in the most comprehensive sense possible. There are some personal letters and statements from various points in Bonhoeffer's career which can support arguments about his own understanding of his political changes. While I would argue that it is possible to reach something that plausibly approaches Bonhoeffer's self-understanding, it is not my explicit aim to provide an answer to the question of why he decided to act differently at different times that might be acceptable to Bonhoeffer himself. It would be difficult or even impossible to state conclusively Bonhoeffer's own understanding of his own behavior. Rather, given both all forms of existing data (personal statements, too) and the other scholarly approaches, I attempt to provide an approach and an answer that ensures the best understanding and explanation of his apparent discontinuities.

2

Bonhoeffer's Early Life:
His Theological, Political, Ecclesial, and Family Contexts

INTRODUCTION

THE FIRST CHAPTER DESCRIBES the problem and the scholarly assessment of the problem and establishes a framework for approaching and offering a solution. As such, the chapter provides the theoretical presuppositions and framework for the entire study. In addition to these theoretical presuppositions, there are important historical, socio-political, ecclesial, intellectual, and family influences from the years before the four operative phases which provide invaluable background for understanding comprehensively the complex changes in Bonhoeffer's theology and forms of political involvement throughout his whole life.

In this chapter I will suggest that Bonhoeffer's family heritage, early life, and academic experiences within the context of the shifting ecclesial and socio-political situation in pre-Weimar and Weimar Germany provide the foundations for his career-long and varied forms of theological and political thinking and behavior. These early formative experiences are especially instructive for understanding Bonhoeffer as they marked him with two potentially opposing and powerful themes that would re-emerge in important and various ways all throughout his career. One theme was a somewhat conservative commitment to, or intense love for, his homeland, including a willingness to take any measure necessary for its continued survival as a nation. Indeed, his early theological mentors, family experiences, and his church tradition were clearly influences in the later healthy and unhealthy nationalist sentiments in his works. The other theme, based in the influence of certain elements in his family heritage, and resulting partially from the interaction with certain theologians, was a radical openness to acting against the dictates of the status quo out of Christian motives.[1]

SOCIO-POLITICAL, FAMILIAL, AND ECCLESIAL CONTEXTS

Bonhoeffer's early life did not, of course, include direct political involvement. However, there were experiences and dynamics from that time that arguably affected, or at least provided an overall context, for his future political thinking and activities. The political stances and socioeconomic statuses of key family members within the shifting German political situation were one important influence on his future political positions. His family's relationship with the German military and the family's reactions to war also provide some important background for Bonhoeffer's later thinking on war. Finally, his family's relationship with, and attitudes toward, the church provide important background material.

Germany was under the Wilhelmine Empire (the *Kaiserreich* founded by Otto von Bismarck in 1871) during the first twelve years of Bonhoeffer's life (1906–1918). The German Empire was at the height of its political and economic power under the *Kaiserreich*. The German sociopolitical situation during the *Kaiserreich*, though, was characterized by the presence of conflicting factions. One faction was the more liberal industrial working class manifest in the Social Democratic Party, the

---

1. Koch, "The Theological Responses of Karl Barth and Dietrich Bonhoeffer," iv. The fact that there is a tension between love of country and conscience throughout Bonhoeffer's career is a main argument in Koch's dissertation. He writes, "Barth's early concerns were primarily ecclesiastical, resisting any attempt to impose National Socialist ideology on the church. His resistance to the Hitler regime became increasingly political, moving to the point where he depicted it as a demonic realm. No such progression is apparent from the works of Bonhoeffer... What one sees in Bonhoeffer's thought is a struggle between his own sense of call and his Lutheran theological heritage. While the possibility of resistance is raised in 'Die Kirche von der Judenfrage,' one finds quite traditional views of church-state relations in *Nachfolge* and *Ethics*." My assessment here is a "filling out" of Koch's idea in his dissertation that there is a tension between Bonhoeffer's "own sense of call" and "his Lutheran theological heritage." The radical independence of thought and desire to act for the benefit of others in spite of the dictates of the expected or status quo corresponds to Koch's "own sense of call" and Bonhoeffer's intense love of the German state in history is a component of his "Lutheran theological heritage."

socialist-oriented Free Trade Unions, and the Roman Catholic Center Party. On the other side were the conservative monarchical-minded anti-democratic aristocrats, military officer corps, state bureaucrats, commercial/industrial elites, and the educated middle classes (the *Bildungsbürgertum*), including the various professions. These latter groups generally supported or identified with the original Bismarckian system. The conflict between the conservative faction, characterized by strong military allegiance having roots all the way back in the Prussian spirit, and the newer more democratically minded socialist faction, would make for a markedly unstable Germany and ultimately lay the foundation for the rise of Hitler's Third Reich.[2]

Bonhoeffer's immediate and extended family members were very well educated and affluent people who fit socioeconomically and logically into a conservative or status quo supporting class.[3] Bonhoeffer grew up privileged and in comfort.[4] Members of his aristocratic and

2. See. Moses, "Bonhoeffer's Germany," 3–21. See also Shirer, *The Rise and Fall of the Third Reich*, 95. The Weimar Republic, in fact, can be seen as an aberration from an otherwise logical straight line from the Prussian usurpation of the German State to the rise of Hitler. Shirer writes, "Bismarck's crowning achievement, the creation of the Second Reich, came on January 18, 1871, when King Wilhelm I of Prussia was proclaimed Emperor of Germany in the Hall of Mirrors at Versailles . . . From 1871 to 1933 and indeed to Hitler's end in 1945, the course of German history as a consequence, was to run, with the exception of the interim of the Weimar Republic, in a straight line and with utter logic."

3. *DB*, 3–18. Bonhoeffer's maternal grandmother, Clara von Hase (née Countess Kalckreuth), took piano lessons from Clara Schumann and Franz Liszt. Her father, Count Stanislaus Kalckreuth, was a member of Prussia's elite art world. Clara's husband, Dietrich's maternal grandfather Karl-Alfred von Hase, was a Church Consistory council member and professor of Practical Theology. He was eventually made chaplain of the Potsdam Court by Kaiser Wilhelm II. His sermons were praised by Wilhelm I and Friedrich III. Bonhoeffer's paternal grandfather, Friedrich Bonhoeffer (1828–1907), of Swabian descent, was a high judicial official for the State of Württemberg. He was politically conservative. His paternal grandmother, Julie Bonhoeffer (née Tafel), was, on the other hand, from a liberal family who challenged the status quo. Dietrich's father, Karl Bonhoeffer, was director of a mental hospital and later accepted the most important professorship for psychiatry and neurology in Germany. Dietrich's mother, Paula, was an extraordinarily gifted person who schooled the children at home. It is clear from this brief description that Bonhoeffer's family was in the socioeconomic elite.

4. *DB*, 16. The Bonhoeffers owned more than one home, some replete with maids and servants. Bethge notes, "By present-day standards the Bonhoeffer household was conducted on an inconceivably lavish scale; but at the same time, the parents strongly disliked personal boasting or pretension." See also, *TF*, 5. Kelly and Nelson add, "Yet the sparks of passion are barely detectable in Bonhoeffer's earliest years spent in an atmosphere of relative affluence. He came from a family that enjoyed abundance, even privilege."

well-to-do family did not, however, fully support conservative political positions in significant ways at various times in Germany's shifting political situation. In fact, Bonhoeffer inherited from his family legacy a strong sense of freedom and independence of thinking and action beyond the accepted. Bethge frames this friction between "the expected" and independence in terms of the tension between a commitment to the socioeconomic and political "status quo" (a conservative nationalism) and the respect for all members of any culture (humanism).[5]

While the presence of radical political positions in the family was low if not negligible, Bonhoeffer's immediate family did include a mixture of those who leaned toward conservative positions and those who leaned in a more liberal direction. This mixture is rooted in the varying political views of his grandparents and their immediate families. Bonhoeffer's ancestry on his mother's side consisted of persons of power and privilege who were affiliated with the Prussian Kaiser. His maternal grandfather, Karl Alfred von Hase, was the son of the famed church historian Karl August von Hase. Karl August became a renowned theologian and eventually enjoyed friendships with, and the respect of, the aristocracy. We can see evidence of Karl August's dedication to the Prussian ideal when Bethge writes of him, "In 1870, he was pleased when his three sons marched into France under the Prussian flag."[6] Karl August's marriage to Pauline Härtel, daughter of a Leipzig publisher, also helped introduce him to cultural elites.

Karl August's son, Karl Alfred, while not as theologically astute, successful, or well known as his father, eventually won the respect of both Wilhelm I and Friedrich III. After serving as senior military chaplain in Königsberg, Karl Alfred was appointed the chaplain of the Potsdam Court by Kaiser Wilhelm II in 1889. Bonhoeffer's maternal grandmother, Clara von Hase (born Countess Kalckrueth), was thoroughly immersed in Prussian sensibilities, her father being Count Stanislaus Kalckreuth, a member of the Prussian military. Bethge offers a general summary of the socio-political perspective on Dietrich's maternal grandparent's side. He writes, "Although not blind to certain aberrations within the German monarchical system, they did not criticize the existing social order and led a full life within it. The national ethos was a central value."[7]

5. Ibid., 9.
6. Ibid., 6.
7. *DB*, 9.

Even with this status quo supporting ethos, one incident from Dietrich's maternal extended lineage illustrates the tension between nationalism and acting on behalf of humanistic ideals. Karl Alfred was made senior military chaplain in Konigsberg in 1876. However, he asked to be released from his position after a short two and a half years. Although Karl-Alfred's published family chronicle did not give precise reasons for the departure, family statements give two reasons. First, Karl-Alfred resisted the Kaiser's attempts to preach. Second, and perhaps more importantly, he "dared to contradict the Kaiser when he characterized the proletariat as a 'pack of dogs.'"[8] Though clearly part of, and in service to, the privileged class, Karl Alfred had the strength and independence to disagree politically with existing powers for the sake of identification with the common people.

Friedrich Bonhoeffer, Dietrich's paternal grandfather, was a high judiciary court official for the state of Wurttmberg. While he disliked local Wurttemberg nationalism, he was politically conservative and was disappointed in Swabian democracy due to its "lax or dismissive position toward the church."[9] Dietrich's paternal grandmother, Julie Bonhoeffer (born Tafel), introduced the more outwardly liberal political sensibilities into the family. Her family was infamously free-spirited, radically democratic, and highly critical of the status quo. Julie's father was one of four brothers, all of whom held radically democratic views in protest against the status quo.[10] A politically significant instance of a collision between independence and acting as expected involves Julie. The remarkable event involves an elderly Julie in Nazi-controlled Germany in 1933. At age ninety-one, Julie "marched past the S.A. (Nazi Storm Troopers) cordons promoting the boycott of Jewish business on 1 April 1933, to shop at the Jewish-owned 'Kaufhaus des Wesens' on Tauentzienstrase in Berlin."[11]

Bonhoeffer's father Karl was a successful psychiatrist who, as noted above, provided a lavish lifestyle for Dietrich's family. His early politi-

---

8. See *DB*, 5–9, for a brief account of Karl-Alfred von Hase's life. See also, *TF*, 5. Geffrey B. Kelly and F. Burton Nelson describe the event as follows, "he [Karl-Alfred] fell 'out of grace' with the kaiser for his bold contradiction of the emperor who had referred to the common people as 'rabble.'"

9. *DB*, 10.

10. See *DB*, 10–13, for a brief account of Julie Bonhoeffer's life, personality, and the politically subversive nature of her father and brothers.

11. Ibid., 11.

cal convictions were of a more conservative nature as evidenced by his participation in the Hedgehogs, a Swabian fraternity founded in 1871 and patriotic in nature supporting the new German Reich. Karl noted that "there were hardly any political differences of opinion. All of us were fairly unanimous in our Bismarckian convictions, revered the elderly Kaiser and were outraged by the black-and-red gold flags of the greater German that hung occasionally before the 'Kaiser's Inn' during the election and other political events. Without reservation, everyone was happy about the united Germany under Prussia."[12] This association with the Hedgehogs would become relevant in terms of understanding the early political leanings of Bonhoeffer and his brothers during the first years of the Weimar Republic.

The Weimar Republic, a democratic regime fashioned out of the wreckage of World War I by a coalition of the Social Democrats (SPD), Democrats (DDP), and the Center Party was, as briefly noted above, a bitterly embattled regime. There were, in addition to the democratically minded parties that formed the Republic, a few important anti-coalition conservative and radical left-wing (Communist) political parties that desired a non-democratic or authoritarian form of government.[13] The Weimar Republic was almost constantly in turmoil, barely withstanding several political and economic crises and attempts at overthrow until its final collapse at the hands of the rising Hitler in 1932–1933.

The SPD, the largest party in the republic, was a working-class party traditionally critical of the monarchist values of the *Kaiserreich* and supported the democratic government throughout. It was not a revolutionary party and was in fact anti-communist, but its sounding of Marxist themes scared the German middle classes who were leery of communism. The DDP, for its part, eventually "became increasingly antidemocratic in sentiment."[14] The German People's Party (DVP), created in 1919 by Gustav Stresemann, was a middle-class party that sometimes worked with socialists for the sake of stability. It, too, because of the influence of conservative business factions, ultimately became increasingly anti-democratic and monarchist.[15] The Center Party was a mostly Roman

---

12. Ibid., 49.

13. Spielvogel, *Hitler and Nazi Germany*, 11. Hereafter this title will be abbreviated as *HNG*.

14. Ibid., 13.

15. Ibid.

Catholic party whose adherents included Catholics among all social classes and geographical regions.[16] Like the SDP, it was critical of the *Kaiserreich* but for different reasons. The Center Party "represented the Roman Catholic population's opposition to the Protestant (*Evangelisch*) and Prussian hegemony in the united Germany."[17] However, in a naive attempt to have a voice in a Hitler-controlled Germany, this party capitulated to him in an important vote which ultimately led to the party's demise.[18]

The German National People's Party (DNVP), consisting of the landed aristocracy, business owners, and the upper middle class, was the most ardent right-wing opponent of the Weimar Republic. As the 1920s progressed, the DNVP decisively turned against the Republic and wanted to eliminate Socialists and Communists from the German political scene. This party became Hitler's coalition partner in 1933. The Republic sustained attacks from the radical left-wing also. The German Communist Party (KPD) attempted a communist "putsch" in 1919 that was ultimately bloodily suppressed by the army and the Free Corps, a band of World I veterans who could not adjust to post-war civilian life. There was also a right-wing attempt at an overthrow in the 1920 Kapp Putsch. A Prussian civil servant named Wolfgang Kapp and the former general Walther von Lüttwitz attempted to create a dictatorship.[19]

Ultimately, the democratic ideal of Weimar, Germany, was constantly troubled by the presence of extreme leftist and extreme rightist factions from its very beginnings to its end. Bitter over what was perceived as a betrayal by the coalition that formed the Weimar Republic,[20] the rightist forces were driven by a yearning for a reinstatement of a pre-war Wilhelmine-like regime. These forces would eventually triumph in the person and political conquest of Hitler and his conservative National

---

16. Ibid.

17. Moses, "Bonhoeffer's Germany," 4.

18. *HNG*, 72–73. See also, Craig, *Germany: 1866–1945*, 581–82, for a description of the party's demise in July of 1933.

19. *HNG*, 13–14.

20. Ibid., 12. This was known as the "stab in the back" theory. It had several formulations. Generally, it was the idea that the German armies were not "really defeated in the field, but stabbed in the back by civilian traitors . . . It was the new government, composed of unpatriotic Socialists (many of them Jews, according to Hitler's version of the myth), who had arranged the armistice, written the new democratic constitution and signed the peace treaty." See also, Borg, *The Old Prussian Church*, 54–55 and 213–15, for a full treatment of the theory and especially its theological underpinnings.

Socialist Party (NSDAP).[21] Hitler was, indeed, perceived by a majority of Germans as the savior of the German Empire; according to this view he was the logical successor in a line of great dictators beginning with Frederick the Great and continuing through Bismarck and Hindenburg. The Weimar Republic, with its anti-Prussian emphasis on liberal democracy, stood only as a temporary obstacle to this otherwise straight and unstoppable progression.[22]

This brief overview of Weimar political dynamics forms the backdrop for evaluating the political positions in Bonhoeffer's immediate family. Bonhoeffer's brothers, Karl-Friedrich and Klaus, refused to join the Hedgehogs. Karl-Friedrich "emphatically refused" to join when he learned they were expected to suppress the uprisings in Stuttgart and Munich.[23] Karl-Friedrich was a supporter of the Social Democrat government that seized power as the result of the November Revolution, a front-line socialist leaning that led to conflict with other branches of the Bonhoeffer family living outside of Berlin. Bethge's comments that Karl Bonhoeffer "let him go his own way" and that this socialist position "made him something of an outsider" in the Bonhoeffer home indicates the moderate political atmosphere in the home. Klaus and his friends' membership in the German People's Party (DVP) and the Democratic Party (DDP), as also noted by Bethge, "represented the family's bourgeois political outlook at the time."[24]

---

21. See *HNG*, 41–56, for a treatment of the early history of the rise of Hitler's party.

22. Shirer, *The Rise and Fall of the Third Reich*, 90–91. Shirer writes, "Nazism and the Third Reich, in fact, were but a logical continuation of German history . . . In the delirious days of the annual rallies of the Nazi party . . . I used to be accosted by a swarm of hawkers selling a picture postcard on which we were shown the portraits of Frederick the Great, Bismarck, Hindenburg and Hitler. The inscription read, 'What the King conquered, the Prince formed, the Field Marshal defended, the Soldier saved and unified.' Thus Hitler, the soldier, was portrayed not only as the savior and unifier of Germany but as the successor of these celebrated figures who had made the country great. The implication of the continuity of German history, culminating in Hitler's rule, was not lost upon the multitude. The very expression 'the Third Reich' also served to strengthen this concept. The First Reich has been the medieval Holy Roman Empire; the Second Reich had been that which was formed by Bismarck in 1871 after Prussia's defeat of France. Both had added glory to the German name. The Weimar Republic, as Nazi propaganda had it, had dragged that fair name in the mud. The Third Reich restored it, just as Hitler had promised. Hitler's Germany, then, was depicted as a logical development from all that had gone before—or at least all that had been glorious."

23. *DB*, 49.

24. Ibid., 30–31.

It is clear from the foregoing that the tension between liberal or humanistic positions and positions more sympathetic to a monarchical status quo supporting conservatism in Bonhoeffer's family, both his extended and immediate, was a microcosm of the larger German sociopolitical situation in both the Willhelmite and Weimar contexts. Four themes emerge from this family history. First, there was no unified political stance expected or required of family members. Second, amidst the diversity, there appears to be a higher concentration of persons in the more traditional or even conservative or status quo supporting mindset, those either in direct service to the monarchy, existing comfortably under the monarchy, or at least bourgeois enough not to be given to open protest. Third, while family members were socioeconomically, logically, and actually in some cases affiliated with the establishment, this did not preclude the strong presence of those who would take what would be considered a counter-position out of a high-minded appreciation of rational humanism (including at least one who was an outright socialist). Finally, no one in the family, besides Karl-Friedrich, was given to extreme political positions or parties (radical rightist or radical leftist). No one in the family became a member of the Nazi Party.[25] As Hans Pfeifer writes in the "Editor's Afterword to the German Edition" of *The Young Bonhoeffer 1918–1927*, "Politically, the Bonhoeffer family was fairly down to earth."[26] All of these themes combine to make any strains of either status quo supporting nationalistic tendencies or readiness for open protest against the Nazis not surprising for Dietrich at any time in his career. Renate Bethge's article makes abundantly clear the commitment the larger Bonhoeffer family had in terms of resistance to the Nazi regime.[27] Bonhoeffer himself, in the last three phases of his life, would, like some of his ancestors, act contrary to the expected for a person of his socioeconomic status.[28]

---

25. Rasmussen and Bethge, *Dietrich Bonhoeffer: His Significance*, 4.
26. Pfeifer, "Editor's Afterword to the German Edition," 566.
27. Rasmussen and Bethge, *Dietrich Bonhoeffer*, 4ff.
28. *TF*, 5. Kelly and Nelson, for example, place Bonhoeffer's activities on behalf of the Jewish community in line with the actions of his grandfather. They write, "Dietrich's grandfather . . . fell 'out of grace' with the kaiser for his bold contradiction of the emperor . . . Dietrich's vocation would take him even further out of step with a German leader's attitude, even to making common cause with the Third Reich's 'rabble,' the Jewish community."

Family Experiences with War

There are also a few instructive anecdotes concerning family reactions to the First World War in addition to his family's socio-political heritage. The first story involves the family's reaction to the war when young Dietrich was only nine years old. Eberhard Bethge, after noting Karl Bonhoeffer's uneasiness about the German entry to the war, writes,

> For the younger children the outbreak of war was a time of great excitement. At the end of July they were hurriedly brought home after a month's holiday in glorious weather in Friedrichsbrunn. When one of the girls dashed into the house shouting: "Hurrah there's a war," her face was slapped. The first German successes filled Dietrich with boyish enthusiasm. When he was nine he wrote his parents from Friedrichsbrunn asking them to send him all the newspaper clippings with news from the front; he had learned from his big brothers and at school how to stick colored pins into a map showing the advance of the front line.[29]

Bethge's account of "the slap" and Bonhoeffer's enthusiasm about the German war efforts indicate a few things. The parental reaction to the war was another instance of "acting against type."[30] More importantly, Bethge's quote also indicates Dietrich's strong sense of pride in his nation and its war efforts. Again, this theme of attachment to his homeland is one that reverberates strongly throughout Bonhoeffer's life, even in the phases where he acts against the existing German government.

The second family experience with war involves Bonhoeffer's two brothers, Walter and Karl-Friedrich, who left the home for combat. Walter was wounded and eventually died on April 28, 1917. The family was devastated. The death "broke his mother's spirit" who "spent weeks in bed at the home of the Schönes next door." The death of his brother and the mother's despondent reaction, moreover, "left an indelible mark on the child Dietrich Bonhoeffer."[31] Brown credits these experiences for the beginning of Bonhoeffer's life-long "keen political interest."[32] Paul

---

29. *DB*, 26.

30. Brown, "Bonhoeffer and Pacifism," 33. Brown writes, "There is not much in Dietrich Bonhoeffer's bourgeois rootage to point to an atypical orientation to the problem of war and peace. Eberhard Bethge does, however, relate the deep impact of the First World War on the life of the family." Brown then tells the story about the slap, suggesting that the parental reaction was somewhat "atypical."

31. *DB*, 27–28.

32. Brown, "Bonhoeffer and Pacifism," 33.

Matheny, in the "Editor's Introduction to the English Edition" of *The Young Bonhoeffer: 1917-1928* argues that "the profound impact of the death of his brother Walter certainly freed him to be able to think more deeply about the nature of war than his tradition would have easily allowed."[33] These experiences with war, influencing Bonhoeffer's eventual embrace of some form of pacifism (a position not common or acceptable in traditional Lutheranism), like the influence of Bonhoeffer's ancestors, also display the tension between thinking as expected (love of the fatherland) and its seeming opposite (pacifism).

Family Experience with the Church

The final family influence of significance is his immediate family's perception of the church. Bethge writes of the Bonhoeffer family, "The Bonhoeffers were not churchgoers in the sense that they active members and participated in the life of a congregation. The children were not sent to church, and the family did not attend church even on the major holidays."[34] In addition, the Bonhoeffers' social network was not made up of ministers or people met at church.[35] Yet, Bethge also makes it clear that Bonhoeffer's mother and Maria Horn, the family governess, did their part to introduce the children to the Bible and to establish "domestic religious customs."[36] Perhaps the most useful anecdote here is the response to Bonhoeffer's declaration of his intention to study theology for the ministry. His brothers and sisters tried to persuade him, saying he was "taking the path of least resistance, and that the church to which he proposed to devote himself to was a poor, feeble, boring, petty and bourgeois institution."[37]

There are three items of import regarding the nature of the Bonhoeffers' religiousness. First, it arguably had direct influence on the nature of Bonhoeffer's own stance toward theologizing in his earliest phase. It has been well established, and especially in light of Bonhoeffer's own statements about his conversion of sorts, that at least his early approach to religiousness was more academically-oriented than faith

33. Matheny, "Editor's Introduction to the English Edition" in *The Young Bonhoeffer: 1918-1927*, 1-16. This quotation is from page 6.
34. *DB*, 34.
35. Ibid., 35.
36. Ibid., 36.
37. Ibid.

centered.[38] Second, Bonhoeffer's first dissertation, for example, is very synthetic and heavily indebted to secular influences such as social philosophy and sociology. In this way, his first dissertation reflected the objective or almost scientific approach reminiscent of his father's empirical proclivities in his own field of psychology, the type of empiricism that would make allegiance to an organized religious tradition unattractive. Third, Bonhoeffer's "confident" response to his brothers and sisters concern about his commitment to the church, "In that case I shall reform it!,"[39] indicates his own early vision of the church as something that can be approached from a forensic standpoint. That is, any prescription of the type of reformation necessary for the church might only come from the perspective of one who approaches it from the outside rather than one who has already blindly bought into its dictates.

SOCIO-POLITICAL, INTELLECTUAL AND ECCLESIAL FOUNDATIONS

Tübingen (1923)

Bonhoeffer began his theological career at Tübingen University in the fall of 1923 where he heard lectures by Adolf Schlatter and Wilhelm Hietmüller and studied with K. Groos.[40] Germany was in its second major regime of Bonhoeffer's lifetime, the ill-fated Weimar Republic (1918–1933). The year 1923 was a particularly volatile year. The French and Belgians, due to the failure of Germany to meet its war debts, occupied the Ruhr in January. In Bavaria, where a right-wing regime was established in 1920, plans were in motion for a march on Berlin to overthrow the Weimar government and install a right-wing dictatorship. The planners even had justification for the overthrow as the coalition

---

38. See Renate Bethge's section "Attitude toward the Enlightenment, Rationality and Empiricism," in *Dietrich Bonhoeffer—His Significance for North Americans*, 16–18.

39. *DB*, 36.

40. Godsey, *The Theology of Dietrich Bonhoeffer*, 20. See also, *DB*, 47. Attending Tübingen, their father's alma mater, for initial studies was a family tradition for the Bonhoeffer children. Dietrich's older brothers, Karl-Friedrich and Klaus, enrolled there in 1919 to study physics and law, respectively. His older sister, Christine, was at Tübingen studying biology when Dietrich began. See also, Robertson, *The Shame and the Sacrifice*, 41. Robertson notes that Bonhoeffer's academic experience at Tübingen was short lived and relatively unimportant. He writes, "But, to be honest, one must admit that Bonhoeffer found little in Tübingen that he could not have found anywhere."

Bonhoeffer's Early Life

of communists and socialists had taken over in Thuringia and Saxony. Hitler had already formed the *Sturmabteilung* (SA), his party's paramilitary unit, which had been recruiting ex-soldiers and some soldiers from the Free Corps. Hitler's paramilitary group was prepared for an attempted overthrow in the spring and summer of 1923. Eventually, though, especially since the Weimar military forces quashed the governments in Thuringia and Saxony, the idea of an attempted takeover of Berlin became unpopular amongst key leaders. Hitler decided to proceed anyway, initiating the move during a November 8 rally in the Munich Beer Hall. The famous Beer Hall Putsch was thwarted when one of Hitler's supposed co-revolutionaries, General Otto von Lossow, head of the Bavarian military district, turned on him and General Erich Ludendorf, Hitler's choice for head of the new army. Because of rightist judges and some crafty propagandizing on his part, Hitler received a lenient sentence and national notoriety that he would use to his advantage later. Ludendorf was simply acquitted.[41]

Bonhoeffer entered Tübingen against this backdrop and other uprisings against the Weimar Republic. I will not address his theology specifically here as his academic experience and pre-dissertation theology at Tübingen would take this project too far afield. Yet, there is one non-theological event from this part of his life that is extremely significant for understanding his mindset later in his first phase. Bonhoeffer joined the Hedgehogs (*Igel*) like his father before him.[42] His father and his father's elder brother Otto were members of the Hedgehogs. As noted above, Dietrich's father was not a radical right-wing supporter although he was pleased with the monarchy and happy about the united Germany under the Kaiser.[43] Dietrich Bonhoeffer, as part of the Hedgehogs, had to undergo an illegal two-week military training session with the Ulms Rifles Troop (as a member of the so-called Black Reichswehr). The training was considered illegal because it violated the terms of the Versailles Treaty. Bonhoeffer had no reservations about joining and seemed to like

---

41. *HNG*, 36–38. See also Craig's chapter "Reparations, Inflation and the Crisis of 1923," in *Germany: 1866–1945*, 434–68, for a more thorough description of the major events in 1923.

42. *DB*, 48–49. See *DB*, 48–53, for a complete account of Bonhoeffer's involvement with the Hedgehogs.

43. Ibid., 48–49.

his experience. He enjoyed the independence and camaraderie in the group.[44]

Bonhoeffer's motivations for joining this group are not entirely clear.[45] In any case, the decision was not an overtly political one. That is, Bonhoeffer's military training was "not based on any secret radical right-wing impulses."[46] On the other hand, Bonhoeffer "had no political reservations about joining the Hedgehogs."[47] This assessment stands in stark contrast to his brothers' motivations for not joining, which were decisively political in nature. It is not, though, important for the purposes of my work here to determine whether Bonhoeffer joined the Hedgehogs out of extreme right-wing or left-wing sensibilities.[48] Ultimately, there are two important things about this brief episode in Bonhoeffer's early life. First, although he may not have been motivated by party politics, he was certainly motivated by a general political concern. That is, he was undoubtedly willing to serve in a military capacity for the sake of the

---

44. Ibid., 50. See also, Robertson, *The Shame and the Sacrifice*, 40. Robertson writes, "He rather enjoyed it, glad that he could stand up to the rigours of camp life and strict training." See 39–40 for a more extensive treatment of Bonhoeffer's brief military training.

45. Ibid., 49–50. Bethge writes, "The fact that Dietrich was the only one of the brothers to join the Hedgehogs may be related to his position within the family. His elder brothers had ample experience in life with their fellows and contemporaries; for him all that lay ahead. It was an opportunity to move beyond the isolation he had felt among his brothers and sisters and in school, a necessary step in self-discovery."

46. Ibid., 53.

47. Ibid., 49.

48. Ibid., 33. Along these lines, there are, in fact, some anecdotes and pieces of information which indicate that Bonhoeffer was, although debatably not fully politically engaged at this time, disdainful of radical political factions on both sides, the left and the right. Bethge writes, "During his final years in school, there is increasing evidence of his opposition to the right-wing radicalism that was becoming more and more obstreperous. When he left for his last school holiday, he wrote to his parents that on the train he found himself sitting opposite 'a man wearing a swastika' and spent the whole time arguing with him. The man [according to Bonhoeffer] 'was really quite bigoted and right-wing.' A few days before, on 24 June 1922, Walter Rathenau had been assassinated. Bonhoeffer heard the shots from his classroom on Königsallee. As one of his classmates reports: 'I still remember Bonhoeffer on the day of Rathenau's murder . . . I still recall my friend Bonhoeffer's passionate indignation, his deep and spontaneous anger . . . I remember his asking what would become of Germany if its best leaders were killed.'" Walter Rathenau was a government official responsible for helping form the German Democratic Party. He was murdered by right-wing extremists after signing the Treaty of Rapallo with the Russians.

Bonhoeffer's Early Life 55

preservation of the German State that he loved. Bonhoeffer "believed he was acting in the service of a state which he approved."[49] Second, Bonhoeffer, whether politically seasoned, mature or savvy at this time in his life or not, was willing to train for violent conflict. That is, Bonhoeffer was certainly no pacifist at this time in his life.[50]

Berlin (1924–1927)

Bonhoeffer attended the University of Berlin for the completion of his theological studies between 1924 and 1927 after brief visits to Rome and Africa in early 1924.[51] Bonhoeffer's experience at Berlin, in comparison with his Tübingen days, provides a more important context for understanding his theology and political stances. This heightened importance is mainly due to the theological and political notoriety, influence, and importance of Berlin's professors. Berlin is where Bonhoeffer would quickly become thoroughly immersed in what Robert P. Ericksen so aptly describes as "The Crisis in Theology," including primarily the dominance of liberal Protestant theology and the beginnings of neo-orthodoxy. Another feature of this crisis includes use of existentialist categories to deal, in part, with problems arising from historical consciousness or historicity.[52] Bonhoeffer's three major influences form an impressive list of names. He had direct interactions with Adolf von Harnack, Reinhold

---

49. *DB*, 53. Bethge also notes that "by nature and family tradition," Bonhoeffer would not have been sympathetic to radical political factions. See also, Robertson, *The Shame and the Sacrifice*, 33. Robertson explains the family tradition of moderate politics, "[The Weimar Republic] was supported, without much enthusiasm, by the Bonhoeffers . . . as the least harmful form of government."

50. Robertson, *The Shame and the Sacrifice*, 40. As Robertson describes, "The afternoon training at Tübingen was canceled because of 'spies' and next day the Tübingen contingent left for Ulm. The family anxiously agreed to his staying and he did two weeks' military training during the second half of November. He rather enjoyed it, glad that he could stand up to the rigors of camp life and strict training. He was no pacifist and was prepared to defend his country." See also, Brown, "Bonhoeffer and Pacifism," 33. Brown writes, "That the more religiously and esthetically sensitive member of the family was not an immediate convert to pacifism can be seen from his membership in the Swabian fraternity, the 'Hedgehog,' at Tübingen in 1923."

51. See *DB*, 56–65, for an extended description of Bonhoeffer's journeys to Rome and Africa. The experience in Rome was especially significant as it provided a foundation for his later works in ecclesiology.

52. See Ericksen, *Theologians under Hitler*, 5–26.

Seeberg, and Karl Barth.[53] Harnack and Seeberg's theology and political affiliations, like most German intelligentsia, were associated with right wing or conservative political ideologies. Karl Barth's Christocentric "crisis" theology, on the other hand, would become the theological source for church criticism of Nazi policy. Bonhoeffer's own theological journey was marked by a more distinct commitment to Barth's thinking, although Bonhoeffer never broke entirely free of liberal influences. Yet, Bonhoeffer's relationship with Barth itself was marked by both personal and theological tension and Bonhoeffer eventually found his own theological and political voice. Ultimately, the influence of Harnack, Seeberg, and Barth is detectable in various ways all throughout Bonhoeffer's theology and his political thinking and action.

The Theology and Politics of Harnack and Seeberg

Harnack and Seeberg were part of the German intellectual elite. Generally speaking, the intellectual elite in Weimar Germany were conservative supporters of a pre-Weimar Germany. They were "anti-enlightenment, anti-materialism, anti-positivism, anti-egalitarian, anti-parliamentarian—all resounded as parts of a polyphony of anti-modernism."[54] They had disdain for "the barren abstraction of a universal and equal humanity" characteristic of Anglo-French political theory.[55] They used "organic analogies" and thought of states as personalized wholes rather than as collections of "egoistic" individuals.[56] States did not consist of a collection of individuals entering into a contract. Rather, they were the manifestation of "suprapersonal spiritual forces which emanate from the

---

53. *DB*, 29. Bonhoeffer's personal relationship with Seeberg was not especially noteworthy. However, his personal relationships with both Harnack and Barth were longstanding and significant. Harnack lived in a house in Grunewald in the same neighborhood as the Bonhoeffers during Dietrich's childhood. Bonhoeffer's father was a regular at Wednesday night meetings with Harnack, Troeltsch, and other famous professors from the neighborhood. Bonhoeffer later developed a friendship with Harnack during his Berlin days and beyond, taking long walks and corresponding by letter. Bonhoeffer even delivered an address at Harnack's memorial service in 1930. Despite the famous disputes between Barth and Harnack, Bonhoeffer had a similarly close relationship with Barth.

54. Zerner, "Dietrich Bonhoeffer's Views on the State and History," 131–57. These quotations are from page 133.

55. Ibid., 133. Zerner is quoting from Fritz K. Ringer's *The Decline of the German Mandarins*, 100.

56. Zerner, "Dietrich Bonhoeffer's Views on State and History," 133.

most important and creative individuals, the volk spirit or the religious aesthetic idea."⁵⁷

This idea of a spiritual force or suprapersonal state embodied in a *Volk* was basically Hegelian in nature. These ideas date back to the early 1800s and were used to support the drive for Prussian unification under Bismarck. For Hegel, the "vocation" of peoples was to achieve statehood and, even more, to expand and compete with other states for dominance. This is, indeed, the natural progression of history and the natural expression of the *Volkgeist* or national spirit. Warfare was thus also expected and even natural for states.⁵⁸ These ideas also became manifest in an important way in the thinking of the great social scientist Leopold von Ranke (1795–1866). For von Ranke and his influential later followers (the Neo-Rankeans) "nations were concentrations of 'moral energy' bent upon expansion and establishing their hegemony, as the behavior of the nation-states in the Napoleonic era so graphically illustrated."⁵⁹ At the end of the 1800s, the Neo-Rankeans (Erich Marcks and Max Lenz, notably) simply applied this thinking to Prussia-Germany; Prussia-Germany was to be the supreme power in Europe.⁶⁰

Harnack and Seeberg would apply this Hegelian-Rankean thinking in the theological disciplines. God's purposes in human history were "unfolding" through the political dominance of the German State. War, then, for Harnack and Seeberg, was inevitable and even a necessary means by which God drives the history of the *Volk*. These theologians tended to emphasize the deeds of God in the world or history rather than look to the Bible for revelation.⁶¹ Harnack, enjoying the confidence of the

---

57. Ibid. Zerner is quoting from Ringer's *The Decline of the German Mandarins*, 100–101.

58. Moses, "Bonhoeffer's Germany," 6–7.

59. Ibid., 7.

60. Ibid.

61. Ibid., 7–8. Moses writes, "Harnack's and Seeberg's point of departure was essentially that of Hegel and von Ranke, namely that peoples were 'ideas of God' and that it was in their nature to compete with each other for domination of the earth. Force was a given in the life of nation; eternal peace, say, as envisaged by the philosopher Immanuel Kant (1724–1804) was certainly not a possibility in this world. Theologically speaking, most German Protestant theologians of the Wilhelmine era were more concerned with the existing world as the venue of Almighty God's self-revelation than with the Bible as the source of revelation. This meant that their theological orientation was determined by their understanding of world history. In a word, it was not so much the activity of God in the Bible that claimed their attention as God's tangible and visible accomplish-

monarchy including the Kaiser himself, was unquestionably the most famous and important theologian at Berlin and perhaps in all of Germany. His name and work is virtually synonymous with liberal Protestantism. In this nineteenth and early twentieth century theological movement, a subjective, historical, humanistic, and rational approach to the Christian message ultimately had the effect of diminishing the radical metaphysical and historical distances or difference between the gospel message and any aspects of contemporary culture.[62]

Harnack was chiefly a historian who sought the recovery of the true meaning or essence of Christianity (or the Gospel) apart from the metaphysically-informed Greek accumulations heaped thereupon throughout history. His task was thus the "completion of the destruction of dogma"[63] with the ultimate goal of showing how the Gospel message can have meaning in any modern context. Like Ritschl and other liberal theologians in the Schleiermacherian line, Harnack started with the religious expressions of humankind rather than with the otherness of revelation. Religion or faith as the individual or collective response to the teaching of Jesus was the focus rather than "Christian faith *qua* faith."[64] Thinking he found the core or kernel of the Christian message, he could study the "adequacy of diverse faith expressions in relation to the 'essence' of the Christian religion."[65] Harnack summed up this "essence" as Jesus's teachings in three categories, "the kingdom of God, God as the Father and the infinite value of the human soul, and the higher righteousness showing itself in love."[66] Jesus Christ, for Harnack, "was not the Son of God who became man, in other words, the incarnate Word of God in the sense of John 1:14, but merely the supreme teacher and revealer of God."[67] Theology thus became an ethical or practical endeavor

---

ments with and for the German people between 1870 and 1914. God, Hegel claimed, 'had been dissolved into history.' The author of the universe could only be conceived of in relation to divine self-revelation, indeed God's Reich on earth. For the German theologians, this Reich was without doubt the Prusso-German Empire."

62. See Rumscheidt, "The Formation of Bonhoeffer's Theology," 50–70. Rumscheidt includes a brief discussion of Harnack and theological method in liberal theology, 53–55.

63. Phillips, *Christ for Us*, 45.

64. Rumschiedt, "The formation of Bonhoeffer's theology," 55.

65. Ibid.

66. Harnack, *What Is Christianity?*, 77.

67. Hartwell, *The Theology of Karl Barth*, 6.

able to evolve to meet various historical or cultural contexts. Theology had as its concern the anthropocentric task of human self-fulfillment in the personal carrying out of ethical directives in whatever historical context a person found him or herself. Theology did not primarily concern the proclamation of an otherworldly, judging, or supernatural Word of God.

Harnack's rationalism or humanism, however, did not, for him, conflict with the more organic or Hegelian models of states or a *Volk* characteristic of the *Kriegstheologie* of many other German intellectuals. In fact, he was able to maintain his emphasis on the value of the "free individual" by arguing that individuals actually became freer or more fulfilled when "subordinating their individuality to the whole."[68] Harnack thus echoed the Hegelian-Rankean concept of nations as individuals with their own particular *Volkgeist* that needed to be nourished and given space to grow.[69] War, for Harnack, actually promoted "liberty, equality and fraternity" amongst the German people by reaffirming equality before God in the common spiritual and political task of fighting for the defense or expansion of the Fatherland.[70]

Ultimately, Harnack's theology, wherein Christianity and larger culture were so closely connected, stripped the gospel of its power to critique aspects of contemporary culture. Gordon Craig, for example, describes the fruits of liberal Protestantism. He writes, "In the long run, the result was a watering-down of dogma and theology to a point where the Protestant religion threatened to become nothing but a bundle of ethical rules, inspired not by divine authority but by social utility. To the extent that this happened, the Church's ability to withstand the competition of secular religions was gravely weakened."[71] In fact, it is not surprising that some perceive liberal Protestantism as being unable to stand against the "secular religion" of Nazism.[72] While not necessarily following Harnack in political matters, Bonhoeffer had a tremendous

---

68. Jenkins, "War Theology, 1914 and Germany's *Sonderweg*," 292–310. Jenkins's full quotation reads, "While acknowledging that people need to cultivate a 'self-contained and free [*geschlossen*] individuality,' he saw a greater freedom in subordinating this individuality to the whole" (303).

69 Ibid.

70. Ibid., 305.

71. Craig, *Germany: 1866–1945*, 182–83.

72. See *HNG*, 130–32, for a description of Nazism as a religious movement.

respect for Harnack's quest for scientific rigor in theological method.[73] Many commentators attribute Bonhoeffer's recurring concern with worldliness and the concrete meaning of Christianity in modern culture to the enduring influence of Harnack.[74]

Bonhoeffer's dissertation mentor Seeberg, for his part, although he denounced to some degree a pacifying over-dependence of the church on the state and thus encouraged church members to engage politically, was basically an anti-Jewish German nationalist who was "critical of capitalism, social democracy, individualism and internationalism."[75] Borg characterizes Seeberg as an anti-Weimar "war theologian" who was critical of the Treaty of Versailles and encouraged the German nation to reclaim its pre-war position. For war theologians, God governed over nations in perpetual conflict and "as nations waxed strong and grew weak, war might justifiably adjust their holdings."[76] Germany's post-war compromised position might be justified, then, according to this thinking. However, Seeberg considered the current situation unjust because "weaker nations collaborated to deny Germany a peace commensurate with its true strength."[77] In fact, at the beginning of the war, Seeberg was one of a group of professors who held that "the enemy must pay for the assault on Germany by being forced to cede territory."[78]

Seeberg held that the German nation would find unity again only in the spirit of a unified *Volk*.[79] Borg thus situates Seeberg among the theologians who made the idea of the German people a central element in their thinking. This notion is part of the potentially dangerous and long-standing German Romantic intellectual tradition affecting all fields (including theology) dating back to the early nineteenth century whereby

---

73. *NRS*, 29–31. See, for example, the text of Bonhoeffer's memorial address at Harnack's funeral service on June 15, 1930.

74. Rumscheidt, "The Formation of Bonhoeffer's Theology," 55. Rumscheidt affirms, "However Bonhoeffer viewed the epistemological concern of Harnack's work, what left a permanent mark on him was the positive character his teacher assigned to the world. In all this, as well as the rigours of scholarship, Harnack was Dietrich Bonhoeffer's eminent teacher." See, also Kaltenborn's "Adolf von Harnack and Bonhoeffer," 48–57, for a detailed account of their similarities and differences.

75. Zerner, "Dietrich Bonhoeffer's Views on the State and History," 134.

76. Borg, *The Old Prussian Church*, 179.

77. Ibid.

78. Craig, *Germany: 1866–1945*, 360–61.

79. Borg, *The Old Prussian Church*, 179.

the notion of a people or a nation was afforded an overly important status as "the highest and unsurpassable object of allegiance and loyalty."[80] *Volk* became theologically significant in combination with an important idea established and used by a few influential Protestant theologians, the "orders of creation." Orders of creation has been defined as "the doctrine that certain structures of human life are not just incidental biological or historical phenomena, but are deliberately ordained of God as essential and immutable conditions of human existence, without which humanity is not humanity as created by God."[81] The orders of creation traditionally included the magistracy, the household, and the church. However, some post-War theologians began to rank *Volk* as another one of the orders of creation, thereby establishing German nationhood as a God-ordained structure of reality. While Borg comes short of listing Seeberg as one of these theologians, he does indicate that "war theology" is consistent with theology that makes *Volk* an order of creation (and he lists Seeberg as a war theologian).[82] Seeberg is certainly a theologian who stressed the importance of communities or orders shaped and driven by the social will over and against any sense of individualism or egoism.[83]

---

80. Clements, "Ecumenical Witness for Peace," 154–72. Clements clarifies the danger, "The Nazi version of it [patriotism], however, not only made the nation the highest and unsurpassable object of allegiance and loyalty, but saw the place of the nation in the world as relying, first, on its military strength and secondly, on its 'racial purity'" (162).

81. See Clements, "Ecumenical Witness for Peace,"163, for a discussion of the "orders of creation."

82. Borg, *The Old Prussian Church*, 178. Borg writes, "These four circumstances . . . appear to have moved theologians and others formally to rank the folk among the orders of creation . . . Conceiving of the folk as an order served their purposes admirably. As an order, the folk received divine ordination. Like the other orders, the folk appeared as one of the structural givens of nature, and thus one ordained by God. Primary responsibilities flowed directly from this crucial assumption. As a God-created given, the folk, like other orders, assumed the form of an involuntary association, a community of 'fate,' into which one was born and by which one acquired responsibilities that could lapse if the folk were merely a voluntary association. Just as the other orders ought to be organically composed to serve the commonweal, so, too, ought the folk, setting a brake on individual class egoism. Only war theology could have stressed more firmly the ethical responsibilities that Christians owed folk short of viewing the national ethics as God's revelation itself."

83. Zerner, "Dietrich Bonhoeffer's Views on the State and History," 134. Zerner, quoting Seeberg's *Christentum und Idealismus*, 71–74, describes his thought: "communities should be shaped in keeping with 'the social will,' not egoism. The aim is to establish each order (such as industry or the state) 'as a useful organ of the social will.'"

There is no evidence that Bonhoeffer chose Seeberg as his dissertation mentor because of Seeberg's views on Jewish persons or any political positions. Bonhoeffer, although closer to Harnack personally, chose Seeberg because he respected and encouraged Bonhoeffer's intellectual independence and adventure and thought a study on "religious community" would be valuable.[84] Nevertheless, elements of Seeberg's thinking, most notably his notions of various institutions (church, state, etc.) as organic wholes, would certainly influence Bonhoeffer in his early writings and arguably for his whole career.

Church-State Thinking, Structure, and Politics of the German Protestant Church during pre-Weimar and Weimar Years

The general theological or theoretical framework for understanding the church-state relationship in Germany was the Lutheran "two kingdoms" or "two Regiments" theory or doctrine. Luther did not write about a "two kingdoms" theory as such, but he did write fairly extensively on the proper roles and interrelations of church and state. So while this complicated set of speculations was never definitively defined by Luther, there have been, in addition to the original thinking of Luther himself, several iterations and interpretations called the "two kingdoms" doctrine since the Reformation.[85] For the sake of organization, Hordern, citing Ulrich Duchrow's work,[86] describes conservative and "more positive" (liberal) interpretations that share some general features.[87] All versions of the doctrine hold both that the church and the state are God-ordained forms or ways of governing the world and that they are in some form of mutually informing relationship or dialectical tension. The church and the state are distinguished from each other by their respective roles. The state makes laws, has the God-ordained power to enforce those laws, and can wage war. The church spreads the gospel. These are, theoreti-

---

84. Zerner, "Dietrich Bonhoeffer's Views on the State and History," 135. See also, *DB*, 81, for Bonhoeffer's September 25, 1925, letter to his parents describing why he chose Seeberg as a mentor.

85. See Hordern's "Lutheran Theology and the Witness of Peace," 133–60, pp. 136–40, for an account of the different formulations. See also, Borg, *The Old Prussian Church*, 13–15.

86. Hordern, "Lutheran Theology and the Witness of Peace," 138. Duchrow and Millwood, *Lutheran Churches—Salt or Mirror of Society?*

87. Hordern, "Lutheran Theology and the Witness of Peace," 138.

cally, non-interfering roles. That is, the state should not interfere with church matters, and the church does not have the power to make laws, enforce laws, or wage wars. Furthermore, the state is not subordinate to the church and the church is not subordinate to the state. They are, rather, "equals with different spheres of responsibility." The individual Christian is responsible to both church and state.[88]

The "more positive" or liberal interpretations are marked by two distinct features. First, they emphasize the idea that "the state should not interfere with church matters." More specifically, the church can protest if the state interferes with the proclamation of the gospel.[89] Second, they allow for the church to protest against certain state directives that do not involve church matters specifically. There are basically two presuppositions that explain the church's power to protest state directives. First, the proponents hold "the two kingdoms [as] represent[ing] different functions in society but not a distinction between two different kinds of moral claims."[90] That is, the same moral principles apply in both realms and to both spheres of responsibility, allowing the church to judge the use of the state's power. The second presupposition is the recognition that the secular order, while divinely ordained like the church, is affected by sin. The pastor thus had as his calling "the responsibility for passing moral judgement on the actions of the magistrate."[91] It should be noted, though, that even in these more liberal interpretations, the church can "not compel secular authority to alter its behavior"[92] and "must not exercise the power of the sword."[93] The church can only "raise a warning voice"[94] or "appeal to the state to exercise its power in a just manner."[95] Christians can only "judge the moral implications of policies of state." They cannot even "prescribe" the content of those policies.[96]

The church's voice in political matters is muzzled in conservative interpretations. These interpretations stressed both the "non-interfering"

---

88. Ibid.
89. Moses, "Bonhoeffer's Germany," 19.
90. Hordern, "Lutheran Theology and the Witness of Peace," 139.
91. Borg, *The Old-Prussian Church*, 15.
92. Ibid.
93. Hordern, "Lutheran Theology and the Witness of Peace," 138.
94. Borg, *The Old Prussian Church*, 15.
95. Hordern, "Lutheran Theology and the Witness of Peace," 139.
96. Borg, *The Old Prussian Church*, 15.

component of the inter-relationship between the two entities and the Christian's responsibility to both realms. The state has the responsibility for the material welfare and government of the nation or people. It does not have as its proper area of concern the spreading of the gospel (the Church's role). The church and the individual Christian, while responsible for carrying out state directives, do not have a role in forging those directives. The church is, rather, primarily responsible for the spiritual welfare of its members or for cultivating individual spirituality and, as such, does not have as its concern the legitimacy of the state's military or other actions. Again, though, the Christian must carry out state directives.[97] Thus, a sort of double-morality operates in this system, ultimately yielding a concentration on an apolitical "religious inwardness." Secular institutions are held as "God-given" and Christians thus "accept existing conditions as beyond the scope of a specifically Christian social ethic or motivation."[98] In their personal lives Christians can suffer injustice without retaliation. As citizens of the secular sphere, they must submit to the authority of the secular leader and fight if necessary.[99]

Duchrow argues that what Hordern calls the conservative interpretation is an outright "misuse" of Luther. Duchrow labels the first type of misuse an "undifferentiated adaptation to the existing power structures" that can happen in three ways (passively, actively, and in a disguised form). While Duchrow acknowledges that the issue of theocracy has not arisen in Lutheran nations, he does argue that

> the problem, rather, has been an undifferentiated adaptation to absolutist political or economic systems. The interests of the church and of theology in such a situation may dictate two possible courses of action: either the church is intent only surviving

---

97. Hordern, "Lutheran Theology and the Witness of Peace," 138–39.

98. Borg, *The Old Prussian Church and the Weimar Republic*, 15. Borg, noting Ernst Troeltsch's account of the situation, writes, "Several years before the First World War, Ernst Troeltsch contended that Luther's dualism had degenerated into a double morality among modern-day Lutherans. Luther's formulations left his followers in a quandary. Should they seek to transform the sinful spirit of the 'world' as it permeated secular orders, or accept it because these orders were divinely ordained? The main thrust of German Lutheranism, according to Troeltsch, was to release the tension of the dualism. Lutherans extolled secular institutions as God given, accepted existing conditions as beyond the scope of a specifically Christian social ethic or motivation, and cultivated religious inwardness." Borg notes from Ernst Troeltsch's *The Social Teaching of the Christian Churches*, 2:465–576, 808.

99. Hordern, "Lutheran Theology and the Witness of Peace," 139.

under a totalitarian system, or else the interests of the majority of the church's membership of leadership tend to overlap with the interests of the system to such an extent that they actively support it (as is the case with nationalism or culturally influenced ethical systems, etc.).[100]

It is significant to note here that Duchrow explicitly connects this particular form of misuse with the German church situation after 1933.[101]

Both types of interpretations, while theoretically leaving the questions of conscientious objection and pacifism somewhat debatable,[102] ultimately frown upon them for various reasons. In liberal interpretations, the church would have the right to judge the state's decision to wage a certain type of war as immoral or may even argue that war represents an intrusion upon the church's proclamation of the gospel. Yet, the church does not have the power to actually do anything about it besides protest. In conservative versions, the disjunction between church or private morality and state or social morality renders the Christian a passive subject to state directives. Luther himself rejected pacifism on the basis of a split between individual or personal adherence to the gospel and the responsibility to protect one's fellows as a citizen of the state. He even argued that "slaying and robbing" in war could, because performed for the purpose of protecting the weak in one's own country, be "works of love." However, Luther frowned upon war and encouraged conscientious objection in cases of unjust wars.[103]

The German theological scene in the pre-Weimar and Weimar years was characterized by a heightened version of the two kingdoms doctrine. This particular version was a "super-conservative" one that ultimately equated the directives of the German nation with the will of God. It thereby rendered questions of conscientious objection or pacifism entirely irrelevant as even aggressive wars on behalf of Germany were not only acceptable, but necessary. As implied above, Bonhoeffer's mentors, in fact, were "fervent patriots" who "incorporated the his-

---

100. Duchrow, *Lutheran Churches—Salt or Mirror of Society?*, 302.
101. Ibid., 301.
102. Hordern's essay is, in many ways, an exploration of pacifist possibilities in the Lutheran tradition.
103. See Douglas S. Bax's "From Constantine to Calvin," 147–71, for a treatment of war and peace positions of several important theologians. See pp. 163–67 for a brief treatment of Luther's positions.

tory of the state into their theology to such an extent that they could virtually equate the foreign policy of the Reich with the Kingdom of God on earth."[104] Harnack, Seeberg, and most other theologians from the pre-Weimar and Weimar era, in fact, "elevated a version of Luther's doctrine of the two kingdoms to dogmatic status. According to this the *Machtstaat*, the power state, was the instrument of God in history, destined to realize God's will for humankind."[105] In this vision "the state [was seen as an] autonomous entity distinct from the society over which it ruled; indeed an entity operating in a sphere above the people in its charge, following its own laws of existence which had been prescribed by Almighty God."[106] Here, the power of the church or individual Christian to critique the state was nullified. Interfering with the state's objectives would be interfering with the will of the Almighty God since the unfolding of Absolute Spirit in history was sovereign.[107]

This state-supporting theology of Bonhoeffer's professors and most other church leaders, which lent itself to a passive acceptance of state directives on the part of church and citizens (in theory and in fact), was consistent with the German ecclesial structure and history in pre-Weimar and Weimar years. There was a long tradition of church support for a monarchical governmental structure in Prussia-Germany during the pre-Weimar years, rooted in an event in Luther's experience itself.[108] For example, in the mid-eighteenth century there was a call by

104. Moses, "Bonhoeffer's Germany," 18–19.

105. Ibid., 19.

106. Ibid.

107. Ibid. Moses continues, "The subjects of the state had no prior right to criticize or judge it in any way; their role was always to obey no matter how unjust or destructive the laws and decisions of the state might appear to be. Ultimately everything that happened was in accordance with the inscrutable will of the Almighty."

108. Klan, "Luther's Resistance Teaching and the German Church Struggle under Hitler," 432–43. Klan states, "In the emergency situation of the Peasants' War, Luther designated the princes 'emergency bishops' to fill the power vacuum by assuming the authority formerly held by the Roman bishops. This absence of authority was the principal cause of the prevailing anarchy. That no steps were taken to remove the princes from their privileged positions points to an inherent weakness in Lutheran doctrine ... The Thirty Years War, the rise of Prussia and the growth of Pietism contributed over the next three centuries to the installation of the 'Lutheran State Church' as the third pillar of the Prussian establishment, after the army and the bureaucracy. Herein lies the genesis of the oft-quoted phrase 'marriage of throne and altar.' This whole development stemmed from the emergency situation of 1525; but Lutherans found it comfortable and convenient, so no step was taken to reverse it," 437–38.

Frederick William III of Prussia, despite both the long-standing presence of various different churches (Lutheran, Reformed, and Roman Catholic churches in the Empire and twenty-eight *Landeskirchen* organized in terms of the individual German states), for a single Protestant Church. This United Prussian Church, made up of essentially a number of the *Landeskirchen* and the churches of the Reformed tradition, met resistance from both Reformed churches in the Rhineland and Lutheran churches in the east. Yet, even with this difficulty, there came to be a United Prussian Church that was treated by the King as a single entity. After 1866, the United Prussian Church was known as the Old Prussian Union. This Old Prussian Union still counted half the total amount of Protestants in Germany during the Weimar Republic even with the separate *Landeskirchen* and the denominational divisions.[109]

The relationship between the state and the churches in the pre-Weimar years was one of financial dependence of the church on the state, the church enjoying privileged status, and the state having bureaucratic control over the church. The churches were actually administered as if they were another department of the state. Germany, in fact, displayed all of the characteristics of a Christian state. There was "state guarantee of church property, theological faculties in universities, religious education in schools, chaplains in the armed forces, hospitals, and prisons —[that were] all maintained by the state."[110] The church even had privileged status as a "corporation with a special legal status" (*Körperschaft des öffentlichen Rechts*).[111] As such, it also enjoyed some of the privileges of a government department. Church officials had the status of civil servants. Churches were even allowed to tax their members and to use the state administration to help in the collection. In order to continue enjoying these privileges the church had to submit to state supervision by means of the *Kultusministerium*, the state bureaucratic mechanism for control.[112]

There was nonetheless a movement toward forging a clearer difference between internal church functioning and state control, driven

---

109. See the "Introduction: The Church before 1918," in Wright, *"Above Parties,"* 1–10, for a brief but very informative treatment of the structure, history, and political leanings of the various Protestant and other churches pre-Weimar.

110. Wright, *"Above Parties,"* 4.

111. Ibid.

112. Ibid., 4–5.

by a desire on behalf of both the state and church leaders for a secular educational system and other concerns. In 1876, the state bureaucracy did, in fact, officially give up control of internal church matters to the *Evangelischer Oberkirchenrat*, a central church authority created in 1850. Theoretically, this move made the church independent from the *Kultusminister*. The edict, however, did not separate the churches from their responsibility to the crown.[113] The churches remained subject to the king as he was "summus episcopus" or highest bishop, a traditional organizational feature of the church-state relationship in Germany since the Reformation.[114] The king, as summus episcopus, "remained the primary source of organizational authority within the church."[115] The king's churchly authority, in theory, was supposed to be nominal compared to his kingly authority. In reality, "the legal distinction between the king's two roles was little more than sleight of hand to conceal the advancement of Protestant and conservative interests and his continuing control of the Old-Prussian church."[116] Furthermore, even with the explicit separation from the state, the churches remained subject to its control and influence. In fact, "the process of separation [of church and state] had not advanced very far, however, before the collapse of the Empire. Until 1918 throughout Germany, the normal conditions of a Christian state were observed."[117]

The notion of *Volkskirche* is another concept illustrating the general conditions of the formal churches in pre-Weimar years. The *Volkskirche* was the longstanding idea, going back to the Middle Ages and emerging strongly in Luther, of an involuntary institution to which people were admitted by birth, encompassing "the entire political community."[118] By positing a connection between the entire populace in any land and the church, this concept encouraged the "folkish" nationalism present in the pro-state perceptions of most pre-Weimar church persons.[119] The

---

113. Ibid., 6. See also, Borg, *The Old Prussian Church*, 9.
114. Wright, "Above Parties," 4.
115. Borg, *The Old Prussian Church*, 9.
116. Ibid.
117. Wright, "Above Parties," 4.
118. Borg, *The Old Prussian Church*, 2.
119. Ibid., 8. Borg is describing the thinking of Julius Kaftan, a Berlin theology professor who, in 1919, reached the vice-presidency of the *Evangelischer Oberkirchenrat*, the highest clerical position in Germany's largest Evangelical church. Borg notes that

Volkskirche, in fact, even had official endorsement by important church leaders and, while arguably a more conservative notion, had the support of both conservative and liberal churches due to a common recognition that "Christian values, nurtured by the *Volkskirche* for centuries, had historically molded German culture."[120] Many people remained in their churches even when an 1873 Prussian law made the Old-Prussian *Volkskirche* no longer "involuntary" by giving citizens the right to "contract out of established churches."[121]

Finally, the notion of *Volkskirche* had not only developed historically in a monarchical governmental structure, but was also logically consistent with that form of government. Democratic forms of government, associated with liberal and humanistic tendencies, were theologically suspect for three interrelated reasons. First, democratic forms of government implied individualism, an idea incompatible with the very notion of a populace as a monolithic folk or organic whole. This individualism, in turn, threatened the ability of the *Volkskirche* to fulfill its perceived long-time role as binding the folk together with agreed-upon Christian moral and cultural values, a necessary role that the state could not fill on its own.[122] The second problem with democratic or parliamentary states vis-à-vis the *Volkskirche* concerns the source of authority. Parliamentary or democratic states (by definition) take their direction from the masses while a Christian state (supported by a unified *Volkskirche*) recognizes itself as an "order of creation" deriving authority only from God. The *Volkskirche*, as an order of creation, was responsible for unifying the nation and culture under the rubric of Christian values, and the monarch was responsible for ensuring that a truly Christian state was possible. Finally, parliamentary states, with their continuously changing personnel and representatives, did not provide the type of continuity demanded for a truly Christian state. Competition and political maneuvering amongst the non-unified masses would divert the state from its "divine purposes."[123]

Kaftan was expressing an idea that "most churchmen expressed from one angle or another in periodicals and synods."

120. Ibid., 2.
121. Ibid., 3.
122. Ibid., 18.
123. Ibid., 19–20.

The political involvement and status of the churches vis-à-vis the state in the period between the establishment of the Weimar Republic in 1918 and the rise of Hitler in 1933 is, in many ways, more complicated than it was pre-Weimar. The obvious source of confusion was the lack of a crown in a parliamentary form of government such as the Weimar Republic, a consistent structural feature in church-state thinking and behavior in Prussia-Germany for hundreds of years. Scholars have undertaken detailed and exhaustive studies of how various churches and political factions within those churches reacted to the 1918 Revolution and the establishment of the Weimar Republic.[124] In very brief summary, while all churches accepted the new form of government on some level, most did so with reservations. Protestant church leadership, while resisting the radical impulses of both the right and the left in some cases, were, as demonstrated by the foregoing, much closer theologically to conservative rather than liberal ideologies.[125] Ultimately, the Kaiser or any monarchical ruler enjoyed the theological and structural support from the mainstream Protestant churches. Moreover, the state-supporting theology and actual church behavior was basically consistent with a conservative interpretation of the two kingdoms doctrine, one manifesting an implicit support of state directives. Bonhoeffer's Germany was, notwithstanding the presence of moderate right-wing and left-wing political factions that supported Weimar Republic at times, basically a conservative and monarchical-minded Germany that never really accepted the Weimar government entirely. The lack of any mass or majority resistance to Hitler on the part of the German Protestant churches is sad testimony to this fact.[126]

---

124. Borg and Wright's works are two excellent examples.

125. Wright, *"Above Parties,"* 74. Wright, for instance, notes that while Protestant leadership "resisted the anti-Republican Right or 'national opposition,'" because its "inability to compromise with the Republic was . . . against the national interest," they did "share many of its political views" and regarded it as "basically sound."

126. See Ericksen, "A Radical Minority," 115–35. Ericksen writes, "Recent scholarship suggests that Christianity and National Socialism mixed more easily than first thought. Many Christians greeted the rise of Hitler in 1933 and most approved his leadership for the next few years, using words like renewal and rebirth to describe this turning point in German history. Even Christians in the Confessing Church often shared this judgement. Although Christian resistance to Hitler developed, it did so only among a tiny, radical minority," 115.

The Theological and Political Impact of Karl Barth

Bonhoeffer was influenced by the thinking of Harnack and Seeberg, was certainly aware of their politics, and familiar with the traditional church-state relationship in his Germany. He also absorbed the "crisis theology" and enjoyed the often times strained personal friendship of the theological giant Karl Barth. Barth's theology would arguably provide him with the resources to look at the church's role vis-à-vis the state in such a way as to make possible adherence to a more liberal version of two kingdoms thinking where the church might criticize the state. Barth, of course, like Kierkegaard before him, was a radical critic of any Hegel-influenced conceptions of God's unfolding in nature and history. Barth emphasized the "infinite qualitative difference" between God and the world, and the otherness of revelation. The marriage of religion and any form of culture, including political culture, was thus potentially revolting to Barth. He wrote,

> For me personally one day at the beginning of August of that year stamped itself as the *dies ater*. It was that on which 93 German intellectuals came out with a manifesto supporting the war policy of Kaiser Wilhelm II and his counsellors, and among them I found to my horror the names of nearly all my theological teachers who up to then I had religiously honoured. Disillusioned by their conduct I perceived that I should not be able any longer to accept their ethics and dogmatics, their biblical exegesis, their interpretation of history, that at least for me the theology of the 19th century had no future.[127]

Barth clearly links political positions with the legitimacy of various theological positions. Political critiques and political matters in general were not, however, the early Barth's primary concern. Nevertheless, his theology, and particularly the way its prevailing themes appeared in the 1934 Barmen Declaration, had distinct political implications contrary to the aims of the majority of those in the German academy.[128]

---

127. Hartwell, *The Theology of Karl Barth*, 7. The original source is Karl Barth's *Evangelical Theology in the 19th Century*, 58.

128. Yoder, *The Pacifism of Karl Barth*, 3. Barth's role in the formulation of the Barmen Declaration provides a good example of how theology was more important than political concerns even in the beginnings of the official church struggle against Hitler. Yoder writes, "The originality of the declaration of Barmen was that of a return to the sources. In its doctrine of the state which 'in the world yet redeemed' should maintain order 'by the threat and the use of force,' there is nothing new. This is the clas-

The logical expectation for Barthian theology would be a disavowal of the connection between theology and specifically political action. Barth's theology, wherein the Word of God was to be safeguarded from any worldly elements, arguably lent itself to a self-involved church concerned only with the purity of its own message. Given Barth's theology, it would seem that the church "must continue to be the church alone" and not try "to govern or to shape state or society."[129] The church's "aim in the midst of state and society was to function soberly and essentially as the church."[130] Some commentators even credit Barth's school of thought with "conditioning the Evangelical churches to silence in the face of the evils perpetrated by the Nazi regime."[131] Nevertheless, Barth, later in his career, did become concerned with political issues outside of the strictly ecclesial, eventually supporting socialist forms of government.[132] Barth's support of socialist forms of government was not popular in the context of the unstable political situation and the general disdain for socialist positions among the German churches and intelligentsia.

Bonhoeffer's relationship with Barth, both in terms of theology and in terms of the various political stances and activities undertaken during the pre-Hitler and Hitler years, was very complicated.[133] Some scholarly

---

sical political doctrine of the churches of the Reformation. The rejection of Hitlerism is therefore not founded politically. It is not in the name of democracy, of international conventions, of respect for the constitution, or in opposition to rising militarism, that objection was raised. The offense of Hitler was more properly 'theological.'"

129. Klan, "Luther's Resistance Teaching and the German Church Struggle under Hitler," 442. Klan explains, "Paradoxically, the dialectical theology of Karl Barth and his school also contributed to the church's impotence in the 1930s. They encouraged the church to be concerned primarily with her own affairs, insisting that the church's role was to defend an 'intolerantly one-sided and transcendental faith laden with paradox.' This theology refused to allow a general revelation and thereby prevented the development of a theology of the natural world. The church must continue to be the church alone. Barth's celebrated line, often misquoted, ran: 'The church has in no way whatever to serve mankind nor the German people. She has alone to serve the Word of God.' It was not for the church to govern or to shape state and society. Her aim in the midst of state and society was rather to function soberly and essentially as the church."

130. Ibid.

131. Ibid.

132. See Hunsinger, *Karl Barth and Radical Politics*, for an extended discussion of Barth's socialism.

133. See Pangritz, *Karl Barth in the Theology of Dietrich Bonhoeffer*, for an extended discussion of their political/theological relationship. See also *DB*, 175–86, for a review of their friendship and summary of the nature of their interactions.

sentiment suggests that Bonhoeffer's motivations for engaging in political action were different from Barth's. Scholars have even implied that Bonhoeffer, unlike Barth, was too rooted in his bourgeois family and life experience to really break away from a conservative version of the traditional Lutheran position on church and state (one that did not encourage political action in the form of criticizing or challenging the state or one that meant engaging politically only in the form of following the state's directives).[134] Some scholars also lament the fact that the impetus for political resistance to the state arguably inherent in neo-orthodoxy did not reach fruition strongly or soon enough for various reasons.[135] In any case, Barth's theology did influence Bonhoeffer. Neo-orthodox theology, to the extent that it emphasized the absolute authority and otherness of God over and against attempts to attribute divine status to any order or element in the human realm, was politically more amenable to criticizing the Nazi regime than theology which directly equated the rise of the Third Reich with the triumph of God's will in history. Some Hitler supporters did, of course, perceive him as divine. To the extent that Barthian themes appeared in Bonhoeffer, then, Barth's thinking eventually contributed to Bonhoeffer's ability to criticize the existing order.[136]

134. This is basically Robert Koch's thesis in his dissertation. See also, Pangritz, *Karl Barth in the Theology of Dietrich Bonhoeffer*, 2–3. Pangritz points out a similar perception of Barth and Bonhoeffer on politics. He writes, "One can no longer reject offhand the contention that the slogan 'positivism of revelation' is used to play off the middle class, liberal Bonhoeffer, whose theology seems to be made believable on account of his death as a 'martyr,' against the Swiss democrat Barth, in particular his socialist leanings. Resistance against the Nazis—yes! as long as it remains within the domain of the middle class and as long as the military plays a decisive part in maintaining security; no! As soon as it tends toward a socialist revolutionizing of the order of society: this is how the message goes."

135. *DB*, 127. Bethge, for example, writes, "Years later we can see more clearly the tragedy of these theologians like Bonhoeffer, who tried in their way to set themselves apart from humanist 'Westernism.' Their 'crisis theology' was colored by strong antiliberal sentiment. In addition, the personal backgrounds of many Barthians prevented them from identifying with those forces that were the backbone of the Weimar Republic."

136. Clements, "Ecumenical Witness for Peace," 163. One example of how Bonhoeffer's acceptance of Barthian theology influenced a political position concerns the controversial "orders of creation" thinking described above. Clements notes, "For Bonhoeffer, by contrast [with the manifesto of the Faith Movement of German Christians who counted race as an order of creation], and in line with Karl Barth's theology of revelation, all such attempts to talk about 'creation' in a general way are spurious. For him, as he made clear in his lectures on *Creation and Fall* given at about

LOOKING AHEAD

Stephen R. Haynes, in a subsection titled "Bonhoeffer and Critical Patriotism" from his excellent work *The Bonhoeffer Phenomenon: Portraits of a Protestant Saint*,[137] referring to Keith Clements's insight, writes,

> Clements observed that Bonhoeffer's life was charged with a tension between being Christian and being German, a tension captured in Eberhard Bethge's description of Bonhoeffer's relationship with his homeland in terms of "exile and martyrdom." As loyalty to Christ and loyalty to country became increasingly incompatible, Bonhoeffer had to face the question whether "one could maintain one's Christian identity other than by distancing oneself from the rest of the people and indeed much of the church."[138]

Many scholars, and even Bonhoeffer himself in the last phase of his life, acknowledge the tension between being a dutiful German and being a faithful Christian within the context of a brutally oppressive political regime. My aim in this brief chapter was not to engage in any extended theoretical debate about Christian responsibility in the political sphere and what that may mean in terms of allegiance to one's nation in times of distress or otherwise. As amply noted, in many ways Bonhoeffer's whole life is an existential working out of that exact problem. Rather, my goal in this chapter was to provide some historical information about Germany's political history, German church history, German political and theologi-

---

this time, it is Jesus Christ through whom we can know both God and the world as God intends it to be. We cannot read God's will and purposes straight off from the world as it is, the fallen world of sin and division. Christian faith cannot be redefined in terms of nationhood. Rather, nationhood has to be understood in the light of the word of God, Jesus Christ." See also, *DB*, 127. Bethge notes of Bonhoeffer, "His almost Barthian theology increasingly provided him with the tools to resist the theological and ecclesial apostles of nationalism." See also, Moses, "Bonhoeffer's Germany: the political context," 19. Moses also argues that Barth's theology gave impetus for Bonhoeffer's critique of the Nazi movement. He writes "This [Bonhoeffer's according the state privileged status in his early years], however, came to be radically modified by his experience of Christianity in other countries (Italy, Spain, the United States and England), with the growing ecumenical movement, and not least by his encounter with his Swiss friend and theological mentor, Karl Barth. All this combined to enable Bonhoeffer to critique the Hitler regime in ways not possible for the majority of his co-religionists."

137. Haynes, *The Bonhoeffer Phenomenon*, 40–45.

138. Ibid., 41.

cal attitudes, and some personal information about Bonhoeffer's family, all in order to explain why he later experienced many profound tensions. The tension between commitment to such a regime and one's spiritual convictions was certainly not unique to Bonhoeffer at this time. Yet, it does seem that Bonhoeffer was one of only a very few persons who experienced it so intensely as to translate into action. Thus, the foregoing account of the German historical, theological, and political context simultaneously illustrates why the vast majority of German church persons and citizens so readily accepted Nazism and just how unique Bonhoeffer really was.

With the problem set up in the first chapter and the important historical foundations addressed in the second, we can proceed to examining the relationship between Bonhoeffer's understanding of the church-world relationship and his forms of political thinking and involvement in the first phase of his writing life (1927–1930). Because of the proximity in time to the above-described historical events and influences, it should come as little surprise that strong traces of the predominantly conservative themes are apparent in his early works. In particular, Bonhoeffer tends toward a status quo supporting or typically German Lutheran church-world vision and political positioning over challenging the state or the status quo from a Christian platform. For example, he echoes *Volk*-related positions on war and uses organic categories to describe the church and state. The seemingly problematic elements of Bonhoeffer's phase one vision are due mostly to his youth and the fact that he had yet to really find his own theological voice. In addition, he had more of an academic mindset and less of personal faith commitment to Christ. Finally, there were no political pressures yet as extreme as the rise of Nazism. However, this does not mean that the effects of these early experiences (as manifest in his early theology) do not later reappear in his uniquely Bonhoefferian church-world and political positions.

3

Phase 1: Church and World in Mild Tension

INTRODUCTION

BONHOEFFER'S RELATIVELY SHORT AND dynamic life contains four phases.¹ The first phase, 1923 to mid-1930, found him in both academic and pastoral settings. He was a student at Tübingen and the University of Berlin, a visitor to Rome and Africa, and a curate in Barcelona. Although characterized by unsettling dynamics between various political factions, the political situation in Germany had not yet reached an outright crisis in this span of years. Thus, Bonhoeffer's worldly involvement in relation to politics, except for a short-lived participation in a military organization and an awareness of various political dynamics, took mostly an academic form consisting mainly of treating issues of church and state and war and peace briefly and in parts of his various writings.

In this chapter I will show how Bonhoeffer's first-phase writings reveal a church and world in a mild tension or even a partnership. In terms of a broad or all-encompassing definition, his particular church-world vision and accompanying political thinking and behavior can be termed "traditional German Lutheranism."² In this mild tension between church and world, both entities, while interacting with each other,

---

1. While a four-phase partition of Bonhoeffer's life and theology is unique, a three-phase scheme has precedents. Different scholars mark the years of these phases off in different ways The chosen overarching framework is what determines the exact years in each case. See John A. Phillips's *Christ for Us*, 19–30, for a critical discussion of how various scholars, given Bonhoeffer's theology and life influences, partition his life and theology.

2. Brown, "Bonhoeffer and Pacifism," 38.

Phase 1: Church and World in Mild Tension

retain their identities with respect to one another. The church is imbued with a distinct message and role which it offers to an outside world or culture. The church struggles to sanctify or justify a reluctant world. For Bonhoeffer this struggle does not imply that the church and world are in an antagonistic relationship. For example, he does not posit the church as a pure sect residing in a hostile world, a world from which the church and Christian should withdraw. Rather, in Bonhoeffer's phase-1 theology there is a marked concern with what is concrete, confrontation with the divine through the time-bound other, and ethical responsibility to the other. Finally, while it remains debatable whether or not Bonhoeffer intends his highly Christocentric vision of the church in phase 1 to extend beyond itself to include humanity outside of church boundaries, the resources are there to make such an argument.

More specifically, we can organize Bonhoeffer's phase-1 church-world theology into four related themes. First, while he does reiterate the traditional Lutheran theme of the church offering Word and sacrament, he does not offer any specific or prevailing content to the Word the church offers the world. This, in turn, leads to an absence of church guidance in terms of any particular world or state-challenging political directives that might be derived from the Gospel (like we see later, for example, where he is fascinated with the Sermon on the Mount). Second, Bonhoeffer is concerned with the concreteness or accessibility of God's reality in the world or through others and the embeddedness of the church in sin-ridden history. Bonhoeffer's church is a sin-ridden institution, among other institutions, firmly embedded in the dynamics of history. The church can exist only as an empirical entity in this sin-ridden history. There is no pure church and it, like other communities, must fulfill its role in history. Third, Bonhoeffer understands transcendence as social or ethical; we encounter God and come to self through interaction with the other person in community who presents an ethical barrier. Finally, his conception of the church as a *Kollectivperson*, a sociological category, emphasizes the importance of authentic interaction with others both individually and in community. Ultimately, these predominant church-world themes establish a vision whereby the church and its members can engage in the worldly.

These church-world theological themes are connected to a few specific political positions for Bonhoeffer (not in direct relationship in terms of the order presented above). First, because the barrier between church and world is limited and somewhat porous, Christians are expected to engage in the world and, specifically, to help the state make history. Accordingly, Bonhoeffer offers a somewhat nationalistic or status quo supporting vision of the church. In addition, because the *Volk* are necessarily part of the church, Bonhoeffer's political thinking is subject to some of the facets of the theology of his contemporaries that rely on *Volkish* themes. This particular form of political thinking supports a more traditionally German understanding of a citizen's or the church's responsibilities vis-à-vis the state, including a disavowal of any form of internationalism (commitment to an ideal other in another place instead of the concrete other within reach) or pacifism (an irresponsible disavowal of the worldly). Finally, although he never explicitly endorses this very controversial idea, certain aspects of his theology (the strong hints of Hegelianism, for example, in his understanding of the church) arguably push him toward "orders of creation" thinking. The Hegelian influence also supports more traditional church-state thinking in line with the prevailing super-conservative interpretation of Luther's Two Kingdoms doctrine in Bonhoeffer's Germany.

Bonhoeffer's forms of political involvement were for the most part consistent with his traditionally German Lutheran church-world vision. He was certainly not involved in radical politics either for or against the state during this first phase. Yet, he did not withdraw from the state or other worldly activities. In addition, Bonhoeffer espoused the expected or typical German Lutheran doctrine on war. Pacifism or conscientious objection (although Luther arguably provides a provision for conscientious objection[3]) were not a particular emphasis for Luther or for successive interpreters of his thought. These political positions were considered unacceptable as they represented an irresponsible lack of commitment to the protection of persons in one's own nation.[4] Any form of pacifism

---

3. Althaus, *The Ethics of Martin Luther*, 127.

4. Hordern, "Lutheran Theology and the Witness of Peace," 136. Hordern describes Luther's position on pacifism: "Martin Luther knew 'pacifism' in two forms. One was the passivity extolled in monasteries as a 'perfection;' the second was the pacifism of some early Anabaptists. In both cases Luther does not seem to have rejected the model of pacifism itself; rather the brunt of his attack was to reject both of these movements for retreating from their responsibilities in the world. Both the monk and the Anabaptist had put themselves in a situation of being cut off from their neighbors in need." See also, Althaus, *The Ethics of Martin Luther*, 137–43.

Phase 1: Church and World in Mild Tension 79

was especially unacceptable in Bonhoeffer's Germany.[5] Bonhoeffer did not meet any minimal definition of pacifism in this first phase. In fact, he echoed sentiments typical of the War Theologians prominent at the time in one of his writings. Moreover, Bonhoeffer was even willing to undergo illegal military training in his early student days.

Overall, Bonhoeffer's church-world theology and his forms of political thinking and involvement are, as noted, consistent with one interpretation of his inherited way of thinking on the church and state, a somewhat conservative interpretation of the Lutheran Two Kingdoms doctrine that arguably haunted him even in later phases of his career.[6] As noted in the second chapter, in most interpretations of the doctrine the church member encounters no barriers to fulfilling his or her duties to the state. Liberal versions stress the church's right to disagree with state policy when that policy threatens the church's ability to fulfill its God-ordained role. Yet, even in these versions, the church is not to act as the state or politically against the state. The typically conservative formulations downplay the right of the church to raise a protest voice, leaving the doctrine open to the criticism that it breeds passive acceptance of

---

5. See Scharffenorth, "Bonhoeffers Pazifismus," 363–87. Scharffenorth writes, "In Bonhoeffers geistlischer Heimat, dem deutschen Luthertum, war kein Raum für einen Pazifismus. Die reformatorische Abgrenzung gegenüber den Schwärmern galt als bindende Entscheidung gegen diese Form des christlichen Friedendienstes" (363). ("In Bonhoeffer's religious environment, German Lutheranism, there was no room for pacifism. The reformation opposition to enthusiasm was regarded as the binding decision against this form of Christian peace-work"). See also, canon #10 of "The Guiding Principles of the Faith Movement of the 'German Christians'" from June 6, 1932, reprinted in Arthur Cochrane, *The Church's Confession under Hitler*, 222–23 (hereafter abbreviated as *CCUH*). Pacifism is regarded as anti-nationalistic. The canon reads, "We want an evangelical Church that is rooted in out nationhood. We repudiate the spirit of a Christian world-citizenship. We want the degenerating manifestations of the spirit, such as pacifism, internationalism, Free Masonry, etc., overcome by a faith in our national mission that God has committed to us."

6. The fact that there may be this continuing influence of traditional conservative Lutheran thinking throughout the various phases of his career is a main argument in Robert F. Koch's dissertation, "The Theological Responses of Karl Barth and Dietrich Bonhoeffer to Church-State Relations in Germany, 1933–1945." He writes, "Barth's early concerns were primarily ecclesiastical, resisting any attempt to impose National Socialist ideology on the church. His resistance to the Hitler regime became increasingly political, moving to the point where he depicted it as a demonic realm. No such progression is apparent from the works of Bonhoeffer . . . What one sees in Bonhoeffer's thought is a struggle between his own sense of call and his Lutheran theological heritage. While the possibility of resistance is raised in 'Die Kirche von der Judenfrage,' one finds quite traditional views of church-state relations in *Nachfolge* and *Ethics*," iv.

state policy amongst the church and its members. As noted, Bonhoeffer was not especially critical of the state as a church member, an academic, or otherwise in phase 1.

I will argue for the connection between Bonhoeffer's church-world thinking and specific forms of political thinking in the individual sections treating his important phase-1 writings. I will cover how this church-world/political thinking connection relates to his particular forms of political behavior in a summary as the penultimate section of the chapter.

SANCTORUM COMMUNIO (1925–1927)

By September 1925, Bonhoeffer had chosen Reinhold Seeberg as a dissertation mentor over Holl and Harnack.[7] He wrote his dissertation, originally titled *Sanctorum Communio: Eine dogmatische Untersuchung*, over a period of eighteen months from fall 1925 to mid-1927.[8] The twenty-one year old Bonhoeffer successfully defended his thesis on December 17, 1927, and earned the Licentiate in Theology with an honor rarely given by the Berlin theological faculty, *summa cum laude*.[9] The work, a study of the church as both a revelatory and sociological reality, represents a brilliant synthesis of the thinking and influence of Seeberg, Harnack, Barth, Troeltsch, Weber and others.[10]

In terms of Bonhoeffer's political context at the time, the Weimar Republic was in a period of stability especially in comparison with the crises accompanying its formation in 1918–1919 and those in 1923.[11] This period of relative economic prosperity and political harmony dated

---

7. See *DB*, 78–81, for an account of the process by which Bonhoeffer chose a mentor and a topic. See also, Clifford Green's Introduction in *Sanctorum Communio*, 7–9, for an account of "The Origin and Publication" of the dissertation. Hereafter this text will be abbreviated as *SC-E*.

8. *DB*, 81. The work has the subtitle, "A Theological Study of the Sociology of the Church," in later translations. See also, *SC-E*, 9.

9. *SC-E*, 9; *DB*, 96.

10. See Bethge, "The Challenge of Dietrich Bonhoeffer's Life and Theology," 22–92. Bethge comments on *Sanctorum Communio*'s remarkable combination of Barth and Troeltsch.

11. *DB*, 65. Bethge notes about Berlin in 1924, "The Berlin to which Bonhoeffer returned was not the stage of world events or of large political demonstrations. It was a city of great art exhibitions and concerts—and of course Max Reinhardt's great theatrical productions, which Bonhoeffer could not have missed."

Phase 1: Church and World in Mild Tension 81

back to 1924. Economically speaking, Germany successfully rectified its chief economic difficulty, the great inflation of 1923, with the creation of the *Rentebank* and its temporary currency (the *Rentenmark*). Moreover, the Dawes Plan, named after the American banker Charles Dawes who chaired the international commission, helped stabilize the economy and even spurred an economic upturn. The plan concentrated on helping Germany finance its reparations payments with loans from American bankers. The loans also helped finance public works and German industry. Finally, by 1928 the German economy was almost operating at full employment.[12]

There was a similar state of relative calm in the political sphere. The developments in the area of foreign policy, and especially the efforts of Gustav Stresemann (leader of the DVP), were of particular importance. His work as foreign minister represented an attempt to soften the "restrictions on German sovereignty by the peace of Versailles" and to reestablish Germany as a power by cooperation with the Allied nations. Stresemann's work included treaties ensuring solid German borders with France and Belgium and the entry of Germany into the League of Nations. He essentially restored Germany to its pre-War position of equality with other nations except for the military.[13] There was also some degree of stability in internal political workings in the form of a consistent right-of-center coalition government for four years (although in 1928 there was a shift away from the right to the benefit of the Social Democrats). Finally, the election of the war hero Hindenburg as president led to at least a "grudging acceptance of the republic."[14]

While not especially active in politics,[15] Bonhoeffer worked in the world (served the church community) in a Sunday School in Grunewald during his dissertation years. Church regulations required pastoral work for candidates for theological examinations. Even with his heavy reading load and dissertation work, Bonhoeffer poured himself fully into his post and became very popular with the children.[16] Bethge

12. *HNG*, 16.
13. Craig, *Germany: 1866–1945*, 498.
14. *HNG*, 16–17.
15. *DB*, 66. Bethge describes Bonhoeffer's Berlin years: "Nor did he try to enter the political student circles, since at the time he wished to associate with neither socialists nor right-wing groups."
16. See ibid., 91–96, for a detailed account of Bonhoeffer's work in the regional church.

notes the life-long import of this episode in the young theologian's life with the following question about Bonhoeffer's own self-understanding: "should practical work be the counter-point to the theme of his theological existence—or should it be the other way around?"[17] The theme of the relationship between thought and action was thus raised early in his career despite his lack of concern for radical politics. In fact, correspondence with a friend indicates that Bonhoeffer was already attuned to the relationship between the practical and the theological.[18] He was already concerned about the implications of theology for engagement with the concrete world. This concern would appear in the theology of his dissertation.

Sanctorum Communio attempts to establish the church as a sociological as well as a theological or revelatory reality. Bonhoeffer declares the aim of his work in an introduction, "My intention is to discuss neither a general sociology of religion, nor genetic-sociological questions; rather, I intend to show that an inherently Christian social philosophy and sociology, arising essentially out of fundamental concepts of Christian theology, is most fully articulated in the concept of the church."[19] Like his liberal mentors in Berlin, Bonhoeffer takes the insights of a discipline outside of theology seriously. Nevertheless, like Barth, he gives precedence to revealed realities. Bonhoeffer thus re-arranges, critiques, or appropriates the contributions of those fields and uses them to the extent that they are "to be made fruitful for theology." The import of these insights is pronounced, however, as he argues that "*all* the fundamental Christian concepts" have a "social intention."[20] Thus, the contributions from social philosophy and sociology would ultimately inform all theological categories, not only ecclesiology.

---

17. Ibid., 93.

18. Ibid. Bethge writes, "After his uncommitted beginnings in Tübingen, it had become plain that there was a gulf between the two realms [practical work and theological work]; but it was also clear that the existence of this gap should not be acknowledged. Thus he spiritedly wrote Widmann that the hardest theological pronouncements of Barth were worthless if they could not be explained thoroughly to the children of Grunewald."

19. *SC-E*, 22. This quotation is from the original version of the preface. It should be noted that all italicized sentences in the text and in the footnotes from *Sanctorum Communio* have been italicized by either Bonhoeffer or the editor.

20. Ibid., 22.

Phase 1: Church and World in Mild Tension

After establishing definitions of sociology and social philosophy,[21] Bonheoffer sets the framework for defining Christian community with two important claims. First, he argues that any analysis of community must begin with an analysis of the human person. Second, since the proper object of the current study is a particular type of community, one already accepted on faith as revealed by Christ, the proper starting point is the specifically Christian concept of person, one that necessarily involves relation with the divine. Bonhoeffer approaches his task by elucidating various classic philosophical approaches to the problem of defining person in relation or "models of social basic relation."[22] He argues that all of these approaches to the problem of the relationship between person, I, or individual and the collective whole of sociality, despite their differences, suffer from an inadequacy. They define the person as atomistic or individualistic with no capacity for legitimate social relationality.[23] Or, they err in the opposite direction. They deny the integrity, value, or defining limits of the person by collapsing the difference between subject and object.[24]

Bonhoeffer designates idealism as his conversation partner to show how these philosophical approaches fail to provide an adequate basis for an understanding of community useful for appreciating the church. The specifically Christian concept of an independent person is established only in encounter with a "fundamental barrier" in the social or ethical sphere. Idealism's intellectual or rational approach does not provide a real person-constituting barrier. Bonhoeffer suggests strongly that it is a faulty or incomplete concept of reality in idealism responsible for the lack of a barrier.[25] He claims that idealism's unique notion of time as it

---

21. Ibid., 27, 33. Bonhoeffer was mostly concerned with definitions that lent themselves to viewing the human person in authentic relatedness to others or the collective whole while retaining individuality. See also, *ATS*, 19–65. Green notes on p. 25 Bonhoeffer's desire to move away from definitions that understand the human person individualistically and atomistically.

22. Ibid., 36–40. Bonhoeffer treats Aristotelianism, Stoicism, and Epicureanism as "metaphysical" and Cartesian as "epistemological." See also, *SC-E*, 41–45. Bonhoeffer also treats the idealists Fichte, Kant, and Hegel.

23. *SC-E*, 38–39.

24. Ibid., 42.

25. Ibid., 46. Bonhoeffer writes, "idealism's 'object' is ultimately no barrier ... The point is the *concept of reality* that idealism did not think through thoroughly, and therefore did not think through at all. Essential reality for idealism is the self-knowing and self-active spirit, engaging truth and reality in the process."

affects ethics is responsible for its inability to establish a real barrier. An individual in a concrete time-bound situation and the ethical responsibility therein are the presuppositions for establishing personhood. Idealism, however, is a closed system wherein acquiescence to universal reason de-emphasizes the encounter with the other in the demanding and anxiety-provoking concrete moment of decision.[26]

The distinctly Christian contribution to the establishment of the barrier and, consequently or simultaneously, personhood, is precisely this notion of ethical encounter in the concrete situation.[27] While admitting that this encounter happens, like in idealism, in spirit or *Geist*, Bonhoeffer makes another extremely important distinction for an explicitly Christian understanding of person. He writes, "*For Christian philosophy, the human person originates only in relation to the divine; the divine person transcends the human person*, who both resists and is overwhelmed by the divine."[28] Idealism, for Bonhoeffer, is decidedly "unchristian, as it involves attributing to the human spirit absolute value that can only be ascribed to divine spirit." Idealism also "universalizes" by making the other a "'bearer' of objective, impersonal value."[29] The other must be a personal concrete being. He or she must be related as an I, with an independent sphere of existence, to a You, also with an independent sphere of existence.[30] I and You are not in the order of "concept" but in the order of the real and the really distinct. Most importantly for Bonhoeffer, the human You encountered as ethical limit is a God-created and God-willed entity. God is thus present in the ethical encounter between persons and in sociality.[31] God's "otherness" is present in the ethi-

---

26. Ibid., 48–49. Bonhoeffer writes, "Idealism has no understanding of the moment in which the person feels the threat of absolute demand."

27. Ibid., 49. Bonhoeffer writes, "It is a Christian insight that the person as a conscious being is created in the moment of being moved—in the situation of responsibility, passionate ethical struggle, confrontation by an overwhelming claim; thus the real person grows out of the concrete situation."

28. Ibid.

29. Ibid.

30. Ibid., 52. Bonhoeffer writes, "I and You are not simply interchangeable concepts, but comprise specific and distinct spheres of existence. I myself can become an object of my own experience, but can never experience myself as a You. Other persons can become objects of my reflections on their I-ness, but I will never get beyond the fact that I can only encounter the other as a You. I can never become a real barrier to myself, *but it is just as impossible for me to leap over the barrier to the other*."

31. SC-E, 54–55. Bonhoeffer writes, "*God or the Holy Spirit joins the concrete You; only through God's active working does the other become a You to me from whom my I*

cal encounter between I and You in concrete, societal, time-bound, and historical human experience, not in an "eternal elusiveness."[32]

In this early work, Bonhoeffer has already established three important ideas that reappear in various ways throughout his writing career. First, he is concerned with the tangible or concrete or the real encounter in time with reality or the world. Other human beings bear this concreteness. The second theme is "ethical," "social," or "this-worldly" transcendence. God is encountered in and through confronting the concrete other in history throughout the structures of sociality, society, or community.[33] Finally, and especially important for the current work, Bonhoeffer argues that the constitution of personhood, the embeddedness in community, and the confrontation with God are "inseparably and essentially interrelated."[34] A person is formed only when he or she

arises. In other words, every human You is an image of the divine You. You-character is in fact the essential form in which the divine is experienced; every human You bears its You-character only by virtue of the divine. This is not to say that it is a borrowed attribute of God, and not really a You. Rather, the divine You creates the human You. And since the human You is created and willed by God, it is a real absolute and holy You, like the divine You. One might then speak here of the human being as the image of God with respect to the effect one person has on another . . . what is holy is the You of God, the absolute will, who here becomes visible in the concrete You of social life. The other person is a 'You' insofar as God brings it about. But God can make every human being a You for us. *The claim of the other rests in God alone; for this very reason, it remains the claim of the other.* In summary, *the person is willed by God, in concrete vitality, wholeness and uniqueness as an ultimate unity. Social relations must be understood, then, as purely interpersonal and building on the uniqueness and separateness of persons.* The person cannot be overcome by a personal spirit; no 'unity' can negate the plurality of persons. *The social basic category is the I-You relation. The You of the other person is the divine You."*

32. ATS, 36. Green confirms, "The transcendence of God means God's presence as 'Other.' God is distinct from but not absent from us; God's otherness is a transforming presence, and not an eternal elusiveness. We do not deal with an invisible God in an invisible world of our wishful fantasy; God is met and heard only in the real world where human personal wills encounter one another; God is to be sought in the real experience of historical, social, ethical existence."

33. Ibid., 35. Green, on Bonhoeffer's idea in *Sanctorum Communio* that the divine is encountered in the other, writes, "*It is the first expression of that characteristic social-ethical-historical transcendence which remains essentially unchanged throughout Bonhoeffer's theological career."*

34. SC-E, 34. Bonhoeffer writes, "What one understands about person and community simultaneously makes a statement about God. *The concepts of person, community, and God* are inseparably and essentially interrelated. A concept of God is always conceived in relation to a concept of person and a concept of a community of persons. Whenever one thinks of a concept of God, it is done in relation to a concept of a per-

is a member of a community where God confronts in and through the concrete other.

To more clearly articulate the relationship between individual and community, Bonhoeffer establishes his own version of an extremely important concept for his work, *Kollectivperson* (collective person).[35] The concept "collective person" expresses the idea that whole communities are the same in structure as individual persons. The collective person transcends all individuals but is "incomprehensible without the correlate of personal, individual being."[36] Neither the collective person nor the individual has priority, though. The individual becomes an individual in sociality and the collective person arises only with the collection of individuals. This important idea also sets up his framework of a three-part "Christian drama"[37] wherein God relates to humanity as a collective person in three distinct phases, the primal state, humanity in Adam, and the church as the collective person of the new humanity. The nature of human relations in community in the different phases marks them off from one another. Bonhoeffer indicates that God desires to relate to a community of human beings rather than individual human beings. God views and confronts humanity as a collective person.[38]

---

son and community of persons. In principle, in order to arrive at the essence of the Christian concept of community, we could just as well begin with the concept of God as with that of person. And in choosing to begin with the latter, we must make constant reference to the concept of God in order to come to a well-grounded view of both God and the concept of community."

35. *SC-E*, 77. See footnote 52. Bonhoeffer takes the idea of collective person from Scheler.

36. Ibid.

37. *ATS*, 44. This is Green's term for an organizing principle of Bonhoeffer's work—the "drama of creation, fall and redemption." Bonhoeffer's chapter 3, "The Primal State and the Problem of Community," corresponds to the type of human relationality present after the creation, his chapter four, "Sin and Broken Community" corresponds to the type of human relationality after the fall and his chapter five, "Sanctorum Communio," corresponds to the type of human relationality present in the redemptive presence of the church.

38. *SC-E*, 80. Bonhoeffer writes, "God created man and woman directed to one another. God does not desire a history of individual human beings, but the history of the human *community*. However, God does not want a community that absorbs the individual into itself, but a community of *human beings*. In God's eyes, community and the individual exist in the same moment and rest in one another. The collective unit and the individual unit have the same structure in God's eyes."

Phase 1: Church and World in Mild Tension

Bonhoeffer's foregoing treatment of human relationality in community and the structure of community itself falls under the title "The Primal State and the Problem of Community." In his penultimate chapter, he treats the second phase of the drama, humanity in Adam. He shows how the I and You relations, described in his treatment of the Christian concept of the person and humanity in the primal state, are re-arranged and altered after the fall. Selfishness and egotism replace the love necessary for human community. Conscience develops and "every person exists in complete, voluntary isolation; everyone lives their own life, rather than all living the same life in God."[39] What Bonhoeffer calls "ethical atomism" enters into history. Humans no longer relate to each other properly and they, therefore, do not relate to God properly. Sin thus breaks the primal community.[40] It is clear, then, that like all other important theological categories, sin must be interpreted in terms of sociality; it must be interpreted in terms of its implications for individuals and their relationship to, and in, community.

The communal consciousness of sin, ironically, establishes humanity as a specifically ethical collective person. Sin, in this sense, though a fragmenting force, actually unites all persons as a "collective person of humanity [*Menschheitperson*]" in the confrontation with God's divine Thou.[41] Sin, and recognition of sin, thus posits humans in a community before God as one in Adam. Or, Adam is the collective person that per-

---

39. Ibid., 108. Bonhoeffer argues, "Whereas in the primal state the relation among human beings is one of giving, in the sinful state it is purely demanding . . . There was no conscience in the primal state; only after the fall did Adam know what good and evil are . . . With sin, ethical atomism enters history. This applies essentially to the spirit form. All natural forms of community remain, but they are corrupt in their inmost core."

40. *ATS*, 50. Green writes, "If this is the nature of sin, its consequence is to 'break' and fragment the primal community of people with God and with one another. This does not mean that people become asocial, but rather that created sociality is torn by a profound inner contradiction."

41. *SC-E*, 121. Bonhoeffer writes, "Wherever individuals recognize themselves both as individuals and the human race, and submit to the demand of God, there beats the heart of the collective person. This ensures its moral unity; insofar as every human being is Adam, the collective person really has *one conscience*. The structure of humanity-in-Adam is unique because it is both composed of many isolated individuals and yet is one, as the humanity that has sinned as a whole . . . Sin is the sign of belonging to the old Adam; consciousness of guilt reveals to individuals their connection with all sinners. When individuals recognize that they belong to Adam's humanity, they join the peccatorum communio [community of sinners]."

sonifies all of humanity in sin. Bonhoeffer, as well as establishing that sociality is the most effective way to understand humanity in its sinful state,[42] also sets up his thinking on the church. If the collective person Adam represents the old humanity of sin, Christ is the collective person of the new humanity. Bonhoeffer offers what has become one of his most recognizable phrases at this point in the text. He writes, "It is 'Adam,' a collective person, who can only be superseded by the collective person 'Christ existing as community.'" "Christ existing as community" is the collective person, "the new humanity in Christ" or the *Sanctorum Communio*. This new community "supersedes" and "restores" the fragmented community in Adam, the *peccatorum communio*.[43]

Bonhoeffer can finally address in his last chapter the third phase of the drama, the Church as *Sanctorum Communio*. He begins with a theological or theoretical treatment of the church. Bonhoeffer describes the church as "God's new will and purpose for humanity. God's will is always directed toward the concrete historical human being . . . this means that it begins to be implemented *in history*. God's will must become visible and comprehensible at some point in history."[44] The church, as God's new will and purpose for the human community, the collective person as Christ, cannot be only a potential reality depending upon humanity for its realization. It is, rather established and realized by Christ finally. However, it must be actualized among the people in history continually by the Holy Spirit.[45]

In addition to describing how the church fits theoretically or theologically into the three-phase drama, Bonhoeffer also describes the church as an empirical or sociological community. His concern here is the relationship between the actualizing work of the Holy Spirit and

---

42. Ibid., 115. Bonhoeffer uses this notion to explain original sin. He writes, "*The human being, by virtue of being an individual, is also the human race.* This is the definition that does justice to the human spirit in relation to the fundamental social category. When, in the sinful act, the individual spirit rises up against God, thus climbing to the utmost height of spiritual individuality—since this is the individual's very own deed against God, occasioned by nothing else—the deed committed is at the same time *the deed of the human race* (no longer in the biological sense) *in the individual person*. One falls away not only from one's personal vocation but also from one's generic vocation as a member of the human race. Thus all humanity falls with each sin, and not one of us is in principle different from Adam; that is, every one is also the 'first' sinner."

43. Ibid., 121.

44. Ibid., 141.

45. See ibid., 145–208, for an extended discussion of the church established and realized in and through Christ and actualized by the Holy Spirit.

the objective spirit of the empirical church community. Bonhoeffer tries to protect the church as a God-initiated revelatory reality against any attempts to divinize a human community or to derive its divine quality from the human interactions within the community itself. He thus strongly asserts a distinct difference between "church" and "religious community." The empirical church is distinct from a general religious community because it is the presence of Christ on earth, because it has his Word. As such, "the objective spirit of the church is the bearer of the historical impact of Jesus Christ and of the social impact of the Holy Spirit."[46] Failing to clearly articulate this relationship leads to two misunderstandings of the church. The first equates the empirical church entirely with sin and the other posits it as "merely . . . the manifestation of the nonreal, ideal church of the future . . . [and] shows that the real church is unattainable in this world."[47]

These views deny the reality that Christ entered history and thus deny that the church is really present in history. Bonhoeffer even asserts, "*The history of the church is the hidden center of world history*, and not the history of one educational institution among others."[48] As such, it is an institution that includes sin, sinners, and imperfection. Bonhoeffer writes, "The very fact that as a sinful community the church is nevertheless still holy, or rather that in this world it is never holy without being sinful—this is what Christ's presence in it means."[49] Bonhoeffer thus distinguishes his thinking from Hegel's. In Bonhoeffer's reading, Hegel equates the action of the collective church community with the action of the Holy Spirit.[50] Bonhoeffer asserts that the reality of sin makes any such equation impossible.[51] Lastly, the idea that the objective spirit of the church includes persons who are not predestined provides Bonhoeffer with "the most compelling proof that objective spirit and Holy Spirit cannot be equated." He argues that these people, though not really be-

---

46. *SC-E*, 210.

47. Ibid., 211.

48 Ibid.

49. Ibid., 214.

50. Phillips, *Christ for Us*, 53. Phillips points out here that Bonhoeffer is also disagreeing with his mentor Seeberg. After offering a quote from Seeberg's *Fundamentals of the Christian Religion*, Phillips writes, "The danger here is readily apparent: Seeberg virtually identifies the action of God with dynamic, interpersonal relationship and personal will. The church is *Christus Prolongus*, the Incarnation of the Holy Spirit."

51. *SC-E*, 214.

longing to the church, can still be used by the Holy Spirit as "creative instruments."[52]

With his emphasis on the difference between objective spirit and Holy Spirit, Bonhoeffer introduces the long-standing and important theological question of the relationship between the "visible" or empirical church and the "invisible" church of Christ that will "become visible only in the eschaton."[53] He has already established that there are those not predestined who are clearly members of the empirical church. There are also members of the empirical church who are members in name only. Bonhoeffer approaches the invisible-visible question with a further distinction between the realities of a *Volkskirche* or church-of-the-people, with several nominal members likely, and a *Freiwilligkeitskirche* or a voluntary or "gathered" church.

How can a church be both voluntary and involuntary? Bonhoeffer answers this question with an analysis of the nature of the Word. It is the nature of the Word (in preaching and the offering of the sacrament) to extend beyond itself and address those who are only potential members.[54] In addition, Bonhoeffer again points to the fact that the church is grounded in history as an explanation for the mutual presence of voluntary and involuntary churches. He writes,

> The second argument for a church of the people is the fact that here in history the wheat cannot yet be separated from the chaff; that separation will be evident only on the day of judgement, and is now being prepared in secret. However, in going beyond itself, the sanctorum communio is at the same time following an impulse back toward the "real" church, toward the becoming real of what is potential. This means the sanctorum communio, which by its nature presents itself as a church-of-the-people, also calls for the voluntary church and establishes itself as such; that is, the sanctorum communio bears the others, so to speak, who have latent potential to become "real" members of the church by virtue of the word that is both the author of the church and of the message it preaches.[55]

---

52. Ibid., 215–16.
53. Ibid., 216.
54. Ibid., 220.
55. Ibid.

Phase 1: Church and World in Mild Tension

So while Bonhoeffer holds that the essential nature of the church is voluntary church, and that "practical church politics" may eventually necessitate a move into a strictly voluntary church, he understands the church-of-the-people to be an extremely valuable reality as it provides potential members.[56] Accordingly, he criticizes the various perfectionist sectarian movements that have arisen throughout Christian history. These movements (the Anabaptists, Pietists, and even socialist movements who seemingly think the Kingdom of God is a historical possibility) do not take seriously the fact that God's revelation takes form as a church that is subject to the sin which accompanies any historical organization or reality.[57] The chaff and the wheat will co-exist in this historical empirical community, and not embracing the chaff is in some ways a denial of God.[58] Bonhoeffer also addresses the problem of how to conceive of the church as a unity given the presence of several different individual existing congregations. Bonhoeffer points to Zwingli's notion of the "universal church" as an answer. Individual churches, to the extent that they express the "one word" in the "one Spirit," manifest "God's historical will for redemption" and form a unity that is the whole church-community. Bonhoeffer uses the classic concept of the "body of Christ" to frame the discussion of unity amidst the diversity of the individual congregations. He warns, however, that this concept is subject to misinterpretation as an organic entity or in a physical or atomistic sense where each individual congregation is a small segment of the sum total body of Christ. It is more accurate to think of the body of Christ in terms of "function" rather than "form." That is, wherever the spirit of Christ is operative in any church community, the whole of the church is manifest.[59]

Bonhoeffer's final topic in the area of empirical church structure concerns the historical and sociological distinction between church

---

56. Ibid., 221.

57. Ibid., 222. Bonhoeffer writes, "In all of these movements we find the attempt to have the realm of God finally present not only by faith but by sight, no longer veiled within the strange forms of a Christian church, but clearly manifested in the morality and holiness of human beings, and in a perfect solution to all historical and social problems."

58. Ibid. Bonhoeffer notes eloquently, "Genuine love for the church will bear and love its impurity and imperfection too; for it is in fact this empirical church in whose womb grows God's sacred treasure, God's own church-community."

59. Ibid., 223–26.

and sect. Bonhoeffer plainly rejects Weber and Troeltsch's distinction between church and sect. His rejection of sectarianism relies not on the fact that the church is subject to sin in history but only on his understanding of the Word.[60] For Bonhoeffer, as long as the Holy Spirit is operating on, through, or within the objective spirit of the community through the Word, there is no real difference between church and sect. The sociological structure of any empirical church itself does not determine whether or not it is truly the church community of Christ. Rather, the "miracle of the divine promise" ensures that wherever the Word is proclaimed it forms a legitimate church-community by its power.[61]

Bonhoeffer's final section, concerning the church and eschatology, is the only place where he explicitly mentions the relationship between the church and the world. He begins with the brute reality of the *sanctorum communio* as it exists in the realm of history. Bonhoeffer argues that there will be two opposing thrusts as long as the church exists in history. There is the attempt of the *sanctorum communio* to penetrate all human communities and societies and the resistance to the penetration. He warns against interpreting this set of circumstances as an oppositional relationship between the church and the world. The church, rather than setting itself up against the world, is engaged in a project of offering itself to culture, "through the word of God and the Holy Spirit" for the purposes of "sanctification and justification of all human communal life."[62] Culture is the ground upon, or arena in, which the church has to operate in history. The church is not against the world. Rather, it is the larger and more pervasive presence of evil in both the church and

---

60. Ibid., 268. Bonhoeffer argues, "The ultimate insight is lacking in Weber and Troeltsch; if it were present, the whole genetic question would disappear . . . However, the social act of will as such, as long as it is guided by the word of God, that is, as long as it consists in love brought about by the spirit, is the same in both church and sect. As long as it has the word, the sect too is community of Christ, *its community is the community of saints. In its basic sociological structure* it is identical with the church" (italics original to translation).

61. Ibid., 271. Bonhoeffer writes, "*To summarize*, the sanctorum communio, the Christian community of love as a sociological type, is dependent on the word of God, and it alone. According to the promise in Isa. 55:11, it is present within every historical form in which the word is preached. The distinction between church and sect suggested by Weber and Troeltsch is untenable both historically and sociologically. Based on the efficacy of the word, we must believe the sanctorum communio to be present even within the sociologically unique structure of the Roman Catholic church."

62. *SC-E*, 283.

Phase 1: Church and World in Mild Tension

the outside culture that presents the permanent problem. Bonhoeffer writes, "*Sanctorum communio and Antichrist* will remain the opposites in history."[63]

Church-World Relationship and Political Thinking

Sanctorum Communio certainly does not have the church-world relationship or church-state relations or political matters as its main focus. Yet, this work does manifest Bonhoeffer's church-world theology directly in brief and in implicit fashion throughout. Bonhoeffer also addresses the issue of war at one point in the text. Given the evidence, I will argue that his general political positioning and his position on war in particular are consistent with his church-world thinking. Finally, I will argue that this consistency makes sense given his intellectual heritage and actual life context.

There are a few themes illuminating the church-world relationship. They all lend themselves to a vision where the church and world retain their respective identities and exist in a tension. This tension, though, does not imply that the church is a sectarian entity of total purity existing uncomfortably in an utterly evil, unredeemable, or hostile outside world, where withdrawal from that world would be required of church members. There is no indication that those inside the empirical church are perfect or purer than those who are on the outside. So while Bonhoeffer does establish boundaries between the church and the world, he leans toward an inclusive vision characterized by an impulse to bring nominal church members to a more active role in the church. Even further, there is a drive toward converting those outside of the empirical church through an offering of the Word and sacrament. This inclusive vision of the relationship between the church and the outside world is generally and logically conducive to church members engaging in the political sphere in some capacity.[64]

---

63. Ibid.
64. Wogaman, *Christian Perspectives on Politics*, 173. Wogaman describes the more inclusive vision and its political ramifications: "it is possible to think of the church ideally as the incorporation of everybody in a whole society into one vast religious community—an ecclesiastical unity of civilization . . . [This vision] is likely to have a positive conception of the state as the temporal aspect of a civilized order of which the church represents the spiritual aspect."

A first theme illuminating the church-world relationship is Bonhoeffer's thinking on transcendence. As noted in the second chapter, Bonhoeffer's specific context was the already-engaged battle between the old guard in liberal Protestant theology and the recent influence of the thinking of Karl Barth. He creatively sought to formulate a Christian understanding of transcendence somewhere between the extremes of God's total otherness and any equation of God and the world. Bonhoeffer's solution is a "this-worldly," "ethical," or "social" transcendence rather than notions of transcendence that rely on traditional or continental philosophy or metaphysics. He holds in *Sanctorum Communio* that all theological categories are social or communal in nature, especially ecclesiology. Transcendence is imbedded in the structures of the church community itself. More precisely, it is the presence of Christ in the church that guarantees this community of persons, both as a collective person and as individuals, as the bearer(s) of transcendence ("Christ existing as community").

Moreover, this transcendence is a specifically ethical transcendence. The concrete barrier provided by the other making an ethical demand is what constitutes Christian person-hood and allows for a conception of church community. Since it is God who confronts in and through the other, it is in this ethical encounter where true transcendence lies. Bonhoeffer's transcendence is thus a Christ-centered, sociological, ethical, ecclesiological, and "this-worldly transcendence" concerned with the concrete reality of lived existence rather than a speculative and metaphysical transcendence or a mystical and inner experiential transcendence. His thinking establishes a vision of the church where the worldly or earthly is not contrary to the aims or reality of the church, whether construed theologically or sociologically. God encounters the world collectively and individually in the real, gritty, worldly, ethical relations between human beings in and as community. The church as an ethical collective person, although formed by Christ and continually actualized by the Holy Spirit, is thus manifest in earthly loving human interaction.

While the possibility of the truly loving ethical community is Holy Spirit-created and, technically, impossible without God's loving presence or grace, it is still a human reality. Structurally, then, or even by definition, the church has a positive relation with the earthly or the worldly in the form of humanity. Moreover, if the establishment and operation of a loving human community defines church, then one might argue

Phase 1: Church and World in Mild Tension

that church exists wherever loving community exists; it does not matter whether or not this community lives within or without the bounds of the empirical church. Bonhoeffer does not hold this position unequivocally in *Sanctorum Communio*. Nevertheless, he does hint at it. In any case, Bonhoeffer's church is certainly not antagonistic to the worldly.

The next and more specific theme, his thinking on the brute fact of the church as an historical entity, serves as a presupposition for Bonhoeffer's treatment of several issues relevant to an analysis of the church-world relationship. Because of its existence within the bounds of human history, the church will necessarily embody the limitations and impediments to fulfillment like any other empirical and historical entities.[65] Theologically speaking, the problem is simply that a church in history will be riddled with sin and imperfection. Bonhoeffer's acceptance of church as an historical entity affects his thinking on the visible-invisible church distinction, the state church versus the voluntary church distinction, and even the church-sect distinction.

In terms of the visible-invisible church distinction, if the only church is the concrete historical empirical church community, with its sin and imperfection, there is no possibility of an otherworldly, invisible or pure copy or version of this sin-ridden empirical church found in history.[66] Therefore, any distinction between the visible and the invisible church is impossible.[67] Bonhoeffer has thus ruled out the possibility of

---

65. *SC-E*, 280–81. Bonhoeffer writes, "Christian thinking, in contrast to all idealist theories of community, considers Christian community to be God's church-community at every moment in history. And yet within its historical development it never knows a state of fulfillment. It will remain impure as long as there is history, and yet in this concrete form it is nevertheless God's community."

66. Kelly, "Bonhoeffer's Theology of History and Revelation," 89–130. This quote is from p. 103. Kelly writes, "In his early ecclesiology Bonhoeffer is insistent that this church be recognized and acknowledged in its actual, empirical form. It is not surprising, then, that he vigorously opposes an idea current in theological circles which would mentally distinguish a visible from an invisible church: one church the gathering of sinners and the other its heavenly, sinless and, therefore, more authentic double. For Bonhoeffer the distinction was meaningless, even when, following Luther's theology, it meant nothing more than the relationship similar to that of body and soul in a church conceived ultimately as one."

67. *SC-E*, 280. Bonhoeffer explains, "But then what does it mean 'to believe in the church'? We do not believe in an invisible church, nor in the Realm of God within the church as coetus electorum [company of elect]. Instead we believe that God has made the concrete empirical church [Kirche] in which the word is preached and the sacraments are celebrated to be God's own church-community [Gemeinde]. We believe that

any segment of the church community designating itself as the holy, set apart, pure, or chosen segment outside of or over and against the general church community. He also therefore rules out the possibility of that set apart segment to actually set themselves apart from its responsibilities in the political sphere.

In addition, Bonhoeffer's answer to the question of what makes this sin-ridden historical entity legitimate, the presence of the Word, influences his thinking on the church-sect distinction and the church-of-the people (or *Volkskirche*) voluntary church distinctions. Bonhoeffer ultimately rejects the sociological distinction of church and sect as it is based on the unreasonable assumption that any segment of the church community can achieve monastic purity or holiness in its concrete historical situation. Rather, any segment of the empirical church community, simultaneously sinful and in the process of redemption, or one that is informed by the Word, shares equally in status as church. The distinction between universal and individual churches and the state and voluntary churches are also rendered meaningless given the sinful church in history and the leveling or unifying work of the Word.[68]

Bonhoeffer does not, at these points in the text or in any other part of *Sanctorum Communio*, have as his main concern the problem of persons outside the bounds of the empirical church community. Thus, it is hard to speak explicitly in terms of church and persons outside the bounds of the empirical community in a definitive way. Yet, he does indicate that it is "in principle possible for God to bring human beings under the divine rule without the mediation of the concrete church community."[69]

---

it is the body of Christ, Christ's presence in the world, and that according to the promise God's spirit is at work in it. We have faith that God is also at work in the others. We do not believe in the call of individuals, but rather in that of the church-community. We believe in the church as the church of God, as the community of saints those who are sanctified by God. We believe, however, that this takes place always within the historical framework of the empirical church."

68. Ibid., 221. Bonhoeffer writes, "The logical and sociological unity of the voluntary church and the church-of-the-people, the essential and the empirical, 'invisible' and 'visible' church is thus established by the word; this is a genuinely Lutheran insight."

69. Ibid., 228. Bonhoeffer writes, "All other cases that might be conceivable in this context only prove that it is in principle also possible for God to bring human beings under the divine rule without the mediation of the concrete church-community. But this is something that falls outside the scope of this study."

Phase 1: Church and World in Mild Tension

He also explicitly states that the "sanctorum communio extends beyond itself and addresses all those who might belong to it even potentially."[70]

Another important theme is the notion of the church and other communities as "collective persons." Bonhoeffer places his notion of communities as collective persons in a three-phase drama. These three phases, and the type of human relationality in community therein, are intended to encompass all of humanity, not just members of the empirical Christian church. Bonhoeffer stresses that "the church is God's new will and purpose for humanity."[71] He also understands the church to be the collective person of the new humanity in Christ. These designations imply that the collective person encompasses all of humanity. Therefore, Bonhoeffer's thinking arguably cannot be sectarian.[72]

Still another theological theme related to Bonhoeffer's church-world thinking in *Sanctorum Communio* is the fact that his references to the Word do not focus predominantly or explicitly on any given biblical text as paradigmatic or even as an example of what in terms of specific content the gospels impart to the world. So there is a sense in which following the gospel or the Word does not require the Christian to act in any way that sets them apart from the world or the worldly. The Word appears more as a concept or as something that plays a certain role or has a certain function (the Word is something that any individual church must have in order to be in unison with other churches, for example) rather than as something that has an explicit content or message that might require some definite forms of response or behavior. In short, Bonhoeffer does not present any biblical texts as if their content might

---

70. Ibid., 220.

71. Ibid., 141.

72. *ATS*, 53. Green affirms, "This Christology and ecclesiology, therefore, is concerned with the rehabilitation and renovation of genuine humanity for all people. Christ is the collective person of the new humanity, superseding Adam as the Kollektivperson of the old humanity. Bonhoeffer's thinking is the very opposite of sectarian exclusivism; it moves, like Paul and Irenaeus, on the level of universal humanity. So the Word of Christ is not only a word to the church. Rather, his presence in and as the church creates a new social reality of human existence, and this is a paradigm, a promise and a challenge which encounters humanity in all human life . . . Thus, when Bonhoeffer describes Christ in the social form of the church as the Kollektivperson of the new humanity, this is a deliberate way of relating Christ to the community as a whole; it is not a way of confining Christ to the church, or of sanctifying any self-righteous ecclesiastical self-preoccupation."

force the believer to act in any way politically other than the way they might normally act.

Finally, the foregoing articulation of an implicit church-world relationship is consistent with what Bonhoeffer says about it explicitly. Bonhoeffer offers a stern warning. He writes, "the sanctorum communio does not place its trust in culture."[73] He warns, in addition, "Consequently, a culture that had absorbed the church into itself is therefore inconceivable." He asserts strongly, though, that "to define the empirical church and world as ultimate opposites would also be wrong."[74] Furthermore, he writes, "the relationship of the sanctorum communio to the world does not consist in a senseless hostility to culture."[75] There is, instead, "a struggle for the justification and sanctification of all human communal life through the word of God and the Holy Spirit."[76]

Bonhoeffer's discussion of the church-world relationship in his first major work thus yields an overall vision where the relationship is characterized by a mild tension. The church, while clearly possessing qualities that make it different from the world, is not antagonistic to the world, worldly realities or those outside the church. Rather, the church is an empirical community firmly embedded in history, a "collective person" formed and informed by the Holy Spirit and imbued with the Word that is constantly in the process of extending beyond itself to a somewhat reluctant culture or outside world. The church is a community, like other communities, wherein membership requires meeting the ethical demand of the concrete other. Bonhoeffer's vision of the church as "the new humanity" suggests that this ethical responsibility may extend to those outside the parameters of the formal church body. The church coexists and interacts with other communities in one single, sin-ridden history or reality.

The relationship between a vision of the church and world in tension or partnership and Bonhoeffer's political thinking begins with a look at his thinking on the church-state relationship. Bonhoeffer's main concern in this work is not church-state relations.[77] Nevertheless, much

---

73. *SC-E*, 282.

74. Ibid., 283.

75. Ibid., 282.

76. Ibid., 283.

77. See Zerner, "Dietrich Bonhoeffer's Views on the State and History," 131–57, for a treatment of his thinking on church-state relations. She notes, in her treatment of

Phase 1: Church and World in Mild Tension

like the above-described church-world relationship, one can formulate a church-state relationship from what Bonhoeffer provides. Bonhoeffer does not yet distinguish between the concepts "state," "nation" or people. His thinking on the state is in the spirit and "Teutonic" tradition of "organism," collective will or collective person.[78] He thinks of the nation in terms of the Hegelian idea of a suprapersonal collection of people or a *Volk* rather than as a social contract entered into for the sake of attaining a certain end or protecting the rights of individuals. As such, the state, nation, or people fall under Bonhoeffer's conception of community rather than society. Communities are timeless or permanent and have a value in and of themselves beyond any rational telos, end or purpose. Societies, on the other hand, are entirely history-bound, goal-oriented, and "constituted in history to realize their purposes."[79] Communities, however, might still embody a "constitutive purpose."[80]

In addition, Bonhoeffer in this early work agrees with Aquinas on the natural political nature of created human beings. People would form themselves into states even without the need to restrain sin.[81] The state is, therefore, like the other communities, a God-willed and organic collective person that exists and has value as an end in itself. It is, while eminently a historical experience, somewhat of a supra-historical entity living permanently (unable to be dissolved) or from "God to God."[82]

Sanctorum Communio, that Bonhoeffer's description of the state in his dissertation is "incidental to his analysis of the church" (135).

78. Ibid., 136–37.
79. *SC-E*, 95.
80. Ibid. Bonhoeffer writes, "Unlike many sociologists, we consider it impossible—however sensitively one tries—to elaborate the telos of a community, a family or a people. A community may have a rational telos, but its very essence is not absorbed by that telos, nor identical with it. Instead, *community* as such is characterized by value, as is history, and, as value-bearing, transcends inner historical limitation. As history by nature finds its telos at the limits of history—thinking eschatologically and supratemporally, that is, in God—so the nature of community is grounded in and willed by God ... So, too, genuine community in marriage, family or people [nation] exists entirely in 'coming from God and going to God.' ... By their very nature all communities are from God to God, whether we mean the *physical* communities of blood such as family and clan, *historical* communities such as people and nation, or *life-shaping* communities such as marriage and friendship."

81. Ibid., 96ff. See also, *ATS*, 47. Green writes, "Bonhoeffer also agrees with the view, which he finds in patristic writings and Thomas Aquinas, that the state, as an agency of order and well-being, belongs to creation."

82. *SC-E*, 95. Bonhoeffer adds, "It is fruitless to try to refute the above description by arguing from the empirical difference in duration. We spoke here of the idea of

Bonhoeffer does not use the phrase "orders of creation" in this work, yet his thinking is arguably close to this most controversial concept.[83] For instance, in one section he writes, "the collective human person has a heart . . . the collective person's heart beats at the point where the individual recognizes himself both as an individual and as the race, and bows to God's demand."[84] This notion of collective-person-as-race, understood as a permanent community "from God to God" as described above, could be taken in a radically dangerous direction, imbued as it is with the immense value of a God-ordained "end-in-itself." Like his mentors, Bonhoeffer's position on the state as an organic collection of wills ordained by God is arguably conservative. As such, Bonhoeffer has even been subject to the types of serious criticisms leveled at other German theologians of that era.[85]

Sanctorum Communio thus posits an implicit vision of the church-state relationship. The state, like the church, is a collective person. They are, therefore, two collective persons existing alongside each other. The church is a God-willed collective person imbued with the Word and charged with the task of offering that Word to the church and beyond. The state is a God-willed collective person with the task of making his-

---

community, not of empirical duration. If wills have joined together for the sake of their bond, if people have said 'yes' to a community in which they find themselves, quite apart from rational purposiveness, then the intentionality inherent in these acts extends to the limits of time, that is to say, to the limits of history, to God—community is from 'God to God.' This is the basis of *all 'holiness' of human community life, and the basis of the relationship of friendship, marriage, and community of people to God, and thus also ideally of the indissolubility of all these life structures*" (italics original to translation).

83. Clements, "Ecumenical Witness for Peace," 163. Clements defines "orders of creation" as follows, "the doctrine that certain structures of human life are not just incidental biological or historical phenomena, but are deliberately ordained by God as essential and immutable conditions of human existence, without which humanity is not humanity as created by God."

84. *SC-E*, 121.

85. Zerner, "Dietrich Bonhoeffer's Views on the State and History," 137. Zerner quotes from Berger's "Sociology and Ecclesiology," in *The Place of Bonhoeffer*, 60–77. Peter Berger criticized Bonhoeffer's position on the state as "sociological Hegelianism" and as a "theological imperialism," 60, 63, 77. Moreover, Berger questions the relationship between corporate ethical responsibility and individual ethical responsibility in visions of communities where "wholes" are emphasized over individuals—where "entities (such as 'the family,' 'the nation,' 'the state') take on the quality of mythological beings that make moral demands over against the imperatives of personal morality" (62). Berger describes this ethical vision as a "pre-Marxian use of Hegelianism" within "a long tradition of German conservative ideology," 64.

Phase 1: Church and World in Mild Tension

tory. There is no confusion of roles. That is, the church does not have as its explicit role the making of history. There is, however, also no evidence that the church or church members, imbedded in the same sin-ridden history as the state, should not take part in the state's task of making history. In fact, the church should take part in making history. A vision of the state colored or influenced by Hegelian categories, the state as a God-willed collective person doing God's will in history, does not generally empower voices of protest against the state's history-making task.

In fact, this idea of action in history is the main place where Bonhoeffer's thinking on church-world and the church-state relationship coincide and find mutual support. Kelly, referring specifically to the Hegelian influence in Bonhoeffer's early works, offers an insight useful for articulating how church-world and church-state are related. He writes, "Even as Bonhoeffer was himself somewhat stymied at first in his theoretical working out of a Christian rationale for and tactic of resistance in the church crisis by the Lutheran doctrine of the two realms, his 'holistic Hegelianism' helped him eventually to overcome that traditional dichotimization of reality into separate spheres of sacred and profane which appeared to justify noninvolvement by church in politics."[86] Kelly suggests two different things here. First, he implies that the Lutheran Two Kingdoms doctrine justifies political noninvolvement on the part of the church. He also implies that an embrace of Hegel's thinking might result in church activity that is critical of the state. In terms of his first point, I would argue that, while the way the Two Kingdoms doctrine was being interpreted in Bonhoeffer's time manifested in a certain political quietism, it did not encourage outright political noninvolvement on the part of the church. There are resources in some iterations of the doctrine for resistance activity on the part of the church. Further, most all interpretations of the Two Kingdoms doctrine carried with them the expectation that church members (and all other citizens) would fulfill their political function by implicitly following state directives or meeting their obligations to the state. Luther's thinking, and the prevailing interpretation of it in Bonhoeffer's context, spells noninvolvement by the church in politics only if involvement is taken to mean actions that are critical of the state or actions that actually determine state policy. Luther's thinking certainly did not encourage total withdrawal from the political sphere. Kelly's second suggestion, that Bonhoeffer's acceptance

86. Kelly, *Liberating Faith*, 92.

of "holistic Hegelianism" was necessary for counter-state political action, only tells one side of the story. I would argue strenuously, and the prevailing right-wing or nationalistic war theology of the majority of Germany's leading theologians who were highly indebted to Hegel's thinking would bear this out, that "holistic Hegelianism" provided as much if not more impetus for endorsing the state on the part of the church as it did for resisting the state.

Even with this disagreement, the general thrust of Kelly's statement (that Hegel's holistic or unified notion of reality, in whatever way in was appropriated by Bonhoeffer in *Sanctorum Communio*, places the church and the world squarely in the same sphere or arena, the historical working out of God's will) is clear and valid. Bonhoeffer does avoid the two-sphered thinking that leads to the withdrawal of the church into an otherworldly escapism that could ultimately justify total removal from the political sphere. Rather, the church, like the state, exists solely in history and sits squarely in the midst of the world. It therefore participates in and is responsible for what happens in history. The church and state are two different collective persons or communities "from God to God" with different roles in the very same world or reality. Being part of the church does not thus force one into some other world or other reality. As such, there are no barriers to partaking in any part of the world, including the state.

Bonhoeffer's understanding of the church in history, as noted above, is also at the root of several positions on the empirical church (church-sect, invisible-visible, and voluntary-involuntary distinctions) that lend themselves to an anti-sectarian vision, a vision logically consistent with forms of pro-state or anti-state political involvement.[87] In fact, it seems that Bonhoeffer's thought, influenced by Hegel and Seeberg and also haunted by "orders of creation" sensibilities, might err in the direction of glorifying the state, the *Volk*, people, or the nation to the

---

87. See van Soosten, "Editor's Afterword to The German Edition," 290–306. Von Soosten writes, "Bonhoeffer's rejection of Max Weber's typology of 'institution' and 'sect,' and his insistence in Sanctorum Communio that the church be considered a distinctive sociological type, has direct consequences for the way the church acts. This certainly becomes apparent at this point, if not before. A church which is governed structurally by the principle of vicarious representative action embodies an ethic of neighborliness [*Brüderlichkeitsethik*] that transcends the dualism of an in-group and out-group morality, an ethic of conscience [*Gesinnungsethik*], and an ethic of responsibility [*Verantwortungsethik*]," 304.

Phase 1: Church and World in Mild Tension 103

extent that these God-willed communities override the power and place of the church. As such, the proper church-state tensions or limits might completely collapse, allowing an unchecked allegiance to state. As noted in my second chapter, scholars have seen German academic support of monarchical forms of government generally, and of Hitler in particular, as an effect of the theological appropriation of Hegel. Other categories treated above also lend themselves to some form of political involvement. For instance, the church as an "ethical collective person," where persons are responsible for the welfare of others in their communities, implies political responsibility toward others in the community. Defending fellow members of the nation or the *Volk* in war would be a duty or ethical responsibility.

It is not surprising, then, that Bonhoeffer does not espouse any of the many possible forms of pacifism in his dissertation. Bonhoeffer is never considered a war theologian. Yet, his thinking on war in this dissertation is very close to Seeberg's and Hegel's.[88] In the only mention of war and peace issues in the text he writes,

> *Where people are called, God's will for their purpose in history is at work*, just as where individuals are called, they experience their history. There is a will of God with a people just as with individuals. Where a people, submitting in conscience to God's will, goes to war in order to fulfill its historical purpose and mission in the world—though entering fully into the ambiguity of human sinful action—it knows it has been called upon by God, that history has to be made; here war is no longer murder. However, not only is God concerned with nations, but has a purpose for every community no matter how small, every friendship, every marriage, every family. And in this sense God also has a purpose for the *church*. There is not only the culpability of individual Germans and individual Christians, but also the culpability of Germany and of the church.[89]

88. *SC-E*, 296. Von Soosten, for example, explains, "The most obvious themes which Bonhoeffer appropriates from Seeberg are a voluntaristic concept of God and Seeberg's insistence that the study have revelation as its starting point, thus making possible 'positive theological knowledge.' Bonhoeffer also agrees with the consequences of Seeberg's voluntarism, as is evident by the fact that in the published version he retained Seeberg's illustrations of the 'ethical collective person.' Bonhoeffer clearly did not yet consider his own statements on people [*Volk*], history and war to be problematic. In Seeberg's view, Bonhoeffer's study quite clearly could be regarded as a contribution to 'modern, positive theology.'"

89. *SC-E*, 119.

The passage reveals consistency with several of the themes treated above. The nation or state is a "people" or a God-willed community ("from God to God") that has as its task, like other communities, fulfilling its God-ordained role in history. Like the church community, the nation or "people" is completely ensconced in earthly history and it is there, with all of its attendant ambiguities and sinfulness, that the nation must fulfill its role. There is no place or sphere a people could or should retreat into or withdraw into. Bonhoeffer implies that nations are fulfilling both God's and their own purpose or mission in the world in human history by going to war.

Ultimately, the church-world and church-state relations developed above are, for the most part, consistent with Bonhoeffer's brief treatment of war. The church is a community like other communities set squarely in the midst of the world. His definition of church does not meet the qualifications of a church-against-world exclusivist sect. There is to be no withdrawal from the world associated with some forms of pacifism. His support of the notion of a *Volkskirche*, traditionally understood to mean an involuntary or state church, suggests an immersion of church members into operations of the state or larger culture.[90] Bonhoeffer does designate the church community as different from culture or world by virtue of the Word informing it, and even in a struggle with outside culture for its ultimate justification or sanctification. Yet, he clearly understands the church as a sin-ridden institution in the midst of a similarly sin-ridden larger culture. This sinful nature of both church and outside world is simply the plain consequence of their existence in history. Bonhoeffer cannot thus encourage any type of withdrawal from state activity on the grounds that it might expose Christians or the church to some type of worldly impurity or sinfulness. Bonhoeffer, in fact, specifically argues that the call to war is a call to enter into the ambiguity of human sinful history.

BARCELONA (FEBRUARY, 1928—FEBRUARY, 1929)

Bonhoeffer was assigned to a post as an assistant pastor of a German-speaking church in Barcelona, Spain, upon the successful public defense

---

90. *SC-E*, 18. Green, in his editor's introduction to the volume, warns, though, that Bonhoeffer's positive assessment of a *Volkskirche* does not imply any excessive racism or nationalism. He writes, "In *Sanctorum Communio* Bonhoeffer certainly does not use the word *Volkskirche* with the racial and nationalistic sense of the *völkisch* movement."

Phase 1: Church and World in Mild Tension

of his theses (he graduated *summa cum laude*) and reception of his dissertation at the end of 1927.[91] This assistant pastorate fulfilled the one-year practical requirement for a career in ministry, academia, or both.

Germany's Weimar Republic was still enjoying relative economic and political calm. Bonhoeffer's work with the parishioners in Barcelona, German "businesspeople with a petit bourgeois outlook," shielded him from political events at home.[92] However, Bonhoeffer was cognizant of the differences in the political situations between Germany and Spain. He also was aware of the differences between the Germans in their homeland and the Germans in the congregation in Spain.[93] Moreover, his range of activities and duties indicate that he was capable of fully engaging in all aspects of the lives of his parishioners as a minister and in the larger Spanish culture. Bonhoeffer's involvement in the parish ranged from playing piano for the local choir and activity in gymnastic societies to committee meetings and other meetings in the German colony.[94] He became very active in the youth ministry, teaching the children and even organizing an elaborate Nativity play with them. Bonhoeffer was very popular with the children, meeting with them frequently, mediating difficulties between them and their teachers, and settling other school problems.[95] In his work with his adults in this expatriate German community, he encountered the contrast of well-to-do businesspersons and poverty.[96]

---

91. *SC-E*, 96.

92. *DB*, 97. See also, Robertson, *The Shame and the Sacrifice*, 46–47. Robertson writes of the Barcelona episode, "This brought him into contact with a world he had never known. Spain was strange to him, although he soon found it fascinating; but the real change was the nature of the congregation—a type of German he did not know. They were businessmen, most of whom were out of touch with the turbulent events of Germany. They regarded change as unfortunate and were still living in the world of yesterday."

93. *DB*, 100. Bethge writes, "Bonhoeffer was shocked by the extreme social contrasts that he saw and was surprised that the signs of revolt were not greater."

94. *DB*, 97.

95. Ibid., 110.

96 Ibid., 106–7. See also, *TF*, 184. Kelly and Nelson, in their introductory remarks before presenting some Barcelona sermons, write, "The pastorate in Barcelona was . . . Bonhoeffer's first encounter with poverty. Many of them were experiencing the effects of the depression then affecting Europe."

Sermons

Bonhoeffer, in his deep involvement with others, sharing intimately in both their joys and pains, surely acted in a manner consistent with his understanding of the church as an ethical collective person placed squarely in a concrete, sinful, and single earth-bound history. His nineteen carefully prepared and delivered sermons for the congregation reflect his intense involvement with the German community in Barcelona.[97] Bethge notes that the sermons do not contain any political references.[98] Feil, moreover, while indicating that Bonhoeffer was concerned in a heightened way with the world, also indicates that he did not establish a "unified conception of the world in these theologically and linguistically still immature sermons."[99] In addition, these sermons do not have as their primary concern the church-world relationship or church-state relations. However, they do address at various points Bonhoeffer's developing understanding of the world in addition to "reveal[ing] the full scope of his theological work and perspective."[100] As such, a brief look at portions of these sermons can indicate the nature of his thinking on the world at this time in his life.

Bonhoeffer's December 2, 1928 sermon for the First Sunday in Advent stresses the simultaneity of God's judgment and God's mercy. This theme suggests the same dynamic from his dissertation between a community entrusted with an authoritative "word" and a world that stands in need of judgment and redemption. Bonhoeffer writes,

> We have grown so accustomed to the idea of divine love and of the coming at Christmas that we no longer sense the awe that God's coming should awaken in us. We have become dulled to the message; we only register what is welcome in it, what is pleasant, forgetting the powerful seriousness of the fact that the God of the world is approaching us on our small earth and now makes claims on us. God's coming is truly and not merely a message of joy, but first of all horrifying news for every person with a conscience. And not until we have perceived the terror of this matter can we then also appreciate the incomparable act of beneficence. God is coming, into the midst of evil, into death, judging evil in

---

97. *DB*, 110–11. Bethge describes the considerable amount of time and care in preparing the sermons.

98. *DB*, 114.

99. Feil, *The Theology of Dietrich Bonhoeffer*, 108–9.

100. *DB*, 112.

Phase 1: Church and World in Mild Tension

us and in the world. And by judging it, God loves us, purifies us, sanctifies us, comes to us with grace and love.[101]

What is of note in this passage is not the idea that God's message judges and heals simultaneously. Rather, this passage is noteworthy for its emphasis on the concreteness or the earth-bound nature of God's involvement with the world. He refers to God as "the God of the world," and writes, "God comes into the very midst of evil and of death." Later in the sermon Bonhoeffer writes, "God is with us now and intends always to be with us always, regardless of where we are, in our sin, in our suffering and death. We are no longer alone; God is with us, we are no longer homeless, a bit of our eternal home has entered into us."[102] Bonhoeffer thus refuses to let any recognition or acknowledgment of sin or God's judgment affect God's involvement with the world.

Bonhoeffer's theme of "this-worldly" or "ethical" transcendence developed in his dissertation is also prominent in this sermon. Bonhoeffer writes,

> But here we are confronted with the terrifying reality; Jesus is at the door, knocking, in reality, asking you for help in the figure of the beggar, in the figure of the degenerate soul in shabby clothes, encountering you in every person you meet. Christ walks on the earth as long as there are people, as your neighbor, as the person through whom God summons you, addresses you, makes claims on you. That is the most serious and most blessed part of the Advent message. Christ is at the door; he lives in the form of the those around us. Will you close the door or open it for him?[103]

As he states clearly in his dissertation, Christ confronts in and as the concrete "other" or "thou" and makes an ethical demand. Bonhoeffer echoes this same theme in another Barcelona sermon on the text of Matthew 28:20 delivered on April 15, 1928. Bonhoeffer reiterates, "Jesus Christ, God himself, speaks to us from every human being; the other person, this enigmatic, impenetrable You, is God's claim on us; indeed, it is the holy God in person whom we encounter."[104]

---

101 Bonhoeffer, *Barcelona, Berlin, New York: 1928–1931*, 544 (hereafter abbreviated as *DBWE-10*).

102. Ibid., 544–45.

103. Ibid., 545.

104. Ibid., 495.

Bonhoeffer's concern with God's presence or immersion in the earthiness or concreteness of human reality also manifested in his thinking about the relationship between time and eternity. He argues that it is only by serving the world fully and completely in the present moment in the world that the eternal, God, can be encountered. In another Barcelona sermon on the text of Romans 12:11c, delivered on September 23, 1928, he writes, "In all of world history, there is always only one genuinely significant hour—the present. Whoever flees the present is fleeing God's hour; whoever flees time is fleeing God. Serve time!"[105] Bonhoeffer explicitly links the importance of serving time with all aspects of one's historical context when he writes,

> Hence Christians are neither modern nor unmodern; rather they serve their own time, that is, they worry not about human beings but about God. And yet—they serve *their own time*, and that means they step into the midst of it with all its problems and difficulties, with its seriousness and distress, and there they serve. Christians are people of the present in the most profound sense. Be it *political* and *economic* problems, *moral* and *religious* decline, concern for the present generation of young people—everywhere the point is to enter into the problems of the present, to enter with all the love and all the energy at your disposal.[106]

Consistent with his thinking about the human community as collective person and the attendant ethical responsibility for meeting the needs of the other, Bonhoeffer connects encountering God specifically with "serving the times" through serving the other in the present.

Feil notes several places in the Barcelona sermons where the depiction of the world is negative.[107] It is clear though, in the sermons and in Bonhoeffer's dissertation, that the world or outside culture, although sinful, is constantly being "acted upon" by the Word entrusted to the church. The negativity does not mean the Christian should withdraw from the world. Rather, Bonhoeffer stresses the reality of God's presence amidst that very sinfulness, even suggesting in places that one can meet God only there. Moreover, echoing a dissertation theme, he implies that the confrontation with God in and through the concrete

---

105. Ibid., 529.

106. Ibid.

107. Feil, *The Theology of Dietrich Bonhoeffer*, 107–13. Feil argues for both a "positive" and a "negative" understanding of the world in the Barcelona sermons.

Phase 1: Church and World in Mild Tension

other in the present situation demands one be of service to one's neighbor. Bethge even makes an explicit connection between Bonhoeffer's thinking on the relationship between the temporal and the eternal and the Christian's participation in the specifically political situation.[108] Although Bonhoeffer is not speaking explicitly about the church-world relationship, he is clearly speaking to a congregation of Christians about the way they should approach the world. These writings present many of the major ideas or themes from the dissertation in sermon form.

Grundfragen einer christlichen Ethik (January 25, 1929)

Bonhoeffer also delivered three evening lectures in the church during his stay in Barcelona.[109] His third and final lecture, "Basic Questions of a Christian Ethic," delivered on February 8, 1929, right before he left Barcelona, shows Bonhoeffer arguing for an ethic based on the direct command of God addressed to the person in a particular moment or situation. While he does not directly treat the church-world relationship in the lecture, he does apply the themes of the earthly, concrete, or worldly from the sermons and his dissertation to his thinking about ethics. Specifically, Bonhoeffer argues that Christian ethics only makes sense when a person engages solely and wholly in the multifaceted and complex situation in the concrete world. This lecture has particular value here as Bonhoeffer treats war and pacifism explicitly and at some length.

Bonhoeffer introduces the topic of the possibility of a Christian ethic with the organizing principle for the piece, the fact that there are no universal moral norms or moral principles accessible for Christianity. Bonhoeffer writes, "Only in the actual execution of a given action do the concepts of 'good' and 'bad' apply, that is only in the given present moment; hence any attempt to explicate principles is like trying to draw a bird in flight."[110] Bonhoeffer even carries this logic toward an ethical relativity amongst different nations.[111] Two familiar Bonhoefferian themes

---

108. *DB*, 114. Bethge writes of the sermons, "he expressed very concrete solidarity with the political, economic and moral present."

109. Ibid., 115–16. The first two sermons on the Old Testament and the Jesus of history/Christ of faith problem were titled "Distress and Hope in the Contemporary Religious Situation: The Tragedy of the Prophets and Its Lasting Meaning" and "Jesus Christ and the Essence of Christianity," respectively.

110. *DBWE-10*, 360.

111. Ibid. Bonhoeffer writes, "Ethics is a matter of blood and a matter of history. It did not simply descend to earth from heaven. Rather, it is a child of the earth, and for

are already evident. First, ethics is meaningful only in a communal context (the nation as an ethical *Kollektivperson* in this case). Second, there is a clear stress on the relationship between the ethical and the earthly, concrete, and historical. That is, the embeddedness of the subject or community in history, including all of the concrete relationships and all other aspects of the historical situation, provides the indispensable context for the ethical.

Bonhoeffer continues with a connection between a Nietzschean insight and the question of a specifically Christian ethics. He argues that it is impossible for the term Christian to qualify ethics. Bonhoeffer writes, "Christianity is basically immoral, that Christianity and ethics represent two entities that at first are not entirely compatible and in fact are quite disparate."[112] The "Christian message," to echo Nietzsche, "stands beyond good and evil." More specifically, the authentically Christian message cannot be molded to fit human conceptions of right and wrong. It cannot be reduced to strictly human aspirations toward goodness as a possible way to God, either. Rather, the Christian message is defined solely by God's free and gracious coming to humans. In addition, God's gracious move cannot be made dependent on any definition by, or level of goodness or evil in, persons. If this were the case, persons "would challenge the power and honor due exclusively to God." Bonhoeffer therefore advocates a childlike communion with God such as that which existed before the fall where God's "limitless love for human beings" prevailed. Bonhoeffer attributes the notion of "beyond good and evil" as originally belonging to Christianity, not Nietzsche.[113]

Bonhoeffer cannot let this seemingly radical lack of ethical direction in Christianity stand because of the presence of moral directives in the New Testament. What about the "so-called New Testament ethic"? He simply argues that there is really nothing "new" in Jesus's ethical commandments, even those in the Sermon on the Mount.[114] The signifi-

---

that reason its face changes with history as well as with the renewal of blood, with the transition between generations. There is a German ethic as well as a French ethic and an American ethic. None is more or less ethical than the other, for all remain bound to history."

112. Ibid., 362.
113. Ibid., 363.
114. Ibid., 364. Bonhoeffer, while acknowledging Christian movements from the third and fourth centuries and beyond as "presenting the proclamation of a new ethic as the center of Christianity; the new commandment, of course, was the command-

cance of Jesus's preaching in that sermon, rather, is that it has the quality of "something quite different." Bonhoeffer explains,

> The significance of all Jesus's ethical commandments is rather to say to people: You stand before the face of God, God's grace rules over you; but you are at the disposal of someone else in the world. You must act and behave such that in each of your actions you are mindful of also acting before God, mindful that God has a certain will and wants to see that will done. Each particular moment will reveal the nature of that will. You must merely be perfectly clear that your own will must in every instance be accommodated to the divine will: your will must be surrendered if the divine will is to be realized. Hence to the extent that acting before God requires utter renunciation of personal demands and claims from us, Christian ethical acts can be characterized as love... There are no ethical principles enabling Christians, as it were, to make themselves moral. Instead, one has only the decisive moment at hand, that is, every moment that is of potential ethical value. Never, however, can yesterday decisively influence my moral actions today. I must rather always establish anew my immediate relationship with God's will.[115]

Bonhoeffer's vision of what constitutes any possible Christian ethic is complete. Following timeless or eternal principles or speculating about what may or may not constitute good or evil actions does not establish a Christian ethic. Rather, Jesus calls the Christian to direct obedience to God's will in any and every new situation and new concrete historical context. Different responses are called for in different situations. The radical contribution of Jesus is "the dismissal of principles, of fundamental rules—in biblical terms, the law." What Jesus does is establish freedom, freedom from "slavery to principles."[116]

With some strong language, Bonhoeffer clarifies the connection with Nietzsche made earlier in the text. Christians, in freedom from principles, even "create their own standards of good and evil." He continues, "Only Christians themselves provide the justification for their own acts... Christians create new tables, a new decalogues, as Nietzsche

---

ment of love," points out that modern historical scholarship shows this ethic to be not exclusively that of Jesus or of Christianity. For example, Rabbi Hillel and the Roman philosopher Seneca both espoused commandments of love very similar to those of Jesus and early Christianity.

115. Ibid., 365.
116. Ibid., 365–66.

said of the Overman."[117] The moral quality of actions can be determined only in the solitary confrontation between the "I" and God. Therefore, Bonhoeffer states radically, "There are no acts that are bad in and of themselves; even murder can be justified. There is only faithfulness to or deviation from God's will."[118] It is in the context of this freedom from principles that Bonhoeffer begins an explicit discussion of the Sermon on the Mount and, ultimately, a treatment of the question of war.

Consistent with the argumentation thus far, Bonhoeffer asserts that even the commandments in the Sermon on the Mount are not to be taken as laws. Making the directives in the Sermon on the Mount into laws would not only be "impracticable," but it would also be clearly against the idea that Christ brought freedom from the law. It would even be "against the spirit of Christ."[119] In each concrete moment or situation the Christian stands face to face before God and must make a decision without reliance on "fixed moral regulations." Bonhoeffer stresses the importance of this moment of decision, indicating that the Holy Spirit is "only in the present, in ethical decision."[120]

Bonhoeffer uses the notion of decision as the starting point for his discussion of war. He admits that his notion of decision in the moment with no eternally binding ethical principles can lead to distress when there is a situation where "God's will seems to contradict itself."[121] The decision for or against participation in war is a continual problem which shows how "the commandment of love might seem self-contradictory."[122] Bonhoeffer gives three justifications for Christian participation in war. He readily admits that the arguments for the Christian's decision against war, based in various parts of the New Testament and manifest in Christian history in the positions of various sects, seem fairly clear and agreeable. Bonhoeffer gives examples such as, "War is nothing but murder. War is a crime. No Christian can go to war."[123] Directly after describing the seemingly obvious Christian position, though, he states, "yet it suffers at the central issue: it is not concrete and as a result does

117. Ibid., 366.
118. Ibid., 367.
119. Ibid.
120. Ibid., 368.
121. Ibid.
122. Ibid., 370.
123. Ibid.

Phase 1: Church and World in Mild Tension 113

not look into the depths of Christian decision. It invokes the commandment not to kill and believes that commandment to be the decision." Bonhoeffer continues, "Here, however, we are overlooking the dilemma that precisely when my own people [*Volk*] are attacked, the commandment of love does extend at least as far as defending them as it does to the commandment not to kill one's enemy."[124] We can find two of the three justifications for participating in war in this statement.

The first justification is a theme developed throughout the lecture. If one makes the commandment of love so definite as to rule out war in every situation for the Christian, then one turns the directives in the Sermon on the Mount and other places in the Bible into laws. Laws, and the "slavish" following thereof, rob the Christian of his or her gift of freedom, his or her call to make a decision face to face only with God's will at any and every given moment. The second and third justifications recall a theme from the brief portion on war in his dissertation, that of *Volk* (which can be translated as "people" or even "nation") as a "divine order" given by God. The commandment of love is indefinite in the question of war because of the dilemma of love directed either toward the enemy or my fellow *Volk* in my own nation. Bonhoeffer refers to Christ's injunction to "Love your neighbor as yourself" to highlight the dilemma. Who is more worthy of love, my neighbor defined in terms of "the powerful notion of universal brotherhood" (every human person regardless of nationality) or as the people in my own nation?[125]

Bonhoeffer ultimately writes off this speculation on the true definition of neighbor to mere theoretical reflection. In the concrete situation, where a decision must be made, the Christian, while recognizing that what he or she must do is "atrocious," will know that his or her family, nation, and *Volk* are the neighbor. Bonhoeffer writes,

> If I ever find myself in the distressing situation of having to decide whether to expose my biological brother, my biological mother, to the hand of the attacker, or to raise my own hand against the enemy, then the moment itself will doubtless tell me which of these two is my neighbor, including before the eyes of God. God gave me my mother, my people [*Volk*]. For what I have, I thank my people; what I am, I am through my people, and so what I have should also belong to my people; that is in the divine order

124. *DBWE-10*, 370.
125. *DBWE-10*, 371.

> [*Ordnung*] of things, for God created the peoples. If for a single dangerous moment I do not act, then I am doing nothing than surrendering my neighbors . . . The situation seems clear to me. In such cases, I no longer have the choice between good and evil . . . I will defend my brother, my mother, my people and yet I will know that I can only do so by spilling blood; but love for my people will sanctify murder, will sanctify war.[126]

Bonhoeffer does admit that the decision represents a crisis of conscience, that raising a weapon against another is "horrible" and will "soil [the soldier] with the world and its laws."[127] In addition, he contends that the soldier is required to love his or her enemy throughout the killing. Yet, Bonhoeffer is no pacifist here. Echoing another theme from his dissertation, he holds that war is an acceptable (and even a necessary) Christian activity born from responsibility to the community.

Bonhoeffer launches into his third justification for the legitimacy of Christian participation in war, a justification that more closely recalls the brief piece on war from his dissertation, after an animated restatement of his argument against taking even the Sermon on the Mount literally.[128] His thought relies on the idea that a *Volk* is called by God to make history in the world. Echoing Hegelian and Nietszchean themes and those of the war theology of some of his Berlin professors and many other German intellectuals, Bonhoeffer makes the strongest pro-war statements in his entire corpus. He likens a *Volk* to a child who develops through stages toward maturity, and he especially highlights the youthful phase with its tendency toward growth and expansion. Moreover, he places this development beyond the question of good and evil.

> Peoples [*Völker*] are like individuals. At first they are mature and need guidance. Then they grow into the blossom of youth, mature into adults, and die. This situation in neither good nor

126. Ibid., 371–72.

127. Ibid., 372.

128. Ibid. Bonhoeffer writes, "If we examine again the argumentation of the other party, we find the decisive point is that they make the New Testament commandments into laws and in doing so they enslave themselves to those laws, whereas they should be making their decisions in freedom. They judge according to the letter rather than according to the spirit of Christ. They act according to principles rather than from the concrete situation of crisis with which God confronts me. Sparks, however, are not created in empty space; sparks are created when hard stones strike against each other. The sparks of the Holy Spirit flash not in ideas and principles but in the necessary decision of the moment."

Phase 1: Church and World in Mild Tension

bad in and of itself, yet profound questions are concealed here. For growth involves expansion; an increase in strength involves pushing aside other individuals . . . Every people, however, has within itself a call from God to create history, to enter into the struggle that is the life of nations. This call must be heeded amid the growth and development so that it takes place before the face of God. God calls a people to diversity, to struggle, to victory. Strength also comes from God, and power, and victory, for God creates youth in the individual as well as in nations, and God loves youth, for God himself is eternally young and strong and victorious. And fear and weakness will be conquered by courage and strength. Now should a people experiencing God's call in its own life, in its own youth, and in its own strength, should not such a people also be allowed to follow that call even if it disregards the lives of other peoples? God is the Lord of history; and if a people bends in humility to this holy will guiding history, then with God in its youth and strength it can overcome the weak and the disheartened. Then God will be with it.[129]

This long, powerful, and somewhat startling quotation reasserts the theme from his dissertation where he argued that sometimes a people (a *Volk*), "submitting in conscience to God's will, must go to war in order to fulfill its historical purpose and mission in the world." The nation "knows it has been called upon God, that history is to be made; here war is no longer murder."[130]

The most radical portion of Bonhoeffer's argumentation is his justification for aggressive war. In some cases a more powerful nation should assert its strength over a weaker nation simply because it is God's will for peoples in history to do so, regardless of the resulting carnage in the weaker, victim nation. The theme of nations as collective persons ("*Voelker* are like men"), suprapersonal or organic wholes who must grow and compete for supremacy in the world, makes an aggressive war not only a moral possibility but even a necessity. The notion of God calling persons to involvement in history, with the possibility of entering into the sinfulness of the world, not only justifies but even *sanctifies* war. Bonhoeffer's "ethical contextualism,"[131] his understanding of responsibility to one's true *Volk* in the moment of decision, and his notion of

---

129. Ibid., 373.
130. *SC-E*, 119.
131. *RR*, 99. Rasmussen describes Bonhoeffer's ethics as "radically contextual."

the development of nations and their God-ordained right and duty to expand and conquer lesser nations, seems to compromise the effect of his statements about the crime-like or sinful nature of war.

In addition to a justification for individual Christians in the decision vis-à-vis participation in war, Bonhoeffer's position on war here is an endorsement for war in general for any nation. As such, it seems to discount some scholars' notions that his ethics during the Barcelona years, compared to the more communal-centered or "ecclesiastical ethics" of his dissertation and the ethics in his *Habilitationsschrift*, *Act and Being*), are entirely an "individualistic" or "solipsistic" enterprise.[132] There is a strong emphasis on the individual Christian's solitary and continual confrontation with God's will in the moment or situation. However, in the area of war at least, Bonhoeffer's ethic is unmistakably communal. God calls Christians specifically as a *Volk* and their chief motivation for engaging in war is responsibility to their *Volk*. In this way, it seems that the ethical demand upon the individual comes, to use Bonhoeffer's language from his dissertation, as much from the human thou in the form of family or nation as it does from the individual confrontation with the divine Thou.

Finally, after his explicit treatment of war, Bonhoeffer ends this essay with a strongly stated echo of the earthly, concrete, or history-confined nature of God's relationship to the world from his dissertation and sermons. Ethics "is a matter of earth and blood."[133] As God is related to concrete history and situations, so the decision-making Christian "must enter into the complicated reality of the world." Christians remain "bound to the earth" where "the window of eternity opens itself up to us."[134] Lastly, in a particularly poignant passage reaffirming the call to radical involvement in the world, Bonhoeffer writes, "Those who would abandon the earth, who would flee the crisis of the present, will lose all the power still sustaining them by means of eternal, mysterious powers. The earth remains our mother just as God remains our father, and only

---

132. See Day, *Dietrich Bonhoeffer on Christian Community and Common Sense*, 47. Day writes, "Further reflection on the nature of that specific community brought a significant shift in Bonhoeffer's appropriation of Nietzsche. In Barcelona he a proposed a superman's ethic for a brave old world. His rugged Christian individualism was that of a Nietzschean over-man who rejects but still lives in and against authoritarian structures."

133. *DBWE-10*, 376.

134. Ibid., 377.

those who remain true to the mother are placed into our father's arms. Earth and its distress—that is the Christian's Song of Songs."[135]

CHURCH-WORLD RELATIONSHIP AND POLITICAL THINKING

Bonhoeffer's ethics as the confrontation between God and the Christian, and the resulting call to decision in the moment, is intimately bound up with the concrete reality of the world. Christians are not permitted to withdraw from the world into the realm of ideas, speculation, or moral regulations in the moment of decision. God's will is available to the Christian only in the present, Holy Spirit-driven concrete call to decision in any and every situation in the world. The Christian must engage in the complex and multi-faceted situation presenting itself in the reality of the world. As in *Sanctorum Communio*, history is another earthly or worldly category serving as a connecting point between the Christian, God, and the world. Responding to God's call places the Christian squarely in the ambiguous ravages of sin-ridden history and, in a move recalling Hegel, even calls him or her to "make history" in response to God's will. Bonhoeffer is speaking in terms of individual Christians and their relationship to the world rather than explicitly about church bodies. However, the call to make history would seem to apply to a collection of Christians if it applies to any individual Christian, especially if nations are collective persons.

Any form of pacifism, and in particular the refusal to take up arms, could, theoretically, be an appropriate response to God's will in a given concrete historical situation, especially given Bonhoeffer's thinking that the confrontation with God's will cannot yield timeless prescriptions for action consistent along different moments (there might be a moment when pacifism is appropriate). However, there are two related reasons, both dependent on Bonhoeffer's understanding of the world, which force him to reject a refusal to take up arms. First, any pacifistic tenets, and particularly the biblical directives in the Sermon on the Mount, represent a reliance on principles and speculation that ultimately forces the Christian out of the concrete situation in the world. Second, the concrete situation in the world presents one with responsibility to others, a responsibility to one's own family, nation, or *Volk*. Bonhoeffer notes that pacifists might argue that there is this same responsibility to others in the sense of a "universal brotherhood" with all humankind. However,

---

135. Ibid., 378.

the concept of "universal brotherhood" with all human persons is somewhat idealistic or theoretical and takes one away from the more immediate, concrete situation involving one's very own family or nation.

Bethge, Rasmussen, and Day, and each in his own way, seem to want to apologize for Bonhoeffer's thinking on war in this lecture. Bethge calls Bonhoeffer's critique of Tolstoy and the conscientious objectors and his statements about a youthful God supporting stronger nations "dreadful phrases."[136] Bethge also notes that Bonhoeffer "was not yet speaking his own language here,"[137] that he never again makes such statements, and that he was later "uncomfortable at having expressed himself this way."[138] Finally, Bethge stresses Bonhoeffer's statements indicating that war is a "crime" and that it "defiles the conscience."[139] Rasmussen, in addition to echoing Bethge's acknowledgment of Bonhoeffer's negative statements about war, notes the "raging contradictions, inconsistencies, and erroneous political judgements in this lecture."[140] Thomas Day notes the same glaring inconsistency as Rasmussen.[141]

These evaluations, though, may be based on how Bonhoeffer's exceedingly nationalistic position on war in the Barcelona lecture looks from the perspective of future political events in Germany and a knowledge of some predominant themes in his later works. The purpose of this current work is to expose the positive relationship between Bonhoeffer's thinking on the church-world relationship and his political thinking and action at discrete stages or phases in his life. There are some theological problems and even some glaring logical inconsistencies in Bonhoeffer's endorsement of war (for example, he employs a principle from outside of the situation, the principle of allegiance to one's family or nation, to offer

---

136. *DB*, 119.
137. Ibid., 119.
138. Ibid., 120.
139. Ibid., 119.
140. *RR*, 99–100. Rasmussen states in a footnote, "The raging contradictions, inconsistencies and erroneous political judgments in this lecture are not the concern here. Suffice it to say that Bonhoeffer is attaching a rather conventional '*Schoepfungsordnung*' ethic of his time to a Barthian *Roemerbrief* stance of man before God in the naked situation. He does not see how the two cannot coalesce. Principles drawn from a crass '*Volkstheologie*' of the orders of creation are freely used at the same time Bonhoeffer asserts that only an atomistic situational ethics is possible."
141. Day, *Dietrich Bonhoeffer on Christian Community and Common Sense*, 40–42. Day discusses several difficulties with Bonhoeffer's "Barcelona ethic."

Phase 1: Church and World in Mild Tension

moral guidance in a situation).[142] His language seems excessively strong, he was young, somewhat undeveloped as a theologian, and influenced by the political thinking of his mentors. Finally, his Barcelona thought seems a dangerous pre-justification for the future horrors of National Socialism. Nevertheless, his words are his words and he clearly disavows pacifism at this phase in his life. He, in fact, supports aggressive wars.

Although there is no explicit treatment of the church-world relationship in the Barcelona literature, there is a correlation between Bonhoeffer's thinking on the God-world relationship and his political positions. Bonhoeffer stresses that the earth, the world, and history are the loci of God's activity and the only places where God calls humans to action and decision. God calls persons to responsibility to their concrete neighbors, their families, and their nations. The earth or world is not considered entirely good. He does indicate that engaging in the world will necessarily "stain" the Christian and situations sometimes present a choice between two evils. Nevertheless, there are several passages in the sermons and the lecture that especially stress the reality of God's presence within the sinful world. Even murder and war, although clearly negative aspects of earthly existence involving difficult and trying demands on conscience, can be sanctified specifically as responses to God's will in the concrete earthly situation. Thus the Christian, and, by extension, the Christian as church member, is called to engage in the world politically as it is the arena of God's presence and God's call.

ACT AND BEING (1929–1930)

Bonhoeffer returned to Berlin in February 1929 to become an assistant lecturer in systematic theology at the University of Berlin. He threw himself into trying to get his dissertation published and writing his postdoctoral thesis (his *Habilitationsschrift*). Bonhoeffer began to recog-

---

142. See *DBWE-10*, 371. The editor's footnote [32.] reads, "Discussing the situation of Christians in times of war, before a German congregation in a foreign country, Bonhoeffer comes closer than anywhere else to the views of the nationalist Protestantism of his era, and in doing so becomes entangled in a contradiction. Allegedly only the moment itself, the concrete situation, can determine which decision a person should make. Nonetheless Bonhoeffer relates the decision to a criterion which transcends the situation, namely ties to one's own people (*Volk*), as a divine order . . . This development corresponded to the prevalent thinking of Protestant theology and proclamation between the world wars and was susceptible to *volkisch* thinking and thereby National Socialist thinking."

nize the stormy political situation in Germany in a way he did not while in Barcelona.[143] Although the end of the Dawes Plan, the beginning of the Young Plan, and the liberation of the Rhineland all signaled some degree of national and financial sovereignty, right-wing forces painted Stresemann's successes as the result of concessions to the Versailles Treaty. Three conservative political groups (the Stahlhelm, the nationals, and the developing National Socialists) even banded together to battle concession to the Young Plan on legal grounds. Church organizations also supported this rightist coalition and denounced the leftist and centrist parties who opposed them. Stresemann's death in early October 1929, and the Wall Street crash later that month, infused the German situation with still more economic and political uncertainty. Street demonstrations involving antidemocratic forces from the extreme left and right were commonplace.[144] The Social Democratic Party, which had a significant role in the relative political stability existing from 1925, withdrew from the government. Finally, in March of 1930, Heinrich Brüning became chancellor and the government was run by the emergency decree contained in Article 48 of the Weimar constitution.[145] The Weimar government was visibly "wasting away."[146]

Bethge, while indicating that Bonhoeffer "sensed" these "ominous political changes"[147] and was surrounded by family members who were more politically active in support of the Weimar Republic, stresses Bonhoeffer's political "aloofness" and concern with theological matters.[148] Bonhoeffer "gave no thought to becoming politically active at this time" and "had nothing to do with the 'national opposition' or the right-wing populism."[149] He was, though, quickly becoming interested in the think-

143. *DB*, 125.
144. Ibid., 126.
145. *HNG*, 54–55. Spielvogel describes Article 48: "The collapse of the Great Coalition and the continuing economic chaos created a parliamentary crisis that opened the door to the so-called presidential system, built upon the extension of the president's constitutional powers. Article 48 of the Weimar constitution gave the president emergency powers to restore law and order in a crisis, including use of the army if necessary . . . This power of the president to rule in an emergency was now enlarged to cover the crisis created by the depression and the failure of the parliamentary parties to cooperate in dealing with economic difficulties."
146. Ibid., 54–55.
147. *DB*, 125.
148. Ibid., 126.
149. Ibid., 127.

Phase 1: Church and World in Mild Tension

ing of Günther Dehn, a preacher whose September 6, 1928, speech on war was denounced by German nationalists in early 1929. Bonhoeffer attended his church in Moabit and thought highly of his preaching.[150]

Act and Being was written amidst these growing political tensions in the summer and winter semesters of 1929. Seeberg encouraged Bonhoeffer to address an historical or biblical problem in his post-doctoral thesis.[151] Bonhoeffer disagreed and threw himself fully into a systematic treatise on "a theology of consciousness and a theology of the child."[152] The jargon and style in this extremely erudite and complicated work, like in his first dissertation, though, makes it difficult to categorize in terms of author's intent or even summarize its contents in a way universally acceptable to scholars.[153] Nevertheless, we can offer a generally acceptable description. Bonhoeffer boldly tried to show how the two main traditional philosophical-theological approaches to understanding Christian revelation, theologies of being (ontology) and theologies of act (the transcendental approach), actually yield faulty notions of both God's revelation and human knowledge of that revelation. He argued that these approaches are legitimate only when they merge in the concept of the church as the concrete social-communal depository of God's revelation.[154]

Bonhoeffer assumes that both the transcendental and the ontological approaches to theology are connected to given theological anthropologies. He begins with the "Transcendental Attempt" and explores what its epistemology implies for theology. Bonhoeffer takes Kant

---

150. Ibid., 120, 127.

151. Ibid., 132.

152. Bonhoeffer, Act and Being. See Floyd, "Editor's Introduction to the English Edition," in ibid., 1–24, for an account of the philosophical, cultural, theological, and life contexts in which the text was produced. Hereafter the text will be abbreviated as AB.

153. ATS, 68–69. Green, for example, gives an account of several scholarly positions on the work.

154. AB, 31. Bonhoeffer argues, "The concept of revelation, therefore, must yield an epistemology of its own. But inasmuch as an interpretation of revelation in terms of act or in terms of being yields concepts of understanding that are incapable of bearing the whole weight of revelation, the concept of revelation has to be thought about within the concreteness of the conception of the church, that is to say, in terms of a sociological category in which the interpretation of act and of being meet and are drawn together into one. The dialectic of act and being is understood theologically as the dialectic of faith and the congregation of Christ."

as his representative of pure transcendentalism and explains that, for Kant, thinking is always being in relation to "something transcendent, which, however, is not at its disposal."[155] Pure transcendentalism's virtue (and what Bonhoeffer reads as Kant's intention) is that it attempts to retain this boundary between the knowing "I" and outside reality. Post-Kantian idealism, however, ultimately collapses the boundary and "thinking [raises] itself to the position of lord over what is nonobjective by taking the process of attainment, the I, into itself in the act of thinking. Here, the I, now thinking itself, simply becomes the *point of departure* instead of the limit-point of philosophy."[156] In this way, the ego or "I" attains knowledge from itself only and not from any confrontation with the external.[157] The ego or knowing "I," in a sense, creates the outside world. When the explicit question of the possibility of knowledge of God arises, both transcendentalism and idealism are inadequate for establishing a truly Christian foundation for revelation. Kant's transcendentalism, while rightly positing a person "in relation to" something transcendent, still cannot establish the concrete reality of "being" outside the "act" of knowledge. It cannot, thus, posit God as an "object" of knowledge.[158] Idealism, for its part, and all of the nineteenth-century and early twentieth-century theology dependent on it, tends to equate God (or any piece of outside realty) with the self; it, epistemologically, "raise[s] substance to the subject" and, theologically, makes "God . . . a prisoner of the consciousness."[159]

Bonhoeffer frames the problem of the "Ontological Attempt" in terms of both establishing a reality outside of consciousness and under-

---

155. *AB*, 34.

156. Ibid., 39.

157. Ibid., 40. Bonhoeffer's writes, "idealism seems to have resolved the concept of being . . . entirely into the concept of act."

158. Ibid., 44. Bonhoeffer writes, "Transcendentalism distinguishes itself from this position in that it does not make the I into a creator but thinks of the I only as something to which the world must be thought of as related. In this way, to be sure, the decisive boundary of the Creator's integrity is honored in principle, that is, to the extent to which this is at all possible in philosophy. Certainly here, too, God cannot be the object of knowledge. Were that possible, God would be oriented with the phenomena of the world as God is towards the I and, consequently would be thought of essentially for the I. Given the transcendental point of departure, the objectivity of God is an impossibility, since all being is understood as something existing [*Seiende*], as what 'there is' in the a priori synthesis."

159. Ibid., 48.

Phase 1: Church and World in Mild Tension

standing the proper relationship between this reality and consciousness. More specifically, the problem centers around being making itself available to knowledge (coming out of itself) so that thinking can embrace it while simultaneously maintaining its integrity. Pure ontology wants "to demonstrate the primacy of being over against consciousness."[160] Bonhoeffer explores how the problematic is addressed in the ontologies of Husserl, Scheler, Heidegger, and Thomism through Przywara. He concludes that they are all, like the transcendental approaches, inadequate for developing a legitimate Christian theology of revelation or person because they ultimately cannot avoid allowing "being [to] fall(s) under the power of the thinking I."[161]

Bonhoeffer sees in these epistemological/metaphysical speculations the philosophical correlate to Lutheran theological anthropology. For Luther, the human person has a *cor curvum in se* or a "heart turned in upon itself." These philosophies of act and being, because they confine the person to him or herself, do not allow the human person to properly understand him/herself or God.[162] They formulate a concept of person that is not disposed to confrontation by an "other." They can, thus, "concede no room for revelation"[163] Genuine transcendental philosophy and ontology are nevertheless useful to theology because they have provided an in-depth analysis of the problem of act and being. They also provide a vision where the person is "in reference to" the other and where thought is "in suspension" in being, positions which "are basically amenable to a theological interpretation and, therefore, of help in the understanding of the concept of revelation."[164]

In his second part, Bonhoeffer addresses how act and being can be useful in the interpretation of revelation. As evident from his thinking so far on traditional notions of act and being, he contends that revelation is contingent (not necessary) and agrees with Barth that it has to be God's breaking in from the outside, from beyond any human speculations or formulations of self-understanding.[165] However, he strenuously

---

160. Ibid., 59.
161. Ibid., 76.
162. Ibid.
163. Ibid., 77.
164. Ibid., 79.
165. Ibid., 82. Bonhoeffer writes, "Revelation, which places the I into truth, which gives understanding of God and the self, is a contingent event that is to be confirmed

disagrees with Barth's reliance on an overly-actualistic or formalistic conception of God's freedom and availability in revelation. Bonhoeffer sees a correlation between an implication of Barth's notion of revelation and the primary drawback of the transcendental approach in epistemology. If the possibility for knowledge of God is understood only in terms of "pure act," then God can never become an object for human knowledge and thus "recedes into the nonobjective, into what is beyond our disposition."[166] The problem is the same here as in his critique of the strictly philosophical application of the transcendental approach. If God cannot be apprehended as object, then how does the receiver of revelation know he or she is being addressed by the divine? The result is that theological thinking is necessarily relegated to the realm of the "profane."[167]

In his answer to this problem, Bonhoeffer writes something that almost all commentators point to as a classic text directed at Barth. He writes,

> In revelation, it is not so much a question of the freedom of God—eternally remaining within the divine self, aseity—on the other side of revelation, as it is of God's coming out of God's own self in revelation. It is a matter of God's *given* Word, the covenant in which God is bound by God's own action. It is a question of the freedom of God, which finds its strongest evidence precisely in that God freely chose to be bound to historical human beings and to be placed at the disposal of human beings. God is free not from human beings but for them. Christ is the word of God's freedom. God *is* present, that is, not in eternal nonobjectivity but—to put it quite provisionally for now—'haveable,' graspable within the church.[168]

---

or denied only in its positivity—that is to say, received as reality; it cannot be extracted from speculations about human existence as such. Revelation is an event that has its basis in the freedom of God, positively as the self-giving or, negatively, as the self-withholding of God."

166. Ibid., 85.

167. Ibid., 90. Bonhoeffer writes, "If the knowledge of self and of God that God has implanted into human beings is considered purely as act, it is for the purpose of excluding any kind of being. The act stays inaccessible to reflection; it runs its course in each time in 'direct consciousness.' That follows from the formal understanding of God's freedom. Theological thought seems, therefore, to remain essentially profane; it can only, in each event, stand 'under God's blessing' (thus Barth)."

168. Ibid., 90–91.

Phase 1: Church and World in Mild Tension

Bonhoeffer thus substitutes a "material" or "substantial" notion of revelation for a formal one. In doing so, he very strongly re-asserts his concern with the "concreteness" of God's availability to, or presence in, reality so pronounced in his first dissertation and Barcelona work. The concern with the concreteness, "graspability," or radical availability of this revelation specifically "within the church" is a theme in direct continuity with his first dissertation.[169]

Bonhoeffer next treats the question of how "being" might be an interpretive lens for understanding revelation. He acknowledges that the approach from the perspective of being is positive in that it rightly and simultaneously asserts a continuity between revelation and human beings and holds revelation to be "objective" and therefore self-existing outside of consciousness, pure act, or an act of faith.[170] Nevertheless, it is not an adequate approach to Christian revelation because it portrays the God of revelation as something that "exists" and is therefore "creaturely." What is creaturely, however, cannot be truly objective or address human existence from outside or beyond.[171] Pure ontology, though, to the extent that it holds thinking to be preserved in being rather than overcoming being, is a step in the right direction.

After the foregoing critique of how both the strictly philosophical and the theological applications of the transcendental and ontological approaches make only partial contributions to the problem of interpreting or articulating Christian revelation, Bonhoeffer finally treats the church. The church is the answer. Only a "socio-ontological"[172] concept of the church as the locus of God's revelatory reality in the world, like

---

169. *DB*, 133. Bethge writes, "Theologically and sociologically, his first book was an argument for the concreteness of revelation in the form of community. The second book argued for the theological and epistemological struggle—basically for the same concreteness."

170. *AB*, 103.

171. Ibid.,105–6. Bonhoeffer writes, "The reason the three possible interpretations of the being of revelation that we have discussed fail to do justice to the Christian idea of revelation is that they understand the revealed God as something existing, whereas all existing things are transcended by act and being. Human beings take all that exists into their transcendental I, which means that what exists cannot be genuinely ob-jective [gegen-ständlich], nor encounter human existence, nor finally interpret theologically the revelation of Christ that impinges on Adam's manner of existence. In other words, something that exists, something creaturely, is not able to encounter the existence of human beings . . . unless God takes hold of human beings and turns them around."

172. *ATS*, 86. This is Green's term.

the one developed in *Sanctorum Communio*, can overcome the shortcomings of the two approaches. Indeed, Bonhoeffer reasserts the main components of his sociologically-informed ecclesiology developed in *Sanctorum Communio* as answers to the shortcomings of the transcendental and ontological approaches to interpreting revelation. First, the church as a community of persons who collectively hear and proclaim the received message of Christ's death and resurrection establish a "suprapersonal" guarantee of the continued presence of Christ. The continued presence of Christ combats the problem of a lack in continuity in the "being" of God's revelation. Second, the continued presence of Christ "existing as community" in the collection of persons, apart from the faith response of any one individual church member, ensures that transcendence is something not created by the self (it is "transsubjective").[173] Third, Bonhoeffer's "Christ existing as community," wherein Christ confronts and places an ethical demand on the person in and through an authentic other, ensures that the existence of human beings is really and truly affected by revelation.[174] Finally, Bonhoeffer has established that the being of revelation is problematic if conceived of as an existing object because it would no longer be relevant to human existence. If, however, it is conceived of as a nonobjective subject, continuity in being cannot be established. The church as a concrete community of persons or as collective person confronting as other ultimately satisfies the demands of true objectivity while retaining its relevance insofar as it is an "existential" encounter.

In the final part of the work, Bonhoeffer reasserts a few more important themes from his first dissertation, humanity in Adam and the new humanity in Christ. In the context of this work, humanity in Adam is described in terms of the major drawback of the philosophies and theologies of act and being treated in the first part of the book, the self-enclosed or self-contained human person creating his or her own world. Humanity in Adam means specifically a separation from God and community.[175] The shift to the new humanity in Christ, on the other hand,

173. *AB*, 113–14.
174. Ibid.
175. Ibid., 137. Bonhoeffer writes, "'In 'Adam' means to be in untruth, in culpable perversion of the will, that is of human essence. It means to be turned into one's self, *cor curvum in se*. Human beings have torn themselves loose from community with God and, therefore, also from that with other human beings, and now they stand alone, that is, in untruth. Because human beings are alone, the world is 'their' world, and other

Phase 1: Church and World in Mild Tension 127

includes within it being part of the church community. He ties his idea of the new humanity in Christ from his first dissertation into the framework of act and being in a more specific way with the notions of faith, conscience, and a distinction between *actus directus* and *actus reflexus*.

Faith, as alluded to above, becomes a possibility only in terms of sociality or being within the context of church community. It is a "direct act," one that places a person in direct relationship with Christ. The faculty of conscience, on the other hand, is a human faculty that directs one solely to self, making faith impossible.[176] Bonhoeffer shows how these insights about conscience and faith as an *actus directus* and his social concept of church and person inform the act-being problem specifically in terms of establishing selfhood for the human person as the new humanity in Christ. Faith is an "act" but cannot be thought of entirely as act or personal self-continuity could not be established.[177] Instead, the confrontation with others from "outside" (*ab extra*) of the person in the form of the concrete community of faith (the church) and the Word assures a continuity in the being of revelation that is prior to or independent of any individual act of faith.[178] Being in the church community in faith is thus the only place where human beings can see themselves as a unity of act and being, where "act is 'suspended' in being just as, conversely, being is not without the act."[179] Coming to faith, entering

---

human beings have sunk into the world of things ... God has become a religious object, and human beings themselves have become their own creator and lord, belonging to themselves. It is only to be expected that they should now begin and end in themselves in their knowing, for they are only and utterly 'with themselves' in the falsehood of naked self-glory."

176. Ibid., 155. Bonhoeffer writes, "The historical human being has conscience, not only in Adam as protection against God's assault, but also in the church of Christ. Conscience is only where sin is. But since the human being in Christ is no longer governed by sin, conscience is something defined in the past in Adam. Human beings have conscience by and in themselves; it does not belong to the things 'to come.' It is the reflection on one's self beyond which human beings in Adam cannot advance. Conscience is primarily not God's but the human being's own voice. If being-in-Christ means being oriented towards Christ, reflection on self is obviously not part of that being."

177. Ibid., 118. Bonhoeffer writes, "The continuity of revelation, like the continuity of existence, is found only in faith, but truly found there, so that faith is suspended only 'in faith,' only in 'the being of the community of faith.' If faith were understood here purely as an act, the continuity of being would be broken up in the discontinuity of acts."

178. Ibid.

179. Ibid., 120.

community, moving from humanity in Adam to the new humanity in Christ, and establishing personhood are simultaneous.

Church-World Relationship and Political Thinking

Act and Being, like *Sanctorum Communio*, does not have as its explicit focus the church-world relationship, church-state relations, or any other political considerations. It is, rather, a treatment of how the philosophies of "act" and "being" can and cannot be useful in establishing truly Christian notions of personhood, revelation, and church. However, this work, like other writings in this phase of his life without these explicit foci, has implications for church-world notions and political thinking. Other scholars who hold this position, though, tend to stress that the seeds for *future* forms of political involvement can be found in *Act and Being*.[180] While those insights are valuable, my aim is to show how his theology is consistent with his forms of political thinking and involvement at the time he wrote the book.

There are only a few themes in *Act and Being* relevant to a consideration of Bonhoeffer's thinking on the church-world relationship. They are consistent with the thinking in *Sanctorum Communio* and the Barcelona literature from this phase. The first theme is the concern with the concreteness of God's availability in the world through revelation. The theological context within which Bonhoeffer asserts this concreteness is different than in the other works from this phase. This new context, though, arguably allows for a more radical assertion of the

---

180. *TF*, 9. Kelly and Nelson, for example, argue that Bonhoeffer's critique of the church in *Act and Being* enabled him to challenge Nazism later. They write, "Only in community, or in God's relationship with us from 'without,' can one encounter God in Christ. The Christian church, Bonhoeffer charged, in its power-hungry appropriation of revelation through doctrine, psychic experience, or institution, had tried to reduce God to itself. His revulsion at what he considered a flirtation with idolatry would later stir Bonhoeffer to criticize and then openly oppose Nazism's claims to be 'positive Christianity in action.'" See also, *ATS*, 95. Green writes, "Bonhoeffer's leadership in the ecumenical movement should be seen as an expression of his theological understanding of the church as the new humanity. His commitment was no mere enthusiasm for a current ecclesiastical fashion, nor simply a pragmatic concern for national and international problems; nor was it just an ad hoc, though admittedly serious, desire that the ecumenical movement recognize the Confessing Church as the legitimate evangelical church in Germany. In his theology, rather, Christ is the Kollectivperson of the church as the new humanity. Therefore, the Oekumene must simultaneously clarify its theological status as *church* and precisely as church speak and act for the peace, justice, truth and freedom of humanity."

Phase 1: Church and World in Mild Tension

concreteness than in the previous works. In *Act and Being*, Bonhoeffer argues (against Barth) that the radical "availability," "haveability," and even "graspability" of God in revelation is absolutely necessary in order even to establish it as revelation and, ultimately, to establish human personhood.

The radicalized concreteness, though, is more a matter of a change in emphasis than in quality. This judgment becomes clear in the consistency in conceptions of the church between the two dissertations. The classic and well-known definition of church as "Christ existing as community" appears in both dissertations. In both cases, the confrontation with the "other" in the concrete church community as limit and ethical demand is what establishes legitimate notions of transcendence, personhood, and revelation. Christ confronts persons as the demand of the other; so transcendence is ethical or this-worldly. Moreover, a person can only establish him or herself by breaking out of isolation in a concrete confrontation with the other. This idea is the same whether the event is explained in terms of sociological theory (*Sanctorum Communio*) or a history of the philosophies of being and act and a theological analysis of their shortcomings (*Act and Being*). Thus, the very same emphasis on God's tangible presence in the midst of the world in the form of church-community appears in *Act and Being*.

Bonhoeffer's relational concept of the church, also reasserted from *Sanctorum Communio*, is another theme indirectly related to church-world thinking. Some commentators have, for example, stressed the connection between Bonhoeffer's relational concept of the church, with its emphasis on the ethical demand presented by the other, and the call to help, suffer with, serve, or be in solidarity with the poor and outcast in the world.[181] These are themes that are characteristic of Bonhoeffer's later Christology and period of political involvement where Jesus is the "man for others."[182]

---

181. *TF*, 65. Kelly and Burton, for example, describe the socially responsible implications of Bonhoeffer's thinking in *Act and Being*. They write, "For Bonhoeffer, God's revelation of the divine self is necessarily a social event. The quest for truth is pursued within the context of what sociality demands of Christians—that Christians engage in self-sacrificing service of others."

182. *DB*, 135. Bethge notes, "From our biographical point of view, the importance of *Act and Being* was that—taken in conjunction with *Sanctorum Communio*—it contained many of the ideas that were to be applied to the 'nonreligious interpretation' in the letters from prison fifteen years later. This fact deprives them of their supposedly fortuitous character; it means that they were better prepared than is generally assumed.

There are conflicting scholarly opinions in terms of the more explicit question of the church-world relationship in *Act and Being*. One side tends to view the conception of the church in *Act and Being* as somewhat exclusivist, where Christ's availability to the world and importance in terms of establishing a loving, serving community is relegated strictly to the institutional church with definite borders. This assessment is generally related to Christology. Bethge, for example (in his appraisal of *Act and Being*), in the sentence immediately after establishing that Bonhoeffer's idea "Jesus, the man for others" is an important point of continuity between the early and later phases of his life, adds, "Here, of course this ['Jesus, the man for others'] applied only to the church. Eventually, Bonhoeffer conceived of this as permanently and essentially freed from all bounds, applied to the world as God's own proper dominion."[183] The boundary between church and world is drawn

---

The ideas of 1930 that seemed to vanish in the subsequent years suddenly reappeared in 1944. *Act and Being* gave the social and ethical transcendence of one's neighbor (which had already been maintained in *Sanctorum Communio* as against philosophical-metaphysical transcendence) the magnificent formulation, 'Jesus, the man for others.'" See also *ATS*, 100. Green, affirming Bethge's insight and referring to Bonhoeffer's classic 'availability' and 'graspability' passage, writes, "This passage, which Bethge rightly sees as the original matrix for the Christological formulation of Jesus as the 'man for others' in the *Letters*, is fundamental to Bonhoeffer's theological development. It demonstrates the *sociality of God as the prototype and possibility of human sociality*: if Christ is God-being-free-for-humanity, then human beings in Christ can find their true humanity in being free for one another and for their communities." Later in the text, Green writes, "Positively, it presents Christ as the free and liberating God who restores a person to true being in community with others; in Christ God is free for humanity, setting people free to participate in the community of the new humanity of which he is the prototype and personification."

183. *DB*, 135. See also Phillips, *Christ for Us*, 70–71. Phillips more explicitly addresses the church-world problematic when he writes, "His essential agreement with the theology of revelation led him, at the same time, to insist that revelation is concrete and apprehensible in the community of revelation, the church. The dangers of his position are reasonably clear: his view of revelation *as* the church leaves open the question of the relationship of Christ and the church to the world *outside* the church. We would like also to see a Christological expression of Christ 'outside' of the church, as her Redeemer and Judge and Perfecter, perhaps in the form of a doctrine of Scripture—which might distinguish his position from the self-contained ecclesiology and revelation of Rome. For a few years Bonhoeffer attempted to work out the difficulties in his position and to broaden the basis of his theology in order to make it more flexible. But history intervened and turned these thoughts inward once more, into an even more radical and exclusive and forceful presentation of his Christo-ecclesiology." Later in the text, Phillips argues that the writings from 1932 and 1933 represent Bonhoeffer's attempt to make the church more relevant to what was outside of it. His involvement with the

Phase 1: Church and World in Mild Tension

such that Christ is not available to the outside world. The other position suggests the opposite. It suggests that "Christ existing as community" pushes beyond itself or spills over into the outside world to affect it in some fashion. Day, for instance, directly argues against Bethge's somewhat exclusivist claim.[184]

Bethge and Day's observations do not cite any particular texts from *Act and Being* for support. However, Bonhoeffer does touch on a theme directly relevant for a consideration of the church-world relationship, the "new humanity in Christ." As in *Sanctorum Communio*, Bonhoeffer argues that the church as "Christ existing as community" consists of those who are the "new humanity in Christ." As such, the notion of church would seem to apply to humanity outside the institutionalized boundaries of any specific church community. Bonhoeffer writes, "Let it be understood that it is precisely as historical that the I is a member of the new humanity. This humanity presents itself here and there in empirical individualized communities, but precisely in the mode of being that belongs to the being of revelation."[185] Bonhoeffer thereby leaves it somewhat unclear as to what types of "empirical individualized communities" serve as places where the new humanity can manifest itself. Green, in addition to arguing that Bonhoeffer's thinking is counter to "sectarian congregationalism," affirms that for Bonhoeffer the universal church exists in "other forms" outside of ecclesial ones.[186] Bonhoeffer

---

church struggle, though, forced him back into his "intractable ecclesiological theory" or a "strict ecclesiological scheme" from which he eventually broke in 1939 (ibid., 74–75).

184. Day, *Dietrich Bonhoeffer on Christian Community and Common Sense*, 44–45. Day writes, "Bonhoeffer's emphasis on the concrete locus of Christian community/ church has led Bethge to simply to say that the realm of Jesus 'is still the closed off church, while later it will be the world.' To the contrary, Bonhoeffer insisted that this real human community is *not* closed off, that its essence is to be open, determined by revelation coming from without, by the future which breaks in upon the ideas and structures of the past. The community based on Christ cannot be closed to the world. Like all truly personal being, its existence is strung between the personal address which calls it into being and the wider human community which it tends to become. Christian community is not shaped by reflection, by self-consciousness, but by response to a Word from beyond itself. The act of faith, rather than reflection upon it, is what makes community. Crucial is how we respond, what we do, not how we articulate it."

185. *AB*, 121.

186. *ATS*, 95. Green's full quotation reads, "In passing we must observe that Bonhoeffer's repetition of his basic proposition that the church is the *new humanity* enables his references to the congregation to be understood in proper perspective. By no stretch of the imagination is he promoting a sort of sectarian congregationalism. The universal church of Christ exists, to be sure, in historical, empirical, spatially-localized communi-

suggests that the new humanity (the being of revelation or church-community) is something of a universal community, potentially present anywhere individuals are confronted by others and realize themselves through being-in-community.

FORMS OF POLITICAL INVOLVEMENT

The attempt to relate Bonhoeffer's thinking and political action during the dissertation years and later in the first phase yields less perfectly consistent results. That is, while Bonhoeffer's church-world thinking and his political thinking are consistent with each other, there is one glaring inconsistency in any attempt to relate his political thinking with his political behavior. If Bonhoeffer's political action were entirely consistent with his Hegelian-sounding and Seebergian themes on war, we would presumably expect him to be involved in a right-wing and possibly militant anti-Weimar faction or at least fall in unquestionably with the war theologians. He clearly was not part of any right wing or radical groups. Nevertheless, he was perfectly willing to undergo illegal military training to potentially engage in armed conflict to defend and stabilize the established order of the Weimar Republic amidst left and right wing uprisings in 1923. That is, his actions indicated a willingness to engage in battle on behalf of the Weimar Republic out of the nationalism implied by his theology. Bonhoeffer was willing to engage in the political sphere for what he thought was an acceptable German state and form of government.

One way to evaluate the consistency between his actual political involvement and his church-world theology is by re-visiting what was happening politically and personally for Bonhoeffer. Hitler had not yet come to power and the Weimar Republic, while riddled with radical left and right-wing factions and some instability, was, as noted, in the midst of a period of uncharacteristic peace. Bethge notes in a few places that Bonhoeffer was more concerned with academic matters than political matters. Yet, this stated political neutrality is not an entirely accurate as-

---

ties. But since Christ is the Kollectivperson of the new humanity, these congregations are therefore spatially localized forms of this new humanity in Christ." In addition, Green, in a footnote concerning the following sentence ending with the clause "empirical, spatially-localized communities," writes, "It also exists in other forms as well." Green thus suggests that "the universal church of Christ" manifests in forms that are not related to the institutional church.

sessment of Bonhoeffer's behavior in the political sphere. Again, he was a bit earlier willing to prepare for battle in a quasi-military organization. Beyond that, Bonhoeffer displayed an implicit support of the existing state. He was not actively involved in any pro-Weimar, anti-radical-right or anti-radical-left political organizations and he was not part of any rightist or leftist factions rebelling against the Weimar Republic. With his lack of engagement in radical politics, he acted like many other well-to-do German Lutherans adhering to the notion of a *Volkskirche* who implicitly accepted the existing Weimar state as a legitimate form of God's governing will in the world.

Another way of linking his church-world thinking and political behavior is by examining two other related themes, the Two Kingdoms doctrine and the possibility of withdrawal from the world or the political sphere. His form of political engagement was in the order of the traditionally conservative or status quo-enforcing interpretation of Luther's Two Kingdoms doctrine.[187] Again, while his political activity was not completely consistent with his conservative Seebergian or Hegelian war themes, his thinking on the church-state relationship and war was consistent with an understanding of the church and/or church members engaging in the world in the traditional or expected ways. The church is an institution with a peculiar role (dispensing Word and sacrament and building community) whose presence and active carrying out of that role, while perhaps moving beyond itself and affecting structures outside of it, does not impede the proper functioning of other institutions or communities. His church-world thinking does not suggest that a Christian should withdraw from obligations in other realms of their concrete human experience. He suggests that the ethical demand presented in confrontation with an other, the person-constituting confrontation available only in community necessary for entering the "new humanity in Christ," can happen outside the bounds of the empirical church community. Bonhoeffer implies responsibility to others in the world outside the church.

Bonhoeffer did, indeed, engage in the world in the form of service to the regional church in Grunewald while writing his dissertation. He

---

187. Koch, as noted in chapter 1, would argue that this is the case for Bonhoeffer's whole career, not just his student days. See also, Zerner, "Dietrich Bonhoeffer's Views on the State and History," 131, 135. Zerner notes the Lutheran influence in his early thought.

was actively engaged in the world in the form of ministerial work and, in particular, challenging his bourgeois, yet suffering, congregation in Barcelona to respond more actively to God's call in the concrete and earthly situation.[188] So while he was aware of political happenings in Germany at this time and not especially active in the political sphere, this involvement should not be read as a withdrawal from the world. It is, rather, the implicit support of the political "status quo" typical of the more conservative German Lutheran adherence to the Two Kingdoms doctrine, where the church does not explicitly criticize the actions of the existing regime. The "status quo" that Bonhoeffer was implicitly supporting may have been the more liberal Weimar Republic rather than the more conservative political parties vying for power. One cannot, though, read this support of a more liberal regime as a radical protest voice against an established or conservative position. The Weimar Republic, after all, had been the government in power for almost a decade by the time of these phase one writings. Bonhoeffer implicitly supported the government he thought was the best for his beloved Germany at the time.

Finally, Bonhoeffer's support of war is also consistent with the conservative (implicitly supporting the status quo) adherence to the traditional Lutheran Two Kingdoms doctrine, a position to be expected from a Tübingen and Berlin-educated young German Lutheran reared in an aristocratic home preaching to a bourgeois congregation.[189] Conservative interpretations of the Two Kingdoms doctrine, while not encouraging political activity contrary to one's state, certainly do not encourage Christians to withdraw from engaging in the political sphere or world, especially when that involvement includes implicit or explicit support of one's state in the form of service in war.[190] Even more mod-

---

188. *DB*, 111. Bethge notes of the Barcelona sermons, "He wanted to say something important, and he believed he had something important to say. People were to be confronted and shaken out of their complacency and won over." See also, Robertson, *The Shame and the Sacrifice*, 49. Robertson affirms, "He tried to stir these stable burghers into a commitment to Jesus Christ."

189. *DB*, 119. Bethge writes of the lecture, "This brought him to the subject of war. What he had to say about this—and the Sermon on the Mount—was quite conventionally Lutheran, although spruced up with the titanic ethics of the immediate present."

190. Ibid. Bethge notes, "Here the later pacifist still proclaimed and defended the relative right of the stronger in the economic competition of the nations and their struggle for life. Better this than a phony rejection of the world!"

Phase 1: Church and World in Mild Tension

erate Germans, like democrats and Stresemann's Volkspartei (the party supported by most of Bonhoeffer's family), espoused the "war slogans" like those in Bonhoeffer's lecture.[191] So Bonhoeffer, while not actively supporting right-wing extremism at this point, remained typically German. He was doing what the typical Lutheran German academic and churchman would do, serving the church and quietly serving the state.

LOOKING AHEAD

At this stage in his career Bonhoeffer did not clearly articulate whether the principle of responsibility to the concrete other extended beyond the bounds of the visible church community. Yet, in *Sanctorum Communio* he did argue that the church is a concrete organic community, placed squarely in the midst of history like other entities that ultimately extends beyond itself to the outside world. *Act and Being* is somewhat less clear on the church's relationship to the world. However, both works rely on the concept of the "new humanity in Christ" as an answer to the "old humanity in Adam." Bonhoeffer's idea of the church as a new type of communal human relationality (in *Sanctorum Communio* humanity in Adam is characterized by lack of true community) or a new form of being in revelation (in *Act and Being* humanity in Adam is characterized by "epistemological" self-enclosedness) implies a form of universalism where all of humanity is potentially church. Furthermore, both his explicit rejection of the concept of sect and his thinking that the church as an historical institution is made up of sinners, clearly militates against an anti-world sectarian concept. Rather, the church is a unique community in the midst of the world among other communities, which neither blindly echoes worldliness nor encourages withdrawal from the world.

Although not withdrawn from the world, Bonhoeffer was not yet politically engaged in a noteworthy way during this mostly academic phase in his life. It should be noted, too, that he, besides the year he spent in Barcelona, was not at this time in his life consistently engaged in the life and workings of his church. While having implications for personal faith development, the ecclesiology in both of his dissertations is somewhat (if not excessively) abstract and theoretical rather than a

---

191. *DB*, 119. Bethge writes, "Such slogans had long since been articles of faith among German nationals in the Evangelical church, but before they were interpreted anti-Semitically and chauvinistically and became the hallmark of right-wing extremism, they were used by democrats and members of Stresemann's Volkspartei."

reflection on his own life in either the church or the world (although some scholars read *Act and Being* as personal reflection dressed up in academic garb[192]). Because of his willingness to serve the church and engage in military training, Bonhoeffer's concern with academics should not be read necessarily as a withdrawal from the world inconsistent with the notion of church-world formulated in this chapter.[193]

At the end of phase 1, Bonhoeffer leaned toward a traditional iteration of Luther's doctrine (with its emphasis on the non-interfering roles of church and state). He was studying theology and on his way to becoming an ordained minister (he was eventually ordained on November 15, 1931), and therefore preparing to work for the church in an official capacity. Bonhoeffer also emphasized the importance of the concrete or the worldly. Thus, it should come as no surprise that he was at this point in his career poised to apply his church-world theology mostly within the context of a deepening commitment to the church with implications for the worldly. All that was necessary was a challenge to the delicate church-state balance and a personal conversion experience to coincide in order for Bonhoeffer to explode into action. Bonhoeffer was ready to engage in the world as a church person in a way that took more seriously the world on its own terms (with its propensity for manifesting sin) in the political sphere. He was ready to push the status quo supporting Lutheran church-state vision into one that emphasized the church's ability to criticize the world's negative aspects.

---

192. *ATS*, 80. Green, for example, argues that Bonhoeffer's concern is partly existential.

193. Day, *Dietrich Bonhoeffer on Christian Community and Common Sense*, 46. Day writes, "His return to the heavy theological phrase signals Bonhoeffer's move from the Barcelona parish back to the Berlin study and not a retreat from the world to the church. His stress remained on the location of individual human existence within the really ambiguous communities of the Christian church. Individual existence can only be considered in communal terms. The church is the necessary social location for understanding what it means to be human. Were this church a self-centered group, Bonhoeffer's assertion would be no more than in-group exclusivism. The church, however, is the eccentric crowd who become a community not by focusing on their own strengths or needs but by selflessly responding to the challenging, demanding Word of God. In this direct act evoked from without and looking beyond itself the church is constituted."

4

Phase 2: Church and World in Heightened Tension

INTRODUCTION

THE SECOND PHASE OF Bonhoeffer's life and thought is marked by two significant and life-shaping experiences. The first was his one-year stay in America. Bonhoeffer was a scholar at Union Theological Seminary in New York, an assistant in a church community in Harlem, and a traveler to Cuba and Mexico. He was introduced to a form of pacifism in a concrete and personal way during the course of a strong friendship with French student Jean Lasserre. Bonhoeffer also became familiarized with racial injustice, both as it applied to individuals and especially in the American churches, in the course of another friendship with African American student, Albert F. Fisher, and in his work in Harlem. The second major experience was Bonhoeffer's confrontation with the worsening political situation in Germany. Bonhoeffer was faced with the rise of National Socialism and its implications for a variety of theological and ecclesial concerns. His involvement in the world consisted of becoming youth secretary for the World Alliance for Promoting International Friendship through the Churches and playing an instrumental role in the movement which would eventually yield the formation of the Confessing Church (*Bekennende Kirche*). The Confessing Church would oppose the majority church, the German Christians (*Deutsche Christen*), who acquiesced to Nazi ideology. Bonhoeffer's ecumenical work included mostly espousing pacifist themes and attempting to establish a theological basis for the ecumenical organization. His work in the early resistance to the *Deutsche Christen* included mostly speaking out against the anti-Jewish Aryan clauses and pushing for a new confession.

I will argue in this chapter that Bonhoeffer's response to these life experiences, including a personal spiritual awakening while in America, manifested itself in a formulation of the church-world relationship where the boundaries and limits of the two entities are more clearly or sharply defined. Specifically, the church and world are placed in a heightened tension when seen in comparison with the church-world relationship in phase 1. In terms of a comprehensive definition of Bonhoeffer's thinking and political involvement, the altered church-world vision wherein the tension between them is heightened is connected to a "worldly or politically active or politically-engaged pacifism." Bonhoeffer's vision of the world and its structures became increasingly negative. Accordingly, he became more entrenched in the church and concerned with the nature of its authoritative and biblically derived and world-challenging message. Bonhoeffer was therefore also able to more clearly define the nature of the church-state relationship. In particular, because of a recognition of the potentially negative aspects of the world, and the state as a component of the world, he was able to see the role of the church as a challenger or critic of the state. Finally, Bonhoeffer began to adopt the Sermon on the Mount as the central component of the Word or message the church offers the world, a message that is by its nature world challenging. Ultimately, in comparison with his first phase position, Bonhoeffer's thinking shifted to a more liberal interpretation of the Lutheran Two Kingdoms doctrine.

Some fairly radical and unmistakable shifts in forms of political thinking came along with this change in Bonhoeffer's church-world thinking. First, rather than continuing to espouse nationalist war positions associated with *volkisch* themes, Bonhoeffer slowly began to embrace a provisional, militant, or protest pacifism both while in America and throughout his involvement with the ecumenical movement. Second, as noted, rather than remaining in a church-state paradigm wherein the church could only engage in the world or state in a state-supporting or non-critical way, Bonhoeffer began to see how the church should challenge the state as a potentially negative aspect of the world. His shift from thinking that looked like the non-critical world or state supporting "orders of creation" positioning to "orders of preservation" thinking, which emphasized the provisional nature of any government, was a result the world more negatively construed in his theology.

Phase 2: Church and World in Heightened Tension 139

Importantly, if the relationship between Bonhoeffer's church-world and political thinking and actual forms of political involvement were not perfectly correlated in the first phase, this is not the case in the second where the relationship between thought and action is very clear and direct. The Nazi regime's passing of the 1933 legislation containing the infamous Aryan clauses became the occasion for Bonhoeffer to manifest his new church-world theology in practical action. In addition to passing legislation directly interfering with church matters, the Nazis exerted influence through their interaction with the *Deutsche Christen*. Bonhoeffer responded to Nazi involvement in the church by joining the Young Reformers, the ecumenical movement, and later the Pastors' Emergency League. In these groups he embodied his thinking whereby the church can criticize the state (when the state oversteps its boundaries) in his actions. Bonhoeffer led a mass exodus of students from a large meeting of the German Christian Student movement at the University of Berlin when support for Hitler's candidate for Reich Bishop was announced. He also risked arrest by visiting the Gestapo offices to protest Nazi interference in above-mentioned church elections. Bonhoeffer also played a role in formulating the Barmen Declaration and wrote an inflammatory pamphlet warning against the implications of the Aryan Clause.[1] Finally, he joined the international ecumenical movement and espoused a form of pacifism. This pacifism, linked as it was with both the authoritative Word of God as manifest in the church and a sense of solidarity with humanity outside of any particular nation, stood as a protest against the excessive nationalistic, decidedly non-pacifistic, or *völkisch* themes.

As in the preceding chapter, I will argue for the connection between Bonhoeffer's church-world thinking and specific forms of political thinking after the individual sections treating his important phase-2 writings. I will cover how this church-world/political thinking connection relates to his particular forms of political behavior in summary form in a section near the end of the chapter.

1. *DB*, 286, 295, 304–5.

AMERICA (SEPTEMBER 1930—JULY 1931)

Bonhoeffer, although not particularly interested in the New World and certainly not impressed with American theology, applied for and won a one-year scholarship for study and pastoral work in America.[2] The Sloane Fellowship to the Union Theological Seminary included classes with Reinhold Niebuhr, John Baillie, Eugene Lyman[3] and pastoral work at the Abyssinian Baptist Church in Harlem. Bonhoeffer also traveled to Cuba and Mexico, delivering a sermon and speaking forcefully about pacifism with a Quaker at a "peace meeting" respectively.[4] Finally, long-fascinated with the East, Bonhoeffer attempted to make plans to visit India on his way home from America.[5]

The situation in Germany during Bonhoeffer's stay in America was beginning to change from the relative stability that existed between 1925 and 1929. The Dawes Plan ended and the new Young Plan was met by resistance from conservative factions. Stresemann's death, the withdrawal of the Social Democratic Party from the government and the start of government by emergency decree all signaled the eventual death of the Weimar Republic.[6] This political instability, accompanied by an economic instability brought on by the October 1929 Wall Street crash, which exacerbated an already down-turning Germany economy, gave rise to a heightened manifestation of extreme leftist and rightist political

---

2. *DB*, 143. Bethge writes, "Still Bonhoeffer hesitated before submitting his final application. He was highly suspicious of what awaited him in America. He was not particularly fascinated by the New World. Was he to become a student again and devote a whole year to whatever placement he received? He had heard about American 'textbook methods,' and he regarded American theology as nonexistent."

3. See *DB*, 159, for a complete list of professors and classes Bonhoeffer took at Union.

4. See Robertson, *The Shame and the Sacrifice*, 57–59, for an account of the Cuba visit and 65–66 for an account of the Mexico trip.

5. *DB*, 105. Bethge traces Bonhoeffer's fascination with the East, and with Gandhi and India in particular, all the way back to the winter of 1924–1925. In 1929, while in Barcelona, he "toyed with the idea of a voyage to Tenerife, for which his grandmother sent him some money. But before the chance arose he had to return to Berlin to qualify as a lecturer, and he put the money aside for the trip to India he hoped to take someday." Bonhoeffer had plans to visit India at least three times in his life for various reasons. These plans never materialized. There is no evidence that the attempted plans in 1930 were born from an interest in pacifism. See *DB*, 147–48, for a description of the 1930 plans.

6. Ibid., 125–26.

Phase 2: Church and World in Heightened Tension 141

groups. Hitler's National Socialist Party (NSDAP), steadily gaining in membership and forging identity since 1926, made major gains in the September 14, 1930, elections.[7] These early electoral successes marked the beginning of Hitler's incredibly rapid rise to the chancellorship of Germany. His party, even at this relatively early juncture, was already engaging in manipulative tactics. Members of the SA (the *Sturmabteilung* or Storm Troops) would, for instance, engage in violent confrontations with the Communists and then criticize the government for not maintaining order.[8]

The Nazis also began their complicated and manipulative interactions with the churches. Hitler, early on, given the anti-Christian racial tenets of his ideology and his need for Christian support and votes,[9] was careful not to offer any clear vision of Nazi policy toward the Christian churches. Hitler's early statement on the relationship of the party to the churches, Point or Article 24, reads as follows:

> We insist upon freedom for all religious confessions in the state, providing they do not endanger its existence or offend the German race's sense of decency and morality. The party as such stands for a positive Christianity, without binding itself denominationally to a particular confession. It fights against the Jewish-materialistic spirit at home and abroad and believes that any lasting recovery of our people must be based on the spiritual principle: the welfare of the community comes before that of the individual.[10]

This 1920 statement of the NSDAP program, "declared unalterable by Hitler in 1926,"[11] with its infamous phrase "positive Christianity," was, even with its deplorable anti-Jewish sentiment, ambiguous enough to not (yet) spark either radical support or mistrust by the German churches. In fact, on a few important occasions Hitler even distanced himself

---

7. *HNG*, 56. The Nazi vote grew from 800,000 in the 1928 elections to a staggering 6.5 million in September 1930. This 18.3 percent showing gave the party 107 seats in the Reichstag, making them the second largest party in the Reichstag.

8. Craig, *Germany: 1866–1945*, 556–57. See also, *HNG*, 59.

9. Wright, *"Above Parties,"* 78. Hitler stated, "I need Bavarian Catholics as well as Prussian Protestants to build up a great political movement. The rest comes later." Wright quotes from the memoirs of Ludendorff's adjutant in W. Breucker, *Die Tragik Ludendorffs* (Oldenburg: Stollhamm, 1953), 107.

10. Matheson, *The Third Reich and the Christian Churches*, 1.

11. Ibid.

from the radically outspoken anti-Christian posturing of his General Ludendorff.[12] In reality, Hitler was jealous of the Roman Catholic Church for its ability to control its followers and hateful toward the Protestant churches for their disunity and lack of centralized authority. Ultimately, though, Hitler was "basically indifferent to all theological questions" and simply saw working relations with the churches as necessary for political advance.[13]

The Protestant Churches were sympathetic to the Nazi cause from the beginning. Mainstream German Protestant theology and churches had always been amenable (with some nuance) to or supportive of monarchical, right wing, nationalist or patriotic positions.[14] The Protestant Churches in the late 1920s did not mount any formal or official opposition to Hitler and his party. On the eve of Bonhoeffer's departure for America, churches would allow members of the Nazi Party to attend in full uniform and decorate entire churches with flags bearing the swastika symbol.[15]

Bonhoeffer was removed from German political events and the church situation while in America.[16] His embrace of pacifistic themes

12. See Wright, *"Above Parties,"* 75–80, for an account of how Hitler distanced himself from Ludendorff's radical position. Ludendorff's departure from the Protestant Church in September 1927 and his turn to a pagan Germanic religion, with its strong anti-Christian sentiment, received much attention in Protestant circles.

13. Conway, *The Nazi Persecution of the Churches 1933–45*, 2–4. Conway writes, "Both Catholics and Protestants could, however, be used for his [Hitler's] own purposes. If they were prepared to participate in his work of national renewal and to become subordinate to his political ends, so much the better. Consequently, throughout the 1920s Hitler refused to campaign against the Christian Churches, fully realizing that, by professing support for the Churches' position in the state and by emphasizing the nationalist aspects of his programme, Catholics and Protestants alike could be persuaded to assist his rise to power," 4. Hereafter, this title will be abbreviated as *NPC*.

14. See my chapter 2, above, for an account of some of the pre-Nazi prevailing theological and political positions of Germany's leading Protestant theologians. See also *NPC*, 9. Conway describes the attitude of the Evangelical Churches: "Here the Nazi Party had gained a substantial following not merely for its political ambitions, but, from a sizeable group of the Evangelical clergy, in the theoretical field as well. Taken as a whole, the Evangelical clergy were politically conservative, patriotic and paternalistic. Many were ardent monarchists; few had reconciled themselves to the establishment of the Weimar democracy."

15. *DB*, 142.

16. Ibid. Bethge writes, "The first major success of the Nazis in the elections of September 1930 created a new situation, but Bonhoeffer had just arrived in New York, and it hardly affected him at first."

Phase 2: Church and World in Heightened Tension 143

and the idea of solidarity with other churches and peoples of other nations (internationalism) came, thus, as something other than strictly a response to the Nazi successes in the September election. One of the factors influencing his move away from the nationalist-sounding themes of his first phase, with their attendant support of war, to the internationalism in the second phase, was his friendships with various people at Union Theological Seminary.

The most influential friendship was the one he had with Jean Lasserre, a young French theologian and avid pacifist. The possibility of a French-German friendship was somewhat challenging given the natural post-WWI resentment on both sides. However, Lasserre was a European person and thinker whom Bonhoeffer could not so easily dismiss as he could American theology or theologians. According to Lasserre, they bonded over similarity in theological viewpoint and style of life.[17] What was most significant intellectually or theologically for Bonhoeffer was Lasserre's "acceptance of the peace commandment that he [Bonhoeffer] had never encountered before."[18] Bonhoeffer would, in his phase-2 writings, wed this pacifist impulse with his own concern for concrete-

17. Kelly, "An Interview with Jean Lasserre," 149–60. In this important interview Lasserre stated, "Given the past history between France and Germany, we were a bit reserved toward each other from the beginning. But . . . as a European, I felt very close to him . . . As Europeans, both from the point of view of general culture and especially from the theological viewpoint, we felt closer to one another than the other Americans. At that time the American students and professors were caught up in a wave of modernism and theological liberalism. Karl Barth hadn't yet penetrated in the United States. And also such a wave of pragmatism that we were a bit struck by it. We were Europeans who liked to reflect before acting, while the Americans gave us the impression of wanting to act before having reflected. All this, I think, brought us close together," 150. See also Nelson, "The Relationship of Jean Lasserre to Dietrich Bonhoeffer's Peace Concerns," 71–84. Nelson relays another instructive Lasserre quotation: "From my first arrival at Union Theological Seminary in New York, I felt myself drawn toward my two companions, on scholarships like myself, who had come from continental Europe. There were three probable reasons for this: a *prosaic reason*—their English, without an American accent, and without too rich a vocabulary, was more accessible to me; a *deeper reason*—their theological approach in the discussion was less superficial, less concerned with immediate practicality, than that of our American fellow-students; and a reason, shall we say *sociological*—these last had, quite naturally from the outset, a mass of friendly ties, of activities, of responsibilities, while we Europeans were let loose in the midst of an enormous city where we knew nobody and no thing" (74). Nelson is quoting from an article translated into English by Allan Hackett, a friend of Lasserre's at Union in 1931, Jean Lasserre, "Remembrances of Dietrich Bonhoeffer," *La Vie Chrétienne, Journal Francophone de l'Eglise Presbyterienne* (October/November, 1981), 1.

18. *DB*, 153.

ness developed in the first phase. Bonhoeffer and Lasserre "shared . . . [a] longing for the concretion of divine grace and the danger of intellectually rejecting the proximity of that grace."[19] Lasserre helped make the "God's word" component in Bonhoeffer's developing concern with "the relationship between God's word and those who uphold it as individuals and citizens of the contemporary world"[20] a word of peace. The message would be concretized in reality in the form of an active or practical commitment to peace within the context of the international church community. The encounter with Lasserre would also start Bonhoeffer off on his journey toward his eventual (phase 3) complete embrace of a nontraditional understanding of the Sermon on the Mount.[21]

Bonhoeffer's "'budding' pacifism,"[22] furthermore, went hand in hand with a counter-nationalistic sense of solidarity with those in other nations. This sense of solidarity with universal humanity outside of his native Germany was eventually accompanied by involvement in the ecumenical movement, a movement uncommon and unacceptable for a Lutheran theologian in Bonhoeffer's historical and theological context.[23] Lasserre offers a story which he thinks "had sufficient importance"[24] in terms of explaining Bonhoeffer's newly found internationalism. In the early spring of 1931 Lasserre and Bonhoeffer went to see the anti-military film "All Quiet on the Western Front," based on Remarque's novel. Bonhoeffer and Lasserre sat horrified and shaken as the American audience enthusiastically applauded and laughed when the Germans killed French soldiers on the screen. Describing the import, Lasserre writes,

> I think it was there both of us discovered that the communion, the community of the Church is much more important than the

19. Ibid., 154.
20. Ibid.
21. Ibid.
22. *TF*, 9. Kelly and Nelson title their section treating Bonhoeffer's American stay, "First American Visit: Budding Pacifism."
23. Clements, "Ecumenical Witness for Peace," 157. Clements writes, "regardless of whatever he actually said in these ecumenical gatherings, within his native German context Bonhoeffer's involvement—and that of other Germans that took part—was seen as highly provocative. Even before Hitler's advent to power, the tide of nationalism in German Protestant circles was rising fast, and there was widespread opposition to anything savouring of 'internationalism.' Church involvement on the wider ecumenical scene was viewed as no less unpatriotic and un-German."
24. Kelly, "An Interview with Jean Lasserre," 151.

Phase 2: Church and World in Heightened Tension 145

national community. I think his reaction was deeper and all the more changed from his pre-conceived ideas of our previous discussions on these things. We had had, in fact, some discussions on the relativity of the national community and on the supremacy of the Church over the nation or on the Universal Church. So I think that made a deep impression on him. That experience in the movie theater was a real experience, tragically real and it must have certainly left its mark on him.[25]

In addition to this experience, Lasserre tells of a trip to Mexico in June, 1931, where he and Bonhoeffer spoke on pacifism with Lasserre's Mexican friend, Herberto Sein. Herberto gathered a large audience of three to five hundred students at the Normal School for Teachers at Victoria, Tamaulipas, to hear Bonhoeffer and Lasserre speak on the meaning of pacifism. Transcripts from this speech do not exist. Lasserre, though, reports that Bonhoeffer spoke as firmly as he, "if not more strongly, on the meaning of pacifism."[26]

It is clear, then, that Bonhoeffer's position moved radically from arguments for nationalist or aggressive wars in early 1929 in Barcelona to his pacifist statements in America in late 1930.[27] The exact type of pacifism arising from the friendship with Lasserre is hard to determine, as Bonhoeffer did not write about this development explicitly. Lasserre's testimony, though, emphasizes Bonhoeffer's developing sense of solidarity with humanity as a whole or with church persons outside of Germany rather than only with those in one's own *Volk*. This new sensibility would provide the basis for Bonhoeffer's concern for international peace. Lasserre's observation corroborates what Bonhoeffer did write explicitly in an American address.

Another significant friendship developed between Bonhoeffer and Albert F. Fisher, an African-American student at Union from Alabama. With the companionship of Fisher, Bonhoeffer made his "only real commitment" in America. It was a commitment to the African-American

---

25. Ibid.

26. Ibid., 152. See also, Robertson, *The Shame and the Sacrifice*, 65–66.

27. Kelly, *Liberating Faith*, 19. Bethge, Kelly, and others have noted both Lasserre's influence and the radical shift in positions on war and peace. Kelly, for example, writes, "Lasserre, a French student-pastor, was an intense committed pacifist, who by the force of his own faith and convictions won Bonhoeffer away from the aristocratic nationalism and enabled him not only to take a detached view toward Germany but also to become a promoter of world peace at future ecumenical conferences."

community in Harlem. Bonhoeffer went with Fisher to the Abyssinian Baptist Church at 128 West 138th Street almost every Sunday. Dietrich preached, taught the catechism, and worked with the Harlem youth in the church as well as participated in many church clubs. He also collected gramophone records of spirituals, read a large amount of Black literature, and collected literature from the NAACP. His experiences helped him to learn firsthand about racism and the disenfranchisement of American blacks.[28] Bonhoeffer was particularly disturbed by the lack of integration of black and white churches.[29] It was in the course of a third friendship with Paul Lehmann that Bonhoeffer may have gained a deeper appreciation of the plight of America's blacks. Bonhoeffer spent part of almost every night with Paul Lehmann and his wife Marion, enjoying meals and arguing about politics and social issues. Lehmann "attempt[ed] to harmonize the gospel with social activism," and may have helped Bonhoeffer apply this dynamic to the race situation in America. That is, Bonhoeffer may have, in the course of both these conversations and in his practical work in Harlem, realized "the church failure and the obvious need of the church to become involved in civil rights and the cause of social justice."[30]

Bonhoeffer's classes at Union also exposed him to an emphasis on praxis over speculation. Bonhoeffer's distaste for American pragmatism, or emphasis on social action over German metaphysical speculative theology and the arguably apolitical Barthian theology, haunted him throughout his stay.[31] Some of his professors, Reinhold Niebuhr

---

28. See *DB*, 154–55, for an account of Bonhoeffer's friendship with Albert F. Fisher. See also, *TF*, 10–11.

29. *TF*, 11. Bonhoeffer's observations on the race issue in America were both stark and astute. Nelson and Kelly write of Bonhoeffer's stance, "if blacks ever became godless, he would hold white America responsible." Nelson and Kelly refer to Bonhoeffer, *Gesammelte Schriften* 1:97–98. Bonhoeffer writes, "und wenn dieser Widerspruch einmal mächtig übergreift, dann wird das weiße Amerika sich schuldig dafür wissen müssen, daß diese schwarzen Massen gottlos geworden sind." ("and if this contradiction powerfully persists, then white America will be responsible [guilty] if these black masses become godless."). See also, *NRS*, 113–14. In 1939 he predicted that dealing with the issue or question of race (*Die Rassenfrage*) would become "one of the decisive future tasks of the white churches."

30. *TF*, 11.

31. *NRS*, 91. Bonhoeffer noted, based on Union's "humanism and the church's social gospel," that Union had "evidently forgotten what Christian theology by its very nature stands for."

and John Baillie, for example, were even "dismayed" with Bonhoeffer's Barthian starting points.[32] While unable or unwilling to see the theological merits of American thinking, Bonhoeffer was nevertheless a fully active and enthusiastic participant in the classes and the sociopolitical activities presenting themselves at Union. He, for instance, showed an interest in understanding the philosophical foundations for the distinctly American way of thinking about theology.[33] Bonhoeffer also took classes that were more explicitly political with C.C. Webber and Harry F. Ward. Webber's class, "Church and Community," included several trips to political and social organizations. The class involved visits to groups concerned with labor problems and civil rights.[34] Bonhoeffer stood by his theological principles, yet "the activity of the churches and students in economic crisis, and the enthusiasm of the 'social gospel,' made an ineradicable impression on Bonhoeffer."[35] Theologically speaking, Bonhoeffer's intense engagement with the concrete realities of the sociopolitical situation in America would force him to ask how the concrete Word of God was relevant to that situation.

"On God's Message of Love to Germany and the Community of Nations"

The only literature from this year period pertinent to his political positions and church-world theology is a sermon he delivered on 1 John 4:16b, "On God's Message of Love to Germany and the Community of Nations."[36] This sermon was possibly constructed in response to some correspondence with Helmut Rössler concerning the political situation in Germany.[37] Bonhoeffer's sermon, written and delivered in English,

32. *DB*, 160. Niebuhr, in particular, was concerned with Bonhoeffer's seeming lack of concern for ethics.

33. Ibid., 161.

34. Ibid., 163.

35. *DB*, 165. Bonhoeffer, for instance, based on the active work by the church on behalf of the unemployed in C. C. Webber's class, did the same with his own class in Berlin in 1932.

36. *TF*, 187–93. This is Kelly and Nelson's title for the sermon. The sermon is listed in Nelson and Kelly's book as occurring in "Autumn 1930." The editors of *NRS* (who print the sermon on pages 76–86), however, indicate that the sermon was delivered several times to different congregations and revised in dialogue with incoming information about Germany.

37. *NRS*, 85–86. Bonhoeffer does not respond directly to this letter. The editors of

arguably answers the nationalistic impulse in Germany presented by Rössler with an internationalist call toward unity amongst persons of all nations and the responsibility of the church to issue a message of peace. The strongly sounded call toward international unity and peace amongst churches worldwide based in a theology of the cross is contrary to Rössler's lack of confidence both in any possibility of "World Protestantism" and the *theologia crucis* as a legitimate solution to the problems facing the church in Germany.[38]

Bonhoeffer directly asserts that it is the sign of the cross of Jesus Christ where the unity of all human persons is brought to mind. He writes,

> Under the cross of Christ we know that we all belong to one another, that we are all brethren and sisters in the same need and in the same hope, that we are bound together by the same destiny—namely being a human being with all his suffering and all his joy, with sorrows and with desires, with disappointments and fulfillments—and most important a human being with his sin and guilt, with his faith and hope. Before the Cross of Christ and his inconceivable suffering all disappear our external differences, we are no longer . . . Americans or Germans, we are one large congregation of brethren, we recognize that nobody is good before God.[39]

Bonhoeffer implores his listeners, in light of Christ's love symbolized in the cross, to come to a realization of human unworthiness and therefore an experience of humility which should translate into a recognition of universal community in need of God's love and help. In a Christian community such as this, people "stand each for one, as a brother stands for his brother." In this vision, Christendom is "one great people composed of persons of every country." Bonhoeffer strongly asserts the church as an "invisible community of the children of God" that is "above all differences of race, nationality [and] custom." Hatred cannot exist in this church, only a desire to understand one another.[40]

No Rusty Swords, though, claim that Bonhoeffer's sermon was written and rewritten for future deliveries based on information he received about the increasingly complicated political and ecclesial situation in Germany. There is no way, however, to determine exactly how Rössler's letter influenced the published sermon.

38. *NRS*, 71–76.

39. *DBWE-10*, 576.

40. Ibid., 581.

Bonhoeffer's sermon then becomes a recognition of the German nation's desire for peace in the midst of this outright despair and a call for peace based on the sense of universal brotherhood or sisterhood mentioned in the earlier part of the sermon. He relays to the congregation his astonishment at Americans constantly questioning the German thinking on a possible future war. He responds that war is something that Germans positively do not want. He then describes how various socio-economic classes in Germany all have the desire for peace.[41] Finally, Bonhoeffer surprisingly asserts that the youth in the country is now, and has been since the end of the first war, consistently pacifistic. Even more surprisingly, he both uses the word "we" in describing the activities of the youth peace movement and describes it as an "enormous power."[42] With his use of "we," Bonhoeffer implies that he was actively involved in a peace movement in his youth. There is no evidence that he was actively political in any peace movements in this fashion. Moreover, even if he meant "we" as referring to the German people as a whole without specifically including himself, there is no evidence that a majority of the German population was pacifistic.

Does the fact that Bonhoeffer espoused pacifistic themes in this sermon mean that he became a pacifist while in America? Moreover, if he did become a pacifist, what kind of pacifist was he? A look at the remainder of the sermon indicates that Bonhoeffer did not really give the details of his own pacifism or prescribe appropriate Christian responses in the event of a war.[43] It is difficult, thus, to answer these questions definitively. What Bonhoeffer does say, though, is in direct contradiction to the nationalistic and anti-pacifistic thinking espoused in the ethics lecture in Barcelona. Expanding on the call for recognition of an international human solidarity from the sermon's first paragraph, he writes,

---

41. NRS, 82–83. The working class, for instance, is "naturally pacifistic." The bourgeois would also "abominate a war more than anything else."

42. NRS, 83. Bonhoeffer writes, "The youth movement which started immediately after the war was in its tendencies entirely pacifistic. In a deep religious feeling we recognized all people as brothers, as children of God . . . The peace movement in Germany is an enormous power."

43. RR, 100. Rasmussen, for example, writes of this American sermon, "Sympathy with peace movements emerges in this address as well, but far too little is said to ascertain Bonhoeffer's own stand on pacifism."

> As a Christian minister I think, that just here is one of the greatest tasks for our church, to strengthen the work of peace in every country and in the whole world. It must never more happen, that a christian people fights against a christian people, brother against brother, since both have one Father. Our churches have already begun this international work. But more important than that is, it seems to me, that every Christian man and woman, boy and girl takes seriously the great idea of the unity of Christianity, above all personal and national desires, of the one christian people in the whole world, of the brotherhood of mankind, of the charity, about which Paul says: ". . . How can the man, who hates his brother, expect grace from God? That is my message as a German and as a Christian to you, let us love each other, let us build in faith and love one holy christianity, one brotherhood, with God, the Father, and Christ, the Lord and, and the Holy Spirit as the sanctifying power. Nobody is too little or too poor for this work; we need every will and force.[44]

This strong sense of international solidarity, based here in Christian love rather than in humility in light of the cross as in the earlier part of the sermon, forms the foundation for the drive for peace. It is, while sounding idealistic, a forceful and moving call for peace. Bonhoeffer, foreshadowing his own later work in the international ecumenical movement, indicates that the churches have begun this international work. It is significant, also, that he uses the word "work." Bonhoeffer's call for peace here is an active struggle requiring work.

Church-World Relationship and Political Thinking

The impact of Bonhoeffer's first American visit on his thinking and behavior is an issue subject to varied interpretation.[45] Bonhoeffer does not appear to be especially politically active in America beyond the involvement required in a few of his classes.[46] However, there are four important events or relationships from Bonhoeffer's first American visit that would

---

44. *DBWE-10*, 583–84.

45. Kuhns, *In Pursuit of Dietrich Bonhoeffer*, 37. Kuhns, for instance, writes, "It is difficult to estimate America's influence upon the young theologian."

46. *DB*, 165. Bethge notes, "When his time in America was up Bonhoeffer had by no means come to terms with the onslaught of information and issues that had bombarded him. Niebuhr and Baillie later recalled that he withdrew into his orthodox European shell: 'He felt that political questions in which our students were so interested were on the whole irrelevant to the life of a Christian.'" Bethge quotes from R. Niebuhr, *Union Seminary Quarterly Review* 1/3 (1946) 3.

Phase 2: Church and World in Heightened Tension

influence his political thinking while in America and especially upon his return to Germany. All of these events, relationships, or realizations are arguably related to a new understanding of the world, and specifically one that recognizes its real or potential negativity. First, Bonhoeffer's reaction to Lasserre's pacifism was based partially on the recognition that the world's unbridled acceptance of violence in war was inappropriate. Second, his sense of the relative importance of his own nation was affected by viewing it from the outside, and especially how Germany might be perceived negatively by other nations. Third, his work with the African-American community introduced him firsthand with racism as a negative aspect of the world and engendered in him a sense of solidarity with those who are oppressed or suffer. Finally, his classes introduced him to the idea that political and social injustices are a negative aspect of the world, and one that churches might involve themselves in practically.

The most significant result of his American stay is his first expression of pacifist themes. Moreover, the drive toward peace can be seen as a result of Lasserre's influence. The drive toward peace was supported by an idea of international brotherhood or sisterhood. Bonhoeffer's position here can be traced partially to his experience of looking at Germany from beyond its borders. The fact that the drive toward peace is an act of solidarity can be traced to his experience with the African-American community in Harlem. Finally, the fact that Bonhoeffer's drive toward peace was an active drive, implying work on behalf of the church, can be traced partially to the awareness gained in his classes that the church has a voice in the political realm.

Bonhoeffer's later pacifism was different. It was based on a reading of the Sermon on the Mount as the Church's authoritative message or Word to the world demanding unmediated discipleship and arguably requiring a break with the world. Bonhoeffer's "call for peace" or "sympathy for peace movements" in his American sermon, on the other hand, is, while also based in the church's Word to the world and motivated by theological concerns, not a demand for a break from the world. It is, rather, motivated by recognition of solidarity with other human beings that implies a concrete response. This response is, moreover, a practical response, a pacifism that calls for work or political struggle.[47] This anti-nationalistic solidarity with all persons, though, while argu-

---

47. RR, 102. Rasmussen writes of the pacifism in this phase, "Bonhoeffer's 'pacifism' is also militant pacifism. Struggle (*Kampf*) is commended."

ably humanistic, does not imply a non-ecclesiological or purely secular call to peace among nations that could be attained without the church or its message. The call to peace is specifically an ecclesial call, it derives from the church's authority and is addressed to the church.

The nature of the church's call or authoritative Word has implications for the church-world relationship.[48] Bonhoeffer, in postulating the church as a body of those who, in unity, should proclaim and accept the call to peace, has essentially established a group of persons who have a commission that marks them off from the outside world. That is, Bonhoeffer has called the universal church to identify itself vis-à-vis the world in its acceptance of the message of peace and its work toward peace. Bonhoeffer has taken his highly theoretical construction of the nature and mission of the church from the first phase and concretized it in this second phase. In his earlier, phase-1 work, the church is distinguished from the world in that it has an authoritative and transforming Word to be made available to a somewhat reluctant outside world. Here, Bonhoeffer designates that theoretical Word as a Word of peace. This designation, and the accompanying clearer definition of the church as opposed to the world, though, does not yield an entirely different dynamic than the one in the first phase. The outside world is not depicted as entirely lost, negative, or unable to be redeemed. The church would thus have no recourse to move to an entirely world-withdrawn or apolitical stance that assumes its work or Word might be arguably ineffectual. There is, rather, justification for the church and church members to both preach and attempt to enact a transformative word of peace. Bonhoeffer's work for peace on behalf of the ecumenical movement in the next few years of phase 2 would be the action component to the message in the American sermon. It would be one of the ways his change in America and the influences from his American visit would become manifest in action.

---

48. Ibid., 100. Rasmussen writes, "Perceptible alterations are visible but a year after Barcelona. The contact abroad gave flesh to the ecclesiastical Christology of *The Communion of Saints*. A New York address shows this by initiating the shift of '*Volk*' from an organic national entity to a supranational, ecclesiological one."

Phase 2: Church and World in Heightened Tension 153

ECUMENICAL WORK AND THE BEGINNINGS OF THE CHURCH STRUGGLE

Bonhoeffer returned to Germany in the fall of 1931 to a political scene much different from the one he left. Hitler's ascent to power took a giant leap forward with the successes in the September 1930 elections. These successes were part of several factors that weakened the already-challenged leadership of Chancellor Brüning's government, a government propped up only by Hindenburg's use of emergency decrees (Article 48). The Nazi successes essentially prevented Brüning from gaining the center-right majority necessary to support his regime. The incidences of violent skirmishes between Hitler's SA and Communist groups in the streets increased dramatically, heightening the sense of Brüning's incompetence.[49] Hitler's party was also wreaking havoc in "legal" ways in the Reichstag by disrupting parliamentary sessions with shouting and even boycotting.[50] Hitler asked President Hindenburg if the Nazis could form a government in October 1931. Hindenburg had a low opinion of Hitler and refused. Hitler had no choice but to run against Hindenburg in the presidential election in the spring of 1932. Hitler lost but Hindenburg failed to gain an absolute majority. A second vote saw Hindenburg gain the requisite absolute majority, but the percentage of the vote for Hitler went up from 30 to 37. Hitler's plan to gain control of the German government had not yet materialized as of mid-1932. However, he was successful in gaining more popular support, more seats in the Reichstag and in de-stabilizing the existing government by "legal" means.[51] Bonhoeffer returned to a Germany on the brink of the Nazi revolution.

The situation in the churches was as important as the larger political developments in terms of understanding Bonhoeffer's church-world theological development in this second phase. As noted in previous

---

49. *HNG*, 59. Hitler's people would create violent chaos and then blame the government for its inability to keep the peace. See also, Craig, *Germany*, 557. Craig writes, "Apart from exaggerating the numbers of his troopers in order to impress his audience, Hitler was drawing a veil of patriotic romance over crimes of assault and murder committed nightly by youthful thugs wearing the insignia of his party. During 1931 hardly a week passed that was not marked by shootings and bombings and deliberately planned 'actions' that left damage to property and casualties in their wake. The real target of these assaults upon the public order was Brüning, but the Chancellor did not fight back."

50. Ibid., 59–60.

51. Ibid., 60–61.

chapters, the German Protestant Church was, in general, theologically, structurally, and traditionally amenable to a monarchical form of government. Even before the official creation of the Hitler-supporting "Faith Movement of 'German Christians'" (*Deutsche Christen*) in June 1932 and the famous "Church Struggle" (*Kirchenkampf*), there were churches supportive of Nazi ideology. These churches were, in effect, forerunners of the *Deutsche Christen*.[52] In addition, these church movements were, for the most part, manifestations of the sentiment of the larger German Protestant Church.[53] However, some saw the incompatibility of the Nazi doctrine with Christianity.[54]

Bonhoeffer involved himself in three distinct forms of activity (academic, pastoral, and ecumenical) upon his return to Germany amidst this tumultuous political and ecclesial backdrop. In the academic realm, Bonhoeffer gave a number of lectures and taught seminars as part of

---

52. *CCUH*, 75–78. The "League for a German Church" (*Bund für deutsche Kirche*), founded in June, 1921, for example, nationalist and anti-Jewish in the extreme, wanted to take the Old Testament from the canon. Cochrane explains further that they wanted "Paul's rabbinic principle of redemption be done away [with]; and that Jesus' death be presented as a heroic sacrifice in line with German mysticism." An even more radical forerunner was the "Thüringian 'German Christians.'" Two pastors, Julius Leuthauser and Siegfried Leffler, thought National Socialism and Christianity to be entirely compatible. Their doctrine, wherein *Heilsgeschichte* was the history of the German people, made the German nation the "new people of God." The immediate forerunner of the "German Christians" was the Christian-German movement, founded in 1930 by Werner Wilm. It was less "racialistic," but still held to the idea that nations were God-willed and "orders of creation." The movement saw Christianity as a stabilizing force in the "body politic." It claimed prominent theologians like Emanuel Hirsch and Paul Althaus as members. See also, Ericksen, "A Radical Minority," 118. Ericksen writes, "My work on Gerhard Kittel, Paul Althaus and Emmanuel Hirsch, for example, is an attempt to show that significant theologians of international reputation supported the Nazi regime. They did so neither grudgingly nor under the political pressure of a totalitarian state, but enthusiastically, because they liked what they saw."

53 *CCUH*, 78–79. Cochrane notes, "Unfortunately there were few who saw in a Nazi victory a threat to the Church. Most churchmen, while critical of National Socialism, recognized merits in it and looked upon it as offering great opportunities for the Church in the future."

54. Ibid., 79–80. These scholars published two volumes titled *The Church and the Third Reich: Questions and Demands of German Theologians*, the first of which was critical of National Socialism. Paul Tillich, for example, was especially forceful in his criticisms. Hitler read the first volume and ordered physics professor J. Stark, who worked in Hitler's Office on Church Affairs, to respond. He wrote, "Never have I seen such an accumulation of ignorance, superficiality, presumption and malicious enmity to the German Freedom Movement."

Phase 2: Church and World in Heightened Tension 155

the theological faculty of the University of Berlin. In the pastoral field, he delivered sermons and lectures and taught a confirmation class. He also engaged in social work, forming a weekend home for students and confirmation candidates and opening a youth club for the unemployed. In his ecumenical activities, Bonhoeffer became a youth secretary in the World Alliance for Promoting International Friendship through the Churches and in the Ecumenical Council for Practical Christianity (Life and Work). He traveled and delivered lectures as part of this organization.[55]

Bonhoeffer's activities in these three capacities were the active manifestation of the influences from his stay in America in response to the German political and ecclesial situation. His pacifistic themes as part of the international ecumenical movement, rooted in the same sense of human solidarity as his American address, were in direct contradiction to the Nazi and generally conservative disavowal of internationalism and pacifism. His essay concerning the Aryan Clause, also in direct contradiction to Nazi ideology, expressed a sense of solidarity with Jewish persons in Germany. Finally, Bonhoeffer's social work in the context of his parish mirrored the social activism he saw in his American classes and in the American churches. His varied activities in this period were accompanied by writings that show a church that has defined itself in a concrete way with a particular message in relationship to the world.

Catechism (July–September 1931)

The first writing in phase 2 dealing with issues of war and peace was a catechism written with a Jewish friend Franz Hildebrandt between July and September 1931.[56] The catechism was a reflection of Bonhoeffer's desire, fresh from his American influences, to produce something of practical theological import. To that end, Bonhoeffer even wrote explicitly about war and peace issues, something uncommon in Lutheran cat-

---

55. *DB*, 174–5. Bonhoeffer espoused pacifistic themes in these lectures and sermons.
56. See *DB*, 186–89 for a description of the catechisms. This was one of two catechisms he wrote in his career (the other he wrote in 1936). See also *NRS*, 141. There is some discrepancy between Bethge and the editors of *No Rusty Swords* over the context for Bonhoeffer's production of the catechism. The editors suggest that he was actively working with his "unusual" catechism class at the time of the writing, whereas Bethge insists he was writing only because he thought a catechism was necessary.

echisms.⁵⁷ In addition to this explicit treatment of war and peace issues, there is some treatment of how the Gospel message interacts with the world and how Christians might act in the world.

For example, in the first question, "What is the Gospel?," Bonhoeffer states plainly that it is the "message of the kingdom of God which is contested in the world."⁵⁸ He thus calls attention to the potential conflict between the gospel and the world. In the answer to another question concerning human reason's unaided ability to come to knowledge of God's act in creation on its own, Bonhoeffer adds "The demons of the world, of money, power, lust, rob us of God's light. God's ordinances are destroyed."⁵⁹ Bonhoeffer's reference here to the destruction of God's ordinances stands as a move away from the prevailing nationalistic interpretation of the "orders of creation." Counter to Luther's original intent, this nationalistic teaching tended to minimize the inherent sinfulness in these orders and treat them as if a people or nation could unambiguously manifest or reflect God's will in creation.⁶⁰

Bonhoeffer next explicitly addresses the nature of various forms of action in the world. After explaining how a "righteous God can permit so much wrong" in the world, he formulates the question as follows, "What then am I to do in the world?" The catechism responds simply to follow God's call in obedience. There is to be no withdrawal from the world. Answers to questions immediately following indicate the difficulties of acting in a world under God's judgment. Bonhoeffer notes that even working and earning money "robs the other man of his food," making work "a curse." The very next question and answer suggests even that it would be better if people did not own private property. When a

57. *DB*, 187. Bethge notes that the "introduction of the subjects of war, peace, or the ecumenical question into the elementary teaching of the church was entirely new."

58. *NRS*, 141. It should be noted that both Hildebrandt and Bonhoeffer are implied as writers when I only state Bonhoeffer.

59. Ibid., 143–44.

60. See Borg, *The Old Prussian Church*, 14. Luther held that "sin permeated the orders of creation; even saints sinned." See also, *TF*, 96–97. Nelson and Kelly describe the prevailing understanding in Bonhoeffer's Germany: "Advocates of these 'orders' [of creation] had made it easy for the churches to overlook the evidence of individual and corporate evil in government policies; indeed, to claim that such evil may have God's own blessing." See also Clements, "Ecumenical Witness for Peace," 163. Clements writes, "[For Bonhoeffer] we cannot read God's will and purpose straight off from the world as it is, the fallen world of sin and division. Christian faith cannot be redefined in terms of nationhood."

Phase 2: Church and World in Heightened Tension

Christian does own private property, he or she should recognize that it has value only to the extent that it can help others. Christians should have an attitude of neutrality toward property.[61]

These canons dealing with the difficulties with human action provide the foundation for his treatment of war as a specific kind of worldly engagement. He begins with a general question about the importance of maintaining one's health and "bodily life." The deliberate ruination of health or body is simply a destruction of "one's own soul and God's property." Bonhoeffer thus begins the admonition against destroying life in the specific context of war. The church, in fact, in explicit and direct contrast to his phase-1 position (where war can be sacred), "knows nothing of a sacredness of war." Rather, the church should "ask God only for peace." The next question shows the unique problem presented in a German context, and one he addressed in phase 1 writings. It states, "Is that not a betrayal of the Fatherland?" Bonhoeffer, in direct contradiction to the prevailing Nazi sentiment that certain blood is different than or even superior to other blood, answers, "God had made of *one* blood all the families of men to dwell on the face of the earth (Acts 17.26)." He continues, "Therefore a national boast in flesh and blood is a sin against the spirit."[62]

Bonhoeffer's line of argumentation does echo themes introduced in both the pro-war Barcelona lecture and the call for peace in the American address. It is a sense of human "neighborhood" or solidarity with brothers and sisters at the root of his call for political action. In the next question about the more general issue concerning the proper Christian political attitudes, for instance, Bonhoeffer writes, "however much he [the Christian] would like to keep his distance from the political struggle, the commandment of love forces him to identify himself with his neighbor here as well."[63] It is unclear whether this identification with neighbor would be the source of a drive toward peace, like in the American address, or war, as it did in the Barcelona address. The next sentence seems to indicate that the sense of love for the neighbor could refer to the responsibility to engage politically for the sake of the neighbor in one's own state. It states, "His faith and his love must know whether

---

61. *NRS*, 144.
62. Ibid., 145.
63. Ibid.

any command of the state may lead him against his conscience."[64] Since states do not generally command peace, Bonhoeffer may be speaking about whether the state's command to war is against one's conscience. Bonhoeffer does not, though, explicitly mention conscientious objection to war.

Like in his American lecture, Bonhoeffer is here not an absolute pacifist who teaches that war is wrong for all persons or nations at all times and in all situations. Moreover, he does not actively encourage conscientious objection. Rather, he asserts the somewhat traditional Lutheran standard that "God has given the state its office that we should serve him as Christians."[65] That sentence, though, is preceded by the ones expressing the unity of all persons and the state's taming citizens' "blind zeal."[66] Bonhoeffer thus hints at a position that he will elucidate in upcoming writings, the idea that there are legitimate ways in which the state should exercise its power. In addition, individual Christians must decide if certain state directives are counter to their consciences. Bonhoeffer asserts the possibility for Christians of a critical stance toward state directives.

Church-World Relationship and Political Thinking

The relationship between Bonhoeffer's church-world thinking and his political positions in this catechism is not as evident as the more general relationship between Christ's message and the world. Clarifying the ambiguity felt by the Christian in the decision to engage in the political, Bonhoeffer writes, for example, "In any decision he feels the irreconcilable cleavage between the peace of Christ and the hate of the world."[67] Bonhoeffer suggests here and in other places that the world's status or condition cannot allow for uncritical engagement therein.[68] Bonhoeffer teaches that worldly structures such as work, property, and states cannot or may not unambiguously reflect God's purpose for them in the

---

64. Ibid.
65. Ibid.
66. Ibid.
67. Ibid.

68. Ibid., 147. Bonhoeffer writes, "Christ is risen, he has robbed the devil of his power. But no one sees that, and Christ and the Antichrist are still fighting in this world. Only to his community does he appear as the conqueror, only to his members does he appear as the head; he makes the church his body and in the church manifests his life."

Phase 2: Church and World in Heightened Tension 159

world. It therefore becomes acceptable or possible for the Christian to decide that the state's political actions are wrong (even war, for example), even while accepting the idea that the state has a God-given authority to govern.

Bonhoeffer's thinking reveals the standard Lutheran theme from his earlier works, the church is a community whose members recognize in it a distinct authority in preaching the Word and administering the sacraments. The church is distinguished from the world in these ways. However, Bonhoeffer does not make the distinction so sharp as to single out the church as an exclusivist sect. He writes, for instance, that "as long as the church exists in this world, no one can decide whom God has chosen for eternity."[69] The content of the preached message emphasized in the catechism, though, is a challenging message that demands obedience. The places where the catechism mentions the message are connected to the desire for peace. He writes, "The church which prays the 'Our Father' asks God only for peace."[70] In another passage he connects the "commandment of love" with the "peace of Christ."[71] In the most explicit description of the message as one of peace, Bonhoeffer writes, "The church knows today more than ever how little it hearkens to the Sermon on the Mount. But the greater the split in the world becomes, the more Christ teaches the peace which prevails in his kingdom."[72]

Bonhoeffer's use of the Sermon on the Mount, and the idea that a theologian might choose it as a focal point of Christ's teaching, is significant as it marks one of the first of many published instances wherein Bonhoeffer takes it as a point of departure for examining both Christ's point of contact with the world and for how Christians might act in the world. Bonhoeffer thus hints at his eventual phase-3 parting with the standard Lutheran understanding of the Sermon on the Mount (this parting will also contradict his stance in the phase-1 Barcelona lecture). The traditional Lutheran understanding makes the Sermon "ideals for an ideal world" or an impossible set of standards meant to indicate how far humanity has fallen and thus not meant to be followed literally.[73] Bonhoeffer does not suggest that the Christian should follow the

69. Ibid., 148.
70. Ibid., 145.
71. Ibid.
72. Ibid., 147.
73. Clements, "Ecumenical Witness for Peace," 155. Clements writes, "The traditional Lutheran response to these words [Jesus' teachings in the Sermon on the Mount]

directives in the Sermon on the Mount literally in this catechism. In fact, despite his description of Christ's call as a world-challenging call to peace and the mention of the Sermon on the Mount, Bonhoeffer is too rooted in the earthly or worldly in this catechism to advocate for an apolitical form of pacifism. Like in the American address, the pacifism here is based as much on recognizing the solidarity existing among the human family as it is in a response to Christ's call of peace in the Sermon on the Mount.[74] It is, thus, a pacifism that might engender active political movement or struggle for peace. Bonhoeffer has drawn the distinction between the church and the world stark enough for the church to question the state's policies, but not so stark as to suggest the Christian should withdraw from the world.

Interlude: September 1931—Winter, 1932: Initial Contact with the Ecumenical Movement and Pastoral Work

Bonhoeffer's next set of activities marks an important development in both his thinking and his form of political activity. Bonhoeffer went to Cambridge in September of 1931 to attend the annual conference of the World Alliance for Promoting International Friendship through the Churches, an ecumenical movement promoting pacifism.[75] His inter-

---

had been to see them as ideals for an ideal world, not the tragically sinful and disordered world in which we are actually living; and not as commands to be followed literally, but, by their very unrealisability, as showing just how sinful and morally bankrupt we are and therefore in need of redemption and grace. Bonhoeffer now began to ask himself whether all such theological explanations were an attempt to escape from the concreteness of Jesus' command." See also Bethge, "Dietrich Bonhoeffers Weg vom 'Pacifism' zur Verschwörung," 119–36. Bethge, describing the common sentiment amongst his peers, writes, "Pazifismus war Scwärmerei, gedankenloser Enthusiasmus und deshalb schlechte Theologie . . . Daß die Bergpredigt nur dazu da war, uns den Spiegel unserer Sündhaftigkeit vorzuhalten, nicht aber dazu, etwas befolgt zu werden, das schien uns theologish klar," 118–19. ("Pacifism was enthusiasm, thoughtless enthusiasm and therefore poor theology . . . That the Sermon on the Mount was only that which put a mirror up to our sinfulness, and not something to be followed, appeared theologically clear to us.").

74. *DB*, 188. Bethge says about the pacifism in this catechism: "He based this bid for peace on the antinationalist principle of the unity of the human family, the argument that he had heard Lasserre use. Bonhoeffer had adopted this ecumenical argument in late 1931, as well as the idea of the church's co-responsibility for the course taken in the political struggles among peoples."

75. Robertson, *The Shame and the Sacrifice*, 69. The "origins and aims" of the World Alliance were "openly pacifist." The organization received "moral and financial" support from the Church Peace Union.

Phase 2: Church and World in Heightened Tension 161

est in the ecumenical movement was incidental at first. Superintendent Max Diestal simply made Bonhoeffer a member of the German youth delegation to the conference. However, he would become a highly committed and important member of the movement, and his involvement would come to shape his theology and political involvement. Bonhoeffer was elected by the executive committee as one of the three European youth secretaries even before his intense involvement in the ecumenical movement.[76]

Bonhoeffer's acceptance of the invitation to the World Alliance was especially noteworthy beyond the general surprise at the involvement of any Lutheran church person or academic in any internationalist movement with pacifist overtones. The World Alliance, being humanist, non-academic, and not solely ecclesiastical, was the least likely choice for the young Barthian intellectual.[77] Nevertheless, the concern for the practical aspect of Christian existence and his interest in pacifism, both attributable to his experience in America, combined to influence his choice for the World Alliance. Max Diestal's persistence was the practical influence in his decision.[78] Bonhoeffer was very active in the World Alliance in late 1931 and 1932, organizing and attending meetings as part of a group of youth secretaries. He was committed to the aims of the World Alliance, including its peace initiative.

Bonhoeffer was also engaged in formal parish work beginning in 1931. He was ordained on November 15, 1931, and assigned immediately thereafter to a student chaplaincy at a technical college in Charlottenburg.[79] A more significant form of parish involvement was his work teaching a confirmation class in the Zion parish in the rough Berlin district of Wedding. Bonhoeffer won over a rowdy bunch of delinquent young boys who drove out the former minister with their unruliness.[80] Bonhoeffer's experiences with the lower class in East Berlin, echoing his experiences in Harlem and in Ward's social action class at Union, spurred him onto his next project. He formed a youth club which "aimed at providing unemployed young men with some creative

---

76. *DB*, 190–91.
77. Ibid., 193. Bethge writes, "Any self-respecting theologian, particularly a Barthian, was bound to have reservations about such an organization."
78. Ibid., 190.
79. Ibid., 226.
80. Ibid., 226–29.

occupation and a sense of belonging in the community."[81] The club was closed down shortly after Hitler's rise to power due to the involvement of communists and socialists.[82]

While attuned to the practical and pastoral, and the church's role as an active force in the international peace movement, Bonheoffer was at this time surprisingly not ready to address publicly the "ominous developments" taking place in the German churches in late 1931 and in the beginning 1932.[83] Hitler realized he needed the support of the church and was thus interested in portraying his party as Christian. He was looking for a united organization to support his cause.[84] It came with Dr. Friedrich Wieneke (from the Cathedral at Soldin) and Pastor Hossenfelder's (minister of Christ Church in Berlin) formation of the National Socialist Pastors' League. The League issued guiding principles for conducting the Church elections and fighting any existing anti-Nazi church leadership under the rubric "Evangelical National Socialists." Pre-election church propaganda was markedly political rather than religious, condemning the standard themes such as the "liberal spirit," "Jewish Marxism," "internationalism," and "pacifism."[85] In the meantime, Pastor Hossenfelder negotiated with the "German Christian League," the "Christian Germans" and the "Thuringian German Christians" and established a union of churches. Hitler immediately ordered a change in the name "Evangelical National Socialists," because it jeopardized the false perception of neutrality.[86]

The "Faith Movement of the 'German Christians'" (*Deutsche Christen*) was officially born on June 6, 1932, with the release of its "Guiding Principles." The *Deutsche Christen*, already sanctioned by the Nazi Party to cover the whole Reich and not just Prussia, called for a unification of all 29 *Landeskirchen* and started the drive to be the official state Church of the Third Reich. Though claiming to stand on an authentic or neutral "positive Christianity," their guiding principles were a compendium of ten racialist, anti-Jewish, and nationalist canons.[87]

81. Robertson, *The Shame and the Sacrifice*, 76.
82. Ibid., 231.
83. Ibid., 232.
84. *CCUH*, 81.
85. Ibid.
86. Ibid., 82.
87. *NPC*, 340. Conway reprints the "Principles of the Religious Movement of 'German Christians,'" issued in June 1932, 339–41, from K. Kupisch, *Quellen zur*

Phase 2: Church and World in Heightened Tension 163

As noted above, Hitler did not think very highly of Christianity. Yet his ambiguous and thus almost unassailable neutral Article 24,[88] and his endorsement of the *Deutsche Christen* as the unified Reich Church, put him in the best position to receive support from the Protestant Churches.

Rather than directly addressing these ecclesial dynamics, Bonhoeffer joined a group of pastors whose purpose was to discuss matters related to "church and ministry."[89] This group of pastors eventually evolved into Martin Niemöller's Pastor's Emergency League, the precursor to the Confessing Church and the first group to produce organized statements of resistance. For now, though, Bonhoeffer, while discouraged by the lack of theological acumen in his fellow group members, was content to discuss theological and ecclesiastical issues with his pastor's group and to minister to the youth in run-down sections of East Berlin. He was thus, even in his practical commitment to the socially disenfranchised, more concerned with internal church theological matters and the nature of the church's message than with the relationship between the church and the outside world. However, Bonhoeffer did not entirely ignore the political happenings outside of the church. His sermons during this time period addressed various socio-political circumstances and events.[90] He did not directly address some of the more startling infractions of the

---

Geschichte des deutschen Protestantismus 1871–1945 (Göttingen: Musterschmidt, 1960), 251–53: "Race, nationality and nation" were, for example, termed "orders of life given and entrusted to us by God." The same canon opposes "racial miscegenation" and states that "the German Foreign Mission has been admonishing the German nation for a long time: 'Keep your race pure!' and has told us that faith in Christ does not destroy but heightens and sanctifies the race." In an anti-Jewish canon, the document warns that the Jewish Mission presents a "danger" to nationality and that marriages between Germans and Jews should not be allowed. In some other significant canons, there is a call for church members to fight against Marxism. Finally, pacifism and internationalism are termed "ruinous phenomena."

88. Matheson, *The Third Reich and the Christian Churches*, 1–2. Matheson reprints a commentary by Hermann Sasse, editor of the *Church Yearbook* of 1932. Sasse writes, "Evangelical theology can enter into dialogue with the National Socialists on all the points of the Party programme, even about the Jewish question and its understanding of race, it may perhaps be able to take seriously the whole rest of the programme. About this article [24], however, no discussion at all is possible."

89. *DB*, 233.

90. Ibid., 235–36. For instance, Bonhoeffer addressed the worldwide "impending unemployment and hunger of that winter" in a Thanksgiving Day sermon in Berlin in 1931. When Franz von Papen took over as German Reich chancellor after Brüning's resignation in early June 1932, Bonhoeffer criticized the Papen government's "misuse of God's name" in a sermon later that month.

Nazi Party in the churches. Bonhoeffer was, however, moving in that direction.

The Theological Basis for the World Alliance (July 26, 1932)

Bonhoeffer's next relevant writing was an address given at the Youth Peace Conference at Ciernohorské Kúpele, Czechoslovakia. He was constantly concerned with establishing the strictly theological foundations for both his own ecumenism and the larger movement in his ecumenical work. Bonhoeffer was unpopular because of this approach. For example, in a heated exchange with a more established participant in ecumenical dealings, Bonhoeffer attacked the "orders of creation."[91] This attack made his implicit theological critique an explicit one and foreshadowed his formal criticism of the Nazi state. In addition, his early concern with the church's proper confession was important as it sowed the seeds for his later concern for identifying the true church during the church struggle. While he continued to organize conferences abroad throughout 1932, his involvement at the conference in Czechoslovakia allowed him to make what was arguably his most valuable contribution to the ecumenical peace movement.[92]

Bonhoeffer's essay begins with a call for the ecumenical movement to develop a theology as a necessary foundation for its self-understanding as church. Recalling the ecclesiological focus of his early academic works, he makes it clear that the theology of the ecumenical movement is based "on quite a definite view of the church" that has the "commission" to offer Christ's Word to the "whole world."[93] While acknowledging the existence of individual churches with distinct geographical limits, Bonhoeffer makes it clear that the ecumenical movement is concerned

---

91. Ibid., 241. In an early conference in Germany on April 29–30, for example, he argued with an older theologian, Wilhelm Stählin, one of the keynote speakers, over Stählin's emphasis on the "orders of creation," the place and importance of the *Volk*, and the need for a confession.

92. Ibid., 247. Bethge notes that the address had "incalculable" implications for many of the delegates. See also, Clements, "Ecumenical witness for peace," 156. The World Alliance, like its related affiliate, Life and Work, was humanistic and practical. Bonhoeffer's emphasis on formulating a solid theology of the ecumenical movement went a long way in encouraging the World Alliance to "take itself more seriously as an expression of the church of Christ, and not simply as an *ad hoc* gathering of like-minded Christians trying to make an impact on the world."

93. Bonhoeffer, "A Theological Basis for the World Alliance," 98–110. This quotation is from p. 110.

Phase 2: Church and World in Heightened Tension

with the Word entrusted to the one church without limits.[94] He also makes it clear that there are no "autonomous spheres of life" unaffected by the Lordship of Christ that need not be offered the Word. The whole world, rather than one holy or sacred part of the world, "belongs to Christ."[95] Bonhoeffer does not thus advocate for a vision of the church as a sect or sect-like. However, he does not imply that the world and the church are the same entity. He heightens the first phase "tension" by articulating the nature and source of the church's authoritative message to the world.

The church derives its authority from the fact that it is the "presence of Christ on earth" or the *Christus praesens*.[96] Bonhoeffer divides the church's message into two categories, the gospel message and the commandment. He reasserts his concern with the church's relation to "worldliness" as he argues that the church's authority depends on the church's ability to "encounter the world in all its present reality from the deepest knowledge of the world." The church must say its word "in the most concrete way possible, from knowledge of the situation." Bonhoeffer is consistent with his Barcelona ethics where he rejects eternal principles. He continues, "The church may not therefore preach timeless principles, however true, but only commandments which are true today, God is 'always' *God* to us '*today*.'"[97]

Bonhoeffer makes a clear distinction between "the gospel" and "the commandment." He uses "Thy sins are forgiven thee" as an example of the gospel and places questions concerning appropriate forms of government and speculation about specific forms of state political activity under the category of commandment. Both the gospel and the commandment are preached with authority when, as noted above, they are spoken in a concrete fashion. Preaching that remains general is "human, impotent, false."[98] The commandment requires the preacher to avoid general principles and make the command as concrete as possible. It is not enough for the preacher to say that "there should really be no war, but there are necessary wars." Rather, the church "should be able to say

---

94. Ibid., 101.
95. Ibid.
96. Ibid.
97. Ibid.
98. Ibid., 102.

quite definitely: 'Engage in this war' or 'Do not engage in this war.'"[99] Bonhoeffer admits to a problem with his thinking at this point. That is, the church would have to have full knowledge of every aspect of the concrete situation in order for it to be entirely confident in the validity of its command. The church can either retreat into the proclamation of general principles or take action. The action can take the form of a "qualified" or "intentional" silence, or the church can venture to preach the commandment "definitely, exclusively, radically."[100] Bonhoeffer also reaffirms the concern with worldliness, arguing that if it is the sacrament that validates the preaching of the forgiveness of sins, it is "knowledge of firm reality" that validates the commandment.[101]

Confident that he has established the church's authority to preach the gospel and the commandment, Bonhoeffer next addresses the source of the church's commandment. Bonhoeffer rejects *The Biblical Law* (which he designates as the *Sermon on the Mount*) as the source of God's revelation of the commandment.[102] He is consistent with his Barcelona ethic wherein he argues that the directives of the Sermon on the Mount cannot be taken as laws. Nevertheless, he does argue that the Sermon on the Mount "in its commandments (it) is the demonstration of what God's commandment can be."[103] He thus reiterates his teaching from the catechism that the Sermon on the Mount might provide more than just a mirror to our sinfulness, that its directives could fall into the category of command. Bonhoeffer next suggests that the church might find God's commandment in the orders of creation. The orders of creation are problematic because they can be used to justify any existing

---

99. Ibid.

100. Ibid., 103.

101. Ibid. Bonhoeffer connects the gospel with the commandment, writing, "The church cannot command without itself standing in faith in the forgiveness of sins . . . The preaching of the forgiveness of sins is the guarantee of the validity of the preaching of the commandment."

102. Ibid., 104. Bonhoeffer writes, "Whence does the church know God's commandment for the moment? . . . The recognition of God's command is an act of God's revelation. Where does the church receive this revelation? The *first answer* could be '*The Biblical Law, the Sermon on the Mount* is the absolute norm for our action'" (italics original to translation). While Bonhoeffer admits that the biblical law of the Sermon on the Mount might be legitimate at one time, it cannot be made into permanent law.

103. Ibid.

order.[104] Orders of creation thinking does not adequately allow for the idea that the present state of the world is fallen and sinful.[105]

Bonhoeffer's disavowal of the orders of creation is ultimately based in Christology. The Christ who has fulfilled the commandment of God and who promises the new creation is the only source of the commandment.[106] All existing orders in the world are relativized with respect to the fulfillment in Christ. They "obtain their value wholly from outside themselves, from Christ, from the new creation."[107] Bonhoeffer introduces his notion of "orders of preservation" as a corrective to "orders of creation." He states, "*all* the orders of the world . . . stand under the preservation of God only as long as they are still open for Christ, they are *orders of preservation*, not orders of creation."[108] No structures are intrinsically valuable. They are not "*per se* 'very good'" and we cannot "perceive the will of God *directly* in them."[109] The orders of the world are legitimate only to the extent that they keep open the possibility of revelation. Bonhoeffer clarifies, "Orders of preservation are forms of working against sin in the direction of the gospel. *Any order*—however ancient and sacred it might be—*can be dissolved*, and must be dissolved when it closes itself up in itself, grows rigid and no longer permits the proclamation of revelation."[110]

Bonhoeffer's Christocentric thinking on the orders of creation-preservation debate had political implications. He writes, "the church of Christ has to pass verdict on the orders of the world."[111] Bonhoeffer thus justifies, on the basis of his understanding of how God relates to the

---

104. Ibid. Bonhoeffer writes, "One need only to hold out something to be God-willed and God-created for it to be vindicated forever, the division of man into nations, national struggles, war, class struggle, the exploitation of the weak by the strong, the cut-throat competition of economics. Nothing simpler than to describe all this—because it is there—as God-willed and therefore to sanction it."

105. Ibid.," 104–5. Bonhoeffer writes, "now sin prevails and that creation and sin are so bound up together that no human eye can any longer separate the one from the other, that each human order is an order of the fallen world and not an order of creation."

106. Ibid., 105.
107. Ibid.
108. Ibid.
109. Ibid.
110. Ibid.
111. Ibid.

world in Christ, the church's ability to criticize the state. If the current form of government, or other orders of preservation, do not allow for the continued proclamation of the gospel, they must be "dissolved." Only orders which "can best restrain the radical falling of the world into death and sin" are legitimate.[112] Finally, Bonhoeffer connects his thinking on the orders of preservation with the commandment in writing, "The church hears the commandment only from Christ, not from any fixed law or from any eternal order, and hears it in the orders of preservation."[113]

With the groundwork laid, Bonhoeffer can address even more explicitly the content of the commandment for the World Alliance. He states plainly that the church has recognized a "quite definite order as commanded by God today" and that order is international peace. Bonhoeffer takes great pains to distinguish this command from "the scandal of pacifist humanitarianism," the tendency of Anglo-Saxon theology to equate peace with the Kingdom of God which makes peace an order of creation.[114] Peace is, rather, an expedient "command of the angry God" in the name of Christ directed toward something else. Peace is not an "ideal state," or "valid in itself."[115] It exists only as a condition for the proclamation of the gospel. Despite his warning against humanist pacifism, Bonhoeffer does not lay the responsibility for peace only on the divine side. Rather, he argues that peace is only possible within the context of a certain form of community, one that "does not rest on *lies* and *injustice*."[116] The quest for truth and justice are the hallmarks of a community capable of enacting God's peace commandment.

Bonhoeffer's notion of peace relies on the concept of "struggle." He argues, "Where a community of peace endangers or chokes truth and justice, the community of peace must be broken and the battle joined." Unlike Anglo-Saxon notions of peace that focus only on the external condition of peace, Bonhoeffer advocates for the necessity of a struggle for truth and justice as the foundations for true peace.[117] Bonhoeffer

---

112. Ibid.
113. Ibid., 106.
114. Ibid.
115. Ibid., 106–7.
116. Ibid., 107.

117. Ibid. Bonhoeffer again criticizes those who would seek to establish peace as if it were a "static" concept (the Anglo-Saxon view) or order or even truth as if it were static (Hirsch and Althaus) or permanent order.

Phase 2: Church and World in Heightened Tension

argues that "Struggle can in some cases guarantee openness for the revelation in Christ better than external peace, in that it breaks apart the hardened, self-enclosed order." This struggle, in addition, can manifest as a form of Christian "action."[118] Bonhoeffer's explicit treatment of pacifism follows upon his treatment of struggle. He quickly dismisses the idea that war can fall under the concept of struggle.[119] Modern warfare is simply too destructive as opposed to past warfare. War, also, because it has become so destructive, cannot serve as an order of preservation.[120] Bonhoeffer's explicit statement about the church's proper position on "war" is as follows:

> Now because we can in no way understand war as one of God's orders of preservation and thus as the commandment of God, and because on the other hand war needs idealizing and idolizing to be able to live, war today, and therefore the next war, must be utterly *rejected* by the church. No word of condemnation of past deeds even in the last war—that is not permitted to us, "thou shalt not judge"—but all the power of resistance, of refusal, of rejection of the next war. Not from the fanatical erection of one commandment—perhaps the sixth—over the others, but from obedience towards the commandment of God which is directed towards us today, that war shall be no more, because it takes away the possibility of seeing revelation. Nor should we be afraid of the word pacifism today.[121]

Bonhoeffer makes clear two important ideas in this statement. First, he is concerned with what is appropriate for today. In his rejection of judgment of past wars he implies that war, as a general phenomenon, is not entirely condemnable. War is, though, unacceptable now. The next (upcoming) war is unacceptable. The question about the war after the "next war" has not been spoken about definitively. Although he uses the word pacifism, he cannot use it as an absolute principle. In fact, since his prior argumentation about the unacceptability of war rested partially on the notion of the horrors of modern warfare, a future war with less destructive weapons may even be acceptable. His second and related idea con-

118. Ibid., 108.
119. Ibid. Bonhoeffer writes, "The right of war can be derived from the right of struggle as little as the use of torture may be derived from the necessity of legal procedures in human society."
120. Ibid.
121. Ibid.

cerns the notion of commandment within a given context. According to his earlier argumentation, the church has to take into account the totality of what is happening in reality in a given situation in order to issue an authoritative commandment. Commandments, for Bonhoeffer, are not therefore laws that must be taken as permanent fixtures in reality applied ahistorically or irrespective of context.

Bonhoeffer concludes his essay with an important question. He writes, "To whom does the church speak?" Bonhoeffer answers that the church speaks not only to its own members but also to the whole world, "telling it to alter its conditions."[122] Consistent with his inherited way of thinking, Bonhoeffer recognizes that the church has no direct transforming impact on the world, and especially no direct transforming impact on the state. He writes, "the voice of the church cannot be authoritative towards it [the state]."[123] Bonhoeffer does show a significant change from his first-phase thinking when he argues that the church's message legitimately criticizes the state's directives. He writes further, "but the state finds in the church a critical limit to its possibilities and thus will have to take notice of it as a critic of its actions."[124] Thus, ultimately, Bonhoeffer espouses a more liberal version of Luther's Two Kingdoms doctrine that stresses the church's ability to criticize the state.

Church-World Relationship and Political Thinking

There are a few important facets of Bonhoeffer's understanding of the church-world relationship relevant to an analysis of his political thinking in this work and his political involvement at the time of this work. As in his American address and in the catechism, his concern here is with defining the church's exact message to the world. Bonhoeffer has articulated more clearly than he did in the first phase the role of the church vis-à-vis the world. He implies a heightened tension with his clearer structural division between the church and the world. He advances this tension further when he states that "the world cannot hear the true voice of the church."[125] Bonhoeffer also implies a heightened tension between the church and a structure or order of the world when he argues that "the state finds in the church a critical limit to its possibilities and thus

---

122. Ibid., 109.
123. Ibid., 110.
124. Ibid.
125. Ibid., 109–10.

Phase 2: Church and World in Heightened Tension

will have to take notice of it as a critic of its action."[126] Finally, his option for orders of preservation over orders of creation further implies that various structures of reality like the state, for example, are only provisional and can be challenged or even dismantled.

Bonhoeffer's heightened tension is still a tension. That is, the church's commandment, while requiring obedience and while being potentially critical of existing structures, is not unrelated to the world or even counter-world. Bonhoeffer states explicitly that the church has to take into account all aspects of the worldly situation when formulating and issuing the commandment. Moreover, he states explicitly that the message is intended for the whole world. Bonhoeffer is, though, very careful to note that the church serves only as a "limit" to the state's "possibilities" and has no authority over the state's directives. Therefore, while establishing that the church is ensconced in the world and has something authoritative to say to the world, he retains the traditional Lutheran teaching that the state should not interfere with the church and the church should not interfere with the state.

Bonhoeffer's form of pacifism in this phase is a reflection of his notion of church and world in heightened tension. The church has defined the commandment as a call for peace and in the context of Bonhoeffer's Germany this commandment is one that certainly challenges the world. The call, however, is not an anti-worldly call requiring withdrawal from the world. Rather, Bonhoeffer's call is a commandment. It is therefore, by his own definition of commandment, a "provisional," "struggle" or even "political" pacifism that must take seriously the multi-faceted reality of the world. It is provisional because commandments, unlike orders of creation, serve the orders of preservation. That is, they are temporary directives that have the purpose of ensuring that conditions exist for the continued proclamation of the gospel.

It follows upon Bonhoeffer's understanding of "commandment" that he does not declare that all wars, especially past ones and even future wars beyond the "next one," are unacceptable. Rather, Bonhoeffer's pacifism is consistent with what is arguably a "situation ethics" established in first-phase writings. The struggle or political component of Bonhoeffer's thinking on peace in this lecture recalls his experience of solidarity with those outcast in America (as expressed in his call for peace in the American lecture in 1931). Bonhoeffer's call is based on

126. Bonhoeffer, "A Theological Basis for the World Alliance," 110.

the creation of a loving community whose aim should be the struggle for truth and justice. This particular form of community would be the actual physical instantiation of the type of community Bonhoeffer described in a theoretical fashion in his first dissertation. The pacifism is political both in sense that the church should work to establish the type of community that must exist as a precondition for peace and also in that it should deliver the call for peace.

Thy Kingdom Come (November 19, 1932)

Bonhoeffer's next significant writing was "Thy Kingdom Come: The Prayer of the Church for the Kingdom of God on Earth." He delivered this lecture as part of a series given during the final week of the church year, the "Week of Repentance."[127] Bonhoeffer does not treat war and peace issues explicitly in the text. However, he does provide what has been described as "one of his clearest statements on church-state relations."[128]

Bonhoeffer wrote the essay against a political backdrop that saw both advances and limited setbacks in the Nazi quest for power. The Nazis did advance from 108 to 230 delegates in the Reichstag during the July 31, 1932 elections and became the largest party in the Reichstag. However, they only received 37 percent of the vote and failed to gain the majority they sought. Sensing that elections were not going to provide the vehicle to complete power, Hitler demanded that he be made chancellor. When he was denied, the SA began to clamor for an illegal or revolutionary seizure of power, but Hitler rejected that course of action. The Nazis, along with the other extreme party, the Communists, accounted for 52 percent of the Reichstag. Hitler knew that any collaboration of these parties in the Reichstag could "wreak havoc" on the government. Papen called for another election in September wherein the Nazi Party's number of seats in the Reichstag actually fell to 196 and their percentage of votes fell to 33. Hitler's party was suffering some setbacks just a few short months before his final ascent to power.[129]

In terms of ecclesial dynamics, there was, as noted above, maneuvering throughout the early and middle parts of 1932 by both Nazi-

---

127. *DB*, 210.
128. Koch, "The Theological Responses of Karl Barth and Dietrich Bonhoeffer," 125.
129. *HNG*, 62–63.

Phase 2: Church and World in Heightened Tension 173

supporting church leadership and certain leaders in the Nazi Party aimed at a takeover of Protestant church leadership. Church elections were to be held in November of 1932 and campaigning was in full swing. The development of the *Deutsche Christen* church was partly motivated by the *Reichsleitung* (Reich leadership). The *Gauleiter* (regional party leaders) were actually instructed by the party to appoint experts in church affairs. While Hitler seemed concerned to appear neutral in church affairs, Wilhelm Kube (the leader of the Nazi Party in the Prussian *Landtag*) and Gregor Strasser (the head of the Nazi Party political organization) were not.[130] Moreover, the party made it obligatory for all of its members to vote.[131] Despite protests by some of the Protestant church leaders who were concerned about political parties interfering with church matters, and especially the church elections, the propaganda campaign proceeded and so did the elections. The *Deutsche Christen*, while not "reaching their goal [of] . . . conquering the church," did win one third of the seats.[132]

Bonhoeffer begins his essay by describing the two extremes. He argues, "we are otherworldly, or we are secularists." He immediately warns, "but in either case this means we no longer believe in God's kingdom. We are hostile to the earth, because we want to be better than it, or we are hostile to God, because God robs us of the earth . . . We flee the power of the earth, or we hold hard and fast to it."[133] The balanced and proper approach for the Christian would be that of a "wanderer" who, realizing that the earth is the only vehicle by which to get to the divine, loves the earth and God at the same time.[134] Bonhoeffer first treats the tendency toward otherworldliness. While acknowledging the fact that Christians are to some extent "otherworldly," he offers a stern warning against a flight from the world mentality.[135] Bonhoeffer admits that this impulse toward otherworldliness is "easy to preach," but it appeals mostly "to the

---

130. *CCUH*, 81. Kube even wrote articles in the *Der Märkische Adler* and the *Völkischer Beobachter* calling for the creation of one single Reichskirche.

131. Wright, *"Above Parties,"* 97.

132. *CCUH*, 82. See also Wright, *"Above Parties,"* 94–6, for a brief account of pre-election dynamics.

133. Bonhoeffer, *Berlin,1932–1933*, 285–86 (hereafter abbreviated as *DBWE-12*).

134. *DBWE-12*, 286.

135. Ibid. He writes, "When life begins to be difficult and oppressive, one leaps boldly into the air and soars, relieved and worry free, in the so-called eternal realm. One leapfrogs over the present, scorns the Earth; one is better than it."

weaklings, all who are only too glad to be deceived and deluded, all the dreamers, all disloyal children of the earth."[136] Christ does not intend the Christian to be weak. Christ "makes the human being strong" and "returns him to the Earth as its true son." Bonhoeffer's Christ does not call Christians out from the world but places them squarely in the world. He ends his section with a strong exhortation, "Do not be otherworldly, but be strong!"[137] Bonhoeffer then treats secularity.[138] Secularism's renunciation of the religious pits the world against the church and worldliness against religion. The implications are tremendous. In this vision, faith "is compelled to harden into religious convention and morality, and the church into an organization of action for religious-moral reconstruction."[139] Christians thus try to build the kingdom of God on their own. They fight a "good fight" and desire to "represent God's cause in this wicked world."[140] Pious Christian secularism tries to speak for or take over for God in the world and operates out of a desire to "earn God his right in the world." In following this desire "we only escape from him, and in our love for the Earth for its own sake and for the sake of this struggle." Bonhoeffer ends this section with another exhortation, "Become weak in the world and let God be the Lord!"[141]

Otherworldliness and secularism are two different manifestations of the very same mistake, "namely, the lack of belief in God's kingdom." Otherworldly Christians hide from the earth and do not find God. A secularist, on the other hand, "evades God in order to find the earth."[142] Those who are to love God must love Him as "the Lord of the Earth as it is." In addition, one who loves God's kingdom "loves it wholly as God's kingdom on Earth." Bonhoeffer does not, though, understand the world or the earth to be perfect. It is a "cursed" earth. Nevertheless, it is into the cursed earth that Christ has come and established the "kingdom of Christ." The kingdom of Christ is, however, hidden. It is the "hidden

---

136. Ibid.

137. Ibid., 287.

138. Ibid. Bonhoeffer defines secularism as follows: "We have succumbed to secularism, and here I mean the pious, Christian secularism. Not the godlessness or cultural Bolshevism at all, but the *Christian* renunciation of God as the Lord of the Earth."

139. Ibid.

140. Ibid.

141. Ibid., 288.

142. Ibid.

Phase 2: Church and World in Heightened Tension 175

treasure in the cursed field." Ultimately, those who want to pray for the coming of the kingdom must do so "only as those wholly on the earth."[143] Bonhoeffer makes two other important points about this need for unity with worldliness. First, it must manifest in solidarity with those who are troubled.[144] Bonhoeffer's second important point is that the solidarity with the earth is a message particularly relevant to what is happening in the world today.[145]

Bonhoeffer frames his explicit discussion of church-state relations using the concept of the kingdom of God. God's kingdom is present on earth in the "duality of church and state." The kingdom of God is manifest in the church to the extent that it testifies to God's miracle in Christ's resurrection from the dead. The kingdom of God is manifest in the state to the extent that it "maintains the order of preservation of life and insofar as it accepts responsibility for preserving this world from collapse and for exercising its authority here against the destruction of life."[146] The form in which the kingdom of God exists in the world is only that of church and state. If one prays for the kingdom of God without taking into account both church and state one is thinking of either otherworldliness or secularity. Bonhoeffer reiterates the traditional Two Kingdoms doctrine: "The church limits the state, just as the state limits the church. And both must remain aware of this mutual limitation and support this tense juxtaposition, which should never be a coalescence. Only thus do both together, and never one alone, point to the kingdom of God, which is here attested in a splendid twofold form."[147] The church prays that it will fulfill its role of witnessing to the miracle of the resurrection and the state must fulfill its function of defending the "orders of the preserved world of the curse."[148] Bonhoeffer indicates that this vision of the mutually limiting and coexisting roles of church and state establish a vision of "Christendom," a somewhat conservative or traditional Lutheran position. He also stresses the importance of "obedience" on the

---

143. Ibid., 288–89.
144. Ibid., 289.
145. Ibid.
146. Ibid., 293.
147. Ibid., 294.
148. Ibid., 295.

part of the people to both the church and the state, another conservative or traditional Lutheran motif.[149]

Bonhoeffer's final portion of the lecture has eschatological overtones. It concerns the relationship between the currently existing kingdom of Christ and "not yet" kingdom of God. He writes, "Christ's kingdom is God's kingdom, but God's kingdom in the form ordained for us; not as a visible, powerful empire, as the 'new' kingdom of the world."[150] The kingdom of Christ is an otherworldly kingdom that has nevertheless entered into the "discord and contradiction of this world" and "appears as the powerless, defenseless gospel of the resurrection." It also appears as the state that maintains order. There will be a time when the kingdom of God becomes fully manifest, when "God will create a new Heaven and a new Earth." At that time there will be no more need for the church and the state.[151] For now, though, God calls us to obedience in the world in the forms of church and state. Bonhoeffer makes a distinction between existing conditions and conditions to come while avoiding discrediting the world.

Church-World Thinking and Political Thinking

Bonhoeffer's lecture has some elements in common with his earlier essay "What is the Church?"[152] There is an emphasis in both these writings, like there was in his first dissertation, on the embeddedness of the church in the world. It should be noted that Bonhoeffer also acknowledges the sinful nature of reality or history in his first dissertation. In these phase-2 works, however, there is both more and more precise attention paid to the conditions of the world the church enters. Moreover, this concentrated attention given to the nature of the world determines

149. Ibid.
150. Ibid.
151. Ibid.
152. See *NRS*, 153–57 for the full text of the essay. Bonhoeffer delivered a series of lectures at the University of Berlin in the summer of 1932. His summer lectures on the nature of the church were the impetus for a later essay entitled "What is the Church?" The essay is very similar to "Thy Kingdom Come" in terms of placing the church squarely in the world. Bonhoeffer writes, for instance, "But the church is a bit of the qualified world, qualified by God's revealing, gracious Word, which, completely surrendered and handed over to the world, secures the world for God and does not give it up. The church is the presence of God in the world. Really in the world, really the presence of God. The church is not a consecrated sanctuary, but the world, called by God to God" (153–54). See also *DB*, 213–14, for a description of the lectures and essay.

Phase 2: Church and World in Heightened Tension

what the church and state actually are, and what roles they should play. The church and state must limit each other. They must make sure that each plays its proper role in manifesting the kingdom of God under the conditions of finitude. Bonhoeffer understands that the world, while being the only conceivable ground upon which the church and state must reside and operate, is cursed or fallen. He also makes a distinction between the kingdom of Christ, which currently exists, and the coming kingdom of God. When the kingdom of God comes finally, there will be no more need for the church and the state. There is, therefore, given both the sinful condition of current reality and Bonhoeffer's eschatological impulse, a temporary, impermanent, or provisional feel to the structures of both church and state.

HITLER BECOMES CHANCELLOR AND THE BEGINNINGS OF *GLEICHSCHALTUNG* JANUARY 1933—APRIL 1933

The year 1933 was a particularly volatile year for the Germany and the church. Papen considered establishing an authoritarian presidential government after the November 1932 elections that would eliminate both the Weimar constitution and the extreme political parties. General Schleicher, the minister of defense, however, convinced Hindenburg to dismiss Papen and to appoint him chancellor. Papen, during Schleicher's maneuverings, plotted political revenge against him. He promised Hindenburg the mass support of the now struggling Nazi Party. Papen and Hitler met at the beginning of January 1933; with his party suffering from financial and other internal problems, Hitler was ready to negotiate with the German right. Papen proposed a new government wherein Hitler would be chancellor and himself vice-chancellor. Hindenburg seemed poised to install the Hitler-Papen government, especially since he was disappointed with some of Schleicher's decisions. Schleicher finally resigned his position as chancellor on January 28 when Hindenburg rebuffed both his pleas to squash the proposed Hitler-Papen government and to eliminate the extreme leftist and rightist parties.[153]

Even with Schleicher's departure and the vacated chancellorship, Hindenburg was reluctant to appoint Hitler as chancellor. Papen, however, tried to convince Hindenburg that he had Hitler under his control. Papen was, in effect, trying to use Hitler and the support of the Nazi

153. *HNG*, 66.

Party as a way to garner support for a Hindenburg government. Papen was confident that the number of conservatives in his cabinet would keep Hitler powerless.[154] He remarked to a suspicious colleague, "within two months we will have pushed Hitler so far into a corner that he will squeak."[155] Finally won over by Papen's arguments, Hindenburg appointed Hitler as chancellor on January 30, 1933.[156] Papen and Hindenburg, thinking Hitler would serve their political purposes, thus made one of the most naive miscalculations in modern history.

Nineteen-thirty-three would, indeed, mark the beginning of a maelstrom of political events centering on Hitler's quick consolidation of, and increase in, power. His total takeover of the government proceeded swiftly in stages. Hitler's first act was to temporarily dissolve the Reichstag on February 1. He was therefore able to rule by presidential decree until March 5 and the next set of elections for a new Reichstag. Hitler appealed to the people, calling for a "national revolution" whereby classes and class warfare would end. He labeled the Communists enemies of the Reich, and convinced Hindenburg to issue an emergency decree on February 4 that made Communist press releases and gatherings illegal.[157] In addition to the political maneuvering against the left, other pre-election activities included violence against the left or any other faction considered to be an ideological enemy of the Third Reich. Under the direction of Herman Göring, the Minister of the Interior, police personnel who were not sympathetic to the Nazi cause were purged and the SA and SS were made auxiliary police and granted the authority to operate independently. Communists and others suffered violence at the hands of the SA and the SS, dispelling Hitler's prized myth that his ascent to power was legal and bloodless.[158] One extremely significant Nazi maneuver came just one week before the election on February 27. When the building that housed the Reichstag burned down, the Nazis blamed Dutch Communist Marinus van der Lubbe and cited the fire as evidence of an attempted Communist Revolution. Hitler used the event as an excuse to have Hindenburg issue a Decree for the Protection of People and

---

154. Ibid., 67.
155. Ibid. Spielvogel quotes from Ewald von Kleist-Schmenzin, "Die letzte Möglichkeit," *Politische Studien* 10 (1959) 92.
156. *HNG*, 67.
157. Ibid., 69.
158. Ibid., 70.

Phase 2: Church and World in Heightened Tension 179

State allowing the police to intervene in any situation deemed to be a threat to public order and safety. In reality, the decree enabled Hitler to begin a reign of terror under the guise of a legally imposed police state. Civil liberties like free speech and the right to assemble were suspended and the SA and SS cracked down violently on political parties other than the Nazi Party.[159]

Bonhoeffer continued in his role as Youth Secretary of the World Alliance throughout Hitler's rise to power. He spent the autumn and winter of 1932 planning the ecumenical program for 1933. However, by March 1933 Bonhoeffer became occupied with matters relating to Hitler's rise to power and resigned from his chair as Youth Secretary.[160] Meanwhile, his lecturing continued at the University of Berlin. In the Winter Semester (1932–1933) Bonhoeffer delivered a series of lectures on the first three chapters of Genesis which was published as *Creation and Fall: A Theological Exposition of Genesis 1–3*.[161] It is important to note this work briefly for three reasons. First, the work marks Bonhoeffer's developing sense of commitment to the Bible as the source of God's authoritative Word. In the general spirit of Barth's *Epistle to the Romans*, Bonhoeffer was not much concerned with theories about the derivation of scriptural texts. Rather, he was interested in what the texts say to the church in its situation today.[162] Second, Bonhoeffer's explicit choice of an Old Testament text for exegesis, implying that the Word of God spoke equally in both testaments, stood in direct opposition to the anti-Judaic trends in his church at the time.[163] Finally, Bonhoeffer argues, as he did

---

159. Ibid., 70–71.
160. *DB*, 254.
161. *DB*, 216.
162. Bonhoeffer, *Creation and Fall*, 83. Bonhoeffer writes, "Our concern is the text as it presents itself to the church of Christ today."
163. Martin Rüter and Ilse Tödt, "Editors' Afterword to the German Edition" in Bonhoeffer, *Creation and Fall*, 147–73. Rüter and Tödt write, "The elimination of the Old Testament or 'Jewish' element for the sake of 'the people,' as Harnack advocated in this passage, and the artificial removal of Jesus from Judaism, became the central demands of National Socialism, and so of the 'German Christians' church politics, once Hitler was named Reich Chancellor on January 30, 1933. This demand began to be made, therefore, while Bonhoeffer was lecturing on 'Schöpfung und Sünde' ('Creation and sin'). From 1933 until the end of his life Bonhoeffer fought against this heresy" (157).

in other writings and contexts in this phase, for the concept of "orders of preservation" over "orders of creation."[164]

If Bonhoeffer's reiteration of the concept of "orders of preservation" represented an indirect criticism of Nazi ideology imbedded in a theological exegesis, his February 1, 1933 radio address "The Younger Generation's Altered View of the Concept of the *Führer*," delivered at the Potsdamerstrasse *Voxhaus*, was more direct. The address was mysteriously cut off before Bonhoeffer could deliver the damning conclusion. While there is no unquestionable proof, there is speculation that the Reich leadership had Bonhoeffer's speech cut short.[165] Bonhoeffer does not mention Hitler's name explicitly or criticize his concept of leadership or authority per se or from a liberal or humanistic stance. Rather, his task is to acknowledge legitimate structures of authority. Bonhoeffer relies on the concept of the distinction between the ultimate and penultimate (developed in his World Alliance talk) in his final paragraph to warn against any form of leadership wherein the earthly leader is confused with the divine.[166] Bonhoeffer's critique of politics is motivated by theological concerns related to the behavior of leaders and followers in a theoretical construct. He does not, as stated above, mention Hitler explicitly in the talk. Nevertheless, it seems fairly obvious that Bonhoeffer was speaking about Hitler. It seems a little more than mere coincidence that his final paragraph got cut off.

Hitler continued his swift rise to total power. The final pre-election tactic included Nazi takeovers of state and local governments. The SA would cause civil unrest and then the Nazis would use the disorder as an excuse for replacing existing governmental leaders. As for the March 5 election itself, the Nazis still could not achieve an outright majority.[167]

164. Bonhoeffer, *Creation and Fall*, 139–40.

165. *DB*, 259–60. The talk could actually be construed as favorable to the Reich without the part that had been cut-off. Bonhoeffer was horrified at this prospect and had the complete paper distributed to his friends and family and published in *Kreuzzeitung*. He was, in addition, able to deliver a longer version of the lecture at the College of Political Science in Berlin in the beginning of March. See also *NRS*, 190. The editors of *No Rusty Swords* state definitively that the Reich leadership cut the speech off. They write, "The authorities recognized the subversive nature of this broadcast shortly after it started and it was cut off before he ended."

166. *NRS*, 204. He writes, "Leaders or offices which set themselves up as gods mock God and the individuals who stand alone before him, and must perish. Only the Leader who himself serves the penultimate and the ultimate authority can find faithfulness."

167. *HNG*, 71.

Phase 2: Church and World in Heightened Tension 181

Hitler introduced the Enabling Act (the Law for the Removal of the Distress of People and Reich) whereby the government could issue laws without approval of the Reichstag. Hitler asked for the operation of this Act for four years.[168] The Nazi Party, meanwhile, continued its propaganda celebrating the bloodless revolution with large public holiday-like displays replete with Swastika flags replacing existing flags. The Enabling Act passed on March 24, 1933 with 444 votes against 94 opposing.[169]

Hitler quickly sought to further consolidate his power with his infamous program of *Gleichschaltung* (coordination). *Gleichschaltung* represented Hitler's attempt to bring all aspects of German life under a unified and centralized structure, like the Reich itself. *Gleichschaltung* also applied to the churches. The process began by making the party *Gauleiters* in the various states the Reich governors (*Reichstatthälter*). A March 31 law made it possible for these state leaders to make laws without the approval of state legislatures. The government bureaucracy was also subject to Hitler's coordination. At this time the main targets in the purging efforts were the Jews and any remaining leftists.[170] It was the April 7 Law for the Restoration of the Professional Civil Service, or the legislation containing the infamous Aryan Clauses, wherein religion and the Reich conflicted. The Aryan Clauses stated, in essence, that persons of Jewish descent could not participate in an official capacity in the church or in the state.[171]

Hitler's Point 24, which assured Nazi support for freedom of religion and for a "positive Christianity," was ambiguous enough, though, that the churches could not accuse the Nazi Party of any malice. The majority of German Protestants, in fact, considered January 30 a "day of liberation" from the despised democratic Weimar Republic.[172] Hitler's March 23, 1933, declaration on Christianity was an attempt to further the perception that the Nazi Party was both somehow Christian and neutral in terms of the various denominations.[173] Behind the scenes, however,

---

168. Ibid., 72.

169. Ibid., 72–73. Spielvogel describes the significance of the legislation: "Parliamentary democracy had been destroyed by parliamentary means."

170. Ibid., 73.

171. Craig, *Germany*, 579.

172. *CCUH*, 14.

173. Ibid., 84–85. Hitler's declaration reads, "The national Government sees in the two Christian Confessions the most important factors for the preservation of our na-

there was no doubt that the churches, because they were traditionally part of state bureaucracy (ministers were civil servants), would be subject to the Nazi project of *Gleichschaltung*. Hitler, in fact, had already begun to lend his support to the notion of a Reich Bishop who would serve as the head of a highly structured and unified Reich Church. All twenty-nine *Landeskirchen* would be united under the Reich Bishop.[174] Hitler personally chose the candidate for Reich Bishop, Ludwig Müller, over the more radical Hossenfelder.[175] Müller, while a committed Nazi and a friend and supporter of Hitler, was a moderate and would cause less suspicion. Hitler had an April 17 meeting with Müller in order to make sure they were in agreement on his role in the process by which the relationship between the Evangelical Church and the Nazi state would proceed. Müller was to make sure the process ran smoothly and eliminate any question as to whether or not the church would accept the Nazi political leadership.[176]

Die Kirche vor der Judenfrage (April 1933)

The event that provided the immediate context for Bonhoeffer's next relevant writing was the official Nazi passing of anti-Jewish policies and legislation. The first act was a one-day boycott of Jewish businesses on April 1, 1933. Hindenburg protested on the basis that Jews who had served in the military should not be subject to any discrimination, and

---

tionality. It will respect the agreements that have been drawn up between them and the provincial states. Their rights are not to be infringed. It expects, however, and hopes that conversely the work upon the national and moral renewal of our nation, which the Government has assumed as its task, will receive the same appreciation. All other denominations will be treated with impartial justice. The national Government will provide and guarantee to the Christian Confessions the influence due them in the schools and education. It is concerned for genuine harmony between Church and State. The struggle against materialism and for the establishment of a true community in the nation serves just as much the interests of the German nation as it does those of our Christian faith. The Reich Government, seeing in Christianity the unshakable foundation of the moral and ethical life of our people, attaches utmost importance to the cultivation and shaping of the friendliest relations with the Holy See. The rights of the churches will not be curtailed; their position in relation to the State will not be changed."

174. *NPC*, 34–35.
175. *CCUH*, 88.
176. *NPC*, 34–35.

Phase 2: Church and World in Heightened Tension

the Reich conceded.[177] The April 7 legislation that forbade Jews any official office in either church or state provided the immediate impetus for Bonhoeffer's essay. This legislation represented a direct intrusion in church affairs on the part of the state.

Bonhoeffer begins by noting that the Jew has been "subject to special laws by the state, solely on the basis of his race and regardless of the religion to which he adheres" throughout history. He asks important questions in light of this historical reality: what attitude should the church take toward the state's actions and what should the church do about the state's actions? He argues as he did in the Czechoslovakian address that an answer relies on a "right concept of the church."[178] Bonhoeffer affirms an idea common to both conservative and liberal interpretations of Two Kingdoms thinking: "the church of the Reformation is not encouraged to get involved directly in specific political actions of the state." The church should not "praise nor censure" the state's laws but must reaffirm the state as one of God's orders of preservation. The church must look at the state's ordinances from a humanitarian point of view and understand that they are "grounded in God's desire for preservation in the midst of the world's chaotic godlessness." [179] The church cannot intervene directly in the state's actions. Bonhoeffer even states that it is the state that makes history, and not the church. He does, however, qualify this statement by teaching that the church bears witness to God's coming in history, and therefore knows the true nature of the state and of history. Nevertheless, he reiterates that the church must let the state continue to make history. In a controversial statement, Bonhoeffer also argues that the "state is entitled to strike new paths" in response to the current Jewish question.[180] That is, Bonhoeffer leaves open the possibility that the state's current actions or any other future actions vis-à-vis the Jewish question would be legitimate because the state must be allowed to fulfill its particular function.

Bonhoeffer distinguishes between "humanitarian associations and individual Christians" or "a church that is essentially regarded as a cultural function of the state" and "the true church of Christ."[181] Humanitarian

177. *CCUH*, 31.
178. *DBWE-12*, 362.
179. Ibid., 363.
180. Ibid.
181. Ibid.

associations, individual Christians, and the church as a cultural institution criticize the state's moral offenses from a humanitarian ideal. The true church, which lives solely by the gospel, cannot and should not criticize the state's history-making decision from a humanitarian ideal.[182] He explains, "The church cannot primarily take direct political action, since it does not presume to know how things should go historically. Even on the Jewish question today, the church cannot contradict the state directly and demand that it take any particular course of action."[183] Just as the essay appears to be heading in the direction of a conservative interpretation of the Two Kingdoms doctrine, Bonhoeffer nuances his definition of the church's nature and role. In fact, it is precisely because the church does not "moralize about particular cases" that it can have a voice in politics. That is, the church becomes more able to concern itself with the larger and more universal question about the state holding to its proper function. Bonhoeffer defines that function as taking actions to keep law and order. The church is thus interested in political actions (or the state's actions) to the extent that they are or are not legitimate actions of a state.[184]

The church is interested in making sure the state remains the state from the perspective of the way God has ordained the two orders in the world. There is a kind of "mystical link" between the church and the state, whereby one's behavior affects the continued existence or functioning of the other.[185] The state, by its decisions and actions, can actually threaten its own existence as state and thereby the church's existence. The issue of the use of force to create law and order in the case of the Jewish question is thus a political concern of the church. That is, the church has the right to ask if the actions of the state are a legitimate manifestation of the state's task of creating law and order.[186] The standard against which the

---

182. Ibid.
183. Ibid.
184. Ibid., 364.

185. Zerner, "Church, State and the 'Jewish Question,'" 190–203. Zerner writes, "there remains a puzzling tension in Bonhoeffer's April 1933 description of the almost mystical link between church and state" (194).

186. *DBWE-12*, 364. Bonhoeffer explains, "The church will have to put this question with the utmost clarity today in the matter of the Jewish question. This does not mean interfering in the state's responsibility for its actions; on the contrary, it is thrusting the entire burden of responsibility upon the state itself for the actions proper to it. Thus the church spares the state any moralizing reproach, referring it instead to the function

Phase 2: Church and World in Heightened Tension

state must be held is whether or not it has either created too much law and order or too little law and order. Bonhoeffer, while admitting that the Christian church tolerated slavery for eighteen centuries, notes that slavery would be an example of "lawlessness." Too much law and order would also be problematic.[187] Finally, the state, while separated from the church by its different role and function, has its rights only to the extent that it recognizes its relationship with the church.

With all of the foregoing as foundation, Bonhoeffer finally gets to the main point of the essay. He argues that there are three distinct ways in which the church can conduct itself with respect to the state. First, the church can engage in "questioning the state as to the legitimate state character of its actions, that is, making the state responsible for what it does." Second, and in line with the sense of human solidarity developed in the earlier writings in this phase, the church can provide "service to the victims of the state's actions" (even those who are not Christians). Finally, in one of the most recognizable phrases in the whole Bonhoeffer corpus, he states that the church has as its responsibility to "not just to bind up the wounds of the victims beneath the wheel but to seize the wheel itself."[188] That is, the church has recourse to direct political action against the state.[189] This form of action is only desirable if the state is failing in its function of creating or keeping too little or too much law and order. In both cases the state would be jeopardizing both its and the church's existence. Bonhoeffer describes how the current situation fits in terms of the problems of too much and too little law. In a situation where a certain group is deprived of rights there is too little law. If, on the other hand, the state intervenes in the church and its proclamation, there is too much law.

---

ordained to it by the One who sustains the world. As long as the state acts in such a way as to create law and order—even if it means a new law and a new order—the church of the Creator, the Reconciler and Redeemer cannot oppose it through direct political action. Of course it cannot prevent individual Christians, who know that they are called to do so in certain cases, from accusing the state of 'inhumanity'; but as church it will only ask whether or not the state is creating law and order."

187. Ibid.

188. Ibid., 365–66.

189. Most all Bonhoeffer scholars equate the phrase "put a spoke in the wheel itself" with direct political action against the state. See for example, *TF*, 130–31. See also, *DB*, 275.

Bonhoeffer considers "the obligatory exclusion of baptized Jews from our Christian congregations" and the "ban on missions to the Jews" as instances of too much law and too little law. He even states that the church would be *in statu confessionis* (in a state where it should make an authoritative statement or confession of faith) and the state would be negating itself.[190] Bonhoeffer notes that, paradoxically, the third option involving direct political action of the church is an "expression of its [the church's] ultimate recognition of the state." Ultimately, though, Bonhoeffer does not recommend the third, most drastic recourse of direct political action against the state on behalf of the church in the case of the Jewish question. Rather, he argues that the first two options suffice and that the third might be a later option dependent on the decrees of an Evangelical Council.[191] Bonhoeffer's reluctance to encourage the third option might be the result of the lingering anti-Semitism he would have been familiar with, given his theological lineage and historical context. He states, for example, that the Jews "hung the redeemer of the world on the cross" and "must endure the curse for its action through a long history of suffering." He also quotes Luther to the effect that Jews "are the most miserable people on earth" and "are plagued everywhere, and scattered about all countries, having no certain resting place."[192] Bonhoeffer offers other patronizing Christian perspectives on the Jews.[193]

Church-World Relationship and Political Thinking

Bonhoeffer's essay is both somewhat unclear and offers some stereotypically anti-Semitic sentiment.[194] One might question whether he is suc-

190. *DBWE-12*, 366.
191. Ibid.
192. Ibid., 367.

193. Ibid. Bonhoeffer argues that the Jews, this people whom God has "loved and punished," are also in line for redemption or "final homecoming . . . And this homecoming will take place in Israel's conversion to Christ." Bonhoeffer, after quoting Luther on the need for Israel to "let go of the sins of its fathers" and "beg for the blood of the Crucified One to come down to reconcile them," argues that "the conversion of Israel is to be the end of its people's sufferings." While recognizing that human efforts cannot bring about the ultimate conversion of the Jews, he argues that efforts must continually be made to that end.

194. See Zerner, "Church, State, and the Jewish 'Question,'" 194–95. Zerner writes, "In Bonhoeffer's essay the most painful and problematic section for Jews and many post-Holocaust Christian thinkers is a string of sentences recapitulating traditional Christian teachings on: deicide, the cursed Jews, the rejected people, the Jewish prob-

Phase 2: Church and World in Heightened Tension

cessful in keeping both the "non-interfering" and "equal" components of the Two Kingdoms doctrine intact. On one hand, the church has no authority to disrupt the history-making decisions of the state and cannot directly address it concerning its political actions. On the other hand, the church, because it alone testifies to God's Word in history, knows better than the state what both history is and what the state is better than the state itself. It is in this sense that Bonhoeffer's argumentation seems to afford the church a higher status than the state. The church, on the basis of this superior position, is authoritatively informed about what role the state should be playing (creating law and order). It is from the platform of this knowledge that the church can define the state's role and even, if rarely, engage in direct political action against the state. The arguably higher status afforded to the church which seems to break the Two Kingdoms teaching on the equality in roles, goes hand in hand with breaking the non-interfering component of the Two Kingdoms doctrine, at least from the side of the church.

Some of the confusion can be explained by the above-noted "mystical link" between the church and state. Bonhoeffer holds that there is a mutually dependent relationship between the two entities. If one entity does not fulfill its role properly, it endangers the other entity's very existence and vice versa. This mutually informing co-existence or tension is ultimately based on an understanding of the church-world relationship or the church-and-state-in-world dynamic. Both the church and the state are firmly imbedded in reality. They simply have different roles. What is different in phase 2 is both the explicit attention paid to articulating how exactly it is that the church is situated in the world, and how it interacts with the state. In this essay he distinguishes the church from the world or "the worldly" with a distinction between the "true church" and humanitarian associations (or the true church and a church that serves as a moral guarantor or any other cultural functions for the state). The true church of Christ "lives solely from the Gospel." The teachings of the

---

lem, the suffering people 'loved and punished by God,' and the final homecoming in the conversion to Christ... When the United States Holocaust Memorial Museum held a ceremony on 29 May 1996 honouring Dietrich Bonhoeffer and Hans von Dohnanyi as righteous Gentiles, who helped save Jews, the invitation included the following: 'Although repudiating Nazism, Bonhoeffer also expressed the anti-Jewish bias of centuries-old Christian teaching.' While Bonhoeffer did not invent any of these categories or concepts, he uncritically quoted some of the earlier exponents of condescension, if not contempt, toward Jews."

true church do not derive from human or worldly realities and cannot be determined by any worldly realities such as the state. The true church does not allow itself to be used by the state to fulfill any functions.

Bonhoeffer's thinking in this essay is consistent with the shift from any hint of "orders of creation" thinking from phase 1 to the "orders of preservation" view which he introduced in his Czechoslovakian address. That is, there is a sense of impermanence or dissolvability of a given state if it does not fulfill properly its function of preserving law and order in the world. Bonhoeffer's thinking in this essay is, therefore, also characteristic of a more liberal interpretation of Luther's Two Kingdoms doctrine. It is the emphasis on the co-presence of the church and state in one shared reality and the simultaneous emphasis on what makes the church different from the state in that reality that accounts for the church's ability to actively or politically critique the state. In a bold move, Bonhoeffer goes beyond an even more liberal interpretation when he argues that the church might even take "direct political action" against the state. He seems, in this sense, to go beyond what would be acceptable by any Lutheran standards.

THE CONTINUING CHURCH STRUGGLE

Bonhoeffer's political thinking from April 1933 until the start of the third phase in October 1933 is consistent with a church-world relationship where the church is seen as having an authoritative message to deliver to an increasingly hostile or fallen world. Political events continued to provide good reason for Bonhoeffer's increasingly negative assessment of the world. Hitler's program of *Gleichschaltung* progressed in the remaining months of 1933. The KPD (Communists) had been officially banned in March and the SPD officially banned on June 22. After the deterioration of all the remaining parties the ultimate goal of a one-party state was realized with a July 14 law.[195]

In terms of the relationship between the Reich and the church, Hitler's superficially non-threatening intrusion into church affairs continued. Müller, Hitler's personal liaison with the Evangelical Churches, took over leadership of the *Deutsche Christen* on May 16, 1933.[196] Meanwhile Dr. Hermann Kapler, head of the Supreme Church Council

---

195. *HNG*, 74–75.
196. Koch, "The Theological Responses of Karl Barth and Dietrich Bonhoeffer," 9.

Phase 2: Church and World in Heightened Tension 189

of the Old Prussian Union, called a meeting of the German Evangelical Church Committee to discuss the movement toward a single unified Reich Church. The Kapler Committee, consisting of representatives from the Lutheran and Reformed traditions as well as Kapler and Müller, could not decide on a candidate for Reich Bishop. The *Deutsche Christen* group decided that their candidate would be Müller at a May 23 meeting in Berlin.[197] The other three in the Kapler Committee nominated Pastor Friedrich Von Bodelschwingh, who was elected over Müller in a series of elections by the German Evangelical Church Confederation.[198] However, the *Deutsche Christen* and other Christian groups protested Bodelschwingh's victory and held the election to be illegal.[199] When Kapler resigned from his position the State replaced him on June 24 with Dr. August Jäger, an "arrogant and narrowminded" lawyer for the *Deutsche Christen* who was more concerned with serving the Nazis than with the wellbeing of the church itself.[200] His first acts as leader of the church council included replacing the existing church administrators with other *Deutsche Christen*, ransacking the offices of the Evangelical News Agency and suspending all Prussian General Superintendents. Bodelschwingh resigned his position as Reich Bishop elect when he heard of Jäger's actions. Müller then proclaimed himself the Reich Bishop designate.[201]

Hossenfelder, a Nazi supporter and Vice-President of the Supreme Church Council of Prussia, ordered the Prussian churches to hold ceremonies recognizing the order that had been restored to the church.[202] However, the public outcry against Jäger's actions led President Hindenburg to force Hitler to rectify the church situation. Hitler reversed Jäger's appointments and set a July 22 date for church elections.[203] Buttressed by a speech by Hitler himself, Müller won the regional elections by a large margin.[204] The most significant of the series of regional synods held after the elections occurred in Prussia and is referred to as

197. *CCUH*, 95.
198. Ibid., 96.
199. Ibid., 98.
200. *NPC*, 36–37.
201. *CCUH*, 98–99.
202. Koch, "The Theological Responses of Karl Barth and Dietrich Bonhoeffer," 11.
203. *NPC*, 38–39.
204. *NPC*, 43–44.

the Brown Synod, where the Aryan clauses were accepted, an oath of loyalty to Hitler was adopted, and the majority of delegates donned the pro-Nazi brown uniform.[205] Finally, Müller was voted Reich Bishop at the September 27 National Synod held in Wittenberg.[206] It should be noted that although Hitler did take some measures indicating support for the *Deutsche Christen*, his and his Reich's "official" dealings with them did not indicate an unambiguous desire to accommodate the goals of their more radical factions.[207] The *Deutsche Christen* were not able to effect a complete church takeover, partly because of Hitler's inconsistencies and Müller's lack of vision.

Niemöller, a patriotic former U-Boat commander and pastor of the wealthy Dahlem congregation in Berlin, recognized the problems with the intrusion upon church operation presented by the Aryan clauses and led the Pastors' Emergency League.[208] The official birth of the Pastors' Emergency League dates to the time directly after the infamous Brown Synod described above, where "The Church Law on the Legal Position of Clergy and Church Officials," including the Aryan Clause, was passed without committee deliberation. The group of pastors that met immediately after the synod became the Pastors' Emergency League.[209] Bonhoeffer and Niemöller drew up a list of four points establishing the position of the League. The original version of the points strongly suggested the need for a church that was committed to the confession of the Reformation and against the Aryan clauses. It stated that those pastors who would enforce the Aryan Clause in their congregations would be excluding themselves from the communion of the church. The points were sent to Boldelschwingh for review and he immediately called some

---

205. See *DB*, 306–7, for a description of this "ominous" synod.

206. *CCUH*, 111.

207. *NPC*, 38–39. Hitler, for instance, reversed Jäger's decision to replace the existing church administrators with other *Deutsche Christen* and his decision to suspend all Prussian General Superintendents. See also Cochrane, *The Church's Confession under Hitler*, 111. Cochrane notes that Hitler thought clear or unambiguous Nazi support of one faction was not conducive to garnering the support of the highest possible number of Christians for the regime. See also, *NPC*, 49–50. Conway notes that Hitler was uncomfortable with the possibility that the strength and the appeal of the *Deutsche Christen* might set up a system of thought and authority which could rival the Nazi Party itself.

208. Koch, "The Theological Responses of Karl Barth and Dietrich Bonhoeffer," 16.

209. *DB*, 309.

Phase 2: Church and World in Heightened Tension

of the pastors for a meeting. Bodelschwingh watered down some of the sentences that implied self-exclusion by those adopting the clauses, thereby leaving the matter up to further debate. The document, along with an appeal to the churches for financial assistance to those who would be affected by the Aryan clauses, was sent to the pastors. There was an additional appeal to the German National synod. The response was overwhelming. By the end of 1933 the number of pastors in the League rose from two thousand to six thousand.[210]

In mid-October, Bonhoeffer finally followed through with his decision to go to London for a two-year commitment. There was some question, given all of his activity on behalf of the opposition, as to whether or not Bonhoeffer would be allowed to leave. Heckel, who had become the German Evangelical Church's official for foreign affairs, and thus Bonhoeffer's superior, warned Bonhoeffer that there might some opposition to his departure. Bonhoeffer, in a face-to-face meeting with Müller, indicated that he would not retract any of his statements, would not support the *Deutsche Christen* cause abroad and would continue to speak for the ecumenical movement. Müller finally allowed Bonhoeffer to leave.[211]

Bonhoeffer's departure for London is significant as it provides insight into his thinking at the time. He was basically misunderstood by the majority of his fellow resistors to the *Deutsche Christen*, especially concerning the seriousness and significance of the passing and possible implementation of the Aryan Clauses. Bonhoeffer, as noted above, even spoke with Hildebrandt earlier in the year about leaving the church entirely. Bonhoeffer was consumed with the idea that the church might draft an authoritative confession that would effectively establish a "free" church apart from the German Evangelical Church. The *Deutsche Christen*, from the perspective of this free church, would be schismatics who had broken away from the church faithful to the ideals of the Reformation.[212] Even Barth, who was clearly influential in Bonhoeffer's theological concern with confession and in agreement that the church was in a *status confessionis* situation, disappointed Bonhoeffer when he

---

210. Ibid., 310–11.

211. Ibid., 321. Bonhoeffer suspected that Müller was less fearful of a "misrepresentation" of the German situation abroad than he was of Bonhoeffer's potential "negative" impact on the churches in Germany.

212. Ibid., 307–8.

advised him to wait until there was a "clash over a more central point" to force a schism.[213] Even Niemöller sent Hitler a telegram on behalf of the Pastors' Emergency League in thanks to him and expressing loyal allegiance to him when Hitler announced that Germany had withdrawn from the League of Nations on October 14. This act indicated the extent to which Bonhoeffer's own allies differed from him.[214]

FORMS OF POLITICAL INVOLVEMENT

Bonhoeffer's understanding of the church-world relationship was consistent with his forms of political involvement during this phase in his life. He was active in the world in the form of extensive work in the ecumenical peace movement. Bonhoeffer, though, was not involved in politics as a politician or specifically in the name of any political party. He was not directly involved in the dynamics of party politics. Rather, he was directly involved in the church and in developing a theology for that church and the ecumenical movement as a whole. Some aspects of that theology had ramifications for political positions, particularly in the area of war and peace. There was, in his vision of the church and world in heightened tension, a sharpened concentration on what that church was as church apart from the world and on what exact message the church had to give to the world. The concentration was intense enough for Bonhoeffer to work strictly as a church person.

Bonhoeffer's first significant opposition activity was his involvement in the Young Reformation Movement.[215] The challenge to the church's sovereignty with the pending imposition of the Aryan clauses led several groups (concerned with theological matters) to form in opposition. Bonhoeffer and an important contact, Gerhard Jacobi, made

---

213. Ibid., 308–9.

214. *DB*, 323. Bonhoeffer and Hildebrandt disagreed with Niemöller's enthusiasm for Hitler's demand of "equal status" for Germany. Bonhoeffer even recognized that the withdrawal from the League of Nations would bring Germany closer to war. Hildebrandt, for his part, turned down Niemöller's offer of a post in the Pastors' Emergency League, citing the hypocrisy of Niemöller's support for Hitler's demand for "equality of status" when his Pastors' Emergency League "refuse[d] to adopt an unequivocal attitude toward a church which denies us [Jewish persons] equality of status." Hildebrandt left Germany to live with Bonhoeffer in London.

215. Koch, "The Theological Responses of Karl Barth and Dietrich Bonhoeffer,"14–15. The *Deutsche Christen* attained a legal injunction that forced the Young Reformers to change their name from the "Program of the Evangelical Church."

Phase 2: Church and World in Heightened Tension 193

a first visit to the Gestapo headquarters to protest the confiscation of Young Reformation literature.[216] In the May 1933 church elections the Young Reformers gave their support to Bodelschwingh.[217] Bonhoeffer also led a mass exodus of students from a large June 19 meeting of the German Christian Student Movement at the University of Berlin when support for Müller's candidacy was announced.[218] Three days later, at a meeting of professors, Bonhoeffer spoke on behalf of the Young Reformation movement against Emanuel Hirsch and others who supported the *Deutsche Christen*.[219] On the basis of a reading of Romans 14, Bonhoeffer warned that a schism was imminent and that a Protestant council would be necessary to define the church's true confession.[220]

In further action, Bonhoeffer protested when Jäger was appointed as the head of the Evangelical High Council. Seeing this as a direct intrusion into church affairs by the state, Bonhoeffer lead delegations to the Reich chancellery and composed a "Declaration of the Ministers of Greater Berlin" which was sent to the Reich chancellor with 106 signatures.[221] The state commissars, as noted above, were eventually removed and the original church office-holders were restored to their positions. Bonhoeffer and his friend Hildebrandt thought that their actions and the actions of the other ministers during the period of the dismissals were not radical enough. Bonhoeffer considered an actual interdict, where ministers would refuse to conduct funeral services. However, other pastors did not understand the Bonhoeffer and Hildebrandt's "political intransigence." Bonhoeffer and his friend even considered leaving the Protestant church altogether.[222]

Bonhoeffer's next activity included making leaflets and lists of candidates in a campaign effort for the July elections. The Gestapo interfered with the elections and with Bonhoeffer's efforts in particular, entering the offices of the Young Reformation Movement in Dahlem on July 17

---

216. *DB*, 281. The Young Reformers also issued a manifesto calling for independence and warning against the church going astray. The manifesto contained, along with Bonhoeffer's, the signatures of thirty-seven important leaders in the church struggle.

217. Ibid., 282.

218. Ibid., 286.

219. Ibid., 287.

220. Ibid., 287–89.

221. Ibid., 291.

222. Ibid., 292.

and destroying the pamphlets and literature. On July 18 Bonhoeffer and Jacobi made their second trip to the Gestapo office to protest to Rudolf Diels, head of the Gestapo. They argued with Diels over the obstructions in the elections and Diels agreed to return the literature if they dropped the title "List of the Evangelical Church" from the pamphlets. If, however, Bonhoeffer and Jacobi broke the terms of the agreement, they would be arrested.[223]

During his very active summer, Bonhoeffer also gave a series of lectures on Christology that would later become one of his most-read books.[224] In these lectures Bonhoeffer argues that Christ is present as the center of history and, since he presupposes that the church is "Christ existing as community," he holds that the church must be understood as the center of history. However, the church must remain the "hidden" center of history. Bonhoeffer's theoretical work here became a direct response to the practical situation when he argued that it is not proper for the hidden center to become visible as in the instance of a "state Church."[225] His sentiment here stands as a direct challenge to the project of the *Deutsche Christen* and also allows him to reiterate the theme of the mutual interdependence of church and state. It is only from its invisible "position" that the relationship between the church and state can be defined. The meaning and promise of the state is actually hidden in the church and therefore the church "judges and justifies the state." The state, "through actions that create law and order should "bring the goals of its people nearer to its fulfillment." Bonhoeffer even argues that the state could not be the state with this particular role without the existence of church.[226] He therefore reiterates the "mystical link" motif from his earlier work.

Bonhoeffer also reiterates the sense of impermanence (or the provisional nature) of a state. The way Bonhoeffer establishes this provisional sense is, however, markedly and explicitly Chistological in these lectures. He argues that it is the cross in particular as that which both fulfills the law and is the "fulfillment of the order of the state." The cross, however,

---

223. Ibid., 295.

224. See Bonhoeffer, *Christ the Center*, 118. The lectures, surviving today only as notes taken by several of Bonhoeffer's students and reconstructed by Bethge are sometimes titled *Christ the Center*.

225. *DBWE-12*, 325–27.

226. Ibid., 326.

Phase 2: Church and World in Heightened Tension 195

while affirming and fulfilling the order of the state, also breaks through and dissolves the order of the state. The state, thus, rather than being a permanent entity or an order of creation, has a precarious existence in light of the cross. Putting the emphasis on Christ as the standard of all reality's structures (rather than how they may exist as natural or intrinsic to creation), Bonhoeffer writes, "As a result, there has been a new relation between state and church since the historical event of the cross. The state has existed in its truest sense only since there has been a church. The true origin of the state is only found together with the church, on the cross, insofar as the cross fulfills and affirms law and order and at the same time breaks through it."[227]

Bonhoeffer received an invitation in August to take a post as the pastor of two German parishes in London. Bonhoeffer declined the offer at the time and headed toward Bethel to work on the opposition church's faith confession against the German Christians. Along with several other theologians, he worked hard on the famous Bethel Confession containing a redefinition of all major theological categories in light of the Reformation and the current theological errors of the *Deutsche Christen*. Bonhoeffer, however, passionately concerned with producing a confession that was in stark contrast to *Deutsche Christen* thinking, became disillusioned by certain dynamics in the writing and production which he considered to be dangerously conciliatory and ultimately refused to work on the final edition.[228] Bonhoeffer's departure for London was delayed by further engagement in the Church struggle, including a renewed battle over the Aryan Clause and the formation of the Pastors' Emergency League. In late August, there was still a question as to whether or not the synods would impose the clauses concerning racial purity in the church. Bonhoeffer wrote an inflammatory pamphlet warning against the implications of adopting the Aryan Clause during the first few months of August.[229] Much to his dismay, he alienated some of the people in the opposition church with some of his language. He even disagreed with Martin Niemöller, the pastor who would lead the Pastors' Emergency League (*Pfarrernotbund*) in the church struggle.

Ultimately, Bonhoeffer's form of political involvement during, and especially at the end of, the second phase, shows a clearer and stron-

---

227. Ibid.
228. *DB*, 302–3.
229. *DB*, 304–5.

ger connection between thinking and action than in the first phase. Bonhoeffer defined the church as having a message that it offers to the world and a role that it must fulfill vis-à-vis the state in the world. The church, while different from the world, must remain in a tension with it in order to make its message available and play its role effectively. The church cannot withdraw from the world. It must remain active therein and engage with the worldly. In this sense, Bonhoeffer remains wholly true to the Lutheran Two Kingdoms doctrine. In this second phase, however, his heightened sense of tension between the church and the world moves him into a more liberal interpretation, where the church's right to protest state interference in the church's role becomes primary.

The particular historical dynamic in Bonhoeffer's life situation that allowed this changed church-world dynamic (and the resulting changed understanding of how church and state should interact) to emerge was the question of the Aryan Clauses. Specifically, Bonhoeffer was concerned that the anti-Semitic ideology of the Nazi Party which resulted in the adoption of the Aryan clauses in the civil realm would become manifest in the church through the maneuverings of the *Deutsche Christen*. Bonhoeffer's actions were thus entirely consistent with his thinking—he battled ferociously with those both inside his camp and those outside of his camp over any compromise in the church's message, confession, or proclamation and over any unwarranted and unwanted intrusion on the part of the state.

While recognizing the extent to which the state could become a negative component of the world, Bonhoeffer did not find it necessary to paint the world or the state in entirely negative terms in his writings. Moreover, he did not find it necessary to withdraw from the world or the state in his actions. It should be clearly noted, though, that Bonhoeffer, while warning against making the leader a god in his February radio address and hinting at the possibility of direct political action against the state in his April address on the Jewish question, engaged primarily in writing about theological concerns and involving himself in church politics. Bonhoeffer did visit the Gestapo offices twice. His intent was, however, to make sure that the new Nazi state would act like a state should act by allowing the church to be the church. Bonhoeffer did not try to actually destroy the Gestapo offices or hinder their operations. He was just calling them to their role in letting the church be the church by allowing pamphlets to be distributed. If Hitler and his Nazi state had

Phase 2: Church and World in Heightened Tension

unequivocally or explicitly accepted the *Deutsche Christen* as the organ of the State, then his Gestapo visits would have been closer to direct political action against the state. Bonhoeffer did not partake in direct political action against the state until his conspiratorial activities and the attempt on Hitler's life during the last phase of his life.

With this in mind, Bonhoeffer remains subject to the criticisms of Koch and others that while certainly exceptional amongst his fellow opposers to the *Deutsche Christen*, he was concerned mostly with the church itself, its theology, and the nature of its confession. He was concerned that the church and state interacted in a way faithful to the parameters of that relationship as it was defined in the German Lutheran tradition. Bonhoeffer involved himself in the church struggle in this phase because the state was in danger of not acting as a state should act. The *Deutsche Christen* too, and to some extent even his fellow opposers to the *Deutsche Christen*, were not acting as the church should act.

THE NATURE OF THE CHANGE

Scholars and interpreters of Bonhoeffer's life and thought recognize and place a shift or change in Bonhoeffer's thinking and behavior sometime between 1931 and 1932. Where they put the change, how they explain it, and what they say actually changed are somewhat different for each scholar. Bonhoeffer himself referred to such a change on at least two occasions. Looking back at his life from his cell in Tegel prison in 1944, he wrote, "I don't think I've ever changed much, except perhaps at the time of my first impression abroad, and under the first conscious influence of Papa's personality. It was then that a turning point from the phraseological to the real ensued."[230] In another letter written in 1936 Bonhoeffer writes,

> I plunged into work in a very unchristian way. An . . . ambition in me that many noticed made my life difficult . . . Then something happened, something that has changed and transformed my life to the present day. For the first time I discovered the Bible . . . I had often preached, I had seen a great deal of the church, spoken and preached about it—but I had not yet become a Christian . . .

---

230. *DBWE-8*, 358. See also, *ATS*, 106. Green emphasizes (in a footnote concerning Bonhoeffer's statement) that, "many years prior to the 1944 statement Bonhoeffer had explicitly identified the *Bible* as the most decisive factor in this 'turning,' not his travels or his father."

> I know that at that time I turned the doctrine of Jesus Christ into something of a personal advantage for myself . . . I pray to God that will never happen again. Also I had never prayed, or prayed very little. For all my loneliness, I was quite pleased with myself. Then the Bible, and in particular the Sermon on the Mount, freed me from that. Since then everything has changed. I have felt this plainly, and so have other people about me. It was a great liberation. It became clear to me that the life of a servant of Jesus Christ must belong to the church, and it became clearer to me how far that must go. And then came the crisis of 1933. This strengthened me in it. Also I now found others who shared this purpose with me. The revival of the church and of the ministry became my supreme concern . . . I suddenly saw the Christian pacifism that I had passionately opposed as self-evident—during the defense of my dissertation, where Gerhard [Jacobi] was also present. And so it went on, step by step. I no longer saw or thought anything else.[231]

Bonhoeffer's personal statements and the writings that make up the bulk of this chapter indicate a change noted by all Bonhoeffer scholars. Bethge, indicating that others surrounding Bonhoeffer also sensed the change, labels it "The Transition from Theologian to Christian."[232] Bethge places the change at the time of the return from America.[233] Kuhns describes the change as follows, "America . . . acted as a watershed. The young man who sailed to New York in September with a keen determination to raise and face substantive theological questions returned, sensing deeply his responsibility to the Church on a level where theology could never be completely accurate."[234] Clifford Green, for his part, locates the change in late 1932. Terrence Reynolds, describing Green's work, shows how Bonhoeffer's newfound interest in Christian piety, regular prayer,

---

231. *DB*, 204–5. Bethge quotes a January 27, 1936, letter from Finkenwalde from *DBW* 14:112–14.

232. See ibid., 202–6 for Bethge's section, "The Transition from Theologian to Christian."

233. Ibid., 173. He writes, "Bonhoeffer's return to Germany in 1931 represented a break in his development that was certainly sharper than the momentous political and ecclesiastical upheaval that followed two years later. The second phase major phase of his career began now, not in 1933."

234. Kuhns, *In Pursuit of Dietrich Bonhoeffer*, 33, 37. Kuhns continues, "Bonhoeffer's later ecumenical drive, his work to create a warm human community in the seminary he would someday operate in Finkenwalde, his growing awareness of the pastoral relationships among churches as being a major ecumenical need: these are probably the fruits, largely, of his year in America."

Phase 2: Church and World in Heightened Tension

Bible study, and worship stemmed from a recognition that his ego and reliance on "knowledge, education, intellectual acuteness, strength and confidence of will" ultimately pitted him against God.[235] Common across all of the interpretations is a spiritual experience or awakening of sorts that included an intense interest in the Bible, the church, personal spirituality, and a move away from academic and philosophical theology.

Scholars' judgments about the nature of Bonhoeffer's changes are interpretations. Bonhoeffer, of course, did not spend much time or effort trying to fit his own statements into any comprehensive framework, theological or otherwise. My work, like other scholarly works, attempts to place Bonhoeffer's statements of self-assessment into a larger framework and thereby draw out their fullest possible meaning. My framework, as described in my first chapter, is the connection between Bonhoeffer's political thinking and behavior and his notion of the church-world relationship. Is the nature and extent of the change of which Bonhoeffer wrote and I have described such that one could reasonably call it an actual break in his thinking and his action with respect to the first phase?

There are a few important themes involving the church-world relationship in this phase which, when compared to their treatment in the first phase, indicate the nature and extent of the change. The first theme concerns whom or what group of people, specifically, constitutes a person's neighbor. In his early writings, he used the Hegelian-influenced language of his dissertation mentor Seeberg and the sociologists to envision the church as an ethical *Kollektivperson* calling for ethical responsibility to the concrete neighbor. The state or nation was also a *Kollektivperson* wherein the same ethical responsibility was implied. While not entirely clear on the relationship between the church and the world or church and state, Bonhoeffer basically argued that the church has the Word and the sacrament that it must offer to a world or culture somewhat reluctant to receive them. The state has the non-interfering role of making history.

Thus for Bonhoeffer there was a tension between the church and the world and the church and the state. However, this tension did not imply a need for the church to withdraw from the world or Christians from the state. In fact, Bonhoeffer's concern with the concreteness of the church in the world and its embeddedness, along with the state, in sin-ridden history, made ethical responsibility an absolute necessity. In the

---

235. Reynolds, *The Coherence of Life without God before God*, 37. Reynolds quotes from Green, *Bonhoeffer: The Sociality of Christ and Humanity*, 166.

specific ethical demand presented by war, Bonhoeffer was very clear that the Christian must partake in this history-making action of the state. More importantly, he was also very clear, echoing Luther and others, in stating that one's own sphere of ethical responsibility in a war situation is limited exclusively to one's own family, nation, or *Volk* rather than to an idealistic (international) notion of humanity as a whole. Allowing one's actions in the ethical sphere to be determined by an abstract idea rather than the concrete thou in a present situation represented an irresponsible avoidance of an obligation. Bonhoeffer's particular understanding of the tension in the church-world relationship in the first phase, with its presupposing concerns both with acting in history and with the demand presented by the concrete other in any situation, forces him to adopt an arguably nationalistic position on war. His use of the concept of the organism-like *Kollektivperson* for the state, where nations have an identity like human persons and grow and expand like individual human persons, allows him to even support aggressive wars in the Barcelona lecture.

In the second phase, Bonhoeffer's heightened appreciation of the tension in the church-world relationship, wherein the church's possession of a message defines it as a distinct type of entity set more starkly against a more negatively construed outside world, establishes a single universal community of Christians in response to the authoritative Word. Now, in the face of the cross and the universal experience of sinfulness in light of it, all Christian humanity, both within and without any particular nation or state, is one. It almost appears as if Bonhoeffer has designated the international body of Christian believers as the *Kollektivperson* from his first phase. Or, as Rasmussen notes of Bonhoeffer's American sermon, he shifted "'Volk' from an organic national entity to a supernational, ecclesiological one."[236] As for the state, there is no more talk of it as *Kollektivperson* in the second phase. In addition, there is no more discussion of a *volkskirche*.

In terms of the new understanding of the church-world relationship and political positions (where the church is now an international community imbued with an authoritative Word of peace in the midst of a larger world) war, for example, is clearly no longer something unequivocally acceptable for the Christian. Bonhoeffer does not espouse absolute pacifism or state that war is always an unacceptable choice for

---

236. *RR*, 100.

Phase 2: Church and World in Heightened Tension

a state. He does not even require conscientious objection for any or all Christians in this universal community. What he does say explicitly is that the universal church should work for peace. In another argument that connects his church-world thinking and political positions, he argues that peace is a condition necessary for the continued proclamation of the gospel. Consistent with the idea of the world and church in a heightened tension, Bonhoeffer argues for a universal community that struggles to establish peace.

Another area where Bonhoeffer's personal transformation influenced his understanding of the church-world relationship and, ultimately, his political thinking and behavior, was his choice of the Sermon on the Mount as a central component of the authoritative message that the church has to offer the world. As Rasmussen notes, it was around 1932 when "Bonhoeffer began his love affair with the Sermon on the Mount."[237] This particular dynamic marks a significant change from phase 1 in a few ways. First, there is the general idea that Bonhoeffer actually designates a concrete theme or biblical motif as the Word about which he spoke in only a theoretical manner in the first phase. The second significant shift involves the content of the Sermon on the Mount itself. The Sermon on the Mount, perhaps more than any other set of biblical directives, presents direct challenges to a Christian's ability to live in a manner that is uncritical of the world and its structures or its normal course of action.

The Sermon on the Mount's world-challenging stance is particularly evident in the area of war and peace. The particular way in which Bonhoeffer understands the nature of the Christian's response adds to the significance of his use of it beyond the obvious pacifist-leaning themes in the Sermon. Bonhoeffer emphasizes in some of these phase-2 writings the need for Christian obedience to the call of Christ as manifest in the Word or the commandment. The change away from the first phase is evident. In his first-phase lecture, Bonhoeffer is adamant that even the directives of the Sermon on the Mount are not to be taken literally or as laws in any given present. In fact, while not dismissing the directives of the Sermon on the Mount as something that may help establish a part of the total context in which an ethical decision is made, Bonhoeffer ultimately gives precedence to a somewhat nebulous idea. He argues that ethical responses are formulated in terms of the claim made by divine command and the concrete need in the situation. In phase 2, he begins

237. RR, 102–3.

to designate the Sermon on the Mount as a specific set of directives to which the Christian should respond.[238] It is no surprise, then, that Bonhoeffer begins to espouse pacifist themes. In his first phase, where the Word was left devoid of content, there was less chance that following it would put one at odds with the state or take any significantly state challenging ecclesial or political action. Designating the content of the Word as the Sermon on the Mount heightened the tension between the church and the world and raised the possibility of undertaking activity or taking positions considered to be anti-state.

Perhaps the most notable change from phase 1 to phase 2 in terms of the church-world relationship/political thinking dyad is his shift from the concept of the nation or state as an "order of creation" to an "order of preservation." Bonhoeffer does not explicitly state that the nation is an order of creation in the first phase and he is therefore not placed in the same category with the excessively nationalistic theologians who did. He did, though, hold in his dissertation that the state is a community (rather than a society) that exists permanently or "from God to God." Furthermore, in his Barcelona lecture he likened a nation to a person who needs to grow, expand, and conquer other nations if necessary. These are positions markedly and undeniably similar to those of the War theologians who were influenced by orders of creation thinking. However, in his second phase, where the church's word, and later Christ Himself, is placed in a centralized or more prominent and distinct position vis-à-vis the world, the orders of the world become relativized. Nations can no longer be thought of as permanent entities or structures given with creation. They are, rather, ways in which God manifests Godself in the structures of the world in light of Christ. Bonhoeffer uses the term "orders of preservation" instead of orders of creation both because they begin with Christ (not with creation) and because these structures that allow for the continued proclamation of the Word in the world have a provisional nature. That is, these structures can and should

---

238. *DB*, 204. Bethge describes Bonhoeffer's behavior in 1932: "More and more frequently he quoted the Sermon on the Mount as a statement to be acted upon, not merely used as a mirror." See also, Bonhoeffer, "A Theological Basis for the World Alliance," 104. It should be noted, though, that Bonhoeffer attempts to avoid making the Sermon on the Mount into a law. He writes, "We have simply to take the Sermon on the Mount seriously, and to realize it. That is our obedience towards God's commandment. To this we must say: Even the Sermon on the Mount may not become the letter of the law to us."

Phase 2: Church and World in Heightened Tension 203

be dissolved if they no longer preserve the possibility for the continued proclamation of Christ. They are not permanent.

Closely connected to his radical shift from orders of creation to preservation is his changed thinking on the relationship between church and state. There was no emphasis on the church's ability to criticize the state in phase 1. In phase 2, and partly because the state was now an order of preservation, the church is now free to criticize the state if it does not act in such a way as to allow the church to continue making its proclamation. If the state does not act as an order of preservation, it can and should be dissolved. The church's ability to fulfill its role is dependent on the state fulfilling its role. Bonhoeffer's emphasis on the centrality and importance of the church's authoritative message, and the accompanying increased tension with the world, has allowed him to more clearly articulate their respective roles and their relationship. The state provides law and order and the church offers the Word and sacrament.

I have argued that Bonhoeffer's actions were "consistently consistent" with his thinking in all four phases. So, if there is a significant change in his church-world thinking from phase 1 to phase 2, there should be a significant change in his form of political activity. This is exactly what we observe. Bonhoeffer's phase-1 activity was not counter-state. Bonhoeffer did not take up a pacifist position, a position which was considered counter-world by Luther himself let alone the ultra-conservative Lutheranism existing in Bonhoeffer's Germany. In fact, while not an ultra-conservative "war theologian," he took positions on war that echoed their voluntarist theology. He was politically active only in the respect that he supported the status quo. Bonhoeffer was, essentially, an adherent of a reasonably conservative version of the Lutheran Two Kingdoms doctrine. He was a typical German Lutheran pastor and academic, his activity relegated mostly to teaching and scholarship.

Bonhoeffer's activity is significantly different in the second phase. Along with his increased concern with the nature of the church's message to the world came a radical concern with the church itself. He became active in the church in Harlem, the ecumenical church, and especially in the church that was emerging in response to the *Deutsche Christen*. His adoption and espousing of a form of pacifism was an expression of both his sense of unity with others in other nations and his choice of the Sermon on the Mount as an important component of the church's message to the world. He placed the world and the church in a more pronounced tension than he did in the first phase but not so pronounced as to preclude action in the world. In fact, in addition to his pastoral and ecumenical work, Bonhoeffer was very active in his struggle against the *Deutsche Christen* project of allowing state-ideology to influence their theology and activity as a church. He was intensely concerned with the nature of the church's confession and its continued freedom to make that confession. He was thus in line with a more liberal interpretation of the Two Kingdoms doctrine, exercising the church's right to protest undue state influence. His action in the church struggle was the impassioned manifestation of his thinking whereby the state must be called to its proper task and the state called to its proper task.

With all of the foregoing in place it is possible to make a judgment concerning the nature of Bonhoeffer's change in thinking and behavior from phase 1 to phase 2. Does it represent a break, a development, or a shift? There is the obvious matter of a radical change in genres. Bonhoeffer's writings in the first phase, with the exception of some existing sermons, are theoretical works for the academy written in dialogue with philosophy and sociology. However, his second phase works owe little to philosophy. Rather, they are biblically based, directly relevant to the church, and reflect a disciplined and dedicated life in the church. This fact in addition to the other significant changes discussed in this present section lean us heavily to the judgment of a break, where both the church-world thinking and its accompanying form of political involvement are different in kind from their counterparts in the first phase.

Labeling Bonhoeffer's move from phase 1 to phase 2 an outright break is tricky, however, because of the presence of some continuity in an important and even foundational area. The church and the world are still in a tension in the second phase. That is, the church, while more self-defined against an increasingly negative world, is never put in an entirely different sphere. This is essentially why the Lutheran Two Kingdoms doctrine still operates in Bonhoeffer's second phase. The other point of continuity is directly connected to the continued adherence to the Two Kingdoms doctrine across the first two phases. While indisputably moving from a conservative to a liberal interpretation of the doctrine in both thought and actions, Bonhoeffer remains, in many ways, subject to the inherently or overall conservative nature of the doctrine itself. That is, even in liberal interpretations, where the church's ability to criticize the state is emphasized, direct political action against the state is not

Phase 2: Church and World in Heightened Tension

encouraged. Direct political action on behalf of the church would, in a sense, release the tension that exists between the church and the state as their explicitly stated distinctive roles would overlap. The church would be acting as the state.

Even with these points of continuity there are two significant ways in which Bonhoeffer manages to stray from a more liberal interpretation of the Two Kingdoms doctrine. The first divergence is the adoption of pacifist sounding themes, which are not prevalent in either conservative or liberal versions (especially the version operating most popularly in Bonhoeffer's Germany). I have argued, though, that while Bonhoeffer is not very specific about what form of pacifist he might be, it is clear that it is not the world-denying absolute pacifism associated with Christian sectarianism. Absolute pacifism releases the tension between church and world by putting them into two separate spheres. Bonhoeffer's form of pacifism, to the extent that it involves struggle or work in the world, stays within the tension between church and world. The second divergence is his suggestion, in his essay on the Jewish Question, that the church have recourse to direct political action against the state. Again, and like pacifism, this is not a common facet of conservative or liberal interpretations of the Two Kingdoms doctrine (and again, especially the version operating most popularly in Bonhoeffer's Germany). It should be noted, though, that while Bonhoeffer raised the possibility of direct political action against the state, he neither engaged in that action nor did he think the church should have done so at that point. The politically-related actions he took vis-à-vis the state were all taken specifically as a church person, in the interests of the church, in the name of the church, and did not involve violence or alignment with any existing political party. To this extent, Bonhoeffer keeps the tension between the church and state in place.

Given the fact that Bonhoeffer maintains the tension between the church and the world (and church and state) in the second phase, it seems appropriate to call his change in the church-world relationship and accompanying political thinking and involvement some form of development. The names I have chosen for the chapters themselves suggest such a development, "church and world in mild tension" to "church and world in heightened tension." However, there is enough outright difference in his thinking and action to label his change a kind of a break. Bonhoeffer's change from phase 1 to phase 2 was a nuanced or "qualified" break.

Finally, looking at Bonhoeffer's career through the lenses of the church-world relationship in terms of his historical context allows us to both pinpoint the time of the qualified break and to understand the remainder of his thinking and action in the second phase in light of where the break occurred. As Bonhoeffer himself and others have suggested, the break happened in America.[239] Bonhoeffer was sounding pacifist themes and getting involved in the church in America in a way that was different than his first phase involvement well before the political crises of late 1932 into early 1933. The German church struggle and the rise of Hitler simply allowed the insights from his personal spiritual transformation in America to manifest themselves in his discourse in the form of a heightened tension between church and world and involvement in the ecumenical church and the church struggle itself.

LOOKING AHEAD

Bonhoeffer's second phase thinking indicated strong worldly themes and similarly strong anti-worldly sentiment.[240] At the end of 1933, Bonhoeffer seemed poised to go in one of two directions. He emphasized the church's embeddedness in the world and offered a more refined definition of what authoritative message the church might have to offer to the world. Accordingly, he adhered to a more liberal interpretation of the Two Kingdoms doctrine. Thus, Bonhoeffer seemed poised to continue his outward (and growing political) battle with the oncoming Nazi regime. He even mentioned the possibility for the church of direct political action against the state or even possibly, if indirectly or accidentally, aligning itself with a political party.[241] One direction might have

---

239. *DB*, 173. I vary from Bethge on this point. I hold, with Bethge, that the break did not happen in 1933. I disagree with his placement of the break upon the return to Germany from America.

240. Ibid., 254. Bethge sums up Bonhoeffer's dualism at the end of 1932 well. He writes, "At the end of this period it appears that the two opposite poles of Bonhoeffer's thought—the eschatological majesty of revelation and the relevance of the real world were more firmly and broadly anchored. His knowledge of the real world had grown personally, geographically and politically. Would these two poles attract or repel each other? Eschatology had undoubtedly gained in intensity, but reality too had become more vivid."

241. *NRS*, 156–57. Bonhoeffer, in his essay "What Is the Church?," raises the possibility that the church might have to make use of an existing political party in carrying out the command. He calls this a "final possibility," an extreme measure.

Phase 2: Church and World in Heightened Tension 207

been a sustained and continued involvement in the world in the form of struggle against oncoming Nazi tyranny. The involvement might have been relegated solely to ecclesial activity, direct political action, or some combination of both. Direct political action on behalf of the church would essentially release the tension between church and world by jeopardizing the mutual non-interference component of Two Kingdoms thinking.

On the other hand, Bonhoeffer was increasingly attentive to both the negativity of the world and to what the church's authoritative message might be to the world. Specifically, he was starting to consider the Sermon on the Mount as a primary component of the gospel message. Adherence to the Sermon on the Mount compelled the Christian to sole and direct obedience to Christ. Bonhoeffer espouses pacifist themes. The form of pacifism was not, though, absolutist (an eternal moral principle valid for all times and places) or the anti-worldly apolitical pacifism associated with exclusivist sects or the historic peace churches. Nevertheless, with his increasingly negative understanding of the world and corresponding developing sense of the church's difference from the world, Bonhoeffer seemed poised to move in that direction. That direction threatened to release the tension between the church and the world or the church and the state by placing them in entirely different spheres.

Bonhoeffer's decision to leave Germany altogether for London pastoral work and an essay given to his students upon his departure ("What Must the Student of Theology Do Today?") provide a clue as to which one of these two paths he would choose. He wrote, "the worldliness which he [the student of theology] likes to assume may yet serve him very ill, and it is really quite impossible to see how unmitigated worldliness can be regarded as the decisive criterion of the good theologian."[242]

---

242. *DB*, 322.

5

Phase 3: Church against or apart from World

INTRODUCTION

THE THIRD PHASE OF Bonhoeffer's life was marked by several important political and ecclesial events. Nazi neutrality in church matters eventually gave way to persecution as Hitler's Third Reich continued to advance in power and control. The resistance to the *Deutsche Christen*, concentrated originally in the Young Reformers and in the Pastors' Emergency League, found its final expression in the official creation of the Confessing Church (*Bekennende Kirche*) at a May 1934 synod in Barmen. Bonhoeffer's forms of involvement included a two-year pastorate in a few German-speaking churches in London, continued participation in the ecumenical movement, and help in the formation of the Confessing Church. His work in the ecumenical realm consisted mostly of trying to get the Geneva-based organizers of conferences to recognize the Confessing Church as the only legitimate church in Germany. His work for the Confessing Church consisted mainly of operating two monastery-like seminaries.

In this chapter I will argue that Bonhoeffer's dissatisfaction with the direction of the resistance and the ecumenical church leadership and his awareness of the increasingly hostile Third Reich manifested themselves theologically in a formulation of the church-world relationship where the two entities are against or apart from each other. While the relationship of opposition seems to maintain some type of tension (what I have called a "mild" or "heightened" in previous chapters), Bonhoeffer actually gets very close to releasing the first and second phase tensions by placing the church and world in separate spheres. He thus removes the necessary foundations for meaningful interaction, leading to a vision of the church that appears to be unconcerned with happenings in the political realm. Bonhoeffer, in tandem with this changed conception of the church-world relationship, makes statements that are the closest to absolute pacifism in his whole corpus in this phase. He arguably approaches a sect-like conception of the church associated with the world-withdrawn, pacifistic, and apolitical historic peace churches. In terms of a broad or all-encompassing definition, his particular church-world vision and accompanying political thinking and behavior gets close to an "apolitical pacifism."

I will, in addition, show how Bonhoeffer's changed understanding of the church-world relationship was consistent with his forms of political involvement. Bonhoeffer was still involved in the ecumenical movement, involved in the official formation of the Confessing Church, and in the continued church struggle. While not entirely withdrawn from the world, he did withdraw dramatically and unadvisedly to London from the center of the heated political and church-political controversy in Germany. Moreover, his work as leader of the monastery-like seminaries, while related to the church struggle, was performed far from the arena of the church struggle. Ultimately, Bonhoeffer's work in the third phase was almost entirely concentrated in and on the church itself with no direct concern with any sphere outside the church, including the political.

As in the preceding chapter, I will argue for the connection between Bonhoeffer's church-world thinking and specific forms of political thinking after the individual sections treating his important phase-3 writings. I will cover how this church-world/political thinking connection relates to his particular forms of political behavior in summary form in a section near the end of the chapter.

LONDON PASTORATE (OCTOBER 1933—MARCH 1935)

Bonhoeffer accepted a position as a pastor in London and moved into the German parsonage in Forest Hill, a South London suburb, on October 17, 1933. He was responsible for two of the six German congregations in London, Sydenham, and St. Paul's.[1] Back in Germany, Hitler's program of *Gleichschaltung* continued in the remaining months of 1933. The KPD (Communists) had been officially banned in March and the SPD offi-

---

1. *DB*, 328–29.

cially banned on June 22. After the deterioration of all the remaining parties, the ultimate goal of a one-party state was realized with the law of July 14.²

The only remaining obstacle to total control actually came from within the party itself, the SA (*Sturmabteilung*). Ernst Röhm, the leader of the SA, deplored Hitler's July 6 announcement that the revolution was over. He was also concerned that Hitler might consider the existing German army as the core of the new military instead of his SA. Hitler favored the army over the SA and made his views clear at a meeting on February 28, 1934. Hitler's actions did not quell the SA's real threat to the newly established Reich. Hitler's response was the forceful "Night of the Long Knives" or "Blood Purge" on June 30, 1934. Hitler personally arrested Röhm and other SA leaders. Röhm and over one hundred others were mercilessly slaughtered. On July 20, 1934, Hitler made the SS independent from the SA, relegating the latter to mere ceremonial functions.³ Finally, Hitler combined the offices of president and chancellor into his own person upon President Hindenburg's death on August 2, 1934. Hitler was the Führer.⁴ His power was complete.

On the church front, the strained relationship between the Reich and the *Deutsche Christen* continued. The *Deutsche Christen* held the infamous twenty thousand person Berlin Sports Palace Demonstration on November 13, where Dr. Reinhold Krause delivered an inflammatory speech.⁵ Müller, in response to the Pastors' Emergency League's protest against the demonstration, denounced Krause's speech and dismissed Krause from his position. However, in a move that earned him the title *Lügen* Müller (lying Müller), Müller encouraged Hossenfelder, another member of the *Deutsche Christen*, to take Krause's place.⁶ In another shocking move, Müller incorporated the Evangelical Youth of Germany

---

2. *HNG*, 74–75.

3. Ibid., 76–79. See also, Shirer, *The Rise and Fall of the Third Reich*, 213–26, for an account of the Blood Purge.

4. Ibid., 79.

5. *NPC*, 52–53. Krause was a district supervisor representing the *Deutsche Christen*. Krause demanded the instatement of the Aryan clauses, the removal of the Old Testament, the discharge of ministers not willing to cooperate with these demands, and the creation of a single unified national church sympathetic to the Nazi cause among other things. See also *CCUH*, 112–13.

6. Ibid., 114.

Phase 3: Church against or apart from World 211

into the Hitler Youth.[7] Müller's response to the opposition was to issue the infamous "Muzzling Order" on January 4, 1934, which stated that ministers could not make any reference to the church controversy in their sermons. Finally, Müller reversed the November 16 law preventing the imposition of the Aryan Clauses. This action effectively re-imposed the Aryan Clauses.[8]

Despite the "Muzzling Order," there was a huge outcry of the Pastors' Emergency League against Müller's actions that forced Hitler to take action. Uprisings in speech or writing against the Reich Bishop were to be reported to the Gestapo.[9] Both sides appealed to Hitler and Hindenburg. The opposition wanted Müller to resign. Disgusted with the Evangelical Church's inability to fall into line, Hitler finally agreed to meet with twelve important members of the churches to discuss the viability of Müller's Reich bishopric. The opposition's hopes for the removal of Müller were dashed when Hermann Göring, head of the Gestapo, read aloud a Niemöller statement recorded by secret phone tap. When Göring read Niemöller's "unguarded" statement about Hindenburg's influence on Hitler, Hitler ranted furiously, accusing Niemöller of trying to drive a wedge between he and Hindenburg Göring also indicated that he had proof that the Pastors' Emergency League had international contacts. Niemöller, who was present at the meeting, did not hesitate to forcefully confront Hitler.[10]

Niemöller's brave confrontation with Hitler, however, could not stop the unfavorable effect the meeting would have on Niemöller and the Pastors' Emergency League. The Gestapo searched Niemöller's home the night of the meeting and a bomb exploded there a few days later. More importantly, Niemöller's statement and response lost him the con-

---

7. Ibid., 117. Müller thus ensured that the thinking of Germany's youth would be informed by Nazi doctrine rather than the Christianity that had been a staple for hundreds of years. Cochrane describes Müller's act as a "most traitorous act . . . that was to have the direst consequences for not only for the Church and for Germany but for the rest of the world."

8. Ibid., 129. See also, NPC, 72.

9. NPC, 72. Some pastors were removed from their posts when they spoke to their congregations about the "Muzzling Decree." One pastor was even dragged from his home and beaten.

10. CCUH, 131. Niemöller reportedly said to Hitler, "You have said that I should leave the care of the German people to you. I am bound to declare that neither you nor any power in the world is in a position to take from us Christians and the Church the responsibility God has laid upon us for our people."

fidence of Hitler and the many bishops who capitulated to Müller's power.[11] Müller was once again given a chance by Hitler to restore order in the Evangelical Church and enjoyed the renewed support of the bishops, who agreed to give him their allegiance on January 27. Müller wasted no time imposing his will on the church.[12]

Even with the ostensible restoration of order, the more radical Nazis (Goebbels, Rosenberg, Göring, and Schirach) stepped up their public criticisms of the churches. They emphasized the squabbling, disorder, and borderline anti-state sentiment in the opposition church and called for a complete separation of church and state.[13] Müller did nothing to quell these types of criticisms with his next major project. He attempted to force the provincial churches that had not yet acknowledged his centralized authority to do so. He created a "Spiritual Ministry" in March and, in a highly controversial move, appointed the infamous Jäger as the legal administrator. Müller and Jäger's task was to dismantle the church administrations of the churches still reluctant to accept Müller's authority. The provincial churches that would not accept Müller's authority were dissolved, many times with the use of police force. Müller and Jäger attempted to force Bishop Wurm of Württemberg into compliance.[14] An April 22 conference at Bishop Wurm's cathedral, wherein the question of an alternate church was raised, marks the unofficial beginning of the Confessing Church.[15]

Müller, Jäger, and their Nazi supporters were horrified at the idea of an alternate church and the planning of a May 1934 rival Synod at Barmen. Hitler, though, refused to take action against the Confessing Church due to the international community's perception of his dealings with the churches.[16] The famous Synod at Barmen, the symbol of the opposition's resentment toward Müller's dictatorial machinations,

---

11. *NPC*, 74. See also Cochrane, *The Church's Confession Under Hitler*, 132.

12. *CCUH*, 132. See also Wright, "*Above Parties*," 150, 159. Müller subjected over two hundred ministers to dismissals, suspensions, and other disciplinary actions. Niemöller was given leave of absence on January 27 and other leaders of the Pastors' Emergency League were even placed in concentration camps.

13. *NPC*, 72–73.

14. Ibid., 82–83. See also, Wright, "*Above Parties*," 159–60.

15. *NPC*, 82–83.

16. Ibid., 83. Conway points out that Dr. George Bell, Bishop of Chichester and leader in the ecumenical movement, declared that Müller's "acts of arbitrary repression had caused very great concern throughout the whole Ecumenical Movement."

Phase 3: Church against or apart from World

would produce the stark and formalized theological statement for the resistance church and mark the official birth of the Confessing Church. Spearheaded by Barth and marked by his distinctive theology, Barmen produced a document stressing the gospel's uniqueness, its sole and unadulterated derivation from God rather than from idolatrous human sources, and the church's ability to preach it without hindrance from the state.[17]

Even with its brave Barmen stand, the Confessing Church did not see itself as an organ of political resistance.[18] While non-political, the Confessing Church nevertheless sparked a Nazi response. The Gestapo confiscated the text of the Barmen Confession in several areas in the country and threatened concentration camps for those who had a copy.[19] The Confessing Church and the *Deutsche Christen*, however, continued to display their passivity when they, along with most of the leadership of the Catholic Church, remained silent when Hitler's people slaughtered several hundred Germans during the above-described "Night of the

17. *CCUH*, 238–39. Cochrane reprints "The Declarations, Resolutions, and Motions Adopted by the Synod of Barmen, May 29–31, 1934," in his Appendix VII. Some notable canons read, "We reject the false doctrine, as though the Church could and would have to acknowledge as a source of its proclamation, apart from and besides this one Word of God, still other events and powers, figures and truths, as God's revelation . . . We reject the false doctrine, as though the Church were permitted to abandon the form of its message and order to its own pleasure or to changes in prevailing ideological and political convictions . . . We reject the false doctrine, as though the State, over and beyond its special commission, should and could become the single and totalitarian order of human life, thus fulfilling the Church's vocation as well . . . We reject the false doctrine, as though the Church, over and beyond its special commission, should and could appropriate the characteristics, the tasks, and the dignity of the State, thus becoming an organ of the State."

18. *NPC*, 84–87. Conway notes some reasons. First, the leaders of the movement were not politicians. They were theologians. The fact that Niemöller's own church was adorned with Nazi flags and that his congregation gave the Hitler salute highlighted the extent to which the motivations of the Confessing Church were theological and divorced from political considerations. Second, most of those in the Confessing Church simply wanted no part in anti-Nazi politics. The members of the Confessing Church who did want to confront Nazism directly were alienated in the Confessing Church. Finally, the Lutheran heritage, wherein the ruling power was afforded respect, insured for the church a certain privilege and status. The fact that the Confessing Church did not set itself up as a "rival free Church," one that would evoke visions of an unacceptable sectarianism, was evidence that the Confessing Church wanted to retain a traditional bourgeois status. The Confessing Church would be the true church and the *Deutsche Christen* a temporary heretical movement.

19. *NPC*, 87.

Long Knives."[20] Many churches, in fact, sent Hitler congratulations and applauded his efforts.[21]

Bonhoeffer was serving in the two German parishes in London during these political and church-political events. He tried to find a quiet parish away from Germany in order to consider his role in the church struggle. Bonhoeffer was unable to avoid it entirely and ended up traveling back and forth from London to Berlin, writing letters, and speaking on the phone with members of the opposition church. His activity, however, especially in the later part of his London stay, concentrated mostly on how the Confessing Church could relate favorably with the ecumenical movement and not so much on the Confessing Church as it existed in Germany. Bonhoeffer would see his role as the interpreter of the events in the church in Germany to the international church community.[22]

Bonhoeffer's other role in London was that of a pastor. His major duty in this capacity was delivering a weekly sermon on Sundays. Bonhoeffer's involvement in the opposition church is not reflected in his sermons. As Bethge and others have noted these sermons are, rather, marked predominantly by eschatological overtones.[23] While not necessarily encouraging withdrawal from the present, Bonhoeffer stresses the power of that which is breaking into the human realm from beyond. For example, in his sermon "On Repentance" he stresses the importance of reliance on God rather than human strength in the face of Christ's final judgment. We are to rely only on God's grace only and not our own work.[24] In his sermon, "Confident Hope," Bonhoeffer again stresses

20. Ibid., 93–94.

21. Ibid., 94. Conway quotes a letter from the Evangelical Bishop of Nassau-Hessen stating, "The Evangelical Church of Nassau-Hessen sends its warmest thanks for firm rescue operation, along with best wishes and renewed promises of unalterable loyalty. We pray for God's blessing on our beloved Führer." In a further letter to his own clergy this same bishop wrote, "The events of June 3th, 1934, have opened the eyes of the blind, and demonstrated to the world, as I have always affirmed, the unique greatness of the Führer. He has been sent to us by God."

22. *DB*, 327.

23. Ibid., 330–31

24. *TF*, 218. Bonhoeffer writes, "Finally, what is 'good and evil' about which Christ asks us? The good is nothing other than that we ask for his grace and take hold of it. The evil is nothing other than fear and wanting to stand before God on one's own, wanting to be self-righteous. Repentance means turning away from one's own work to the mercy of God."

Phase 3: Church against or apart from World

God's power in otherness rather than human activity or human agency.[25] There is a sense in which the Christian, in his or her experience of this world, must recognize that it is relative in the face of his or her final destination. His Advent sermon, "Come, O Rescuer," similarly discounts the experience of the worldly in the face of God's redeeming and even rescuing work in Christ. Bonhoeffer writes, "Look up, you whose eyes are fixed on this earth, you who are captivated by the events and changes on the surface of this earth. Look up, you who turned away from heaven to this ground because you had become disillusioned. Look up, you whose eyes are laden with tears, you who mourn all that the earth has snatched away. Look up, you who cannot lift up your eyes because you are so laden with guilt. 'Look up, your redemption is drawing near.'"[26]

The only sermon in which he addresses a political event, his Trinity Sunday Sermon on July 8, 1934, addressing the Blood Purge, does not call the Christian to deal with that event on political grounds. The sermon, "The Way that Leads to Renewal," encourages, rather, the Christian to respond to events in the world with a humble repentance. In addition, and with an interesting reference to Gandhi, Bonhoeffer suggests that the oppressed should not judge the oppressor. The oppressed should, rather, repent as he or she recognizes his or her own sharing in the negative qualities of the oppressor.[27] Bonhoeffer's recommendation for how

25. Ibid., 221.

26. Ibid., 225. Bonhoeffer writes, "But once again: There is no room for selfish questioning. Rather knowledge and hope come when we look to God and put everything in his hands . . . Now we cannot hear about this world of God which is not our world without an immeasurable longing, an indescribable homesickness for the world creeping over us, just as anticipation creeps over the children before Christmas morning when there will be abundant joy and blessed peace. The persons who are themselves not homesick and waiting from that time on, joyously waiting for the redemption of the body, have never really believed in God and the kingdom."

27. Ibid., 233. Bonhoeffer writes, "A great man of our time, Mahatma Gandhi, is a non-Christian. Yet one is very tempted to say he remained a heathen Christian. This man tells his life story how he once ran a school and gave his support to one young man there to the best of his ability. One day the young men of the school perpetrated an injustice on this boy that deeply shocked him. From this incident he did not hear the call to punish or judge the students, but only the call to repent. He went and did penance for days by fasting and practicing various forms of self-denial. What did that mean? It means first that he recognized in the guilt of his students his own guilt, his own lack of love, patience and truthfulness. Furthermore, he knew that only in a spirit of humility that recognizes one's own sin could he once again yield to the Spirit of God. Finally, he saw here that there is faith and love and hope in repentance alone. We have not yet believed enough, we have not yet loved enough—can we be judges? Jesus says to us: 'I tell you no!'"

Christians should "overcome the world of the newspaper, the world of terrors, and the world of judging" is the way of repentance.[28] In addition to this reference to Gandhi, Bonhoeffer preached several times on the Sermon on the Mount.[29]

Bonhoeffer's London sermons thus emphasized God's gracious agency in the world rather than human agency. They, for the most part, stressed the coming of God's gracious love into the world from beyond history, and the human response of hope, repentance and humility. They recommended an approach to the world wherein it is overcome by humble repentance and love. They were, ultimately, more concerned strictly with the individual's relationship with God rather than with how that relationship might affect action in the political sphere.

Beyond the delivery of these sermons Bonhoeffer engaged in some interactions with the German churches from his London post (I will treat his activities in detail in a section near the end of the chapter). Meanwhile the opposition began to define itself more strongly against the German Christian Church with the synod at Barmen. Müller's above-noted appointment of Jäger as the "legal administrator of the churches" and the attempt from Berlin to forcibly consolidate the regional churches awoke an opposition formerly quiet.[30] Bonhoeffer did not actually attend the Barmen Synod. His work related to Barmen remained in the ecumenical sphere. He concentrated on getting the ecumenical church community to recognize the Confessing Church as the only church in Germany. Bonhoeffer, against others in the ecumenical movement like Wilhelm Menn, thought that a real separation from the Evangelical Church in Germany was not only imminent but also necessary.[31] Bonhoeffer's help in preparing Bishop Bell's letter to members of the World Council of Churches warning them against recognizing the Evangelical Church in Germany was his contribution to Barmen.[32]

---

28. Ibid.
29. *DB*, 330. Unfortunately, texts of these sermons no longer exist.
30. Ibid., 366–67.
31. Ibid.
32. Ibid., 370–72.

Fanø Conference: The Church and the Peoples of the World (August 28, 1934)

Bonhoeffer's next move was in direct continuity with his pre-Barmen efforts in the ecumenical sphere. His official roles at the Fanø (Denmark) conference included those of a lecturer and organizer of the youth portion of the conference. Off the record his task was to get the organizers of the conference to allow the Confessing Church to participate as a legitimate entity apart from the recognized German Evangelical Church. His activity as youth secretary involved weeding out potential *Deutsche Christen* delegates from the other German delegation to the conference.[33] Bonhoeffer's task of making sure the Fanø organizers invited the Confessing Church officially brought him into some controversy.[34] He did attend the conference and push (despite the opinions of some both inside and outside of Germany who had misgivings) for a resolution whereby the ecumenical council, the Universal Christian Council, would recognize the Confessing Church in an official capacity. Bonhoeffer's August 8 letter to Ammundsen, for example, appealed passionately for help in supporting a clear resolution.[35] In a way that he had never been up to this point, Bonhoeffer was adamant about the disjunction between the Nazis and the Christian church.[36] Bonhoeffer's behind-the-scenes work paid off as a committee was appointed to write a resolution. The resolution, including recognition of the abuses of the Reich church, a pledge of sympathy for the Confessing Church, and a

---

33. Ibid., 375–76.

34. *DB*, 378–81. Bonhoeffer's initial letter to Henriod, one of Bell's Universal Council secretaries in Geneva, did not meet with success. Henriod's July 7 letter simply stated that there were not provisions in the statutes for inviting two separate delegations from Germany. Bonhoeffer then turned to Bishop Bell for help. Bell's interactions with Bishop Ammundsen, Chairman of the World Alliance, manifested in an invitation to Bonhoeffer, Koch, and Bodelschwingh to come to Fanø in "no official capacity." Ammundsen essentially placed the decision in the hands of Bonhoeffer and his colleagues. The Church Foreign Office in Berlin heard of the invitation and unsuccessfully tried to put a halt to it. Koch and Bodelschwingh decided not to go because of the political situation.

35. Ibid., 381.

36. *TF*, 407. Bonhoeffer writes, "Precisely because our attitude to the state, the conversation must be completely honest, for the sake of Jesus Christ and the ecumenical cause. We must make it clear—fearful as it is—that the time is very near when we shall have to decide between National Socialism and Christianity."

resolve to maintain a close relationship with the Confessing Church, passed on August 30.[37]

Bonhoeffer was satisfied with the accomplishments at Fanø; he believed that the recognition of the Confessing Church was the beginning of a fruitful and long-term relationship between the ecumenical churches and the Confessing Church.[38] Many commentators, however, consider his August 28 sermon, "The Church and the Peoples of the World," to be the event of enduring significance regarding the council. Bonhoeffer's initial draft of his required lecture and sermon was the source of controversy because he concentrated on the question of war. Pastor Hans Schönfeld, Research Department Secretary for the Ecumenical Council in Geneva, wanted Bonhoeffer to change his writing to address more specifically the proper meaning of the concept *Volk*, the role of the church in the nation, and issues concerning the orders of creation and preservation.[39] Bonhoeffer ignored the criticisms and did not change either the lecture, delivered on August 28, or the sermon delivered the same day. There is no existing manuscript of the lecture. The recorded responses to the lecture indicate, though, a marked similarity to the content of the sermon.[40]

Bonhoeffer's relatively short sermon is an extremely important text for any analysis of church-world thinking or political positions because he argues for an extreme form of pacifism, a form different from the one he espoused in phase 2. His sermon also displays a church at odds with the world. Bonhoeffer begins his sermon by hearkening back to a theme he introduced in his 1932 Czechoslovakia speech, God's commandment given to and preached by the church in any given situation. He writes, "Between the twin crags of nationalism and internationalism

---

37. *DB*, 383. Heckel smartly responded to the resolution in a few ways. First, he added a clause to the resolution opening the door for future recognition of the Reich Church in ecumenical dealings. Second, he recorded a protest in the minutes wherein he denied the allegations against the German church. He cited the election of Bonhoeffer and Koch explicitly as evidence of the biased nature of the conference in terms of the internal affairs of the German church. Bishop Bell's article in *The Times* highlighted the council's support of the Confessing Church and the rejection of the use of force. The *Junge Kirche*, on the other hand, emphasized the fact that the Confessing Church was not officially represented at Fanø and applauded Heckel's protest and reiterated opposition to foreign influence in the German church.

38. Ibid., 384–85.

39. Ibid., 386.

40. Ibid., 387.

Phase 3: Church against or apart from World 219

ecumenical Christendom calls upon her Lord and asks for guidance. Nationalism and internationalism have to do with political necessities and possibilities. The ecumenical church, however, does not concern itself with these things, but with the commandments of God, and regardless of consequences it transmits these commandments to the world."[41] Bonhoeffer's thinking here is different than it was in previous phases. Bonhoeffer stated explicitly in the Barcelona lecture on ethics and in the 1932 lecture in Czechoslovakia that all aspects of the reality into which the command enters (and requires response) are important. So the commandment and the response thereto necessarily engage the political component of reality in some way or another. However, in this Fanø sermon, the commandment requires one to somehow bypass (or ignore) the political aspects of the context into which the message is spoken.

Bonhoeffer's description of how the church should respond to this commandment anticipates what he would write shortly in his *Discipleship*. He sounds a forceful call to complete obedience and surrender to the command for peace. He writes, "Our task as theologians, accordingly, consists only in accepting this commandment as a binding one, not as a question open to discussion. Peace on earth is not a problem, but a commandment given at Christ's coming."[42] Bonhoeffer characterizes all of the practical questions surrounding the quest for peace as a choice against "the unconditional, blind obedience of action" and a choice for the "hypocritical question of the Serpent." Questions such as "Has God not understood human nature well enough to know that wars must occur in this world, like laws of nature?," "Did God say you should not protect your own people?," and "Did God say you should leave your own a prey to the enemy?" are attempts to complicate or evade the responsibility of obediently following God's simple peace command. Bonhoeffer states that command unequivocally, "No, God did not say all that. What God has said is that there shall be peace among men—that we shall obey Him without further question, that is what He means. He who questions the commandment of God before obeying has already denied God."[43]

---

41. Bonhoeffer, *London, 1933–1935*, 285–86 (hereafter abbreviated as *DBWE-13*). This quote is from 307.
42. *DBWE-13*, 307.
43. Ibid., 307–8.

The next phase of Bonhoeffer's argumentation relies on thinking that places the cause of Christ and the world in an antithetical relationship. The command of peace is given for the sake of the church of Christ, a reality that is not bound by the limits of national identity. The natural ties of nations such as "common history," "blood," "class," and "language" all become relative in light of the word of Christ.[44] Bonhoeffer emphasizes, in direct contradiction to his Barcelona lecture, how faith in Christ can put one in opposition with family and other natural structures of the world. Bonhoeffer writes further that Christians are not ashamed, "in defiance of the world," to speak of eternal peace.[45] He is aware that the call for peace is a counter-world call.

The next phase of Bonhoeffer's sermon hearkens back to another one of the "questions of the serpent" asked at the beginning. He asks, "Must God not really have said that we should work for peace, of course, but also make ready tanks and poison gas for security?"[46] Bonhoeffer argues that peace implies a risk on the part of those who are commanded to seek it, that trying to avoid the risk of peace by political or other means is wrong-headed. He writes,

> How does peace come about? Through a system of political treaties? Through the investment of international capital in different countries? Through the big banks, through money? Or through universal peaceful rearmament in order to guarantee peace? Through none of these, for the single reason that in all of them peace is confused with safety. There is no way to peace along the way to safety. For peace must be dared. It is the great venture. It can never be made safe. Peace is the opposite of security. To demand guarantees is to mistrust, and this mistrust in turn brings forth war.[47]

Bonhoeffer thus reiterates his idea about the uselessness of political machinations, an idea stressed in the introductory paragraph of the lecture. There are no sure means to establishing peace. There is only obedience in faith to the command.

What is perhaps more important than the theoretical concerns about following God's command in unquestioning obedience or taking

---

44. Ibid., 308.
45. Ibid.
46. Ibid., 307.
47. Ibid., 309.

on risk are the actual implications for action in accepting the command and the risk of peace. Bonhoeffer writes further,

> To look for guarantees is to want to protect oneself. Peace means to give oneself altogether to the law of God wanting no security, but in faith and obedience laying the destiny of the nations in the hand of Almighty God, not trying to direct it for selfish purposes. Battles are won, not with weapons, but with God. They are won where the way leads to the cross. Which of us can say he knows what it might mean for the world if one nation should meet the aggressor, not with weapons in hand, but praying, defenseless, and for that very reason protected by "a bulwark never failing"?[48]

Bonhoeffer thus makes his argument for the most extreme form of pacifism, refusing to take up arms in a defensive war. This is also the most extreme pacifist statement in the entirety of his corpus. The statement clearly makes the point that a certain inactivity comes along with accepting the risk or giving all power to God in political matters in relationship to war. It also fleshes out the implications for action in the world for some of the rhetorical (serpent) questions from the early part of the sermon. Engaging in a build-up of arms for the purpose of protection, for example, is clearly unacceptable because it represents an attempt by political means to ensure peace. The answer to the question about protecting one's own people or leaving them "prey" to the enemy must be leaving them prey because action geared toward protecting one's own people would be both reducing risk and participation in a defensive war. Bonhoeffer's logic and theology here spell out a complete political and military passivity.

In the final portion of the sermon Bonhoeffer uses anti-world language to call on the ecumenical church to take a stand for peace. An individual Christian could raise his voice but "the powers of this world [would] stride over him."[49] Only the ecumenical church can speak out for peace in a world that will "gnash its teeth."[50] Only the ecumenical church can proclaim the peace of Christ "against the raging world."[51] Bonhoeffer depicts the world powers as entities full of fury and the world as "choked with weapons." Bonhoeffer argues that the ecumenical church is the only

48. Ibid.
49. Ibid.
50. Ibid.
51. Ibid.

church that can offer Christ's word of peace to the hardened and dangerous world.[52] It is in this way that Bonhoeffer's vision in this sermon is a church against world vision.

Church-World Relationship and Political Thinking

Bonhoeffer's phase-3 Fanø "peace sermon"[53] differs from the phase 2, pacifist literature (and the phase-2 literature in general) in the intensity of the pacifism and the extent to which the world is set against the church. More specifically, it is different in terms of the extent to which following Christ's peace command sets the church against the world. The Fanø peace sermon also has an apolitical tenor not evident in the phase-2 writings. For instance, Bonhoeffer argued for the possibility of the church engaging in direct political action in his essay about the Jewish question. He also spoke of pacifism as if it were something for which the church could work. However, it is clear in this sermon that political speculation or considerations are only a hindrance to following God's command. The church is only to proclaim Christ's command for peace, it is not to engage in war as a means to ensure peace or even approve of wars in which fellow Christian countries are in imminent danger. One might argue that the proclamation of Christ's peace command is itself a political action. From the evidence presented in this sermon, it seems that Bonhoeffer would have disagreed. He is clear that its character as command places it somehow beyond or against the political.

Post-Fanø London

Bonhoeffer returned to London from Fanø in early September of 1934. Back in Germany Hitler continued to consolidate his power with economic reform, a drive for rearmament, and the growth of the SS.[54] His

---

52. Ibid.

53. *DB*, 387. Bethge points out that this sermon "has become known as Bonhoeffer's Fanø 'peace speech.'"

54. *HNG*, 92–93. The Reinstadt Plan, in full swing by late 1934, included allocating a billion Reichmarks for public works projects. The German government even created a new and secret financial instrument that did not officially show up in the government's budget or in the Reichsbank's ledgers. Rearmament significantly lessened Germany's unemployment. Hitler also met with his cabinet in February 1933 to discuss the need for rearmament. He warned against starting too quickly for fear of repercussions by the Allies for breaking the Versailles Treaty. By late 1934, however, financing for rearmament was in full swing.

Phase 3: Church against or apart from World

renewal of the economy and his drive for rearmament were geared towards establishing Germany as an independent and autonomous nation. Another measure geared toward further unification included the further development of the *Schutzstaffeln* or SS, a quasi-religious organization replete with their own symbols, rituals, and ideology concerning racial purity and moral integrity.[55] Himmler, the leader of the SS, ultimately wanted to replace Christianity with Nazi ideology.[56] The separation from the SA after the Blood Purge and Himmler's complete takeover of the Gestapo and all German police forces made him accountable to Hitler alone.[57] Himmler formed a special group within the SS, the *Sicherheitsdienst* or Security Service (SD) that carried out the fear-inspiring activities.[58] For instance, the SD and the Gestapo would act as "block wardens," conducting weekly searches of all households on the block and forcefully prosecuting "undesirables."[59] The concentration camp, created by the SS during the first few months of Nazi control, was the primary symbol of Nazi terror.[60]

Having made significant progress on the domestic front, Hitler also began dealings in the international arena. His late 1933 withdrawal from the Geneva Disarmament Conference and the League of Nations gave the impression that Germany would no longer be subject to domination by the European nations. Hitler, though, made it perfectly clear that he was willing to engage in bilateral agreements with other nations if Germany was to be treated as an equal.[61] Hitler's first move, a ten-year non-aggression pact with Poland signed in January 1934, shocked other European nations.[62] Another success included the re-incorporation of

---

55. Ibid., 106. Himmler wanted to eliminate all factions of society considered counter to his version of Nazi ideology by terror methods. The list of enemies to the *völkisch* state included Communists, Socialists, several Christian groups, Freemasons, pornographers, homosexuals, artists, and writers and musicians who were even mildly critical of the Nazi regime. Jews were especially suspect.

56. Ibid., 102–4.

57. Ibid., 105–6.

58. Ibid., 104.

59. Ibid., 105.

60. Ibid., 107. Temporary stays in concentration camps were seen as a legitimate means to purify groups considered counter-Nazi. The Jews, however, according to Himmler, needed to be eliminated entirely from a racially pure German society.

61. *HNG*, 197. See also, Craig, *Germany 1866–1945*, 679–80.

62. *HNG*, 198. See also, Craig, *Germany 1866–1945*, 680–82. The Poles, because they were leery of a German attempt to retake areas that were given to Poland after

the Saar region back into Germany.⁶³ Now very confident, Hitler decided to break outright certain terms of the Versailles treaty. After denying accusations of rearmament for a few years and sensing that France and Britain wanted to avoid war, he boldly stated publicly on March 8, 1935, that Germany had developed an air force. This plain admission of breaking the Treaty was followed one week later by a public renunciation of the military provisions of the Treaty altogether. France, Great Britain, and Italy were not pleased with Hitler's moves and held a conference at Stresa in April 1935, where they vowed future action if Germany broke any more terms of the Treaty. However, Hitler assured other nations that Germany wanted only peace and would be willing to sign non-aggression pacts with all its neighbors in a May 21, 1935, speech to the Reichstag.⁶⁴

The church struggle continued during Hitler's political successes. Jäger placed the churches in Hanover, Bavaria, and Württemberg under a special Commissioner after promising that no force would be used in coordinating recalcitrant churches. Church offices were searched and occupied by the police. In addition, Jäger and a contingent from the Gestapo entered unannounced into the Munich offices and declared the Bavarian churches under his own control.⁶⁵ Müller and Jäger's activities were the cause of bad press from the international community.⁶⁶ Hitler did not approve of their heavy-handed measures as he was concerned that Europe would not perceive his rise to power as smooth and peaceful. He summoned Müller to his office on September 29 and told him he would no longer support him if Müller could not unite the Evangelical Church without force or controversy.⁶⁷ The Confessing Church responded to Müller and Jäger's measures with another Barmen-like synod in Dahlem on October 19–20.⁶⁸

World War I, had even considered a preventative war against Germany when the Nazi regime was established. Hitler's work was considered a diplomatic success.

63. *HNG*, 198–99. The Treaty of Versailles granted it to the League of Nations for fifteen years. A plebiscite held there in 1935 gave its inhabitants the choice of German or French control. Germany won by a 90 percent vote.

64. Ibid., 199.

65. *NPC*, 99.

66. Ibid., 100.

67. Ibid., 99–100.

68. See *DB*, 393–95, for a description of the Dahlem Synod.

Phase 3: Church against or apart from World

Sensing that Jäger and Müller were becoming a serious political liability, Hitler attended a late October meeting at the Reich Chancellory and demanded that Jäger resign. Hitler did not share the opinion of some that Müller should also resign.[69] Hitler, in fact, was appalled at the resistance of the Protestants in the southern provinces. His reversal on Jäger and his anger with Müller were not based on theology or on any sympathy with the church opposition. Hitler was simply disturbed by the political risks of their behavior and was likewise growing in his sense of overall disdain for the churches and their leaders.[70] His specific answer to the most recent church controversy was to tell his *Gauleiters* in a November 1 speech to be neutral in church matters and to make it look like the church struggle was an inter-Christian farce. Further, in light of the above-noted plebiscite concerning the re-incorporation of the Saar, the church struggle was to be kept quiet to avoid further international reaction. Hitler forbade any interference in church matters by any official Nazi body.[71]

After the successful plebiscite in the Saar, the Nazi Party encouraged anti-clerical speeches. Other measures were put into place to take away the privileged position of the church in society, especially in the areas of social welfare and education. The government also cut its financial support for the churches, and the *National Socialist Monthly* was instructed to propagandize against the churches.[72] By the start of 1935 Hitler had become frustrated and dissatisfied with Müller and essentially dropped

---

69. *NPC*, 100–101. See also, Wright, "*Above Parties*," 150.

70. *NPC*, 101–3. Hitler, for his part, began to look upon Christianity with hatred. He stated, "I promise you that, if I wished to, I could destroy the church in a few years; it is rotten and hollow and false through and through. One push and the whole structure would collapse." He did not, though, advocate the outright destruction of the churches, but rather surmised that they would eventually die out on their own. He stated further, "I shall give them a few years' reprieve. Why should we quarrel? . . . The church was something really big. Now we are its heirs. We, too, are the Church. Its day has gone."

71. *NPC*, 102.

72. Ibid., 104–8. The Nazi Party also gave temporary support to a new religious movement called the *Deutsche Glaubensbewegung* (German Faith Movement) and its radical leader, professor Jakob Hauer. The German Faith Movement was a combination of mystical Eastern religions, an emphasis on existential living, and a radical allegiance to Germany. In February 1935, the Movement, with its combination Nazi swastika and golden sun flag as a symbol, began massive propaganda efforts, including rallies in the Sports Palace in Berlin. Hauer and his movement were not entirely anti-Christian. They were only against any aspects of the Churches that were dogmatic and not radically Germanic.

him. Müller, for his part, had ceased to have any authority but retained the Reich Bishop title.[73] Hitler and his party, even with the foregoing actions, still had no stable or consistent policy for the churches.[74] A possible solution to Hitler's need for a more permanent policy directive presented itself with a January 1935 memo from Dr. Wilhelm Stuckart, a young secretary of the Ministry of Education. The memo ran through three possible ways to control the churches.[75] Stuckart's third suggestion, exerting pressure on the churches through the control of appointments to church offices and the control of finances by putting the churches under the power of a governmental department, seemed to appeal to Hitler.[76] Hitler appointed Hans Kerrl, a senior party member and former Prussian Minister of Justice, as the Minister of Church Affairs.[77]

SEMINARIES

Bonhoeffer's preachers' seminaries were not a new feature in the German Protestant churches. They were, however, both very rare and somewhat frowned upon, because most theological training was controlled and conducted by state-appointed professors at the major universities.[78] Bonhoeffer's April 26, 1935, meeting with his class at Zingst marked the beginning of nearly five years of conducting his own monastery-

---

73. Wright, *"Above Parties,"* 160.

74. *NPC*, 102. Rosenberg thought the nation should be converted wholesale to a Nazi ideology that would effectively replace Christianity. Von Schirach thought that capturing and indoctrinating the youth was the way eventually to overcome Christianity. Himmler wanted to avoid conflict in public and preferred intimidation by police methods to quash Christianity.

75. Ibid., 117–19. The first, using a movement like the German Christian movement sympathetic to the Nazis, was an option that already failed. The second option, an entire separation of church and state, where the church would receive no money at all from the state, might unite all the churches against the Nazi government.

76. Ibid., 119–20.

77. Ibid., 128–31. See also Wright, *"Above Parties,"* 152, 160. Müller's authority and power were effectively nullified, and Kerrl was expected to accomplish what Müller could not—conformity of the church with the Nazi state. Kerrl did not want to engage in theological arguments. He did not want to establish a State Church. Kerrl wanted his office to act as an external control over the various factions of the church and to ensure that the churches realized that their continued existence hinged upon allegiance to the German race and the Nazi party.

78. *DB*, 419–20.

Phase 3: Church against or apart from World

like seminary training pastors for the Confessing Church.[79] The Nazis ultimately shut all of these places down by the start of the 1940s. His seminary work falls basically into two phases. The Zingst-Finkenwalde seminary existed from April 1935 until the Gestapo shut it down in 1937. The Köslin and Gross-Schlönwitz seminaries were operational from December 1937 until the Gestapo shut them down in March 1940.

Bonhoeffer stayed in Zingst for two months until the seminary moved to Finkenwalde in June of 1935.[80] In the political realm, Hitler's Reich continued its march toward war between 1935 and 1937. On June 18, 1935, Hitler signed an agreement with Britain agreeing to form a navy that was only 35 percent the size of the Britain's navy with the same number of submarines. The agreement represented another diplomatic victory for Hitler; it was evidence that the British condoned the Germans' outright breaking of the Versailles Treaty. Hitler was convinced that the Western powers would not respond forcefully to his aggression and next moved to occupy the demilitarized Rhineland. Hitler's troops marched into the Rhineland on March 7, 1936, and swiftly established occupation. Britain and France did not respond.[81] At home, Hitler's quest for rapid rearmament, once something that helped the economy, was now pushing the economy to its limits by 1936. Hitler responded by instating a four-year plan designed to get the German economy ready for war by 1939/40. Ultimately, Hitler succeeded in both developing a military as big or bigger than those of his neighbors and restoring the economy to health. By the beginning of 1937, Hitler was talking about expansion

---

79. *TF*, 24–25. Nelson and Kelly quote Bonhoeffer's letter to Erwin Sutz, "I no longer believe in the University, and never really have believed in it—a fact that used to rile you. The entire training of young theologians belongs today in church, monastic-like schools in which the pure doctrine, the Sermon on the Mount, and worship can be taken seriously which is really not the case with all three things at the university and, in present-day circumstances, is impossible." Nelson and Kelly also write, "The regimen at Finkenwalde was built around a monastic-like schedule. The Seminarians began and ended the day with a half hour of common prayer drawn from the Psalms and read antiphonally, a hymn for the day, the readings from the Hebrew and Christian Scriptures, extempore prayer, recitation of the Our Father, and a closing hymn. On Sundays there was a full liturgical service with the usual sermon. In the mornings this was followed by a half-hour meditation."

80. *DB*, 425.

81. *HNG*, 199–202.

eastward to gain the *Lebensraum* or the "living space" necessary to meet Germany's needs.⁸² War was just around the corner.

In the ecclesial realm, Hitler had just appointed Kerrl. The more extreme members of the party wanted to continue to harass and undermine the Christian churches. Kerrl wanted to find a way to forge a positive relationship between church and state. Hitler, for his part, was content to continue to use whatever happened in the churches to meet his political ends. At the Nuremberg Rally of 1935, he once again made a public pledge of neutrality by the state toward the churches and even set a date for another set of church elections. Many Protestants, as they had in the past, and even many in the Confessing Church, took Hitler at his word.⁸³ In September 1935, Kerrl started to untangle the mess that Müller and Jäger left by first granting amnesty to all pastors who were punished under them. At the end of September he promulgated a Law for the Safety of the German Evangelical Church which reestablished the authority of the provincial churches. On October 3 Kerrl appointed a number of commissions to give the churches a sense of order to remedy the chaos left by Müller and Jäger.⁸⁴

Several members of the Confessing Church welcomed these measures and especially lauded the appointment of General Superintendent Zöllner to the chair of a national commission. Niemöller, however, was less than optimistic about Kerrl's project, in part because the charter of the new National Commission read, "We welcome the Nationalist Socialist popular evolution (*Volkwerdung*) on the basis of Race, Blood and Soil."⁸⁵ The differing opinions on Kerrl by two factions of the Confessing Church came to a head after its Prussian synod in late September. The churches in Hanover, Bavaria, and Württemberg split from those associated with Niemöller, whose adherence to the Barmen principles, the purity of the Word of God over any political agency, seemed extreme to

---

82. Ibid., 94–96. Hitler's economic plan centered around establishing Germany as a self-sufficient economic entity. It included developing raw materials needed for military and industrial growth as well as the expansion of Germany's borders for fulfilling agricultural needs

83. *NPC*, 134–35.

84. Ibid., 135.

85. Ibid., 135–36. Niemöller even sent a letter to his supporters in the Confessing Church warning that the new church structure was not in line with the Barmen Declaration.

Phase 3: Church against or apart from World 229

some.[86] The divide between those in the Confessing Church who supported Kerrl and those who supported Niemöller became official at a long national synod of the Confessing Church held at Oeynhausen in Westphalia in February of 1936.[87] The disunity gave the Nazis more ammunition against Niemöller's faction and the churches in general. Kerrl's frustrations with the Confessing Church took the form of an executive order preventing the church from exercising authority where any of the commissions had already been established.[88]

Kerrl's project of attempting to coordinate and control the church while maintaining some form of relationship between the church and the state was ultimately in constant peril due to two factions. There was Niemöller's above-mentioned wing of the Confessing Church who refused to accept Kerrl's authority. There was also the extreme wing of the Nazi Party, which thought Christianity should be replaced with Nazism.[89] The Dahlemites, those who supported Niemöller's faction, responded to what they saw as Kerrl's abuses with a late August 1936 memorandum directly to Hitler himself. The bishops, wishing to avoid public confrontation, wanted to keep the memo private.[90] The results of the memo were embarrassing. Hitler ignored the letter entirely. The memorandum was leaked to the foreign press and was printed in Switzerland, England, and elsewhere, forcing the authors to accept responsibility. Those inside Germany, both in the government and in the church, accused the authors

---

86. Ibid., 137.

87. Ibid. Those who followed Niemöller thought that cooperation with Kerrl indicated an abandonment of the claim that the Confessing church was the one true evangelical church in Germany. They formed a new Provisional National Administration. The other faction thought cooperation with Kerrl was compatible with adherence to the Gospel.

88. Ibid., 137–39.

89. Ibid., 161–62.

90. *NPC*, 162–63. See also, *DB*, 531–32. This unprecedented and bold letter voiced six major areas of concern: 1) they wanted to know if the efforts to de-Christianize Germany, in direct contradiction to Hitler's most recent public statement about state neutrality in church matters, were official state policy; 2) they stated that the notion of positive Christianity was theologically suspect; 3) they questioned arbitrary intervention by the Gestapo in church matters; 4) they accused the state of interfering with the Church's work by limitations of church matters in the press, radio and public education; 5) they expressed concern over the incompatibility of anti-Semitism and the presence of concentration camps with Christianity and 6) they expressed concern that the nation was setting itself up as divine, with Hitler himself being something like a high priest mediating between God and the people.

of action against the state and siding with Germany's enemies. The leaders of the Confessing Church did not respond valiantly. They formally dissociated themselves from the man who authorized the publication in Switzerland, Dr. Weissler. Dr. Weissler was arrested by the Gestapo, sent to the Sachsenhausen concentration camp, and brutally beaten to death a few months later.[91] The Dahlemites, in an attempt to redeem themselves, issued a watered down version of the memorandum on August 23, which was rejected by the faction of the Confessing Church wanting to maintain a working relationship with the Nazi Party and Kerrl.[92]

By the end of 1936 it was becoming clear that Kerrl's attempts to unify the Protestant church were going the way of Müller's. His relative ineffectiveness in mitigating the effects of both the Dahlemites and the extreme Nazis opened the door for Himmler and other Nazi leaders to initiate an intense form of intimidation and persecution in the churches. Himmler targeted the churches' press and radio mechanisms and their schools and set up a special section of the Gestapo to deal with the churches. By the middle of 1937 the Nazi campaign against the churches was in full swing and yielding favorable results from the Nazi perspective.[93] Kerrl, for his part, still thought a positive relationship between church and state could be formed in early 1937. A strongly worded document from the Dahlemites, however, once again laying out the position of the Confessing Church vis-à-vis the State and Kerrl's own authority, prompted him to take control of the church's administration. Kerrl's harsh measures and the Confessing Church's response made the Nazis realize that Kerrl's efforts to solve the church problem would

---

91. Ibid., 163–64. See also, *DB*, 533–37.

92. *NPC*, 164. Conway notes, "The revised document was rejected by the South German Bishops and by Bishop Marahrens of Hanover, on the grounds that its proclamation would prevent 'profitable negotiations' with the Nazi hierarchy."

93. *NPC*, 168–72. Himmler and Eichmann even hired ex-Evangelical pastors and ex-Catholic priests (Albert Hartl, notably) who knew internal church workings well to assist in intimidation and repression. Hartl oversaw a conference in July 1937 which served as a plan of attack against the churches. The conference produced a document wherein several directives were recommended, including monitoring the sexual behavior of seminarians, infiltrating the church administrations with informants, ascertaining the political attitudes of theologians in the various universities, scrutinizing both theological journals and church press activity as well as other invasive procedures. The effects of the conference were quickly felt as the Gestapo began investigating and prohibiting various church activities. The schools were pressured to replace Christian teaching with Nazi ideology.

not be successful.[94] The Nazis decided that a course of action marked by outright repression of the churches would be the best measure. By November 1937 the Gestapo arrested over 700 pastors, including Niemöller. Finally, the Gestapo shut down all of the private seminaries, and the state refused to pay the salaries of those who had been educated in one of those seminaries.[95]

"The Question of the Boundaries of the Church and Church Union" (April 1936)

One writing of significance in this phase was Bonhoeffer's lecture to his students at Finkenwalde in April of 1936, "The Question of the Boundaries of the Church and Church Union." The writing sparked an enormous amount of controversy.[96] The writing, later published in *Evangelische Theologie*, was originally a lecture given to his ordinands in order to clear up issues not settled at the Oeynhausen synod. The synod had not stated definitively if Confessing Church members should join Kerrl's committees.[97]

Bonhoeffer is adamant that the question of setting visible boundaries of church union is a legalistic one not usually called for except in extreme circumstances. He also makes clear the impossibility in the Lutheran tradition of saying who is a definitively a member of the elect. There are, for instance, "no theoretical statements about the saved and the lost" and "no verdict 'This person belongs to the church, that person does not.'" Rather, the church is content to joyfully proclaim the gospel and administer the sacraments, wherever that might happen. Bonhoeffer writes, "the nature of the church is not determined by those who belong to it but by the word and sacrament of Jesus Christ which, where they are effective, gather for themselves a community in accordance with the

---

94. Ibid., 208.

95. Ibid., 209–10.

96. *DB*, 517. The essay, like his support of pacifism, earned him the criticism that he was a fanatical enthusiast and even caused many within the Confessing Church to dissociate from him theologically.

97. *DB*, 518–20. He wanted to address important questions such as what the ramifications were of joining Kerrl's committees, the continuing authority of Barmen and Dahelm, and the value of the positions of the various factions in the Confessing Church. Bonhoeffer's lecture was meant to answer the questions that the synod left unanswered.

promise."[98] The church is grateful that it has the word and the sacrament and is not concerned with the question of where else church may or may not be.

The church must, however, recognize boundaries when it is opposed from the outside.[99] What forces the church to make clear the boundaries between it and the outside world always comes from the outside world.[100] Bonhoeffer thus sets up a church against the world vision in which the "boundaries are drawn arbitrarily by the world, which shuts itself off from the church by not hearing and believing."[101] Bonhoeffer also enumerates the various types of boundary-creating situations coming from the outside. Attacks can come from the world, an anti-Christian church, or from another church.[102] The intention of the aggressor is another factor in determining the setting of boundaries. If the church with the false teaching has the intention of totally annihilating the true church, communion is not possible. The church, according to Bonhoeffer, must set boundaries for the sake of the true proclamation of the gospel.[103]

Bonhoeffer shifts the discussion from the theoretical to the practical, the synods of Barmen and Dahlem. He urges church leaders and laypeople to examine the synods and what they mean in terms of his discussion up to them. He stated plainly that the National (Reich) Church had cut itself off from the Christian church and that the Confessing Church was the true church in Germany.[104] Bonhoeffer raises all kinds of specific questions that appear as a result of his position (has each German Christian pastor cut himself off from the church of Christ?, Can a pastor in the Confessing Church have German Christians in his congregation?, etc.). Bonhoeffer also asks whether or not the statement

---

98. Bonhoeffer, *The Way to Freedom*, 75.

99. Ibid., 78. Bonhoeffer writes, "This is where the question of the extent of the church, of the boundaries, of the distinction between the elect and the rejected arises. Wherever the call to salvation is not heard, the church's claim becomes judgement, it divides those who hear it from those who do not hear it."

100. Ibid., 79. Bonhoeffer explains further, "It is not the church that sets the boundaries; it comes up against boundaries that are set from the outside. Now the church experiences the call to salvation as the law which judges the world, as the boundary that cannot be passed. Now it must take account of the situation."

101. Ibid.

102. Ibid., 84.

103. Ibid., 85.

104. Ibid., 86.

Phase 3: Church against or apart from World

of heresy implied by the Dahlem synod applied to the current debate over participation in Kerrl's committees. Bonhoeffer argued that definite answers must be given for all of these questions because the church demands obedience.[105] He calls "pernicious" the obscurity of the debate in the Confessing Church over the church committees.[106] Bonhoeffer next provides concrete answers to his questions. He states definitively that the German Christian ministers had cut themselves off from the true church. He argues that it would be better for congregations "to abstain from all ministerial acts of a false teacher for the sake of the Word of God and the salvation of their souls, and to live and die without the sacrament rather than go to a false teacher."[107] He also argued that a congregation should pass judgment on a minister who espoused false teaching. Finally, Bonhoeffer argued that the Confessing Church must hold that whoever agrees to participate in the committees has cut him/herself off from the true church.[108]

Bonhoeffer's next segment of the essay provides another one of the most famous and controversial passages in his corpus. He writes,

> *Extra ecclesiam nulla salus.* The question of church membership is the question of salvation. The boundaries of the church are the boundaries of salvation. Whoever knowingly cuts himself off from the Confessing Church in Germany cuts himself off from salvation. That is the recognition which has always forced itself upon the true church. That it its humble confession. Whoever separates the question of the Confessing Church from the question of his own salvation does not understand that the struggle of the Confessing Church is the struggle for his own salvation.[109]

Bonhoeffer was careful to distinguish his own position from that of the Roman Church, which he considers to be heretical on this point. The heresy of the Roman Church was not that it linked salvation with the church or the church with salvation. The heresy, rather, would be to take the *extra ecclesiam nulla salus* as a "theoretical truth about the saved and the lost." The statement is legitimate as a statement in faith of the offer-

---

105. Ibid., 87.
106. Ibid., 88.
107. Ibid., 91.
108. Ibid., 92–93.
109. Ibid., 93–94.

ing of salvation in the visible church where the pure gospel is preached.[110] Finally, Bonhoeffer argues that God can be known only in the visible church. He again warned that *extra ecclesiam nulla salus* should not be used by the pious to speculate about the saved and the lost. The statement, rather, points persons to the visible church where the pure gospel message was preached. As such, the setting of boundaries in the phrase *extra ecclesiam nulla salus* is an act of mercy on the part of the church toward its members.[111]

The fact that a bitter debate raged over Bonhoeffer's essay in general, and his use of the phrase *extra ecclesiam nulla salus* in particular, is in some ways a testimony to his lack of clarity. Bonhoeffer was charged with being a fanatic and accused of Romanism, adopting a legalistic interpretation of Protestantism,[112] and being part of a sect.

> This Confessing church shaped according to the wishes of Barth and Asmussen, as distinct from the confessional movement upheld by the Lutheran churches, is a sect, the worst sect in fact ever to have set foot on the soil of German Protestantism. Anyone who doubts this should read the papers by Bonhoeffer and Gollwitzer in the June issue of *Evangelische Theologie*. Founded on the miracle of Barmen, held together by Barth's *Theologumenon* on the worthlessness of the remnants of natural theology to which Calvin and Luther adhered, beaten down by the harsh experience of the church struggle, there stands the alleged church.[113]

Did Bonhoeffer adequately protect himself from the charges levied against him? He tries to avoid sectarian or extreme thinking in a few ways. First, he repudiated legalism throughout the essay. He used the fact that the church must be able to recognize boundaries spontaneously and make decisions about those boundaries, and that those decisions

---

110. Ibid., 94.

111. Ibid., 96.

112. *DB*, 520. New Testament professor Hans Lietzman, for example, wrote, "and recently, a highly gifted but now altogether fanatical teacher, declared *extra ecclesiam nulla salus*, that is, whoever cooperates with the Reich church committee stands outside the church of salvation." See also, *DB*, 521–22. Pastor Duensing of Hannover wrote, "Has not another revelation now been placed alongside Holy Scripture as the sole rule and guiding principle, thus throwing the door wide open to fanaticism? Or again, the question might be asked: Is this not the same claim on the part of the 'Confessing church' an exact repetition of the claim raised by the pope?"

113. Ibid., 522. This quote is from one of Bonhoeffer's staunch allies from Bethel in 1933, Hermann Sasse.

Phase 3: Church against or apart from World

could be overturned at future dates, as evidence that his notion was not legalistic. Sects, presumably characterized by legalism, have already decided to cut themselves off from the world before any encounter with unbelief.[114] In addition, Bonhoeffer, makes the point several times throughout the essay that the church's task is to proclaim salvation to the world and not merely to the members of an exclusive sect. The setting of the boundaries was, in fact, in the service of proclaiming the pure gospel to the entire world.[115]

Church-World Relationship and Political Thinking

There would have been no controversy if Bonhoeffer's (implicit) attempts to avoid the charges of fanaticism or sectarianism were entirely convincing. A look at the implicit understanding of the church-world relationship sheds some light on Bonhoeffer's positions. It is clear, even if Bonhoeffer states that the setting of boundaries is actually in the service of proclaiming the gospel to the whole world, that the motivation for establishing the boundaries in the first place was a recalcitrant outside world, unwilling or unable to hear the gospel. The fact that Bonhoeffer paints the decision to establish boundaries as a defensive one, or one that the church is pushed to in recognition of an outside world hostile to the church, implied a church against world stance. In addition, while Bonhoeffer tried to justify the Confessing Church's decision to set up clear boundaries as a special decision in an unusual circumstance, where the church encounters boundaries being imposed from the outside, it seems that these circumstances were not extraordinary at all. That is, all Christian churches at all times exist in a situation where certain factions of the world or the world in general are reluctant to hear and obey the pure gospel. Bonhoeffer's defense against legalism is also somewhat questionable. He has essentially laid down a number of rules that govern when a church can and should set boundaries between itself and the outside world, all the while claiming to avoid legalism. His disjunction between a theoretical statement of who is and who is not saved and a

---

114. Bonhoeffer, *The Way to Freedom*, 79. Bonhoeffer writes, "The boundaries of the church are always decided only in the encounter between the church and unbelief; the act is a decision of the church. If it knew the answer beforehand it would have separated itself from the world and would be unfaithful to its commission to proclaim salvation."

115. Ibid., 86. Bonhoeffer writes, "The church's decision on its boundary is in the last resort a merciful act to both its members and to those outside. It is the last, the 'strange,' possibility of making the call to salvation audible."

church setting boundaries while the whole time holding that the question of church boundaries was the question of salvation seems inconsistent at best. Bonhoeffer's church against world stance, one that necessitated the establishment of boundaries, is too strict for him to avoid all suspicions of sectarianism or fanaticism.

What is markedly different in this phase is how the church against world stance does not allow Bonhoeffer to posit overlap. The concept over which the change comes to light in this particular case was purity. In the previous phases, Bonhoeffer made it clear that the church would never be pure as long as it was in history (phase 1) or because it was a part of the lost and godless world (phase 2). Bonhoeffer never states in this current essay that this church which has set boundaries against the world consisted of a mixture of the saved and unsaved, or the pure and impure. Bonhoeffer did not speak, for example, as he did in phase 1, of a *Volkskirche* and a voluntary church. The church in this essay is rather a visible community that knows itself to have the pure and unadulterated gospel message. It is clearly cordoned off from the attacking outside world. Bonhoeffer's friend, Helmut Gollwitzer, tried to defend Bonhoeffer's essay on the church by saying that Bonhoeffer was really talking about the universal church.[116] Bonhoeffer's emphasis on the visible church having the pure message, and his further argument that its only members are those who obediently and visibly respond to it, negates the concept of *Volkskirche* or a church which includes all members of a people or nation regardless of explicit belief and action.

Finally, the way Bonhoeffer uses the Roman Catholic Church in his argumentation is another indicator of his change from previous phases. In phase 1 Bonhoeffer argued that "based on the efficacy of the word, we must believe the sanctorum communio to be present even within the sociologically unique type of the Roman Catholic church."[117] In the current essay he writes,

> But what if the Gospel [the word] were now preached purely in a single congregation of the Roman Church or the National Church? Is not then the true church there also? There is no pure proclamation of the gospel independent of the whole church. And if someone preached the Gospel as purely as the Apostle Paul and was obedient to the papacy or to the government of the

---

116. Ibid., 99.
117. *SC-E*, 271.

Phase 3: Church against or apart from World

National Church, he would be a false teacher and a misleader of the congregation.[118]

Bonhoeffer thus suggests that it is identifying oneself with a certain church administration that assures correct teaching and correct leading rather than the operation or preaching of the word itself.

Discipleship (1937)

Bonhoeffer's other significant writing from his Finkenwalde days is arguably his most famous, *Nachfolge*, translated originally as *The Cost of Discipleship* and most recently as *Discipleship*. Bonhoeffer wrote the work in stages between 1933 and 1937. His letter to Erwin Sutz in 1934 indicated a desire to preach and teach about Christian obedience and discipleship. Bonhoeffer preached on the Sermon on the Mount and had discussions about it with Hildebrandt during his London pastorate. Student notes and fragments from lectures reveal, however, that the main source material for *Discipleship* was his three courses at Finkenwalde between 1935 and 1937.[119] The work is very long. I will treat only the portions relevant to the connection between Bonhoeffer's church-world thinking and his political positions.

Bonhoeffer's work begins with his famous diatribe against cheap grace and his positing of costly grace as an antidote. Cheap grace, "the mortal enemy of our church . . . grace as bargain-basement goods . . . doled out by careless hands without hesitation or limit," is grace given so freely and abundantly that it makes no demands on receivers.[120] Bonhoeffer sets up his thinking on the world right away in this first section when he argues that this grace makes no demands. It therefore allows the Christian to go along freely with the world "and not venture (like the sixteenth-century enthusiasts) to live a different life under

---

118. *The Way to Freedom*, 94.
119. Bonhoeffer, *Discipleship*. The section "The Writing of *Discipleship*" (pp. 24–28) from Kelly and Godsey's "Editors' Introduction to the English Edition" contains a description of the sources and stages of the writing. See also, *DB*, 450–51. Bonhoeffer treated the call to follow Jesus, the visible church, the Sermon on the Mount, and Paul's ethics in his Finkenwalde lectures. The work was finally published in book form in mid-1937.
120. *Discipleship*, 43.

grace from that under sin!"[121] Costly grace, on the other hand, requires discipleship on the part of recipients.[122]

Bonhoeffer laments the loss of awareness of costly grace that came with the spread of Christianity and the process of secularization in the church.[123] He credits the Roman Church with maintaining a "remnant" of the awareness of costly grace in the form of monasticism.[124] Monasticism was a "living protest against the secularization of Christianity, against the cheapening of grace."[125] This positive move was, however, ultimately negative for the concepts of grace and discipleship because the larger church accepted monasticism. The church, now able to establish a distinction between extraordinary Christians and regular Christians, could paradoxically justify its own process of secularization. Bonhoeffer faults monasticism for allowing itself to become the province of extraordinary persons. He uses the story of Luther's re-entry into the world from the monastery to make an important point about discipleship. Namely, God made Luther fail in the path of monasticism to show him that "discipleship is not the meritorious achievement of individuals, but a divine commandment to all Christians." Bonhoeffer thus suggests that all Christians follow the difficult path of costly grace.[126]

Luther's re-entry into the world was not, though, a simple call for Christians to embrace the world fully or even as a positive realm. Bonhoeffer explains,

> Luther had to leave the monastery and reenter the world, not because the world itself was good and holy, but because even the monastery was nothing else but world. Luther's path out of the monastery back to the world meant the sharpest attack that had been launched on the world since early Christianity. The rejection which the monk had given the world was child's play compared to the rejection endured through his returning to it. This time the attack was a frontal assault. Following Jesus now had to

---

121. Ibid., 44.

122. Ibid., 45. Bonhoeffer writes, "Costly grace is grace as God's holy treasure which must be protected from the world."

123. Ibid., 46. Bonhoeffer writes, "The world was Christianized; grace became common property of a Christian world. It could be had cheaply."

124. Ibid. Monasticism was "the place where the awareness that grace is costly and that grace includes discipleship was preserved."

125. Ibid., 47.

126. Ibid., 47–48.

Phase 3: Church against or apart from World

be lived out in the midst of the world. What had been practiced in the special, easier circumstances of monastic life as a special accomplishment now had become what was necessary and commanded for every Christian in the world. Complete obedience to Jesus' commandments had to be carried out in the daily world of work. This deepened the conflict between the life of Christians and the life of the world in an unforeseeable way. The Christian had closed in on the world. It was hand-to-hand combat.[127]

So while Bonhoeffer does not use Luther's experience as a way to justify a full withdrawal from the world, he does suggest that activities associated with living in discipleship, when performed in the world, place one against the world. For Luther, "a Christian's secular vocation is justified only in that one's protest against the world is most sharply expressed."[128] Bonhoeffer warns further against interpreting grace in Luther's teaching on justification by grace alone as cheap grace without discipleship. Grace should not allow the Christian to live his or her secular existence "in the world and like the world . . . not being different from it . . . Not being permitted to be different from it."[129]

Bonhoeffer goes on in chapter two to describe more fully the nature of the call to discipleship. Its main feature is that it requires a response in deed, a deed of simple obedience to Christ's call. There is a direct and unmediated attachment to Christ's person as Son of God, not as a teacher who lays out a programmatic way of life.[130] The call to discipleship also creates a new situation and forces one into a whole new existence wherein there is a separation from one's former life.[131] The true disciple lives directly in terms of his or her relationship with Jesus. Bonhoeffer's next chapter, "Simple Obedience," clarifies further the nature of obedience. He uses the story of the young rich man to illustrate how "conscience, responsibility, piety [and] even the law and

---

127. Ibid., 48–49.
128. Ibid., 49.
129. Ibid., 50–51.
130. Ibid., 57–58. Bonhoeffer writes, "What is said about the call of discipleship? Follow me, walk behind me! That is all. Going after him is something without specific content. It is truly not a program for one's life which would be sensible to implement."
131. Ibid., 62. Bonhoeffer writes of the true disciple, "Now his call to discipleship dissolved all ties for the sake of the unique commitment to Jesus Christ. Now all bridges had to be burned and the step taken to enter into endless insecurity, in order to know what Jesus demands and what Jesus gives."

the principle of scripture intervened to inhibit this most extreme, this lawless 'enthusiasm,'" associated with simple obedience.[132] He explains how, if Christ were to give the same commandment today, we would attempt to avoid the call to simple obedience. We would, for instance, take Jesus's admonition to sell our goods and give to the poor as a call for inward conversion in faith rather than as a call to simple obedience in deed.[133] Bonhoeffer calls this the "paradoxical" response to the call and argues that it is only acceptable for those who have already taken simple obedience seriously and "stand in community with Jesus, in discipleship, in expectation of the end."[134] He argues that it would be easier to simply follow the command literally.[135] Bonhoeffer's concern is, again, the concern with cheap grace. The paradoxical response can easily become a justification for cheap grace.

Bonhoeffer's next chapter explores the connection between following Christ and suffering and rejection. Christ's suffering and his and our being rejected cannot be separated. He also makes a distinction between suffering stemming from natural existence and suffering that comes from following the call of costly grace. Bonhoeffer writes,

> The cross is not suffering that stems from natural existence; it is suffering that comes from being Christian. The essence of the cross is not suffering alone; it is suffering and being rejected. Strictly speaking, it is being rejected for the sake of Jesus Christ,

132. Ibid., 77. The editors add a footnote here describing the nature of Bonhoeffer's theological disagreement with some of his contemporaries. They note, "Here Bonhoeffer objects to the way simple obedience was labeled a 'heresy' against the Reformation, an accusation that some Lutherans liked to make; for example, see Althaus, *Der Geist der lutherischen Ethik im Augsburgischen Bekenntnis*, 45: 'Even among us today, what the reformers called enthusiasm is a powerful element' in the form of 'Christian-pacifist and other irrational options.'"

133. Bonhoeffer, *Discipleship*, 78.

134. Ibid., 80. This paradoxical response is "the last possible form of Christian existence, a possibility of living in the world, only in light of the expectation that Christ would return in the immediate future. It is not the first and simplest possibility."

135. Ibid., 81. Bonhoeffer continues, "Understanding Jesus' call paradoxically is the infinitely more difficult possibility. In human terms it is an impossible possibility, and because it is, it is always in extreme danger of being turned over into its opposite and made into a comfortable excuse for fleeing from concrete obedience. Anyone who does not know that it would be the infinitely easier way to understand Jesus' commandment simply and obey it literally—for example, to actually give away one's possessions at Jesus' command instead of keeping them—has no right to a paradoxical understanding of Jesus' word."

not for the sake of any other attitude or confession. A Christianity that no longer took discipleship seriously remade the gospel into only the solace of cheap grace. Moreover, it drew no line between natural and Christian existence. Such a Christianity had to understand the cross as one's daily misfortune, as the predicament and anxiety of our natural life. Here it has been forgotten that the cross always means being rejected, that the cross includes the shame of suffering. Being shunned, despised and deserted by people, as in the psalmist's unending lament, is an essential feature of the suffering of the cross, which cannot be comprehended by a Christianity that is unable to differentiate between a citizen's ordinary existence and Christian existence.[136]

Bonhoeffer thus sharply separates, like he did in the first chapters, old existence in humanity from new existence in Christ. He furthermore argues that all Christians, not just a specialized few, are required to take up their crosses and suffer.[137] In addition, he reaffirms the counter-world ramifications of the call to discipleship when he writes, "The first Christ-suffering that everyone has to experience is the call which summons us from our attachments to this world."[138] There will be a daily struggle and intense suffering for the Christian who takes up his or her cross because the world is counter-Christian.

Bonhoeffer's next chapter, "Discipleship and the Individual," continues the theme of necessary separation from old existence and from the world. Bonhoeffer writes, "Jesus' call itself already breaks the ties with the naturally given surroundings in which a person lives. It is not the disciple who breaks them; Christ himself broke them as soon as he called. Christ has untied the person's immediate connection with the world and bound the person immediately to himself. No one can follow Christ without recognizing and affirming that the break is already complete."[139]

The counter-world mediator Christology becomes pronounced at this point in the text. Bonhoeffer continues:

> In becoming human, he put himself between me and the given circumstances of the world. I cannot go back. He is in the middle. He has deprived those whom he has called of every immediate

---

136. Ibid., 86–87.
137. Ibid. Bonhoeffer writes, "It [great suffering] is laid on every Christian."
138. Ibid.
139. Ibid., 93.

> connection to those given realities . . . He stands not only between me and God, he also stands between me and the world, between me and other people and things . . . Since Christ there has been no more unmediated relationship for the human person, neither to God nor to the world.[140]

Bonhoeffer suggests further that the illusion of immediacy to the world hinders faith and obedience. He argues that even the most intimate relationships (husband to wife, child to parents, etc.) are characterized by Christ's mediatorship. The relationships that are particularly important for understanding Bonhoeffer's changes from previous phases include the blood relationships between family members and those between citizens and nation.[141]

Bonhoeffer is especially forceful in his understanding of how direct attachment to Christ has anti-world ramifications. He argues,

> But because any delusion which hides truth from us must be hated, immediacy to the natural given things in life must also be hated, for the sake of Jesus Christ, the mediator. Anytime a community hinders us from coming before Christ as a single individual, anytime a community lays claim to immediacy, it must be hated for Christ's sake. For every unmediated natural relationship, knowingly or unknowingly, is an expression of hatred toward Christ, the mediator, especially if this relationship wants to assume a Christian identity.[142]

This quote, as well as being a thinly veiled reference to Hitler and the *Deutsche Christen*, indicates the extent to which attachment to Christ means enmity toward the world. Bonhoeffer continues with a warning against reading Jesus' mediation between God and humans as a stamp of approval for relating directly with the world. Attachment to Jesus requires a break with immediate relationship with "God given realities" of the world.[143]

---

140. Ibid., 93–94.

141. Ibid., 95.

142. Ibid.

143. Ibid., 96–97. Bonhoeffer says the break is inevitable and says it can take different forms—"externally in a break with one's family or nation . . . visibly [to] bear Christ's shame, to accept the reproach of hatred for humans . . . or whether the break must be borne hidden, known by the individual alone who, however, is prepared to make it visible at any time."

Phase 3: Church against or apart from World

Bonhoeffer's next chapter, "The Sermon on the Mount," begins with an interpretation of the Beatitude, "Blessed are the poor in spirit, for theirs is the Kingdom of Heaven." He establishes clearly that the disciples are, with Jesus, distinct from the larger crowd of people. They have been called, they have responded, and they have been set apart from the larger community. He reiterates the enmity between the called and the world when he writes, "there will be enmity between the disciples and the people until the end. Everyone's rage at God and at God's word will fall on the disciples."[144] Bonhoeffer, moreover, introduces a theme of lostness, homelessness, or lack of rootedness on the earth when he argues that the disciples have "no security, no property to call their own, no piece of earth they could call their home, no earthly community to which they might fully belong."[145] Bonhoeffer argues that every Beatitude widens the breach between the disciples and the people and the disciples and the world. The blessed mourners "are rejected as strangers in the world" and "cannot be brought into accord with the world."[146] They see the oncoming end of the world rather than the world's material progress. They do not avoid suffering.

Bonhoeffer is quick to note, though, that the disciples do not "withdraw into willful contempt for the world."[147] They bear the suffering that is laid upon them. The Beatitude, "Blessed are the meek, for they will inherit the earth," also shows the counter-world stance. Bonhoeffer argues that the disciples, the "community of strangers in the world," renounce all rights in the world for the sake of Jesus Christ. He writes, "When they are berated, they are quiet. When violence is done to them, they endure it. When they are cast out, they yield. They do not sue for their rights; they do not make a scene when injustice is done to them."[148] Bonhoeffer has essentially removed all impetus for any type of response in the economic, political, or social spheres. Disciples, according to the next Beatitude, "Blessed are those who hunger and thirst for righteousness," cannot actually do anything but hope for a future righteousness.[149]

---

144. Ibid., 101.
145. Ibid., 102–3.
146. Ibid., 103.
147. Ibid., 104.
148. Ibid., 105.
149. Ibid., 106.

The next significant Beatitude with implications for action in the world is the one concerning making peace. Disciples are to "maintain peace by choosing to suffer instead of causing others to suffer . . . They renounce self-assertion and are silent in the face of hatred and injustice. That is how they overcome evil with good."[150] Bonhoeffer does not indicate that disciples should actually work for peace in the form of political protest. Ultimately, true Christian discipleship means living a counterworld stance. It means being different from the world and causing the world to reject, take offense, and even persecute.

Bonhoeffer next lays out his teaching on nonviolence. He points out that Jesus raises the "eye for an eye" teaching to the level of all the commandments. Jesus, again, demands that his followers renounce their own rights for his sake. The "eye for an eye" teaching stands as just retribution for evils, ensuring the integrity of a just community. For Jesus and his disciples, just retribution happens in not resisting evil. Bonhoeffer writes,

> With this statement, Jesus releases his community from the political and legal order, from the national form of the people of Israel, and makes it into what it truly is, namely, the community of the faithful that is not bound by political or national ties. God's chosen people of Israel did exist in a political form in which, according to the divine will, retribution consisted of returning a blow for a blow. For the community of the disciples, which makes no national or legal claims for itself, retribution means patiently bearing the blow so that evil is not added to evil. That is the only way community can be established and preserved.[151]

Bonhoeffer's call to the sphere of discipleship, like the command given in the Fanø speech, places one outside the sphere of political involvement. It is significant that Bonhoeffer does not distinguish between particular forms of nationality or legal structures, like for instance an evil government or evil regime in a particular nation. Rather, he indicates that adherence to the community of disciples means release from any or every political and legal structure.

The implications of Bonhoeffer's view on discipleship for political resistance or action in the world are made clear when he writes,

---

150. Ibid., 108.
151. Ibid., 132–33.

Phase 3: Church against or apart from World

The overcoming of others now occurs by allowing evil to run its course. The evil does not find what it is seeking, namely resistance and, therewith, new evil which will inflame it even more. Evil will become powerless when it finds no opposing object, no resistance, but, instead, is willingly borne and suffered. Evil meets an opponent for which it is not a match... Suffering passes when it is borne. The evil comes to an end when we permit it to pass over us, without defense. Humiliation and debasement are revealed as sin when the disciple does not commit them, but bears them without defense. Assault is condemned by not being met with violence . . . Our voluntary renunciation of counter-violence confirms and proclaims our unconditional allegiance to Jesus and his followers, our freedom, our detachment from our egos. And it is only in the exclusivity of this adherence that evil can be overcome.[152]

Bonhoeffer does not distinguish between, or even use, the terms active and passive resistance. Discipleship is not a program of political action or a strategy for political or societal change. It is, rather, simple obedience to Christ's call. Bonhoeffer does away with the traditional Lutheran distinction between the Christian as private citizen and the Christian as bearer of public office. The Reformation justifies war by arguing that a Christian as holder of a public office can return violence with violence in the name of love. Jesus, however, does not speak of this distinction between the private and the official. He expects his disciples to follow him obediently.[153] Bonhoeffer answers the major objection (that refusing to fight is an irresponsible enthusiasm because it fails to recognize the reality of sin or evil in the world[154]) by arguing that Christ's

152. Ibid., 133.

153. Ibid., 134–35.

154. Althaus, *The Ethics of Martin Luther*, 63–64. Althaus describes the Lutheran understanding of enthusiasm. He writes, "Luther was confronted by the Enthusiasts'— for example, the Anabaptists'—interpretation and application of the Sermon on the Mount. They too assert that the Sermon on the Mount and life in this world as it now is are in irresolvable contradiction to each other. If Christians really want to obey their Master, then they must leave this world. They neither may nor can participate in the institutions of this world, such as property, law, oath-taking, the exercise of authority, affairs of state, police work, the penal system, any kind of use of power, and war. Tolstoi asserted that true disciples of Jesus may not even participate in marriage, and similar opinions were current at the time of Luther . . . Luther . . . does not in any way weaken the Sermon on the Mount . . . Luther [though] recognizes—as Clement of Alexandria did earlier—that the freedom from the world of which Jesus speaks does not consist of outward but of inner distance."

position is actually the ultimate recognition of evil in the world.[155] He also argues that refusal to fight would be enthusiasm if Jesus' statement that "evil will only be conquered by good" were to be taken as "general secular wisdom for life in the world." He writes,

> That really would be an irresponsible imagining of laws which the world would never obey. Nonresistance as a principle for secular life is godless destruction of the order of the world which God graciously preserves. But it is not a programmatic thinker who is speaking here. Rather, the one speaking here about overcoming evil with suffering is he who himself was overcome by evil on the cross and who emerged from that defeat as conqueror and victor. There is no other justification for this commandment of Jesus than his own cross. Only those who there, in the cross of Jesus, find faith in the victory over evil can obey his command.[156]

Bonhoeffer thus arguably contradicts himself by reasserting the bifurcation between the secular and the Christian realm that he said Jesus avoided with the command. He also comes short of saying that pacifism should be adopted by all persons. He is clear though that true Christians are part of an exclusive community of holiness and therefore must not fight.

Bonhoeffer also interprets Jesus' command to love enemies. This command is an "extraordinary command" because it "is not only an unbearable offense to the natural person [but also] demands more strength than a natural person can muster, and it offends the natural concept of good and evil."[157] Bonhoeffer argues that the love required of Christians in this instance is the type of love required in all Christian acts. It is an extraordinary love beyond the natural.[158] In another criticism of current attitudes in Germany about the natural, he claims, "It is the great mistake of a false Protestant ethic to assume that loving Christ can be the same as loving one's native country, or friendship or profession, that the better righteousness and *justitia civilis* are the same."[159] The Christian, rather,

---

155. Ibid., 135.
156. Ibid., 136.
157. Ibid., 138.
158. Ibid., 144. He writes, "what is Christian is 'peculiar,' περισσόν, the extraordinary, irregular, not self-evident. This is the 'better righteousness' which 'outdoes' that of the Pharisees, towers over them, that which is more, beyond all else."
159. Ibid.

Phase 3: Church against or apart from World

cannot conform to the world. The περισσόν is unworldly, it is "the way of self-denial, perfect love, perfect purity, perfect truthfulness, perfect nonviolence."[160]

Bonhoeffer's section on the "Simplicity of the Carefree Life" addresses specifically the question of attachment to the world or earthly goods. He states clearly that the disciple sees Christ alone and not "Christ and the world." Bonhoeffer continues to see the world as something that is counter-Christ when he writes, "If the heart clings to the appearances of the world, to the creatures instead of the creator, then the disciple is lost. It is the goods of the world which try to turn the hearts of Jesus' disciples."[161] He argues that the heart's attachment to the goods of the world closes it off to the call of Jesus. Bonhoeffer suggests, as he did in the other situations where Christ's call forces one to give something up, that it would be simpler to take the command literally than to ask questions designed to soften the command. Bonhoeffer concludes his section on the Sermon on the Mount with a final cry for direct obedience to the call.[162]

Bonhoeffer's next significant section, "The Visible Church-Community," contains some of the strongest church-against-world sentiment in the book. Bonhoeffer treats explicitly the church as a visible community and its relationship to the world. The church must have a living space (*Lebensraum*) because it is a physical reality set in space and time. The church "gains space for Christ," but the members of the church are not part of the world. He continues, "all who belong to the body of Christ have been freed from and called out of the world."[163] Since their lives are, however, still in this world, they must bear witness to their separation from the world in the world. They live in their designated sphere to show disdain for the world. When they enter a secular calling, they do it to show just how far Christ's sphere is away from the worldly sphere. Bonhoeffer writes,

160. Ibid., 145. Bonhoeffer states that the "extraordinary" occurs in both the crucified Christ and in his community. Bonhoeffer says of the disciples, "Here are those who are perfect, perfect in undivided love, just as their Father in heaven is."

161. Ibid., 161–62.

162. *Discipleship*, 181. Bonhoeffer writes, "From the human point of view there are countless possibilities of understanding and interpreting the Sermon on the Mount. Jesus only knows one possibility: simply go and obey. Do not interpret or apply, but do it and obey."

163. Ibid., 236.

> Christians are to remain in the world, not because of the God-given goodness of the world, nor even because of their responsibility for the course the world takes. They are to remain in the world solely for the sake of the body of Christ who became incarnate—for the sake of the church community. They are to remain in the world in order to engage the world in a frontal assault. Let them "live out their vocation in this world" in order that their "unworldliness" might become fully visible. But this can take place only though visible membership in the church-community. The world must be contradicted in the world. That is why Christ became a human being and died in the midst of his enemies.[164]

Bonhoeffer continues with his church against world motif with further reference to Luther's return to secularity from the monastery. He writes,

> The value of the secular vocation for Christians is that it allows them to live in the world by God's goodness and to engage more fervently in the fight against the things of this world. Luther did not return to the world based on a "more positive assessment" of this world, or even by abandoning the expectation of the earliest church that Christ's return was imminent. His return rather was meant as a protest and criticism of the secularization of Christianity within the monastic life. By calling Christians back into the world, Luther in fact calls them to become unworldly in the true sense.[165]

Bonhoeffer thus reasserts the idea of being in the world only for the purpose of showing how different the Christian is from the world. He also emphasizes that this return to the world is in the service of reestablishing the idea of otherworldliness.

Bonhoeffer continues by arguing that, while Christians are to be and act in the world, there are limits to what they might do in their secular vocations. That is, "in certain cases the call into a secular vocation must of necessity be followed by the call to leave that worldly vocation." He describes that eventuality as one in which the "space the body of Christ claims and occupies in this world for worship, offices and the civic life of its members" clashes with the "world's own claim for space."[166] In this instance, the church can make a visible profession of faith. The world, in this instance, can either concede ground to the church or re-

---

164. Ibid., 244.
165. Ibid., 245.
166. Ibid.

Phase 3: Church against or apart from World

sort to violence. Bonhoeffer also makes the point that the church sometimes initiates the withdrawal from secular professions. He cites acting, policing, and being a soldier as examples of professions that the early church deemed unacceptable for the Christian.[167] Because of the embrace of secularization, the church-world relationship became such that those professions became acceptable for Christians. Bonhoeffer argues that the clash between the church and secularity grows more intense as history proceeds, and the world's efforts to rid itself of Christians will intensify.[168]

While again stressing the fact that the body of Christ is necessarily in the world, Bonhoeffer ultimately emphasizes the extent to which it is called to not conform to the world. The church is involved with the world but there are times when a "complete separation remains visible, and must become even more visible." Christians, whether in separation from the world or working in a separated way within the world, must obey Romans 12:2 which states, "Do not be conformed to this world, but be transformed to a new form (μεταμορφοῦσθε) by the renewing of your minds, so that you may discern the will of God."[169] Bonhoeffer argues that there is an illegitimate way of both remaining in the world and of separating therefrom. He continues,

> In either case we become conformed to the world. But the community of Christ has a "form" that is different from that of the world. The community is called to be ever increasingly transformed into this form. It is, in fact, the form of Christ himself. He came into the world and in infinite mercy bore us and accepted us. And yet he did not become conformed to the world but was actually rejected and cast out by it. He was not of this world. If it engages the world properly, the visible church-community will always more closely assume the form of the suffering Lord.[170]

Bonhoeffer again emphasizes the importance of establishing a visible disavowal of the world. The form of Christ is ultimately different from that of the world. He also reiterates the suffering the community must experience for having attached itself to Christ. The church's conforming to Christ rather than to the world will earn for it the world's disdain.

167. Ibid., 246.
168. Ibid., 247.
169. Ibid.
170. Ibid., 247–48.

The church can only suffer for having attached itself to Christ. It can do nothing else.

Bonhoeffer's concluding chapters, "The Saints" and "The Image of Christ," offer still more church-against-world argumentation. Bonhoeffer writes, for example, that the "'ekklesia' of Christ, the community of disciples, is no longer subject to the rule of this world."[171] He does argue, like he has in other chapters, that the church "still lives in the midst of the world." It has, however, been made into one body and has a "territory with an authority of its own, a space set apart."[172] God has chosen this church-community, reconciled it, and purified it. The church-community is "the fulfillment of God's will to establish a holy community . . . [that is] set apart from the world and sin as God's own possession, the body of Christ is God's realm of holiness in the world."[173] Bonhoeffer explains that the church-community is actually sanctified by separating itself from the world. Sanctification requires first of all a "clear separation from the world." Bonhoeffer writes,

> The church-community's claim to a space of its own within the world, and the concomitant separation from the space of the world, attests that the church-community is in a state of sanctification. For the seal of the Holy Spirit seals off the church-community from the rest of the world. By the power of this seal, God's community must insist on God's claim to the whole world. At the same time, it must claim a specific space for itself within the world, thus drawing a clear dividing line between itself and the world.[174]

Bonhoeffer does claim that the church claims the entire world. It is clear though, from prior argumentation, that until the end, there will be the stark break between the church and the world.

Church-World Relationship and Political Thinking

Bonhoeffer's work, while a well-regarded and powerful classic of contemporary Christian spirituality and devotion, is fraught with unresolved problems. It has been the source of radically different and even conflicting scholarly interpretation. Some commentators seize on Bonhoeffer's

---

171. Ibid., 253.
172. Ibid.
173. Ibid., 254.
174. Ibid., 261.

Phase 3: Church against or apart from World

argumentation that the church claims a visible space and remains in the world as evidence that he is not advocating for a sect-like, otherworldly, escapist, or apolitical notion of the church.[175] Others see *Discipleship* as a detour from the consistency in the worldliness between the early part and the last part of Bonhoeffer's life.[176] The resolution of the diametrically opposed scholarly sentiment rests in an examination of the connection between his understanding of the church-world relationship and his political positions. It is clear, given the foregoing summary of the text, that Bonhoeffer holds to a church-against-world vision. In response to the call, disciples are removed from the sphere of the world and placed in the sphere of the church community. They are strangers in this world. They do not act in the ways that the world dictates for persons. They are counter-cultural and counter-worldly.

Perhaps most importantly, disciples not only experience persecution, rejection, and suffering for their counter-world stance. They also expect and even welcome poor treatment. This dynamic appears to be the underlying reason for Bonhoeffer's call to reenter the world so strongly pointed out by those who would argue that his vision is not entirely counter-world or counter-cultural. The disciples or church-community stay in the world only so that, in their visible suffering, they can

---

175. Ibid., 14–20. John Godsey and Geffrey Kelly, for example, in their "Editors' Introduction to the English Edition" of *Discipleship*, argue that Bonhoeffer's counter cultural stance was understandable given the widespread acquiescence to Nazi ideology in the church. They write, "This counter cultural perspective was not a flight *from* the world, but a struggle to establish a critical church presence in the world. Hence *Discipleship* contains ample exhortations for the church to engage positively for the world." They acknowledge the tendency of some critics to see the book "as too otherworldly and impractical in how Christians had to deal with an enemy such as Nazism— so dangerous to Christian civilization and so entrenched in power militarily." They continue, "Some critics see *Discipleship* as more of a detour along the way to the more realistic actions of Bonhoeffer the conspirator, the affirmer of a world come of age in the prison letters." They argue that these commentators "fail to appreciate Bonhoeffer's ever-shifting dialectic in pitting the Christian disciple against the wiles and twisted values of what he depicts as a world plunged into widespread iniquity."

176. See Davis, "Gandhi and Pacifism," 49. Davis argues that Bonhoeffer's particular form of pacifism (Gandhian pacifism) throughout his life allowed for entry into the political conspiracy except for the form in *The Cost of Discipleship*. See also, Phillips, *Christ for Us*, 104. Phillips writes, "For *The Cost of Discipleship*, transcendence means primarily from the world . . . Christology was given concrete form in discipleship, and discipleship meant nothing less than a 'breach with the things of this world.' But in the [later] prison letters, the 'boundaries' which delineated this breach of the world have disappeared."

show just how counter-worldly is their churchly sphere. More suffering and rejection means a purer form of discipleship. Ultimately, Bonhoeffer has established a two-sphered reality, even if the otherworldly sphere sits side by side with the worldly sphere. The overlap between the two spheres has no content other than the wide gap between them.

Bonhoeffer's two-sphered vision of reality (the sphere of the worldly, secular, or cultural and the otherworldly sphere of the church-community) is, furthermore, a prescription for political passivity. The fact that Bonhoeffer places the church back into the world does not mean, as some of Bonhoeffer's commentators assume, that it has anything other than an accidental or implicit political status as a physical entity, organization, or "polis" within the world. Even if the church does not withdraw entirely from the larger world, it stands only as a "sign of contradiction" in the world. Further, the church's prescribed actions in the world have the nature of a withdrawal. It is hard to further argue that this withdrawal stands as a contrived political protest aimed at changing various political systems or circumstances (nonresistance aimed at effecting political change, for example) when Bonhoeffer argues specifically that disciples are to be concerned only and solely with clinging to Christ (and not with how that clinging might affect anything else). They must suffer passively as a result of this clinging as they wait for God to usher in the end.

An analysis of Bonhoeffer's treatment of some explicitly politically related issues illustrates my point. He has a whole section on Paul's letter to Philemon. He argues that slaves should remain slaves because they, having been called to discipleship and to the church-community, are already liberated. Slaves should remain in the condition they were in when called.[177] They, as members of Christ's community, "gained the kind of freedom which no rebellion or revolution could have brought them or could ever bring them."[178] They are to remain in their condition and renounce revolution.[179] The idea that Christ's kingdom is coming in the future forms a significant part of the political passivity.[180] Slaves

---

177. *Discipleship*, 237.

178. Ibid., 238.

179. Ibid., 239. Slaves, by "renouncing rebellion against the forms of order in this world . . . express most convincingly that they expect nothing from the world but everything from Christ and his coming realm."

180. Ibid., 239. Bonhoeffer continues, "That is why slaves are to remain slaves!

Phase 3: Church against or apart from World 253

are also to take comfort in the fact that Jesus, himself, "took the form of a slave" when he was on the earth. Bonhoeffer even comes close to arguing that slavery is, because it entails a forced distance from the natural, a situation helpful for showing the world's hatred of Christ and therefore a favorable situation for discipleship. Bonhoeffer concludes, "Therefore, slaves ought to suffer not as a consequence of being rebellious but as members of the church-community and the body of Christ! That is how the world is getting ripe for its demise."[181] Christians, with their feet in the churchly sphere and their eyes set on the otherworldly sphere to come, have no recourse to any action upholding their rights in the worldly sphere. They are to suffer passively only for the purpose of showing their allegiance to Christ and difference from the world and not to effect political change, until Christ comes again.

Bonhoeffer moves from the specific issue of slavery to the general issue of allegiance to authority. He argues, like Calvin and Luther, that Christians should obey worldly authority. He writes, "The world rules; Christians serve." Bonhoeffer is not arguing about general authority, but about particular leaders in particular situations. He writes,

> They [Christians] are to take comfort from the fact that God will use the authorities as an instrument through which to work for their welfare, and that their God is Lord over the authorities. But this statement must be more than an abstract consideration and idea about the nature of authority (ἐξουσία—note the singular!) in general. It must determine the attitudes of Christians to the actually existing authorities (αι δὲ οὖσαι . . .). Whoever resists them resists what God has decreed (διατγῇ τοῦ θεοῦ), the God who intended the world to exercise authority, and for Christ and the Christians belonging to him to gain victory through service. Christians failing to recognize this fact would become subject to judgement (v. 2), for they would once again no longer be any different from the world.[182]

Christians are to be concerned only with doing good and doing the will of God. They are to be concerned only with the realm or sphere of the church, and not the realm or sphere of the world. Any other concern, in-

---

Because this world is not in need of reform, but ripe to be demolished—that is why slaves are to remain slaves! They have God's promise of something far better!"
181. Ibid., 239.
182. Ibid., 240.

cluding judging the good or evil nature of the particular leader, indicates an inappropriate reentry into the world.

According to Bonhoeffer's interpretation of Paul, it is Christians and not the leaders themselves who are called to Christian purity.[183] Christians, furthermore, should not be concerned with whether or not they gain the approval of the ruling authorities. Rather, they should endure suffering at the hands of the authorities and remain obedient even in persecution. They can endure suffering even though they are innocent because "they know that in the end it is God that rules, not the authorities, and that any authority is ultimately God's servant."[184] Again, according to this two-sphere thinking, the church-community should be concerned with the proceedings and purity in its own sphere and be indifferent to the same qualities in the worldly sphere. Furthermore, the church-community, knowing that the victory Christ has already effected will eventually manifest itself fully in the world, can endure suffering until that day. The church stands only as continued testimony to the enmity between Christ and the world.

The question of nonviolence has been treated above. Rather than engaging in activity that would establish the worldly sphere as a legitimate space (claiming rights in the world, for example), disciples are to cling to the person of Christ only. Violence is to be met with love and the willingness to suffer in order to show the large gap between the worldly sphere and the sphere of the community of Christ in the world. Bonhoeffer further asserts the breach between the sphere of the secular and the sphere of the Christ-community when he argues that this position of nonviolence does not apply to the secular sphere. That would be a "godless destruction of the order of the world which God graciously preserves."[185] It should be noted that Bonhoeffer does not address specifically the contradiction between the church-community's unwillingness to participate in war and its duty to obey the secular rulers. It would

---

183. Ibid., 242. Bonhoeffer argues that Paul addresses Christians and not the leaders "not because the way this world is ordered is so good, but because its good or bad qualities are irrelevant compared to the only thing that is truly important, namely, that the church-community submit and live according to God's will."

184. Ibid., 242–43. He continues, "Authority as the servant of God—here speaks someone who knows that all powers and authorities of this world have already been stripped of their power, that Christ has already led them to the cross in triumphant victory, and that it will be but a short while until all this must become manifest."

185. Ibid., 136.

Phase 3: Church against or apart from World

seem that participating in war would be one of those secular vocations no longer a possibility for the Christian.[186]

The positions on all three specific political situations (slavery, the submission to ruling authority and nonviolence) illustrate the connection between Bonhoeffer's specific church-against-world stance and political passivity. Bonhoeffer's church-world position cannot properly be considered an outright church-withdrawn-from-world vision. He does, after all, advocate for a return back into the world or a living-in-the-midst-of-the-world notion of the church even if it is just to show the enmity between the church and the world or the difference between the church and the world. There remains, nevertheless, a question as to whether Bonhoeffer is guilty of sectarianism. He does explicitly discount the notion that the church should act like a sect in terms of its mission to offer the gospel to the entire world.[187] Bonhoeffer also argues that the church-community is not entirely pure.[188] He does, however, assume that the aim of the church community is to seek absolute purity in a law-like discipleship with respect to the directives of the Sermon on the Mount. The church is not defined as an entity that might accept, include, or patiently endure those who do not aim for purity. This quality, along with the strict or literal adherence to the Sermon on the Mount requiring nonviolence, places Bonhoeffer close to Troeltsch's definition of "sect" and the stances common to the sect-like historic peace churches.[189]

---

186. Ibid., 245–47.

187. Ibid., 196. Bonhoeffer writes, "The gospel should not become some sectarian affair. Instead it is to be preached in public."

188. Ibid., 269. Bonhoeffer writes, "The community of saints is not the 'ideal' church-community of the sinless and the perfect."

189. Wogaman, *Christian Perspectives on Politics*, 173–74. Wogaman describes Troeltsch's concept of sect: "Or, at the opposite end of the pole, one can understand the church as the company of the truly committed—a sectarian island of holiness or redemption in the larger sea of secularity or fallenness . . . The second type, the sectarian, is likely to envisage the church as withdrawn from the political realm." See also Bainton, *Christian Attitudes*, 154–55. Bainton's description of the Anabaptists is close to Bonhoeffer's vision. He writes, "His [Christ's] kingdom they held to be based on the Sermon on the Mount and his injunctions to be literally obeyed, not only with regard to war but also with regard to the oath. Here, then is a New Testament legalism. Obedience, discipleship and the imitation of Christ are the recurrent words in the Anabaptist confessions. They suggest something more than individual behavior and stand in the context of a program for the Church which must itself first be restored to the purity of the apostolic time, when Christianity was persecuted rather than supported by the state."

Overall, Bonhoeffer has constructed a church set apart from the larger community, one that is called to a greater purity than the secular, and one that does not conduct itself by the same set of rules or values as the secular. This church sits in a "holding pattern," passively accepting conditions as they are until the end. So even though this church sits in the midst of the world, its manner of operation and sphere of concern affords it no real concern with secular matters. The church is concerned with itself, its discipline, its following Christ, and an attachment to Christ that makes attachment to the world tenuous at best and totally unnecessary at worst. The church is in its own sphere and is unconcerned about the secular. It does not remain in the world, therefore, because of any particular responsibility for the course of the world. The church is to renounce the rights afforded it by the secular realm and to stay in its position and suffer patiently and passively as Christ did, knowing that the world's increasing encroachment on the church's space signals the final liberation.[190] In light of Bonhoeffer's two-sphered thinking in *Discipleship*, the church would have no political recourse against Hitler. Taking an active political stand against Hitler would be a non-Christian or non-church act. It would be truer to the call to discipleship to let Hitler or any other political regime to take over and wait for God to usher in the Kingdom. The world can go on in whatever direction it will.

The Collective Pastorates (January 1938—June 1939)

Bonhoeffer's next commitment was to two Finkenwalde-like vicarages in eastern Pomerania, Köslin and Gross-Schlönwitz.[191] These places were shut down by the Gestapo in March 1940. I will, however, only treat

---

190. Ibid., 247. Bonhoeffer writes, "But the older this world grows, and the more sharply the struggle between Christ and Antichrist grows, the more thorough also become the world's efforts to rid itself of the Christians . . . In the end, Christians are thus left with no other choices but to escape from the world or go to prison. But when they have been deprived of their last inch of space here on earth, the end will be near." See also ibid., 250. Bonhoeffer writes, "but they [the church-community] will even do what must seem incomprehensible to the world, namely, to prefer to be taken advantage of and to suffer injustice rather than to insist on their rights before a pagan court of law . . . In suffering [the church-community] is patient and joyful, taking pride in its tribulation."

191. *DB*, 589. They were set up under a name different than "preaching seminary" in order to avoid the prohibition of training pastors in illegal seminaries.

Phase 3: Church against or apart from World

Bonhoeffer's experience up to June 1939, when he traveled to America for the second time.

The political scene between 1938 and June 1939 involved primarily the beginning of Hitler's war. Hitler set his sights on neighboring Czechoslovakia after successfully annexing Austria. Convinced that Britain and France would not act to defend Czechoslovakia, Hitler ordered his troops to invade it in March 1938. Hitler then decided to take Poland.[192] On the church front, events between 1938 and mid-1939 were characterized by increasing hostilities on the part of the state toward the church.[193] In light of the general church disruption, Kerrl announced that the church elections proposed by Hitler would be suspended indefinitely. On December 10, Kerrl also proposed a new administrative initiative giving him control over the provincial churches. He also handed the disciplinary control of pastors to Dr. Werner (a German Christian). Kerrl's newest efforts, though, proved to be an ineffective means of forging a working relationship between a unified Evangelical Church and the state.[194] In addition, his public propaganda case against Niemöller leading up to his trial in February 1938 was unsuccessful. Niemöller was found "not guilty" by the court. Hitler still had Niemöller arrested on direct orders and sent to the Sachsenhausen concentration camp and then to Dachau, where he stayed for the next seven years despite ecclesial and international outcry.[195]

The Confessing Church was, for its part, starting to experience a heightened sense of confusion and disunity. Werner issued an order in the *Legal Gazette* on April 20, 1938, demanding that all pastors take

---

192. *HNG*, 207-9. The Treaty of Versailles made the German city of Danzig a Polish seaport. Hitler now demanded the city back. When the Polish accepted an Anglo-French offer of protection against Germany, Hitler revoked his nonaggression pact with Poland at the end of April 1939. Hitler would soon attack Poland.

193. *NPC*, 209-11. The arrest of over 700 pastors by November 1937 was accompanied by the removal of preaching rights, ejections from parishes, and deprivation of stipends. Kerrl made public threats to reduce state subsidies to the churches wherein the Confessing Church element refused to repent. Pastors affiliated with the Confessing Church were not allowed to teach in state schools, and pastors who had taken their ordinations at Confessing seminaries were denied stipends. All theology students were forced to join Nazi organizations. An evangelical publishing house was seized, and a large Protestant church in Munich was demolished.

194. *NPC*, 209-11.

195. Ibid., 212-13.

an oath of allegiance to Hitler.[196] The Confessing Church allowed the pastors to take the oath provided that certain conditions were fulfilled.[197] Most of the pastors in the Confessing Church signed the oath even after a strong negative minority opinion was expressed at a July 1938 synod. Martin Bormann, leader of the Nazi Party in Munich, dealt a heavy blow to the Confessing Church, however, when he sent a letter stating that the Nazi Party did not recognize any nuanced interpretation of the oath. Any pastor who signed the oath did so on the authority of the *Führer* or the party, regardless of their attempts to avoid this implication.[198]

The Confessing Church was weakened by the arrests. It was also hurt by the embarrassment over signing the oath. The disarray in the Confessing Church was perhaps highlighted best by the lack of united response to the infamous November 9, 1938 *Kristallnacht* (Crystal Night) attack on the Jewish population. The Nazis burned down 177 synagogues and arrested over 20,000 Jews. There were only a few notable responses from the Protestant or Catholic leadership.[199] Some churches even supported Hitler by passing decrees that banned Jews from entering their churches. The provincial churches of the *Deutsche Christen* created an institution "for the research and removal of Jewish influences on the Church life of the German people."[200]

196. Ibid., 211. See also *DB*, 600. The text of Werner's ordinance included the following: "In the recognition that only those may hold office in the church who are unswervingly loyal to the Führer, the people of the Reich, it is hereby decreed: Anyone who is called to a spiritual office is to affirm his loyal duty with the following oath: 'I swear that I will be faithful and obedient to Adolf Hitler, the Führer of the German Reich and people, that I will conscientiously observe the laws and carry out the duties of my office, so help me God.' . . . Anyone who was called before this decree came into force . . . is to take the oath of allegiance retroactively . . . Anyone who refuses to take the oath of allegiance is to be dismissed."

197. *DB*, 601.

198. Ibid.

199. *NPC*, 223. Conway notes, "the Church leaders, both Catholic and Evangelical, turned a blind eye. Exhausted and demoralized by previous efforts, they fell silent even in the face of such monstrous outrages. The only voice raised in dissent was that of Fr. Lichtenberg, the Catholic Provost of Berlin, who on the following day led his congregation in prayer for the persecuted non-Aryans among the German community. His action immediately made him a marked man, and destined him to suffer imprisonment and finally death for his courageous act. Nonetheless, his example was promptly followed by the Evangelical Pastor Grüber, who established an office in Berlin where Christian Jews could receive advice and assistance in escaping from the country, until he himself was arrested in December 1940."

200. *NPC*, 230.

Phase 3: Church against or apart from World

Bonhoeffer's activities between early 1938 to June 1939 indicate more frustration with the Confessing Church. He continued preaching and teaching in the collective pastorates as he had at Finkenwalde. He also traveled to various places and continued to try to lead the Confessing Church back to the spirit of Barmen and Dahlem. He attended the July synod concerning the oath of loyalty to Hitler, and supported the minority opinion to no avail. Bonhoeffer was ashamed and embarrassed that the majority of Confessing Church members took the oath.[201] He was also involved in the controversy over "legalization," or the official statuses of those pastors trained in the illegal seminaries. Church consistories pressured the illegal pastors to officially apply for legal church status. The illegal pastors thus had to decide whether to hold fast to the resolutions of Barmen and Dahlem or to officially register as legitimate pastors in the eyes of the Reich Church. Bonhoeffer was in favor of a non-compromise position.[202]

Bonhoeffer was also faced with the real possibility of a call to military duty. He pursued international travel (first to England and then to America) as a way to avoid conscription. Major von Kleist, the head of the local recruiting station, was a friend of the Bonhoeffer family and pushed through swiftly his application to go to England for two months.[203] Bonhoeffer's time in England was spent in a questioning anxiety over the issue of his military service. He wondered if his refusal to enter the military would dangerously and publicly label his Confessing Church as an anti-state church. He wondered if it would be more useful to offer his theological expertise to the ecumenical church worldwide than to enter the military. He also wondered whether even the Confessing Church would not see his refusal of military service to be a "destructive and iso-

---

201. *DB*, 601–3. Bethge writes, "Bonhoeffer was ashamed of the Confessing church, the way one feels shame for a scandal in one's own family. This Confessing synod had approved the oath to the Führer when it already knew of the impending order that non-Aryans must have a large 'J' stamped on their identity cards—an omen of worse things to come, and the thing that finally moved his twin sister's family to flee" (603).

202. Ibid., 612–3. Bonhoeffer spoke at a "extraordinary convention" in Pomerania in October 1938, where he also warned against compromise. Bonhoeffer also acted in Westphalia, for instance, when four-fifths of the illegal pastors voted to compromise. Bonhoeffer reacted forcefully in writing, encouraging pastors to stand by their convictions.

203. Ibid., 634.

lated course."²⁰⁴ Bonhoeffer ultimately decided to delay the decision by procuring an invitation to America. He sought out Bishop Bell's advice while in England. He also sought out Reinhold Niebuhr, who was in Scotland delivering the Gifford Lectures at the time. Niebuhr was very helpful and procured for Bonhoeffer a formal invitation to New York.²⁰⁵

When Bonhoeffer returned from England the problem of his military conscription was not yet settled. He was formally called up to the military in mid-May and was to report on May 22. In an act of desperation, Bonhoeffer called on his father to speak to Major von Kleist. The intervention was successful. Bonhoeffer was granted permission to leave for America on June 2, 1939. Without this intervention he would have had to decide whether to enter the military or to appear before a court-martial as a conscientious objector.²⁰⁶ Bonhoeffer was not entirely clear about why he made the decision to leave for the United States. In a letter to Bishop Bell he pointed to the military conscription as the major reason.²⁰⁷ In another letter to Henry Smith Leiper a few weeks later he cited his role as international contact for the Confessing Church in the ecumenical church as the primary reason for his decision to leave for America (with military service being a secondary concern).²⁰⁸ Bethge describes the decision as a "flight" and finds in Bonhoeffer's diary entries regarding this matter evidence that Bonhoeffer considered it a flight as well.²⁰⁹

One extremely significant final event from phase 3 was Bonhoeffer's initial contact with the explicitly political resistance to the Nazi regime. Bonhoeffer's brother-in-law, Hans von Dohnanyi, was the link between Bonhoeffer and the formal political resistance. Dohnanyi served in several capacities which allowed him access to inside information concerning Nazi horrors.²¹⁰ He introduced Bonhoeffer to Major General Hans

---

204. Ibid., 636.

205. Ibid., 639.

206. Ibid., 634–35. Hermann Stöhr, a member of the Fellowship of Reconciliation, was arrested and shot when he registered as a conscientious objector.

207. Ibid., 637.

208. Ibid., 637–38.

209. Ibid., 636, 638.

210. Ibid., 624. Dohnanyi was a personal information officer to justice ministers and Reich Minister of Justice Franz Gürtner. He became a Supreme Court judge in Leipzig in September 1938.

Phase 3: Church against or apart from World

Oster, Head of Military Intelligence Wilhelm Canaris, head of the army's legal department Dr. Karl Sack, and General Ludwig Beck.[211] All four were members of the quickly developing political resistance to Hitler. There is, however, scant evidence proving that Bonhoeffer at that point knew of the plans to overthrow the regime or was even in close contact with the conspirators.[212] However, Bethge does list the dilemma of the possibility of active and direct anti-state political action (a course of action not traditionally available to a German Lutheran) as one of the factors influencing his decision to escape from Germany in June 1939.[213]

FORMS OF POLITICAL INVOLVEMENT

Bonhoeffer's forms of activity in this phase range from those associated with London to his seminary experience. While in London his activity beyond the delivery of the sermons included continued participation in the church struggle. Yet, his engagement in this struggle was somewhat tempered by his distance from it in London. Often the news from Germany was either hard to obtain or partly inaccurate. Nevertheless, Bonhoeffer and Hildebrandt (Bonhoeffer's young minister friend of Jewish descent) did respond to certain events in Germany. The first event was the November Sports Palace Rally. When Bonhoeffer and Hildebrandt heard that some German bishops had decided to negotiate with Müller, they wrote a letter to Niemöller encouraging him to remain firm in his convictions. Bonhoeffer and Hildebrandt suggested that earlier synods of the Pastors' Emergency League be dissolved and that any potential new members be subject to screening and disciplinary review. Bonhoeffer sent another encouraging telegram to Niemöller when he heard that Niemöller was confused about how to proceed. Bonhoeffer had just persuaded all of the London pastors to join the Pastors' Emergency League and could not withstand any backsliding on the part of its leader.[214]

211. Ibid., 625.
212. Ibid., 625–26.
213. Ibid., 636. Bethge writes, "Finally, Bonhoeffer had a growing sense that if he remained in Germany, he would be drawn more deeply into the conspiracy against Hitler. Was it right for a pastor and a theologian to go beyond the role of accessory, to actively participate in such a conspiracy? Wouldn't it be easier to avoid this dilemma? Everything suggested that it might be easier for him to arrive at a definite conclusion on these matters outside Germany."
214. Ibid., 335–38.

In further activity, Bonhoeffer sent a series of telegrams to the Reich Church government indicating the London pastors' continued lack of confidence in Müller as Reich bishop when Berlin requested a London delegation be sent to Müller's consecration.[215] Bishop Theodor Heckel (church leader in charge of the Ecclesiastical Foreign Ministry) responded to the telegrams by encouraging all the pastors abroad to concentrate on the tasks in the foreign churches rather than on the German church situation. Concerned that the London pastors would inform the world press and the ecumenical movement about the German church situation, Heckel also planned an actual visit to London. He ultimately wanted the London pastors to give their allegiance to the Reich bishop.[216] In preparation for Heckel's visit Bonhoeffer and his colleagues wrote a six-point memorandum wherein they expressed their indignation at Müller's recent abuses.[217] Bonhoeffer was the first to speak after Heckel's speech to the London pastors during his February visit. According to the notes taken, he questioned Heckel as to why his concerns were with church unity rather than the theological mistakes of the German Christians, especially those concerning the Old Testament and the Aryan clause. Bonhoeffer even suggested that the most important concern should be possible secession from such a church.[218]

Bonhoeffer's ecumenical involvement also continued throughout his London days. One of his most significant relationships was forged with the Bishop of Chichester, George K. A. Bell. Bell had an important position as the Chairman of the Universal Council of Churches. Bonhoeffer came highly recommended to Bell as someone who had extensive knowledge of the German church crisis. Bell even suggested that Bonhoeffer consult with certain politicians, but Bonhoeffer refused because he thought it would put him in a "questionable position."[219] His correspondence with Bell indicated his main concern. Bonhoeffer was mostly concerned that the ecumenical movement regard the opposition church as the true Evangelical Church in Germany. His concern would force Bell, as the chairman of the ecumenical organization, to pressure Müller into choosing which faction in the German church was the legiti-

---

215. Ibid., 338–43.
216. Ibid., 334–36.
217. See Ibid., 347–48 for a listing of the six points.
218. Ibid., 349.
219. Ibid., 357.

Phase 3: Church against or apart from World 263

mate one. Bell did so in writing.[220] Bonhoeffer's interactions with Bell, and his ecumenical activities in general, would give rise to suspicion from the church authorities in Berlin.[221] On Bonhoeffer's recommendation, Bell wrote a letter to Müller in response to the events of January 1934 suggesting that Müller was no longer capable of dealing with the ecumenical movement. Bell also wrote to Hindenburg. These letters, combined with the fact that Heckel's February visit found a Bell who was very well-informed about the German church situation, were enough for the authorities in Berlin to take some form of action concerning Bonhoeffer's "disturbing influence" on Bell.[222] Heckel finally decided to address Bonhoeffer's activities when he learned that the Archbishop of Canterbury was to meet directly with Bonhoeffer to discuss the happenings in the German church. Heckel demanded that Bonhoeffer refrain from ecumenical activities and asked him to sign a written agreement. Bonhoeffer's March 18 letter to Heckel stated that he would not sign the document and would continue his "purely ecclesiastical, theological, ecumenical work."[223]

Bonhoeffer's activities at Fanø also indicated other signs of concern for the church's freedom to assert itself as church against external interference. His choice of topic or content for both his lecture and his sermon is a somewhat interesting phenomenon. Schönfeld and the research committee wanted material on "the church's responsibility for what is intrinsic to a nation" among other things.[224] Given the climate in Germany, where the *Deutsche Christen* did not have an adequate understanding of their role in the nation and where certain factions of the Nazi Party were overstepping their boundaries vis-à-vis the church, that topic seemed to provide a platform tailor-made for Bonhoeffer. Instead, against advice

---

220. Ibid., 356–57.
221. Ibid., 362–64. There was a rumor in Berlin that Bonhoeffer was involved in the London *Times*'s "embarrassingly accurate" descriptions of the church struggle. In addition, Lord Lothian, an influential politician with connections to *The Round Table*, an important English monthly magazine, wanted to run an article about the situation in the German Protestant church. Bonhoeffer was asked to write the article but he declined, and Bell wrote the article with the provision that Bonhoeffer would look over the draft. The Church Federation Office, however, somehow found out that Bonhoeffer was helping Bell with the article.
222. Ibid., 364.
223. Ibid., 365.
224. Ibid., 386.

and counsel, Bonhoeffer chose to concentrate on a pacifism that was specifically theological and apolitical, a form different from the more political form espoused in the second phase.[225]

Bonhoeffer's later activity at Fanø included a further push for pacifistic and other resolutions at the youth conference. The conference debated the issue of conscientious objection. The more controversial issues involved the wording in two specific resolutions. Bonhoeffer wanted to propose a resolution that allowed the foreign press to criticize Germany for incidents involving the church. When this proposal came up for a vote, though, many of Bonhoeffer's own students voted against it. The next proposed resolution saw Bonhoeffer pushing for the council to state that it rejected support for "any war whatsoever." Bonhoeffer and his pacifist friend Jean Lasserre, part of the French delegation, battled with the Polish and Hungarian delegation who wanted to use "aggressive wars" rather than "any war whatsoever." The conference finally agreed to retain Bonhoeffer and Lasserre's wording.[226]

When Bonhoeffer returned to London after Fanø his activities continued along the lines of establishing separation. He attempted to get the Confessing Church government to continue to assert itself as distinct from the Reich Church. Bonhoeffer did not attend the October conference in Dahlem. He did, though, encourage the Confessing Church government to uphold the resolution from that synod whereby the Confessing Church would not recognize any Reich church directives.[227] A November 5 meeting of the German churches in London produced their own resolution pledging support for the Confessing Church. Bonhoeffer was overjoyed at the resolution, which was essentially a decision to try to secede from the Reich Church. He saw it as the fruits of his labor.[228] Bonhoeffer and his colleagues saw another victory in Hitler's statement of government neutrality in church matters, seeing in it the possibility that the Confessing Church be considered an official church body.[229] The Confessing Church, for its part, despite having successfully

---

225. Ibid. Bethge writes, "Compared with 1932, he showed a new forthrightness that ruled out any exception from this command and its realization. It was a foretaste of the intellectual climate of *Discipleship*; his terminology was highly provocative. Never before had he declared that there could be no justification for war, even a defensive war."

226. Ibid., 390–91.

227. Ibid., 394–95.

228. Ibid., 395.

229. Ibid., 396–99.

Phase 3: Church against or apart from World 265

established two synods, lacked theological uniformity, funds, and a set system of church governance. The Provisional Church Administration, formed officially on November 22, was in constant flux and in constant disagreement over the level of intensity in its resolutions.[230]

Bonhoeffer's activities continued to be controversial and geared toward separation. Heckel attacked the November 5 resolutions by arguing that, legally, each German congregation in England would have to issue its own declaration of secession. If the pastors did so, though, they would be subject to legal actions including the loss of their right to be pastors when returning to Germany (and the accompanying loss of pension money). Bonhoeffer and the London pastors hired a lawyer to make sure their decision to secede was legally protected. On January 4, 1935, Bonhoeffer and the London pastors reaffirmed the November 5 statement with another strongly worded resolution.[231] Ultimately, however, after Bonhoeffer left London, the German pastors there got caught up with other theological concerns. In addition, Heckel's Church Foreign Office informed the pastors that their secession had not been put on record. Bonhoeffer's triumphs in London were either nullified at worst or short-lived at best.[232]

Bonhoeffer spent his last month in London trying to decide what to do next. Much to the consternation of Barth and others, Bonhoeffer was determined to travel to India, meet Gandhi, and explore the ways in which his methods of non-resistance might be useful in the German church struggle. Bonhoeffer got Bishop Bell to write Gandhi a letter on his behalf and procured a letter of invitation from Gandhi himself.[233]

230. Ibid., 400–402.
231. Ibid., 403–4.
232. Ibid., 405–6. Bethge describes, "No sooner had Bonhoeffer disappeared from the London scene than the majority of German congregations in England began to see the church struggle in a different light. During this new era of General Superintendent Zoellner's church committees, most fell under the spell of a new slogan, the preservation of the '*Volkskirche*.' The files of the English Pastors' conference reveal that the phrase 'Bible and Confession' was decisive during Bonhoeffer's period there. After 1936, concern for the *Volkskirche* prevailed. Pastor Schönberger ceased to play any role in the cause, devoting himself to work on behalf of the National Socialist Party in London . . . The minutes of the pastors' conference of June 1936 record the isolated remark of a participant: 'You will, I hope, not think too ill of me if, having been subjected for years to Bonhoeffer's influence, voluntarily or involuntarily . . . we stand more on the side of the Confessing church!'"
233. Ibid., 408–9. Bonhoeffer made contacts with English pacifists who followed Gandhi, did research, got clothing suited for the East from a friend who had been there,

Bonhoeffer did not follow through with the India plans. Instead, he decided to become the headmaster of a monastery-like seminary designed to train pastors for the Confessing Church. Bonhoeffer toured three Anglican monasteries in the beginning of March in preparation for his next assignment.[234]

Bonhoeffer's London pastorate produced only one major piece of writing of significance for understanding the relationship between his church-world thinking and political matters. His Fanø peace sermon is a strong argument for an absolute and mostly apolitical pacifism accompanied by a negative vision of the world. Bonhoeffer's other extant literature, some sermons delivered to the London congregations, show a Bonhoeffer more concerned with spiritual matters than with any concrete political situation. His actual activity in London is significant mostly for how it shows the nature of Bonhoeffer's continued struggle against the Reich Church. Bonhoeffer is indeed concerned, like he was in phase 2, with the identity of the church. What is different in this phase was his obsession with separation, with trying to get the ecumenical church to see the Confessing Church as a separate and legitimate entity apart from the Reich Church. This obsession forced Bonhoeffer into an entrenched position in the church against the world. Accordingly, Bonhoeffer engaged in activity solely in the ecclesial realm.

The theme of separation, considered before the London pastorate,[235] became manifest during this phase-3 London pastorate. Bonhoeffer's speech during Heckel's February visit provides a good example of how he conceived of separation. The objection was a theological one about what it is that actually constitutes a true Christian church.[236] Bonhoeffer held the Confessing Church up against the Reich Church and judged, based on ecclesiology, that the Confessing Church was purer. His efforts in the ecumenical realm were geared toward making the various ecumenical organizations realize this greater purity. The ramifications

---

and even went to a medical facility to see if he was physically ready to withstand Indian climates. See also Bonhoeffer, *The Way to Freedom*, 119. Barth wrote to Bonhoeffer, "Do you know the only thing I knew about you for a long time after that business of the 'ship after next'? The strange news that you intended to go to India to take over from Gandhi or some other friend of God there a spiritual technique, for the application of which in the West you promised great things!"

234. Robertson, *The Shame and the Sacrifice*, 120–21.
235. *DB*, 308–9.
236. Ibid., 349.

Phase 3: Church against or apart from World

of Bonhoeffer's notion of separateness for the political sphere are clear in his letter to Bishop Ammundsen just before the Fanø Conference. Bonhoeffer stated definitively that being part of the Christian church precluded one from taking part in the prevailing political system in Germany.[237] His solution to the presence of an unacceptable political regime did not, however, include direct action against the state. It included defining a church against it and pushing for resolutions emphasizing separation.

Bonhoeffer's pacifism in this phase was based on a similar separateness leading to a distance from the political realm. The ecumenical church's obedient acknowledgment of Christ's message of peace defines it as distinct from the other churches and from the world, including its political aspects. Bonhoeffer states explicitly the lack of concern for "political necessities and possibilities" in the Fanø peace sermon. He also advocates for the form of pacifism most closely associated in the Lutheran tradition with separation from the political sphere or political responsibility, refusal to participate in defensive wars. In addition, he pushed hard at Fanø for a resolution allowing for conscientious objection, another unacceptable position in his German Lutheran tradition.

Bonhoeffer's presence in London itself, given the political situation in Germany and the situation in the German churches, stands as a separation. Hitler's ruthless consolidation of power and build up of arms was an ominous harbinger of things to come. Müller and Jäger's actions in the ecclesial sphere were intrusive and deplorable. Bonhoeffer, while frequently making trips back to Germany, was content mostly with trying to get the London churches to make resolutions about secession and with making sure the ecumenical churches formally recognized the Confessing Church at conferences. He did not directly confront the church-political situation in Germany. It is unclear whether his talk of the world being armed and on the brink of war in his Fanø peace speech was a direct reference to Germany's rearmament. In any case, a speech delivered in Denmark is something quite different than a formal protest in Germany.

Bonhoeffer's publicly active involvement in the church struggle from March 1935 to the closing of Finkenwalde in 1937 was even more limited than it was during his London pastorate. His activities were not a series of direct responses to events in the church struggle or political

237. Ibid., 381–82.

realm. Bonhoeffer's activity, rather, consisted mostly of reaffirming separation and acts of withdrawal in the ecumenical sphere. He was invited to Hanover for a preparation meeting for the 1937 Oxford conference. Bonhoeffer argued there that the ecumenical leaders could not expect the Confessing Church and the Reich Church to work together. He also insisted that the Research Department firmly acknowledge the claims made at Barmen and Dahlem. Bonhoeffer accused Geneva of still not taking a legitimate stand on the issue of the real church in Germany, evoking a paper from Schönfeld defending Geneva's attitude.[238]

Bonhoeffer was also supposed to lead the ecumenical youth conference in Chamby in 1935, where he wanted to address the issue of conscientious objection. He lacked faith that the conference would adequately address Christ's peace command. This, in addition to the increasing distaste for Bonhoeffer at the Geneva office, helped him decide not to attend.[239] The Geneva office thought that the ecumenical youth conference in Fanø was a bit radical. They split the youth conference from the larger conferences and appointed Edwin Espy, an American, to the post of youth secretary. Espy asked Bonhoeffer to assemble a delegation for an upcoming 1936 youth conference. Bonhoeffer's refusal to choose any representatives other than those from the Confessing Church prompted Schönfeld to write a letter expressing lack of support for Bonhoeffer. He wrote, "I have long found it inexcusable that this part of the work should be determined exclusively—or almost exclusively—by a man like Bonhoeffer."[240] Bonhoeffer's insistence on the absolute and exclusive claims of the Confessing Church was beginning to seriously affect his relationship with Geneva. Finkenwalde, and the refusal to support Kerrl's committees, were beginning to earn Bonhoeffer the reputation of a "radical" outsider even in the context of the Confessing Church.[241]

The extent to which Bonhoeffer was falling out of favor with certain elements of the Reich Church became clear after an innocent trip to Sweden with his Finkenwalde seminarians in March 1936. The trip came under much scrutiny by the state and church authorities in Germany when the newspapers in Stockholm reported extensively on the voyage

---

238. Ibid., 472–73.
239. Ibid., 476.
240. Ibid., 478.
241. Ibid., 505.

Phase 3: Church against or apart from World 269

of these "persecuted" church visitors.[242] Heckel and his group reacted to the trip by sending a letter to Archbishop Eidem in Sweden accusing him of siding with the Confessing Church against the Reich Church. Heckel wrote another letter to the Prussian church committee, a devastating one that was to become famous. In it, he described Bonhoeffer as "a pacifist and an enemy of the state." Heckel also wrote, "it might be advisable for the provincial church committee to disassociate itself from him [Bonhoeffer] and take steps that he will no longer train German theologians."[243] The Reich Ministry of Education, in a shocking turn of events, did just that. Bonhoeffer received a written notice on August 5, 1936, permanently revoking his right to teach in German universities.[244]

Bonhoeffer attended the Chamby conference in August 1936. His behavior there, however, was markedly different than it had been at other ecumenical gatherings. Bonhoeffer remained absolutely silent during the debates and discussion between the delegates from the Confessing Church and the Reich Church over the feasibility of a joint delegation to the Oxford conference in 1938.[245] The February 1937 meeting in London concerning the youth commission to the Oxford conference saw Bonhoeffer commit another act of withdrawal. In a meeting attended by Henriod and Schönfeld, he expressed his intention to resign from the youth conference entirely. Bonhoeffer simply could not be involved in any ecumenical organization that either expected joint-delegations from the opposing German churches or for him to send delegates from both churches.[246] His withdrawal from ecumenical activity meant the Confessing Church lost its most powerful voice in that arena. Important figures from the Confessing Church did not attend any more ecumenical conferences. Heckel's office, however, sensing its chance to have the Reich Church represent the German church, continued to send representatives.[247]

---

242. Ibid., 508.

243. Ibid., 511–12.

244. Ibid., 515–17. They cited both his breach of the Reich church decree concerning teaching at a banned seminary and his unauthorized travel to Sweden. Heckel's letter was not considered officially responsible for Bonhoeffer's dismissal.

245. Ibid., 552–54.

246. Ibid., 558.

247. Ibid., 560.

Bonhoeffer's final significant activity was attendance at a meeting of the Confessing Church in Stettin in October 1936 to discuss whether or not the churches there should join Kerrl's committees. Bonhoeffer argued against a faction that wanted to go with the church committees. A vote was taken and the results were favorable for the faction supporting the Dahlem and Barmen synods. Eventually, though, the numbers supporting the committees grew larger.[248] Things were starting to look bad in general for the opposition church. The state brought almost all Confessing Church activities to a halt, declared collections taken at Confessing Church services illegal, revoked passports, and arrested hundreds of members of the Confessing Church for violating various laws.[249] When Bonhoeffer and Bethge went to Niemöller's home on July 1, 1937, in response to the arrest of another important Confessing Church leader, Niemöller had just been arrested. The Gestapo was still at the house and detained Bonhoeffer for several hours, making him watch the ransacking of Niemöller's home while Bonhoeffer's mother, who heard of Niemöller's arrest, circled around the house in the family car peering frantically out of the window.[250] Bonhoeffer was allowed to return to Finkenwalde later that week. The Gestapo, however, finally shut Finkenwalde down in September of 1937.[251]

Bonhoeffer's activities during his Finkenwalde days were consistent with an apolitical church-against-world stance. He was not active in any political sphere whatsoever. Bonhoeffer did not publicly protest Hitler's military actions in the Rhineland. Bonhoeffer did not publicly protest Hitler's swift and ominous rearmament and breach of the Treaty of Versailles. In action consistent with the passive acceptance of the world encroaching on the church's space he espoused in *Discipleship*, Bonhoeffer did not protest Kerrl's reliance on the strong-armed tactics of the Gestapo. Bonhoeffer did not, furthermore, participate in the writing of the infamous direct memorandum to Hitler. Bonhoeffer did not protest Himmler's violent persecution of the Confessing Church. Finally, the removal of his right to teach theology in state universities in Germany was prompted by an innocuous visit to Sweden, one that he informed church officials about; the state action was not the result of any

248. Ibid., 573–75.
249. Ibid., 577–79.
250. Ibid., 580.
251. *DB*, 583–84.

Phase 3: Church against or apart from World

direct political protest against the state. His actions vis-à-vis the political realm were consistent with his thinking developed in *Discipleship* and his essay on church boundaries. Bonhoeffer was concerned with establishing a self-contained church with sharply defined borders entrenched against a hostile outside world.

An analysis of Bonhoeffer's behavior in the church during his Finkenwalde days does not reveal someone whose isolating concern with his church forced him out of church politics. His record in that realm was, however, also one characterized by a distancing himself from other church members. He spent most of his time training pastors for the Confessing Church. His travels outside of Finkenwalde were mostly in the service of the ecumenical church. His activity in that capacity was characterized by an unwillingness to cooperate in conferences where the Research Department in Geneva invited delegations from the Reich Church. Eventually, Bonhoeffer withdrew from ecumenical activity altogether. In doing so, he took away the Confessing Church's most effective voice in that arena. His withdrawal allowed Heckel and the Reich Church to be the sole representatives from Germany at future conferences. Ultimately, in the ecclesial sphere, his actions were consistent with the ecclesiology developed in his writings. The church was to be a unique entity concerned solely with its own purity.

Bonhoeffer's post-Finkenwalde phase-3 activity has much in common with his Finkenwalde activity. It was characterized by a lack of direct political confrontation with the state, and ecumenical activity wherein he continued to uncompromisingly emphasize the unique nature of the Confessing Church as an entity with distinct boundaries according to his reading of the Barmen and Dahlem synods. Bonhoeffer still found the mutual presence of the Confessing Church and the Reich Church at ecumenical conferences unacceptable. His attempt to influence the illegal pastors in their recognition of the uniqueness of their church was consistent with his aims in the ecumenical sphere.

There are some glaring instances of lack of direct political involvement, too. Bonhoeffer did not publicly address the horrible *Kristallnacht*. He did not take a public stand on the Nazi persecution of the churches or the closing of Finkenwalde. In addition, he responded to his military call-up with what has been described as a flight from the country. Bonhoeffer could have taken this opportunity to make a political point with a visible or public display of resistance against the state. In this sense, one could argue that he was inconsistent with his thinking in *Discipleship* in a few ways. First, he argued that church members should suffer passively and publicly the consequences of a separation from the world in the world. His public disavowal of military service would have been an example of separating from the world visibly, and consequently suffering dire consequences. Second, he argued that church members should respect the authority of the state's decisions, making military service a required action. Military involvement, though, according to other parts of the text, was an activity inconsistent with discipleship. Military involvement is perhaps one of those secular vocations that had become unacceptable for true disciples because the world and the church had become too antithetical in regard to one another. In any case, the particular nature of his decision to flee from military conscription was that of a withdrawal from political engagement interpreted in any possible sense. That is, his fleeing from the military draft to America was a withdrawal from pro-state political engagement lacking the character of a political protest in the name of the church against the state.

THE NATURE OF THE CHANGE

Bonhoeffer's phase-2 vision included a church in a heightened tension with the world. He set the church against the world more starkly than he did in phase 1, allowing him to examine and emphasize the unique nature of the church's message to the world. This particular church-world vision raised the distinct possibility that the church's authoritative message might run counter to the world, especially the political or governmental component of the world. Bonhoeffer thus moved from his somewhat conservative first phase adherence to Luther's Two Kingdoms doctrine to a more liberal version where the church specifically as church might raise a protest voice against the state. While carefully articulating the roles of church and state according to traditional Two Kingdoms thinking, he went beyond the doctrine by suggesting that the church might undertake direct political action against the state. Bonhoeffer's works indicated a heightened perception of the world as a negative entity, pushing him toward a form of pacifism wherein the church was to publicly proclaim its peace witness and struggle or work for peace. His growing fascination with the Sermon on the Mount and his designation of it in some of his writings as a possible source of specific content for the church's authoritative word to the world also contributed to his paci-

Phase 3: Church against or apart from World

fism. Bonhoeffer tried to avoid the legalism associated with following the Sermon on the Mount literally by stressing that such pacifism was provisional.

Bonhoeffer's form of political involvement was consistent with his thinking on the church-world relationship. He proclaimed the message of peace to the world, took a public stand against the church that adopted the state's policies against the Jewish population, and tried to call the church and state to their proper roles. His ecumenical involvement was consistent with his form of pacifism, which saw the church as a union of Christians not bound by national identity but having the mission to proclaim a message of peace and work toward peace. His work in the early resistance against the *Deutsche Christen* was consistent with holding the church to its role of formulating a confession and proclaiming the true gospel unpolluted by political concerns or any racially based ideologies. Finally, it is extremely important to note that the church and the world, while in a heightened tension, were not set into different realities or spheres. Bonhoeffer stated this position explicitly in various places in his phase-2 writings. There might be justification for the church to criticize the world's structures, for it to adopt a pacifism based in some form of worldly engagement, or even for the church to engage in direct political action in the world. Yet, the phase-2 church-world vision does not support splitting reality into two spheres and any accompanying withdrawal into one sphere to the total exclusion of some form of involvement in the other.

In phase 3 Bonhoeffer essentially places the church and world in different spheres. He is concerned mostly with the church's attachment to Christ leading to a separation from the world. The Christian's response to Christ's call pulls him or her out of the world into an otherworldly holiness. Bonhoeffer emphasizes the qualitative difference between the types of interactions that govern reality in the churchly sphere and those in the worldly sphere. Bonhoeffer's obsession with defining his version of the Confessing Church against the Reich Church (and even some factions in the larger Confessing Church) made the church perfectionist, withdrawn, and sect-like. *Discipleship* seems to lay out more comprehensively the details of the visible church-community described in Bonhoeffer's controversial 1936 essay on the visible church.

Bonhoeffer's strongest pacifist statements accompanied this church-world stance. The negative view of the world starts in the London sermons, continues in the Fanø speech, and culminates in *Discipleship*. Bonhoeffer's Fanø argument that church members are not to engage in the political sphere even in defensive wars, his strongest and the most extreme pacifist position, indicates the extent to which the church might remove itself from the worldly. *Discipleship* also encourages following the Sermon on the Mount wherein the call to follow Christ requires a break from the world. The way the Sermon on the Mount functions in the third phase writings is different than the way it functioned in the second phase. In the second phase Bonhoeffer simply begins to designate the Sermon as the basic content of the provisional command given to the world. In phase 3 the Sermon functions almost like a series of laws that the Christian must follow obediently without any equivocation or hesitation. Any questioning of these directives constitutes disobeying the command.

Finally, a change in behavior came along with this change in thinking about the church-world relationship and thinking on war and peace. Seen in comparison with his phase-2 behavior, Bonhoeffer's actions were a series of withdrawals. Bonhoeffer withdraws from Germany to London during the intensifying church struggle. Bonhoeffer withdraws into the clandestine seminaries in Finkenwalde and the backwoods of Pomerania. Bonhoeffer spoke out for the rights of Jewish persons in phase 2. In phase 3 he, along with most other church leaders, remained silent during the infamous *Kristallnacht*. He did not directly address Gestapo crackdowns against the clergy in phase 3, activity that would be entirely justifiable or acceptable given his phase 2 thinking. His predominant activity in phase 3 was involvement in the ecumenical sphere. Even here, though, his activity was geared toward distinguishing the Confessing Church as the unique, distinct or other. Bonhoeffer eventually withdrew from activity in this realm too.

An important consideration in judging the nature of Bonhoeffer's change from phase 2 to phase 3 is an examination of his relationship with Luther's Two Kingdoms doctrine. Some commentators, because part of the prevailing interpretation of the doctrine in Bonhoeffer's historical context included a passive acceptance of state directives, mistake his political passivity in this phase with adherence to a conservative or traditional version of the doctrine.[252] Yet, there are distinct differences

---

252. Koch, "The Theological Responses of Karl Barth and Dietrich Bonhoeffer," iv. Koch, for example, writes, "one finds quite traditional Lutheran views of church-state relations in *Nachfolge*."

Phase 3: Church against or apart from World

between the classic Two Kingdoms doctrine and Bonhoeffer's phase-3 vision, which ultimately rest on the different church-world visions. The political passivity associated with agreeing to pro-state activities is actually motivated by the overlap between the church and the world. Being a citizen of a state does not force one from the churchly sphere and being part of the church does not force one from his or her duties in the worldly, secular, or governmental sphere. So what is sometimes labeled political passivity does not mean the church is actually disengaged from the political sphere. In a conservative or traditional (Bonhoeffer's phase 1) vision it means engaging in the world mostly in the form of pro-state rather than anti-state activities. In a more liberal (Bonhoeffer's phase-2) vision it means following state directives with the possibility of criticizing them.

The passivity in phase 3 derives from the opposite church-world vision. It derives from a qualitative break between the sphere of the church and the sphere of the world. The church and its members are to concern themselves with adhering to the strict and demanding call to moral perfection in answering the directives in the Sermon on the Mount. The church constitutes a band of persons whose behavior is so pure and therefore counter-worldly that it is essentially in its own sphere. The overlap of the two separate spheres presupposing any form of engagement in the world or in the political sphere is not a function of a shared or reconciled reality. The church re-engages the world or throws itself back into the world as an alien entity only to display the disparity between the churchly and the worldly sphere. So Bonhoeffer's advocating for the church obeying secular authority, while it mimics the political passivity from phase 1, does not rest on the same church-world vision espoused in phase 1. The church is to obey secular authority not as an affirmation of the shared space or overlap between the church and the world but only so it can suffer in the world visibly as Christ did. The church is not motivated by politics in this case. There are instances, though, where the gap between church and world does actually become visible in terms of disallowing certain secular vocations. Bonhoeffer does not explicitly state that participation in war would be a secular vocation no longer permissible. The preponderance of evidence in *Discipleship* does, however, clearly and strongly suggest that war is one such instance where the gap between the church and the world disallows soldiering as a secular vocation. War calls one to act in a way that is not consistent with the purity demanded by the Sermon on the Mount. Politics does not serve as motivation in the case of Bonhoeffer's pacifism either, even though it earned him the label "enemy of the state."

As noted in other parts of my text, most scholars divide Bonhoeffer's life and thinking into three phases. They generally include *Discipleship* in the phase that goes from roughly 1933 to 1940, thereby including early pacifist literature with later pacifist literature. The fact that Bonhoeffer no longer holds the church and the world as interacting or sharing in the same sphere of concern in the later thirties is enough to call the change from phase 2 to phase 3 a real break in his understanding of the church-world relationship.[253] A political or "struggle" form of pacifism, based even partially in the recognition of a common humanity regardless of national boundaries and in the nature of the type of weaponry in existence, is distinctly different from a pacifism based entirely in the response to the call of Christ requiring a break from the outside world. In addition, a pacifism that takes the Sermon on the Mount literally or perhaps even legalistically is distinctly different from a provisional pacifism where the commandment of God is only applicable to any given today. There was a corresponding break in his form of political involvement. Bonhoeffer's was involved in the church struggle in Germany, spoke out for the rights of the Jews and suggested that direct political action against the state might be acceptable in phase 2. These are distinctly different and different in kind from living in London, heading up monastery-like seminaries, and working in, and gradually withdrawing from, the ecumenical sphere.

---

253. It should also be noted that Bonhoeffer's phase-3 eschatology (especially in *Discipleship*) is markedly different from his eschatology in previous phases. This eschatology, where God's consummation of history is imminent (where, in Bonhoeffer's language, the world is overtaking the space of the church to the point where persecution of the pure church is widespread and heightening) is related to his church-world relationship and therefore his political thinking and behavior. See for example, Wogaman, *Christian Perspectives on Politics*, 172–73. Wogaman writes, "a doctrine of eschatology that emphasizes the realization of divine purposes in history is open to an important role for politics ... if one's eschatological conception envisages the fulfillment of history altogether as the work of God—without any direct contribution by human action—then politics can be taken as irrelevant or to be part of the 'principalities and powers' that God must and will overcome." Bonhoeffer's eschatology translates into political passivity for the church. Church members are to passively and patiently endure suffering and persecution (they are not to involve themselves meaningfully in the political sphere) as they simply wait for God to usher in the soon-coming end.

Phase 3: Church against or apart from World

A final consideration in appreciating Bonhoeffer's break into phase 3 concerns testimony or perception (his own self-perception and the responses from those who surrounded him). His departure for London marked the entry into phase 3. Bonhoeffer was at that time disappointed in the direction the resistance was taking. Barth had refused to recommend the movement toward an absolute schism or the creation of a Free Church[254] and Niemöller sent Hitler a congratulatory note and a promise of allegiance after Germany's withdrawal from the League of Nations. At the time Bonhoeffer wrote,

> although I am working with all my might for the church opposition, it is perfectly clear to me that this opposition is only a very temporary transition to an opposition of a very different kind, and that very few of those engaged in this preliminary skirmish will be part of the next struggle. And I believe that the whole of Christendom should pray with us that it will be a "resistance unto death," and that the people will be found to suffer it. Simply suffering—that is what will be needed then—not parries, blows or thrusts such as may still be possible or admissible in the preliminary fight; the real struggle that perhaps lies ahead must simply be to suffer faithfully, and then, then perhaps God will once more confess his church with his Word.[255]

Bonhoeffer thus recognized that he would have to pursue a different course than the one he had been pursuing in phase 2. Prefiguring the thinking in his *Discipleship* (which was to be written a few years later), that course would not involve fighting, but rather a willingness to suffer. Barth's letter of November 30, 1933, also highlights the extent to which the departure for London signified a break in Bonhoeffer's behavior. Bonhoeffer waited until he already left for London to ask for Barth's opinion. Barth replied scathingly:

> Once you had this thing on your mind you were quite right not to ask for my wise counsel first. I would have advised you against it absolutely, and probably by bringing up my heaviest guns. And now, as you are mentioning the matter to me *post eventum*, I can honestly not tell you anything but "Hurry back to your post in Berlin!" What is all this about "going away," "the quietness of pastoral work," etc. at a moment when you are just wanted in Germany? . . . Look, I gladly suppose, as I have already said, that

---

254. *DB*, 308–9.
255. *TF*, 411.

this departure was personally necessary for you! But I must be allowed to add, "What does even 'personal necessity' mean at the present moment!" . . . I just will not allow you to put such a private tragedy on the stage in view of what is at stake for the German church today . . . No, to all the reasons or excuses which you might perhaps still be able to put in front of me, I will give only one answer: "And the German church?"—until you are back again in Berlin to attend faithfully and bravely to the machine-gun which you have left behind there . . . the German church is lost. But one simply cannot become weary just now. Still less can one go to England! What in all the world would you want to do there? Be glad that I don't have you here in person, for I would let go at you urgently in quite a different way, with the demand that you must let go of all of these intellectual flourishes and special considerations, however interesting they may be, and think of only one thing, that you are a German, that the house of your church is on fire, that you know enough and can say what you know well enough to be able to help and that you must return to your post by the next ship. As things are, shall we say the ship after next?[256]

Bonhoeffer's two proposed trips to India to study Gandhi's pacifism and passive resistance were met with similar criticisms. Barth's criticism of Bonhoeffer's India plans at the end of the London pastorate actually made reference to the "ship after next?" phrase from the November 1933 letter. Niebuhr responded to Bonhoeffer's mid-1939 desire to travel to India by pointing out that Britain's political liberalism was more amenable to Gandhi's techniques and that the Nazis would not feel at all guilty about slaughtering any persons practicing passive resistance.[257] Bonhoeffer's phase-3 thinking, motivations, and behavior were, ultimately, noticeably different from those of his contemporaries and colleagues.[258]

---

256. *NRS*, 237–40.

257. *RR*, 213.

258. *DB*, 372. Bethge notes, "his [Bonhoeffer's] colleagues in the Confessing church viewed him as an outsider because of his constant concern with the Sermon on the Mount. Yet among his ecumenical friends . . . he was isolated because of his insistence on the confession and the repudiation of heresy."

Phase 3: Church against or apart from World

LOOKING AHEAD

Bonhoeffer engaged in two major church bodies during the church struggle, the international ecumenical church and the Confessing Church. He worked hard to forge a vision of them as different than, or apart from, the German Reich Church. By the end of this third phase, Bonhoeffer had become dissatisfied with both the ecumenical movement and the Confessing Church. Those in the Ecumenical Research Committee in Geneva did not acknowledge the importance of consistently viewing the Confessing Church as the only legitimate church in Germany. The Confessing Church, for its part, had spilt into two factions. One faction recognized the dangers of Kerrl's committees and steadfastly held to the resolutions of Dahlem and Barmen. The other faction acquiesced to Kerrl's committees. Some more radical form of thinking and action would be necessary for Bonhoeffer if he was to pursue the restoration of Germany's churches and restore his nation's integrity. The fact that he started making contacts with the formal political resistance during the collective pastorates provides a clue as to the direction he would choose.

6

Phase 4: Church as World

INTRODUCTION

THE FINAL PHASE IN Bonhoeffer's life has garnered the most attention. Bonhoeffer became an active participant in the explicitly political sphere, acting as a double agent for the *Abwer*, the counterintelligence agency of the armed forces in Nazi Germany. As part of this organization, Bonhoeffer made use of ecumenical contacts from earlier phases to make further contacts with nations outside of Germany. His main political goals were to assure the Allies that a significant resistance existed and to find out if and how these nations would negotiate with a post-Hitler Germany. Bonhoeffer was also involved in various ways in support of plots to actually murder Hitler. His activity in the ecclesial realm lessened and ultimately gave way to exclusive involvement in the political.

In this chapter I will argue that Bonhoeffer's stark move from a narrow concern with the church to involvement in the political realm was accompanied by a similarly stark change in his a church-world vision. He moves gradually from a church against world or apart from world vision to something approaching a church as world vision in his *Ethics* and a more complete articulation of a church as world vision in his *Letters and Papers from Prison*.[1] In terms of a broad or all-encompassing

---

1. *ADOB*, 52. Bonhoeffer's embrace of the world or secularity in his final phase has led some commentators to question whether he left room for an organized church at all. Hopper, for instance, writes, "In Müller's view, Bonhoeffer anticipated a declericalization and desecularization of the church, one that would involve the surrender of all status and privilege. This would call for the abandonment by the church of all outwardness, all visibility."

Phase 4: Church as World

definition, the political position associated with his church-world vision for Bonhoeffer is a just war stance (including the possibility of tyrannicide). At the end of phase 3, Bonhoeffer was faced with a series of situations and he found himself in a position that made adherence to his phase-3 theology impossible. His frustration and disappointment with the ecumenical movement and the Confessing church in the face of Hitler's domestic tyranny and posturing toward war forced him to take a drastically different approach to the role of the church and the Christian in the world.[2]

Bonhoeffer's dramatic move in 1939 from seclusion to a full embrace of the world is captured in his letter to Reinhold Niebuhr.

> I have come to the conclusion that I made a mistake coming to America. I must live through this difficult period of our national history with the Christian people of Germany. I will have no right to participate in the reconstruction of Christian life in Germany after the war if I do not share the trials of this time with my people. My brethren in the Confessing Synod wanted me to go. They may have been right in urging me to do so; but I was wrong in going. Such a decision a man must make for himself. Christians in Germany will face the terrible alternative of either willing the defeat of their nation in order that Christian civilization may survive, or willing the victory of their nation and thereby destroying our civilization. I know which of these alternatives I must choose; but I cannot make that choice in security.[3]

Bonhoeffer could have continued his isolation from events in Germany in the safety of America. Instead, he abandoned his two-sphered thinking (which made adherence to the church a prescription for world-avoiding passivity) in favor of a church whose members must engage radically in the world. Bonhoeffer's phase-4 church-world vision, seen in terms of the previous phases, represents a release of the tension between the church and world by dramatically lessening their difference. At the very end for Bonhoeffer, there were thus no longer any qualifications regarding direct and anti-state political action, including those associated with both liberal and conservative interpretations of the Two Kingdoms doctrine. There was ultimately no difference between acting as a secular person and a acting as a church person.

2. Kuhns, *In Pursuit of Dietrich Bonhoeffer*, 230.
3. *TF*, 479–80.

As in the preceding chapters, I will argue for the connection between Bonhoeffer's church-world thinking and specific forms of political thinking after the individual sections treating his important phase-4 writings. I will cover how this church-world/political thinking connection relates to his particular forms of political behavior in summary form in a section near the end of the chapter.

ETHICS (MID-1940—APRIL 1943)

Bonhoeffer's thought had not yet moved into a mature church as world vision in his *Ethics*. He does, though, reverse his strong hints of sectarianism from the third phase and immerse the church back into the world, making possible meaningful involvement in it for the church and its members. That is, political engagement is motivated by a legitimate appreciation of the world and its structures rather than to highlight the world's fallenness. There is thus some similarity between his thinking here and his thinking in phase 1, where the church is also embedded firmly in the world (and the state is a legitimate means by which God rules the world). In addition, there is some similarity with his phase-2 thinking where the church is also embedded firmly in the world and can thus try to make sure the state fulfills its role properly. Bonhoeffer does indeed reiterate traditional two kingdoms thinking in *Ethics*. There is a sense, though, in which the immersion of the church in the world is so pronounced in *Ethics* that Bonhoeffer is able to challenge the constraints of typical German Lutheran thinking on church-state relations.

Bonhoeffer never completed *Ethics*. It was edited after the war and published posthumously in 1949 by Bethge.[4] The fragments were written in various locations from mid-1940 until his arrest by the Gestapo in Berlin.[5] Bonhoeffer wrote the work in the political context of Hitler's war and the implementation of the "final solution," the attempt to exterminate all Jews in Germany and the conquered territories. On the war front, Hitler's plan to take Poland included signing a non-aggression pact with the Soviet Union in August 1939. He did so to prevent a two-front war in case the Western powers decided to retaliate. Germany attacked

---

4. See Bonhoeffer, *Dietrich Bonhoeffer: Witness to Jesus Christ*, 221–22, for a brief description of the order in which the fragments were written. See also, *ATS*, 302–3.

5. *DB*, 685. *Ethics* was written primarily in three locations: 1) the Benedictine monastery at Ettal in the South; 2) a Kleist estate in Kieckrow; and 3) another Kleist estate at Klein-Krössin.

Poland on September 1 and by September 28, 1939, Hitler's alarmingly effective *Blitzkrieg* warfare had destroyed Poland. Russia and Germany then divided the land between them. Hitler tried to take countries one by one and quickly in order to prevent a Europe-wide war. Britain and France, however, declared war on Germany two days after the attack on Poland.[6] Germany continued its military operations and invaded the Netherlands, Belgium, and France in April and May 1940. Belgium and the Netherlands fell quickly and by the end of June, Germany occupied three-fifths of France (Germany allowed the other two-fifths to remain under French rule).[7]

Hitler would next turn his attention toward Britain and Russia. He wanted to avoid war with Britain and tried to get Britain to accept his rule peacefully. Britain did not respond favorably and in the beginning of August 1940 Germany launched a major air offensive. Germany underestimated British resolve, wasted a number of aircraft in a poorly planned offensive, and eventually lost the Battle of Britain by mid-September. Hitler tried to strike at British naval power in the Mediterranean. He could not get Spanish support and decided to oppose Britain by letting the Italians fight them in North Africa. The Italian military offensive against Egypt, begun in September 1940, was unsuccessful. Hitler responded with a full-scale military campaign of Germans and Italians led by Rommel, which reached the Egyptian frontier by May 1940. Germany's insufficient troops and supplies forced a stoppage.[8]

Convinced that the presence of inferior Jewish-Bolshevik leadership in Russia would signal a quick defeat, Hitler broke the non-aggression pact and attacked Russia in June 1941. There were early German successes, but Hitler ultimately grossly underestimated Russian power and resolve and failed to achieve his military objectives. By late 1941 many German units were stuck freezing in the Russian winter, but Hitler would not sanction a retreat. Another strategic move would mean the eventual defeat of Hitler. He declared war on the United States.[9] Hitler saw some successes in early 1942. His submarine attacks on Allied ships in the North Atlantic theater were beginning to weaken British power. His troops in North Africa were getting close to Egypt. In late 1942,

6. *HNG*, 210–12.
7. Ibid., 213–14.
8. Ibid., 215–17.
9. Ibid., 218–21.

though, things started to turn around. Rommel's forces in North Africa failed to take El Alamein, and the British forced a German retreat back into the desert by late 1942. The Germans were met on the other side of the desert by British and American forces who, partly on Stalin's request for a two-front war, had launched a major amphibious offensive in Morocco and Algeria in November 1942. Axis troops surrendered in Tunisia in May 1943 and the Allied powers were poised to cross the Mediterranean and enter Europe through Sicily. The Russians attacked German positions on the outskirts of Stalingrad and defeated the Germans in that battle in February 1943. By mid-1943 it became clear that Hitler was not going to defeat the Soviet Union. Germany began to lose the war.[10]

The other significant political event was the implementation of the "Final Solution." Hitler's desire to exterminate the Jews was based in his desire for more *Lebensraum* and his adoption of pseudo-biological racial theories from the nineteenth century.[11] The roots of Hitler's anti-Semitism are complicated but in some ways his mindset was a reflection of the cultural and religious anti-Jewish racial ideology held by German nationalists and many other Germans. Hitler's first act was to partition Poland along racial lines and set up a civil administration for displaced Jews. A special strike force called the *Einsatzgruppen* was ordered to move Jews from rural to centralized urban areas. The second phase included sending *Einsatzgruppen* into Russia after the June 1941 invasion. These "mobile killing units" would round up Jews, tell them they were being moved to settlements, and then mercilessly execute them. There was another "sweep" in 1942. This form of persecution lowered morale for the executioners, so the Nazis built concentration camps in Poland. European Jews in areas under German control would be sent by train and killed in gas chambers. Auschwitz was chosen as a central location but there were a number of camps all over Europe. The major centers were built and put into operation in 1941 and 1942. The "Final Solution" continued until the very end of Hitler's regime in 1945.[12]

On the church front, Hitler realized both the absolute necessity for the population's support during the war and the need for a percep-

---

10. Ibid., 221–23.

11. See Shirer, *The Rise and Fall of the Third Reich*, chap. 4, "The Mind of Hitler and the Roots of the Third Reich," 80–113, for a description of Hitler's influences.

12. *HNG*, 274–80.

Phase 4: Church as World

tion of unity from other nations. He demanded that "no further action should be taken toward the Evangelical and Catholic Churches for the duration of the war."[13] The Evangelical Church responded by issuing a proclamation in support of the war in September 1939. Furthermore, the churches did not protest Hitler's quick destruction of Poland.[14] Even with the Evangelical Church's compliance, the more radical anti-Christian members of the Nazi regime decided to take advantage of the church's vulnerability. Heydrich (head of the SD), in particular, did not see the church's support of the war effort as particularly significant. He sent a lengthy report to Hitler in October 1939 describing his plans for further persecution of the church, including the scaling down of church subsidies and concentration camp incarcerations for any religious leaders who opposed the war. Religious journals were forced to cease publication, church bells were melted down, and the Gestapo ordered that all pastors who had been trained at the illegal seminaries of the Confessing church be considered unemployed and be reassigned for more meaningful employment. In September 1940, the Ministry of Labor ordered that no more novices were allowed to join the priesthood or other religious orders.[15]

Seemingly unaware of the current crackdown on the churches, Kerrl made his final effort to bring them into line with Nazi ideology. He and Dr. Engelke, a member of the *Deutsche Christen* and one of Müller's deputies (Müller still had the title Reich Bishop even though he had been ineffectual for years) proposed a pre-1918 idea to Hitler. Müller suggested that the leader of Germany be the head of the Evangelical Church, the *Summus Episcopus*.[16] Hitler outright refused this proposi-

---

13. NPC, 232. See also, HNG, 258. Hitler proclaimed that "every German should do his duty and that every soldier should, if need be, go to his death bravely . . . If, in that connection, religious belief is a help and support to him . . . it can only be an advantage, and any disturbances in this connection could conceivably affect the soldier's inward strength."

14. NPC, 234.

15. Ibid., 235–38.

16. Ibid., 247–48. The letter, in part, reads, "To the Führer and Reich Chancellor Adolf Hitler: The Evangelical Church transfers itself to you with all its possessions, lands, buildings and institutions. It thereby desires to prove that it wishes to be considered as nothing apart from the State, but rather feels itself bound up with the prosperity and fate of the State. It would bring an end to the unfortunate processes of the past by which the church became a separate state within the State and often became a power opposed to the State. The Church makes this transfer at the present time because it

tion and the Nazi hierarchy used it as more evidence of Kerrl's incompetence.[17] Kerrl's attempts to unify the Churches into one state church were further complicated by Rosenberg and Bormann's continued persecutions of the church. Rosenberg and Bormann, moreover, had assurance from Hitler that he no longer wanted a united Evangelical Reich church.[18] Kerrl's power was almost nonexistent. He was not even consulted when the Nazi regime undertook confiscation of the monasteries in 1941. Kerrl's request to meet personally with Hitler was denied. Kerrl died in December 1941.[19]

From the end of 1941 through the remainder of the war, the battle between the churches and the Nazi State centered around the taking of church property, the racial persecution of the Jews, and the replacement of Christianity with Nazi ethical principles (including primarily the question of euthanasia). Catholics presented the most resistance to property seizure.[20] The churches' response to the racial persecutions of Jews was nothing short of alarming.[21] The *Deutsche Christen*, for example, issued a statement affirming that the current war was "hatched by the Jews" and approving the "Reich Police regulations of marking the Jews as the born enemies of the Reich and the world." They argued that "from the crucifixion of Christ to our own day the Jews have combated Christianity and abused or falsified it in pursuance of their selfish goals" and that the German Evangelical church has "no room" in it for

---

desires to show its deep gratitude that you have brought our German people from the depths and weakness to the height of power and world-importance . . . In our position as Evangelical Christians we have internal freedom to place our Church, our teachings and ourselves under strict examination to learn from history and from the present, and in particular to exclude every influence of Jewish thinking on Christianity."

17. Ibid., 249.
18. Ibid., 249–52.
19. Ibid., 253.
20. Ibid., 260.
21. Ibid., 261. Conway writes, "In the circumstances, therefore, it is not surprising that the most terrible outrage of the whole Nazi era—the attempted extermination of the Jews, with all its attendant horrors of mass murders and gas-chambers—was not loudly and urgently denounced by the Churches. At a time of unprecedented challenge to the moral courage and conscience of the German people, all save a handful of German churchmen continued to turn a blind eye on events, retreated into apathetic indifference, and even manifested a sort of sympathetic acquiescence. The resolute protests which, as some critics maintain, might have in part at least mitigated these awful atrocities, were never made."

Phase 4: Church as World

Jewish Christians.[22] The Confessing church did not make any statement until 1943. The Confessing church was at this time in disarray and still in internal disagreement over the Jewish question. The statement actually came from a group of laymen rather than the church leadership. When Bishop Wurm of Württemberg finally decided to write a letter to the Church Ministry on March 12, 1943, he emphasized the injustices against Jewish Christians and Jews married to Christians who were transported to the East.[23]

The Nazi practice of euthanasia was one area wherein the churches led a successful protest. The Nazis euthanized the elderly, the mentally ill, orphan children, and others deemed a drain on Germany's resources. Evidence suggests that the Nazi use of gas chambers in killing these parties helped them to find the most effective means of eliminating larger numbers of undesirables in the concentration camps. Some members of the Catholic and Protestant church leadership publicly denounced the practice of euthanasia in early August 1941 and Hitler ordered a stop to the practice on August 28. The practice continued in a highly secretive manner and to a lesser degree.[24] The presence of this relatively small resistance from the churches prompted Hitler again to order his party to stop church persecutions. This order was not in any way an indication that Hitler began to respect the churches or that he desired their presence in the Third Reich. In fact, he planned to deal forcefully with them after the war. However, some of Hitler's radicals could not abide by his orders. One of Rosenberg's staff, for example, recommended the creation of an "executive committee to establish training centers for

---

22. Ibid., 263.

23. Ibid., 262-64. Bishop Wurm's letter reads in part, "The measures taken against the Jews, in particular, so far as they do not take place in the scope of the laws at present in force, have for a long time been depressing many circles in our nation, particularly the Christian ones. In the present difficult circumstances, the question automatically arises in many minds whether our nation has not made itself guilty of bereaving men of their homes, their occupations and their lives without the sentence of a civil or military court. In view of a possible political exploitation of a public protest by the enemy countries, the Christian Churches have exercised great restraint in this respect. They cannot, however, possibly be silent when lately even Jews living in mixed marriage with Christian Germans, some even being themselves members of Christian Churches, have been torn from their homes and occupations to be transported to the East."

24. Ibid., 282-84. See also Dietrich, "Catholic Resistance to Biological and Racist Eugenics," 137-55.

ideological shock troops" for the purpose of eliminating anti-Nazi sentiment during the war.[25]

Bonhoeffer's activities during these political events had moved in large part from the churchly sphere to the political sphere. He became involved in the explicitly political wing of the resistance against Hitler. *Ethics* is a lengthy work whose entire content is somehow related to church-world issues. I will only treat sections dealing explicitly with church-world themes and how they relate to political thinking and political issues.

Bonhoeffer reiterates themes from his Barcelona ethic (the domain of the ethical is the confrontation with reality, for example). Bonhoeffer treats and dismisses several traditional ways of approaching ethics. Most importantly, he dismisses "private virtuousness" as paradigmatic.[26] Private virtuousness is simply not comprehensive enough to encompass the totality of what ethics might mean as it precludes public action in the world in the face of injustices or wrongs. As such, it and all the other approaches or traditional methodologies employed in ethical systems cannot, for Bonhoeffer, serve as a proper foundation.[27] The proper foundation is Christological. Jesus Christ became man in the world and Jesus is still present in the reality of the world. Bonhoeffer connects Christ with the world in a way not possible in phase 3. He writes,

> No one can look at God and at the reality of the world with undivided gaze as long as God and the world are torn apart. Despite all efforts to prevent it, the eyes still wander from one to the other. Only because there is one place where God and the reality of the world are reconciled with each other, at which God and humanity have become one, is it possible there and there alone to fix one's eyes on God and the world together at the same time. This place does not lie somewhere beyond reality in the realm of ideas. It lies in the midst of history as a divine miracle. It lies in Jesus Christ as the reconciler of the world. As an ideal, the unity of simplicity and wisdom is as much doomed to failure as are all other efforts to face reality; it is an impossible, highly contradictory ideal. Grounded, however, in the reality of the world reconciled with God in Jesus Christ, the command of Jesus gains

---

25. *NPC*, 287–88.

26. Bonhoeffer, *Ethics*, 80. This text will be abbreviated as *DBWE-6*.

27. *DBWE-6*, 78–80. Bonhoeffer lists and describes ethical approaches based in reason, moral fanaticism, conscience, duty, free responsibility, and private virtuousness.

Phase 4: Church as World

meaning and reality. Whoever looks at Jesus Christ sees in fact God and the world in one. From then on they can no longer see God without the world, or the world without God.[28]

Bonhoeffer makes clear the Christological formulation which reconciles the spheres of God and the world. Clinging to Christ no longer serves as a call out of the world. He writes, "This love of God for the world does not withdraw from reality into noble souls detached from the world."[29] Bonhoeffer's further statements reinforce the role Christ plays in terms of understanding a reality without spheres. The reconciliation of the two spheres (the Godly and the worldly) in Christ also allows Bonhoeffer to construct an ethical system based on "Conformation." Christians and the world are to be "conformed" with or to the Incarnate, Crucified, and Risen Christ. They do not become anything "alien" but rather what they were intended to become, persons before God.[30] The focus for Ethics becomes what actions taken conform to the reality of Christ in the world (or the Christocratic[31] structure of reality) rather than those dictated by the other ethical programs (duty, knowledge, private virtuousness, etc).[32]

The church-world relationship comes to the fore in Bonhoeffer's treatment of conformation. He writes, "'Formation' means therefore in the first place Jesus Christ taking form in Christ's church."[33] Bonhoeffer's concept of the church in the world moves radically past any hint of phase-3 sectarianism when he argues that all persons are taken up by Christ into Christ's body, the church. Bonhoeffer argues that the church "now bears the form that in truth is meant for all people."[34] Bonhoeffer does not argue that all humanity is actually church. Rather, he argues that "the church is nothing but that piece of humanity where Christ has really taken form."[35] Nevertheless, he does argue that in the process

---

28. Ibid., 82.

29. Ibid., 83.

30. Ibid., 94–96.

31. RR, 23. "Christocratic" is Rasmussen's term for Bonhoeffer's understanding of Christ's embeddedness in the structures of reality.

32. See RR, 23. Rasmussen explains, "With this methodology moral action is action that conforms to Christ's form in the world (that accords with reality); immoral action is action that deviates from Christ's form in the world (from reality)."

33. DBWE-6, 96.

34. Ibid., 97.

35. Ibid.

of formation what happens in the church is, if only an "indirect" way, "meaningful for all human beings."[36] Bonhoeffer explains further,

> But here again it is not as if the church has been set out as a model for the world, so to speak. Rather, we can only speak of the formation of the world in such as way that we address humanity in light of its true form, which belongs to it, which it has already received, but which it has not grasped and accepted, namely, the form of Jesus Christ that is its own. Thus humanity is—so to speak, proleptically—drawn into the church. It is still the case that, even where one talks about the formation of the world, only the form of Jesus Christ is meant.[37]

The true form of humanity is the form of Christ in the world, which is the church. The fact that all persons have not yet responded to the call explicitly does not change the fact that all humans are called to their true selves in the call of Christ in the church.

Bonhoeffer is clear, also, that ethical conformation to the world requires engagement with the totality of the worldly (not just the religious) because the real world has been conformed to Christ in the church. He writes, "its [the church's] first concern is not with the so-called religious functions of human beings, but with the existence in the world of whole human beings in all their relationships. The church's concern is not religion, but the form of Christ and its taking form among a band of people."[38] Bonhoeffer uses the term "reality" in his description of the dominion that has been conformed to Christ. He writes, "Christ does not abolish human reality in favor of an idea that demands to be realized against all that is real. Christ empowers reality, affirming it as the real human being and thus the ground of all human reality."[39] Bonhoeffer, echoing his phase-1 concern with the complete confrontation with reality, therefore sees Ethics as dealing primarily with action in the concrete world rather than with formalism or casuistry.[40]

Bonhoeffer's section "Christ, Reality and Good" has the subtitle "Christ, Church and World" and therefore also deals with the church-world relationship. Bonhoeffer makes it absolutely clear that conform-

---

36. Ibid., 98.
37. Ibid.
38. Ibid., 97.
39. Ibid., 99.
40. Ibid., 99–100.

ing oneself to Christ places one directly in the world or reality. Christian Ethics presupposes "God as the ultimate reality beyond and in all that exists" and "the reality of the existing that is real only through the reality of God."[41] He continues,

> In Christ we are invited to participate in the reality of God and reality of the world at the same time, the one not without the other. The reality of God is disclosed only as it places me completely in the reality of the world. But I find the reality of the world always already borne, accepted, and reconciled in the reality of God . . . The Christian ethic asks, then, how this reality of God and of the world that is given in Christ becomes real in our world. It is not as if "our world" were something outside of this God-world reality that is in Christ, as if it did not already belong to the world borne, accepted and reconciled in Christ.; it is not, therefore, as if some "principle" must first be applied to our circumstances and our time. Rather, the question is how the reality in Christ—which has long embraced us and our world within itself—works here and now or, in other words, how life is to be lived in it. What matters is participating in the reality of God and the world in Jesus Christ today, and doing so in such a way that I never experience the reality of God without the reality of the world, nor the reality of the world without the reality of God.[42]

Bonhoeffer makes his point even more explicitly in his section, "Thinking in Terms of Two Spheres." He argues that dividing reality into spheres has plagued the history of Christian Ethics. The "two realms [*Räume*] bump against each other: one divine, holy, supernatural, and Christian; the other worldly, profane, natural, and unchristian."[43] Scholastics, for example, made the realm of the natural subordinate to the realm of the supernatural. Pseudo-Lutheranism pits the "autonomy of the orders of this world" against the "law of Christ." Enthusiasts, for their part (and similar to Bonhoeffer's own phase-3 thinking), pit the "church-community of the elect" against a hostile world.[44] These positions problematically assign Christ a place within the limits of reality or assume that there are realities that exist outside of Christ. Bonhoeffer explains the results. He writes, "This division of the whole of reality into

41. Ibid., 54.
42. Ibid., 55.
43. Ibid., 56.
44. Ibid., 56–57.

sacred and profane, or Christian and worldly, sectors creates the possibility of existence in only one of these sectors: for instance, a spiritual existence that takes no part in worldly existence, and a worldly existence that can make good its claim to autonomy over against the sacred sector."[45] Bonhoeffer cites certain groups as examples. There is the monk who closes himself off to secular existence and the nineteenth-century Protestant secularist who dismisses the spiritual.[46]

Bonhoeffer again proposes the answer as a reconciliation of the two spheres in the person of Christ. He writes,

> As long as Christ and the world are conceived of as two realms [*Räume*] bumping against and repelling each other, we are left with only the following options. Giving up on reality as a whole, either we place ourselves in one of the two realms, wanting Christ without the world or the world without Christ—and in both cases we deceive ourselves... As hard as it may now seem to break the spell of this conceptual framework of realms, it is just as certain that this perspective deeply contradicts both biblical and Reformation thought, therefore bypassing reality There are not two realities, but only one reality, and that is God's reality revealed in Christ in the reality of the world. Partaking in Christ, we stand at the same time in the reality of God and the reality of the world. The reality of Christ embraces the reality of the world within itself.[47]

Bonhoeffer's profoundly Christological or Christocratic understanding of the nature of reality clearly eliminates the possibility of two-sphered thinking. Christian existence clearly means existence fully in the world or reality. Bonhoeffer continues,

> Whoever confesses the reality of Jesus Christ as the revelation of God confesses in the same breath the reality of God and the reality of the world, for they find God and the world reconciled in Christ. Just for this reason the Christian is no longer the person of eternal conflict. As reality is one in Christ, so the person who belongs to this Christ-reality is also a whole. Worldliness does not separate one from Christ, and being Christian does not

---

45. Ibid., 57.
46. Ibid.
47. Ibid., 58.

Phase 4: Church as World

separate one from the world. Belonging completely to Christ, one stands at the same time completely in the world.[48]

In addition, Bonhoeffer makes a very important point about the nature of Luther's foundation for his Two Kingdoms doctrine. He argues that Luther's intention was to establish and reassert this unity of God and the world in Christ.[49] Without this unified understanding of reality there exists the danger of separate laws, the law of the world and the law of Christ which stand in opposition to each other.[50] Bonhoeffer's strong assertion of a reconciled reality in Christ is, of course, important for his vision of what is ethical. Bonhoeffer writes, "Since ethical thinking in terms of realms is overcome by faith in the revelation of ultimate reality in Jesus Christ, it follows that there is no real Christian existence outside the reality of the world and no real worldliness outside the reality of Jesus Christ. For the Christian there is nowhere to retreat from the world, neither externally nor into the inner life."[51] Ethics is the conformation of the Christian to reality that is, in effect, Christ. There is, as Bonhoeffer states, no otherworldly sphere into which the Christian can or should retreat. Being Christian means understanding that Christian action can take place only in the one reconciled reality in the world.

Bonhoeffer's thinking on the reconciled two-sphered reality brings him back to questions about the limits of the church and the outside world. Bonhoeffer warns against understanding the sectors or spheres as static and unchanging categories. Nevertheless, he does ask, "Are there really no ultimate static oppositions, no realms that are definitively separated from each other? Is not the Church of Jesus Christ such a realm that is divided from the realm of the world?"[52] Bonhoeffer confirms, as he did in *Discipleship*, that the church occupies a definite space in the

---

48. Ibid., 62.

49 Ibid., 60. Bonhoeffer writes, "In the name of a better Christianity Luther used the worldly to protest against a type of Christianity that was making itself independent by separating itself from the reality of Christ. Similarly, Christianity must be used polemically today against the worldly in the name of a better worldliness; this polemical use of Christianity must not end up again in a static and self-serving sacred realm. Only in this sense of polemical unity may Luther's doctrine of the two kingdoms [*Zwei Reiche*] be used. This was probably its original meaning."

50. *DBWE-6*, 60.

51. Ibid., 61.

52. Ibid., 62.

world. He argues, though, that "it would be entirely wrong to interpret this space in a purely empirical sense." He writes,

> When God in Jesus Christ claims space in the world—even space in a stable "because there was no other place in the inn"—God embraces the whole reality of the world in this narrow space and reveals its ultimate foundation. So also the church of Jesus Christ is the place [*Ort*]—that is, the space [*Raum*]—in the world where the reign of Jesus Christ over the whole world is to be demonstrated and proclaimed. This space of the Church does not, therefore, exist just for itself, but its existence is already always something that reached far beyond it. This is because it is not the space of a cult that would have to fight for its own existence in the world. Rather, the space of the church is the place where witness is given to the foundation of all reality in Jesus Christ ... The space of the church is not there in order to fight with the world for a piece of its territory, but precisely to testify to the world that it is still the world, namely, the world that is loved and reconciled by God.[53]

Bonhoeffer thus tries to acknowledge the difference between the church and the world while avoiding positing them as conflicting entities defined by empirical space. As he argued in various phase-2 writings, the world's true nature or proper self-understanding is dependent on the Church being able to function as the place where Christ is proclaimed. Even more, the Church is actually the primary bearer and standard of reality against which the world must define itself. The Church "can only defend its own space by fighting, not for space, but for the salvation of the world."[54] It is in this sense that the world and church are not defined by physical space but rather by their proper interrelationship. The Church also has as its task to proclaim and witness to Christ to the whole world and not just the church itself. It is in this way that "this space has already been broken through, abolished, and overcome in every moment by the witness of the church to Jesus Christ."[55]

Even with his strong argumentation thus far, Bonhoeffer is not convinced he has articulated fully the difference between the church and the world in non-spatial terms. He looks to the Bible for some guidance

---

53. Ibid., 63.
54. Ibid., 64.
55. Ibid.

Phase 4: Church as World

and asserts an important concept, mandates, as the answer.[56] According to scripture, whether the world is conscious of it or not, it is related to Christ and that relatedness to Christ "becomes concrete in certain mandates of God in the world." Bonhoeffer is very careful to argue that these mandates (labor, marriage, government and Church) are different from "divine orders" because they are "divinely imposed tasks [*Auftrag*], as opposed to determinate forms of being."[57] Bonhoeffer places the emphasis on God's active or dynamic word in terms of the existence and functioning of these mandates in the world rather than how they may be operating or the nature of their very existence itself. Furthermore, these mandates place the Christian squarely in the world. Bonhoeffer explains, "God has placed human beings under all these mandates, not only each individual under one or the other, but all people under all four. There can be no retreat, therefore from a 'worldly' into a 'spiritual' 'realm.' The practice of the Christian life can be learned only under these four mandates of God. It will not do to depreciate the first three mandates as 'worldly,' over against the last. It is a matter of 'divine' mandates in the midst of the world, whether they concern work, marriage, government, or church."[58] The fact that these mandates have their origin, continuance, and goal in Christ in a reconciled reality disallows their separation into secular and spiritual. They are geared toward establishing unity. A Christian's participation in Christ is as legitimate through secular activity as it is in spiritual activity.[59]

56. Ibid., 68. Bonhoeffer writes, "This belonging together of God and the world that is grounded in Christ does not allow static spatial boundaries, nor does it remove the difference between church-community and world. This leads to the question of how to think about this difference without falling back into spatial images. Here we must ask the Bible itself for advice, and it has its answer ready."

57. Ibid., 68–69.

58. Ibid., 69.

59. Ibid., 73. Bonhoeffer writes, "Since a person is at the same time worker, spouse and citizen, since one mandate overlaps with the others, and since all mandates need to be fulfilled at the same time, so the church mandate reaches into all the other mandates. Similarly, the Christian is at the same time worker, spouse and citizen. Every division into separate realms [*Räume*] is forbidden here. Human beings as whole persons stand before the whole earthly and eternal reality that God in Jesus Christ has prepared for them. Only in full response to the whole of this offer and this claim can the human person fulfill this reality. This is the witness the church has to give to the world, that all the other mandates are not there to divide people and tear them apart but to deal with them as whole people before God the Creator, Reconciler, and Redeemer—that reality in all its manifold aspects is ultimately one in God who became human, Jesus Christ.

Bonhoeffer's concepts of the ultimate and the penultimate also reiterate his concern with positions that vary from the notion of a unified, sphere-less reality. The ultimate is the justification of the sinner by grace alone. The penultimate, on the other hand, is "all that precedes the ultimate—the justification of the sinner by grace alone—and that is addressed as the penultimate after finding the ultimate."[60] These categories, however, are not static or theoretical categories. Rather, they refer to goals or ends in light of which a whole range of Christian activity or ways of daily living are framed or ordered. Bonhoeffer's thinking on the world comes to light in his analysis of certain extremes in the way the ultimate and the penultimate relate to each other. These relations are really extremes in the Christian stances toward reality. They are the radical solution and the compromise solution.

The radical solution focuses on the ultimate to the exclusion of the penultimate. Everything worldly is therefore against Christ. Bonhoeffer writes, "The radical solution sees only the ultimate, and in it sees only a complete break with the penultimate. Ultimate and penultimate stand in mutually exclusive opposition. Christ is the destroyer and enemy of everything penultimate, and everything penultimate is the enemy of Christ. Christ is the sign that the world is ripe to be consigned to the fire. Here there are no distinctions; all must come to judgment. In the judgment there is only one division: to be for or against Christ."[61] The implications of this vision are a relinquishing of responsibility for the course of the world. Bonhoeffer continues, "What will happen to the world as a result is no longer important; the Christian has no responsibility for that. The world must burn in any case."[62] The other position, the compromise solution, is cause for a similar sense of lack of responsibility for the world. The penultimate, in this vision, "retains its inherent rights, but it is not endangered or threatened by the ultimate." The ultimate has no impact on the everyday and therefore the world can carry on self-enclosed and unaffected. There is therefore an "eternal justification for all that exists" or for the status quo.[63]

The divine mandates in the world are not there to wear people down through endless conflicts. Rather, they aim at the whole human person who stands in reality before God."

60. Ibid., 159.
61. Ibid., 153.
62. Ibid.
63. Ibid., 153–54.

Phase 4: Church as World

The radical and the compromise solutions represent extremes because they sanction one position to the exclusion of the other. Radicalism, for its part, consciously or unconsciously hates the world or creation and gives rise to withdrawal from the world or efforts to improve it. The compromise solution attempts to protect the sphere of the world and life within it from encroachment on its territory by the ultimate.[64] The answer to holding to one of these ultimate or penultimate positions to the exclusion of the other, and to the negative ramifications of these extremes, is Christology.[65] Bonhoeffer speaks of the Christological answer in terms of Christ's incarnation, crucifixion, and resurrection. The incarnation is the affirmation of God's love for his creation. As such, it ensures that the human realm is neither totally "self-sufficient" nor to be destroyed.[66] Bonhoeffer's incarnational theology lends itself to legitimate action in the world. If, however, the incarnation is torn apart from the crucifixion and resurrection, emphasis on the incarnation leads to an uncritical engagement in the world, the compromise solution. The crucified Jesus, who stands as God's "final judgment on fallen creation," corrects this overemphasis on uncritical acceptance of the world. Emphasis on the crucified Christ to the exclusion of Christ incarnated leads to the opposite extreme, radicalism or enthusiasm.[67] Bonhoeffer's solution is a Christology that holds all three moments in balance in a Christian life lived fully in the world.[68]

The major themes in *Ethics* show a Bonhoeffer decisively (and even explicitly) reversing the two-sphered thinking from phase 3. The ethical demands the Christian's conformation to Christ who is the structure of reality. The mandates serve as specific biblical warrants for engaging in a reality not divided into the secular and the spiritual. The Christology

---

64. Ibid., 156.
65. Ibid., 157.
66. Ibid., 158.
67. Ibid.
68. Ibid., 159 Bonhoeffer writes, "Christian life means being human [*Menschsein*] in the power of Christ's becoming human, being judged and pardoned in the power of the cross, living a new life in the power of the resurrection. No one of these is without the others. Concerning the relationship with the penultimate, it can be concluded that Christian life neither destroys nor sanctions the penultimate. In Christ the reality of God enters the reality of the world and allows us to take part in this real encounter. It is an encounter beyond all radicalism and all compromise. Christian life is participation in Christ's encounter with the world."

related to the concepts "ultimate" and "penultimate" places the Christian back into the world. Ultimately, Bonhoeffer's positions in *Ethics* make a commitment to Christ the occasion for full and legitimate engagement in the world as "action in accordance with Christ is action in accord with reality."[69] Finally, Bonhoeffer's explicit church-world theorizing shows him arguing for a church whose borders with the outside world, while defined, are not done so in spatial terms which lend themselves to visualizing the church and the world as residing in mutually impenetrable spheres. Rather, church is where Christ makes possible the calling of all of humanity to its proper form (i.e., to the form of Jesus Christ in the world). As such, church is not synonymous only with a group of persons who mark themselves off from the world by following a highly specialized set of biblical directives. Church exists where persons conform themselves to the form of Jesus Christ in the world. The church is therefore constantly moving out beyond itself rather than closing itself off from the segment of humanity who has not explicitly accepted the gospel (or a particular part of the gospel, like the Sermon on the Mount as in his phase-3 thinking).

Church-World Relationship and Political Thinking

We can examine the relation between his church-world thinking or his thinking on the world and his political positions with all of the foregoing in place. Because he places the church legitimately back into the reality of the world (common to his phase 1 and phase 2 visions), his positions on political matters have returned to those more properly in the Lutheran Two Kingdoms arena. Here, the church and state both participate in the same reality and therefore meaningfully interact. Bonhoeffer, in his chapter on "State and Church," is markedly Christological in his theorizing. The state, as is true for any existing entity, must be related to Christ as the Mediator between created reality and the Creator. If one fails to conceive of government as mediated by Christ one establishes it as an entity outside of Christ's proper dominion. Thus, one must conceive of government in terms of natural law. Yet natural law, based as it is in the sinful nature of humanity as it exists, opens the door for imperialism and revolution, two positions irreconcilable with a government grounded in the reality of Christ.[70] Bonhoeffer's explicit teaching on the

69. Ibid., 229.
70. Bonhoeffer, *Conspiracy and Imprisonment: 1940–1945*, 512. This text will be abbreviated as *DBWE-16*.

Phase 4: Church as World

nature of government through and in Christ thus appears to be reasonably conservative. The Christian owes the government obedience. The Christian is neither able to nor obliged to question the government's directives in any particular case. The Christian is compelled to obey even in cases of doubt. There is, furthermore, no right of revolution for the Christian.[71] The government fulfills its role of wielding the sword and keeping order, and the citizen responds and fulfills his or her duty as a member of the *polis*.

Bonhoeffer's church-state thinking in *Ethics* is thus far consistent with the conservative elements of the Two Kingdoms doctrine (phase 1). However, he does not remain there. For instance, Bonhoeffer argues that "the duty of the Christian to obey binds them up to the point where the government forces them into direct violation of the divine commandment, thus until the government overtly acts contrary to its divine task and thereby forfeits its divine claim."[72] Bonhoeffer thus reiterates his position in phase 2 whereby the church and state should expect each other to fulfill their respective roles. Along these lines, the church has as its task to call the government to its proper duty.[73] Bonhoeffer also reiterates the "mystical link" thinking from phase 2 whereby only the church brings government to an understanding of itself. The church has the political responsibility to make the government aware of its "failures and mistakes that necessarily threaten its governmental office."[74] Bonhoeffer is somewhat unclear about the possibility of direct political action against the state for the church and its members in his sections that deal explicitly with government or church-state relations. However, other parts of *Ethics* and an essay written during the same time period ("After Ten Years"[75]) contain an implicit program of political resistance against the government, and even tyrannicide.[76]

71. Ibid., 525.
72. Ibid., 516–17.
73. Ibid., 522.
74. Ibid., 525.
75. *DBWE-8*, 37–52.
76. See *RR*, 129–73. See also Green, "Bonhoeffer's Christian Ethics in Resistance to Tyranny and Genocide." Both Rasmussen and Green argue that there is a program of resistance to the state and a justification for tyrannicide in these writings. It should be noted that their analyses (and my own acceptance of their conclusions) can be criticized on the grounds that they are speculative since Bonhoeffer did not explicitly state that tyrannicide was acceptable.

Bonhoeffer's positions on the government are not surprising given what he has said about the Christocentric nature of reality and the mandates. Participating in a government is participating in the reality of Christ in the world. Bonhoeffer writes, "In obedience to government the Christian obeys Christ. The Christian as citizen does not cease to be a Christian, but he serves Christ in a different way. In this way the content of the legitimate governmental claim is already sufficiently determined as well. It can never lead the Christian against Christ; rather it helps Christians serve Christ in the world. In this way the person in government becomes for the Christian a servant of God."[77] Conforming to reality, conforming to Christ, and obeying the government, which is itself one of the ways in which Christ is present as a structure of reality, are simultaneous moments. Acting in the world to make sure the government fulfills its role properly can also be a legitimate conformation to reality.

It is also no surprise, given Bonhoeffer's church-state thinking, that he does not argue for pacifist positions or even use the word "pacifism" in *Ethics*. His positions are much closer to traditional "just war" thinking. Bonhoeffer's rationale for both war and tyrannicide are presupposed by his section "The Structure of Responsible Life"[78] as well as the general themes concerning the church-world relationship. Bonhoeffer describes the structure of responsible life as vicarious representative action (*Stellvertretung* was previously translated as "deputyship"), accordance with reality, taking on guilt, and freedom. Vicarious representative action includes primarily responsibility for individuals and the larger community.[79] Bonhoeffer, in a significant departure from his phase-3 writings, implies that this sphere of responsibility lies outside the church as well as inside of it.[80]

---

77. *DBWE-16*, 522.

78. Green, "Bonhoeffer's Christian Ethics in Resistance to Tyranny and Genocide," 11.

79. *DBWE-6*, 257–61.

80. *RR*, 41. Rasmussen, in the concluding paragraph of his section describing Responsibility and Deputyship in the *Ethics*, writes, "Deputyship, then, is a possibility and a standard for all men, and it is a characteristic of normal human conduct as life is lived out in its divinely commissioned framework, the mandates. By meeting the built-in obligations as, for example, a husband, father, laborer, citizen, and churchman, a man conforms to Christ's form, whether cognizant of it or not. The christological and ecclesiological understanding of deputyship in Bonhoeffer's writings of the thirties becomes a christological and universal humanist one in the forties."

Phase 4: Church as World

Bonhoeffer's explication of the theme of accordance with reality has much in common with his 1929 Barcelona ethic. The responsible ethical agent responds to reality as it is, without recourse to ideas or laws. Ethical action is in total accordance with reality. Bonhoeffer explains, as he does throughout the work, using a Christology wherein Christ reconciles God with humanity and humanity with the world. He writes, "The origin of action that is in accord with reality is neither pseudo-Lutheran Christ whose only purpose is to sanction the status quo, nor the radical, revolutionary Christ of all religious enthusiasts who is supposed to bless every revolution; it is rather the God who became human, Jesus Christ, who took on humanity and who has loved, judged, and reconciled humanity, and with it the world."[81] There is thus a sense in which responsible action in the world in accordance with reality is beyond the question of conservative or liberal responses. There is no abstract ethic or theoretical basis for Christian action in the world that can govern ethical decisions. An abstract ethic would lead to "a number of mutually irreconcilable laws."[82] There is only participating in Christ from whom "human action occurs that is not crushed by conflicts of principle, but springs instead from the already accomplished reconciliation of the world with God. This is an action that soberly and simply does what accords with reality, an action done in vicarious representative responsibility."[83]

Bonhoeffer's treatment of the craft of political governance or *Staatkunst* contains one of the instances of his teaching on war. Bonhoeffer argues that in everything "there is an intrinsic law that is grounded in its origin." He argues further that the correspondence of responsible action with reality also involves the finding out and complying with this law.[84] There is a technical component of these laws whose operation is relatively unproblematic when the object does not involve human existence. When human existence is involved, though, the detection and operation of these laws becomes questionable. Statecraft is an example of an entity which, while having a technical side with discernible operating laws, is also directly concerned with human existence.[85] Responsible

---

81. *DBWE-6*, 263.
82. Ibid., 264.
83. Ibid., 266.
84. Ibid., 271.
85. Ibid., 271–72.

action must thus go beyond that which can be circumscribed by laws. Bonhoeffer writes,

> However, it is precisely at this point that appropriate action is inevitably forced to recognize that these laws of statecraft do not exhaust the content of the intrinsic law of the state, and indeed that the law of the state ultimately extends beyond any legal definition, precisely because the state is inextricably linked to human existence. And it is only at this point that responsible action reaches its most profound expression. There are occasions when, in the course of historical life, the strict observance of the explicit law of a state, a corporation, a family, but also of a scientific discovery, entails a clash with the basic necessities of human life [*Lebensnotwendigkeiten*]. In such cases, appropriate responsible action departs from the domain governed by laws and principles, from the normal and regular, and instead is confronted with the extraordinary situation beyond ultimate necessities that are beyond any possible regulation by law.[86]

Bonhoeffer uses Machiavelli's term *necessità* to describe this situation where "the craft of political governance [*Staatskunst*] becomes political necessity [*Staatsnotwendingkeit*]."[87] These necessities, while beyond the rational, when acted upon constitute behavior in accordance with reality. They are, therefore, actions which conform to the form of Christ and demand the free responsibility of the agent.

The situation of *necessità* is an extraordinary one that confronts human reason with an *ultima ratio*. In the realm of statecraft or politics the *ultima ratio* situation is that of war. It is a situation that "lies beyond the laws of reason," an "irrational action" that cannot be treated as if it were normal. War is, nevertheless, an activity that can be legitimate given the fact that *necessità* and *ultima ratio* both constitute action that can be in accordance with reality.[88] Bonhoeffer is no pacifist in *Ethics*.[89] Further thinking confirms his acceptance of war. The section, "The Right to Bodily Life," treats war in the context of the arbitrary taking of life. He writes, "The first right of natural life is the protection of bodily life from

86. Ibid., 272–73.
87. Ibid., 273.
88. Ibid.
89. *RR*, 112. Rasmussen writes, "Bonhoeffer may have been a pacifist earlier, but not at this time and above all not because he felt war justifiable solely as *ultima ratio*! This does not match even the minimal definition of pacifism."

Phase 4: Church as World 303

arbitrary killing."[90] Arbitrary killing is an instance where innocent life is destroyed. When a person or a nation engages in a conscious attack on life in another nation, the killing which results in the response is no longer arbitrary. Even if a particular combatant (or presumably a citizen who is killed in war by mistake without direct intention) is not "personally guilty," in war they must "share the consequences of bearing the common guilt."[91] Bonhoeffer, in addition to legitimizing the taking of life in the context of a defensive war, also lays down principles concerning conduct in war. Killing of innocents in war, for example, if not directly intended, is not arbitrary killing and thus acceptable. Bonhoeffer's thinking on war in *Ethics* thus resembles a just war position where certain rules govern the decision to enter war and the conduct therein.[92] Finally, in many places in *Ethics* Bonhoeffer argues that engaging in reality fully in responsible action will necessitate the taking on of guilt.

There are two more considerations in Bonhoeffer's positions on war and peace, conscientious objection and tyrannicide. Bonhoeffer argues that, if the state is not understood apocalyptically, military service is one of the obligations to the government.[93] He also argued, as noted above, that obedience to the government was required by Christians except in cases where the "government forces them into direct violation of the divine commandment, thus until the government overtly acts contrary to its divine task and thereby forfeits its divine."[94] Since in the case of war, Bonhoeffer suggests that arbitrary killing is the only problematic government directive, it appears that military service which does not demand arbitrary killing would be acceptable.

Bonhoeffer scholars, notably Rasmussen, see the *Ethics* as evidence for a decidedly non-pacifist position. Both Green and Rasmussen, as noted above, also see in it (and "After Ten Years") a justification for tyrannicde. Bonhoeffer does not argue directly for tyrannicide in *Ethics*

---

90. *DBWE-6*, 189.

91. Ibid.

92. Ibid. See also, *RR*, 113. Rasmussen writes, "In short, once war as *ultima ratio* has begun, killing of the enemy and of civilians is justified, providing the latter is the unintended outcome of necessary military action. That this is not a pacifist position is clear beyond cavil. It belongs instead to the adherent of 'just war' theory, a position in rather sharp contrast with pacifism."

93. *DBWE-16*, 517.

94. Ibid.

for obvious reasons.⁹⁵ His theological arguments for tyrannicide must thus be inferred from his thinking on violent action (war), disobeying governmental directives (breaking laws), and his veiled references to Hitler as tyrant. Bonhoeffer mentions tyranny and, although he does not use Hitler's name, describes him as the despiser of men. This person is a brutal "tyrannical despiser of humanity" who exploits human weaknesses. The whole time he disguises the "basest contempt for humanity" behind "the most holy assertions of love for humanity."⁹⁶

Some Bonhoeffer scholars argue that he considered the German situation an extreme one calling for responsible action by responsible persons even though he did not state specifically in any text that the presence of Hitler as tyrant created an *ultima ratio* situation.⁹⁷ War, as has been shown, can be responsible action in accordance with the Christocratic structure of reality if conducted in accordance with certain rules. The thinking that undergirds tyrannicide is, as an another *ultima ratio* act of violence performed in responsibility, the same as that which supports war.⁹⁸ Bonhoeffer's "After Ten Years" provides indications that he understood the contemporary situation as *ultima ratio*. He writes,

> Have there ever been people in history who in their time, like us, had so little ground under their feet, people to whom every possible alternative open to them at the time appeared equally unbearable, senseless, and contrary to life? Have there been those who like us looked for the source of their strength beyond all of those available alternatives? Were they looking entirely in what has passed away and in what is yet to come? And nevertheless,

---

95. Green, "Bonhoeffer's Christian Ethics in Resistance to Tyranny and Genocide," 4–5. Green writes, "But Bonhoeffer does not appeal directly to the traditional arguments for tyrannicide, nor structure his ethics of resistance around them. Why was this? Prudence seems an obvious answer: you don't give the Gestapo evidence to convict you by laying out your rationale for an assassination, should they confiscate your writings—as indeed happened with some of Bonhoeffer's manuscripts."

96. *DBWE-6*, 86.

97. *ATS*, 304–21.

98. *RR*, 111. Rasmussen writes, "This relation of free responsibility to the *ultima ratio* was shown to be Bonhoeffer's rationale for conspiratorial breaking of law. Times do arise which demand violence as *ultima ratio* action, but the employment of this violence must never be made normative for other times. The use of violence must never be made *prima ratio* . . . War is also among the examples of the *ultima ratio* case. In short, Bonhoeffer conceptualizes conspiracy and war in the same way!"

without being dreamers, did they await with calm and confidence the successful outcome of their endeavor?[99]

Given the unique and extreme situation in which the church and country found itself, Bonhoeffer questions the effectiveness of the traditional ethical options (conscience, duty, complete freedom, and private virtuousness).[100] Bonhoeffer's treatment of two options, duty and private virtuousness, arguably make the most direct (if veiled) references to Hitler and tyrannicide. He argues that "duty is so circumscribed that that there is never any room to venture that which rests wholly in one's own responsibility, the action that alone strikes at the very core of evil and overcome it. The man of duty will in the end have to do his duty to the devil as well."[101] He writes that the person who chooses private virtuousness, "must close his eyes and mouth to the injustice around him. He can remain undefiled by the consequences of responsible action only by deceiving himself."[102]

Bonhoeffer offers another description of the extraordinary nature of the current German situation. While not making explicit reference to the German population, he describes persons and a situation characterized by "stupidity." Bonhoeffer's answer to this situation is, arguably, another reference to tyrannicide. He writes, "Yet at this very point it becomes quite clear that only an act of liberation, not instruction, can overcome stupidity."[103] Bonhoeffer's answer throughout the essay is consistent with his thinking in *Ethics* in the section the "Structure of Responsible Life." There is a need for a free act of responsibility. He writes, "Who stands firm? Only the one whose ultimate standard is not his reason, his principles, conscience, freedom, or virtue; only the one who is prepared to sacrifice all of these when, in faith to and in relationship to God alone, he is called to obedient and responsible action. Such a person is the responsible one, whose life is to be nothing but a response to God's question and call. Where are these responsible ones?"[104]

---

99. *DBWE-8*, 38.
100. Ibid., 38–40. These are the same positions he question in *Ethics*.
101. Ibid., 40.
102. Ibid.
103. Ibid., 44.
104. Ibid., 40.

In another section he adds, "But civil courage can grow only from the free responsibility of the free man. Only today are the Germans beginning to discover what free responsibility means. It is founded in a God who calls for the free venture of faith to responsible action and who promises forgiveness and consolation to the one who on account of such action becomes a sinner."[105] One more significant portion in considering the nature of a responsible act is Bonhoeffer's section "Sympathy." He argues that the responsible moral agent is called to respond to the sufferings of his or her fellow human beings.[106]

Finally, we can formulate a few sentences describing Bonhoeffer's thinking on the possibility of tyrannicide given what has been presented in *Ethics* and "Ten Year's After." Tyrannicide is a deed of free responsibility in response to God's command in a time of extreme necessity in the service of those who are suffering. The action, while a sinful one outside the bounds or laws governing normal ethical existence and thus one requiring the agent's willingness to take on guilt, is still an action which is in accordance with reality and thus in service to Christ. The responsible person would be able to enter a conspiracy or kill a tyrant if necessary.[107]

In terms of conscientious objection, it should be noted that Bonhoeffer also has a brief statement from the final paragraph of his *Ethics* from 1943 where he advocates for its possibility. Bonhoeffer writes, "Finally, there is also a frightening confusion or arrogance on the part of countless Protestant Christians with regard to Christians who refuse to take an oath [*Eidesverweigerer*], conscientious objectors,

---

105. Ibid., 41.
106. Ibid., 49.
107. Green, "Bonhoeffer's Christian Ethics in Resistance to Tyranny and Genocide," 22–23. Green sums up his own position as follows: "Bonhoeffer's ethics of resistance can be summed up in the following statements. Christian ethics, in his context, is a matter of doing the will of God, not of 'being good' according to some human standard. The Christological themes of reconciliation, incarnation, cross and resurrection frame the ethical analysis of the context and inform the ethical action within it. In extreme situations where life itself is at stake, the killing of a tyrant may be wagered. This is a particular act, not the enactment of a general principle; it occurs only in a specific case of extreme necessity. The act is one of vicarious responsibility, and its purpose is healing and the peace of human community. It is not justified by any principle of human ethics, but is a wager, with its risk, about the will of God. It is done in freedom, with appropriate analysis of the situation, and with a willingness to take on guilt. This free, responsible action is an act of faith."

Phase 4: Church as World

etc."[108] His statement here would seem to be inconsistent with other elements of this phase wherein reengagement with the world in the form of war is the political position consistent with his church-world vision. This would seem to be the case especially if one considers conscientious objection to fall under a definition of world-withdrawn pacifism. It is clear, here, though, that Bonhoeffer is not denouncing war or the possibility for Christians engaging in wars that they see consistent with their consciences. The footnote in the *Ethics* text clarifying and supporting Bonhoeffer's brief and undeveloped statement about conscientious objectors relays a piece from Maria von Wedemeyer's diary which reads, in part,

> He [Bonhoeffer] said it was a tradition with us that young men should volunteer for military service and lay down their lives for a cause which they mightn't not approve at all. But there also must be people to fight from conviction alone. If they approved of the grounds for war, well and good. If not, they could best serve the Fatherland by operating on the internal front even by working against the regime. It would thus be their task to avoid serving in the armed services for as long as possible—and even, under certain circumstances, if they couldn't reconcile it with their conscience, to be conscientious objectors.[109]

Bonhoeffer is arguing for the possibility for some to make a decision to not engage in war only if the "grounds" for the war are not acceptable in terms of their consciences. This would seem to be consistent with the earlier text noted above wherein he argues that, in general, military service is required unless the government's directive "directly compels him to offend against the divine commandment." Again, the position here is the possibility of conscientious objection for some under certain circumstances but, generally, a just war position.

The connection between Bonhoeffer's church-world thinking and his political thinking is somewhat complicated given the fragmentary nature of the writings and questions concerning which texts were altered for fear of Nazi confiscation and reading. In a general sense, though, the connection between his church-world thinking and political thinking is extremely clear. Bonhoeffer, through the mandates, his warning against two-sphered thinking, the concepts of the ultimate and the penultimate,

---

108. *DBWE-6*, 407.
109. Ibid.

and the structure of responsible life, has made it clear that reality has a Christocratic structure. Reality is not broken up into spheres. The church and the world, while different, are united in Christ in this one reality. Since, according to the mandates, connection to Christ becomes the occasion for engagement in all worldly structures, and government and church are mandates equal in value, Christian faith is not in any way incompatible with full engagement in the political realm. There is simply no otherworldly sphere of holiness or purity into which the Christian can go in order to shield him or herself from this full engagement, which includes obligations such as paying taxes, participating in war, or even potentially tyrannicide.

In his more specific church-world analysis, Bonhoeffer does reiterate his phase-3 teaching on the church as a visible community with its own space and particular function. The church is not an invisible or strictly spiritual community. These parts of *Ethics*, implying some form of tension between the church and the world, would be consistent with adherence to some interpretation of Luther's Two Kingdoms doctrine as in phase 1 and in phase 2. There are parts of *Ethics* where Bonhoeffer does seem to adhere to the more conservative aspects of the doctrine, one emphasizing the non-interfering aspect of church-state relations. There are also parts where Bonhoeffer adheres to a more liberal interpretation, one which emphasizes the church's right to criticize state action or call the state to its proper function.

Bonhoeffer's thought in *Ethics*, though, also falls outside Two Kingdoms thinking in places for the same reason his thought in phase 3 does. In both cases the church and the world are no longer in any meaningful tension. There are indeed facets of his theology in *Ethics*, beyond his specific statement about the church reaching far beyond itself, that indicate a church whose boundaries with the world have been severely compromised or perhaps even nullified. Deputyship, acts of free responsibility, the willingness to take on guilt and to suffer with and for others are all acts (or ways of being) demanded of all persons in the world (Christian or not, religious person or secular person) in all contexts. It is in this way that the Lordship of Christ, if not the visible church itself, extends over all persons. This is not surprising given that Bonhoeffer considers all of reality to be Christocratic in its very structure. Responsible action performed by anyone and anywhere is action in conformation to reality and thus a response to the call of Christ. It is in this sense that

Phase 4: Church as World

Christ's Lordship over the whole world (Bonhoeffer's "Christo-universal vision"[110]) eclipses the difference between action as a church member and activity as any secular person.[111]

The political issue which shows how Bonhoeffer's church-world vision forces him past accepted interpretations of Two Kingdoms thinking is his implicit approval of tyrannicide. There was no unambiguous provision for killing a tyrant in most interpretations of the doctrine and especially the ones with which Bonhoeffer would have been familiar. Bonhoeffer's phase-2 thinking did allow for the possibility of direct political action against the state. This possibility arose from a heightened tension between the church with an authoritative identity and Word on the one side and the world depicted as increasingly hostile on the other. Bonhoeffer did not assign any specific content to the direct political action in phase 2. He did not, furthermore, indicate that the person engaging in this direct political action was to do so in any other capacity than as a churchperson. The result of releasing the tension between the church and the world in the particular way that Bonhoeffer has done in some of his argumentation in *Ethics* has made it virtually impossible to distinguish responsible action as a churchperson and responsible action as a secular person.

LETTERS AND PAPERS FROM PRISON
(APRIL 1943—DECEMBER 1944)

There are several Bonhoeffer letters, written mostly to Bethge and various family members from prison, first published by Bethge in 1951. Bonhoeffer wrote the letters against the backdrop of a political situation which saw Hitler begin to lose the war. The Allies invaded Sicily in mid-

110. *RR*, 21.
111. Ibid., 40. Rasmussen, noting the difference between *Cost of Discipleship* and *Ethics* on this point, writes, "Furthermore, this deputyship [as described in *The Cost of Discipleship*] is an action for the sake of the world . . . Yet being in the world for the world is at considerable distance from deputyship seen in the profane acts of secular men or deputyship viewed as permeating all worldly reality. Thus a new and decisive dimension is given deputyship in *Ethics*, despite the foretaste in *The Cost of Discipleship*. In *Ethics* deputyship is found throughout the whole range of Christ's dominion. It is no longer a thoroughly ecclesiological term, although it remains a thoroughly christological one. Deputyship draws out its universal dimensions as Bonhoeffer's Christology draws out its theocratic breadth. Now it is seen in the behavior of *all* 'responsible' men, whether Christian or not. The whole of life, rather than almost wholly the Church, is the locus for discovering and exercising deputyship."

1943 and began their slow move up the peninsula. The more significant event was the allied landing in Normandy on June 6, 1944. The Allies liberated Paris by the end of August and continued on through northern Germany.[112] Hitler and others, thinking that the West would not permit the Communists to overtake parts of Europe, were still confident in a German victory. The Allies, who had been slowly retaking Europe from the West, and the Soviets, who made tremendous advances coming from the East, however, met up with American troops in Berlin in April 1945. The successes of the Allies and the Soviets and the realization of internal difficulties, which manifested themselves in the unsuccessful July 20, 1944, assassination attempt, forced Hitler into seclusion in his bunker in January 1945.[113] The death of President Roosevelt added a last hope for Hitler. He eventually realized the war was lost and announced his intention to commit suicide at an April 22 military conference. Hitler and Eva Braun committed suicide on April 30, 1945. On May 7, 1945, the Third Reich surrendered unconditionally to the Allies.[114]

The situation in the ecclesial sphere from April 1943 until the end of the war was basically the same as the period between 1940 and the beginning of 1943. The notable exception was the continued activities of Bishop Wurm. He sent two letters in July and December to government officials (and later circulated them around the parishes) arguing that the extermination of non-Aryans stood in "the strongest possible opposition to the commandments of God and destroy[ed] the foundation of all our Western thought and life, in particular our fundamental belief in the God-given right to human existence and human dignity."[115] Finally, in October 1943 the Prussian synod of the Confessing church issued a statement to congregations laying out the obligations of the Fifth Commandment.[116] On the whole, though, the Protestant church leadership on the whole was ineffective and silent.[117]

---

112. *HNG*, 225–27.

113. Ibid., 227.

114. Ibid., 228–29.

115. *NPC*, 265.

116. *NPC*, 266–67. The pastoral letter read, "The State is not entrusted with the power to take away life, except in the case of criminals or war-time enemies... Terms like 'eradication,' or 'unfit to live' are not known in the law of God. The murdering of men solely because they are members of a foreign race, or because they are old, or mentally ill, or the relatives of a criminal, cannot be considered as carrying out the authority entrusted to the State by God."

117. Wright, '*Above Parties*,' 170. Wright writes in a footnote, "Wurm's attitude

Phase 4: Church as World

The papers and letters from Bonhoeffer's prison experience do not address political matters explicitly. There are, however, some extremely important and controversial letters that deal with general theological themes (religion, metaphysics, secularity, and worldliness). While these themes do not deal explicitly with the church-world relationship, they do have direct implications for the way Christians and the church might embrace or act in the world.

Bonhoeffer wrote several letters concerning the meaning, status, and function of the religious or religion. His thinking on religion is connected to the themes of worldliness and metaphysics, two areas that have implications for understanding Christian existence in the world. Bonhoeffer notes that Barth started the move toward criticizing the concept religion in modern Christianity. Barth, however, did not go far enough and essentially reasserted a "positivism of revelation" in its place.[118] Bonhoeffer wants to go beyond Barth's answer to the problem of religion with his notion of "religionless Christianity." While not clear on what religionless Christianity would ultimately look like, he was clear that the world has "come of age" and cannot be considered religious in the ways that it had been formerly. The age of religion is over. Bonhoeffer argues that "people as they are now simply cannot be religious anymore. Even those who honestly describe themselves as 'religious' aren't really practicing that at all; they presumably mean something quite different by 'religious.'"[119] Bonhoeffer argues that the presupposition held throughout the history of Christian preaching and theology, the "religious *a*

---

hardened during the war with the experience of Nazi mass murder and because he came to the conclusion that the Nazis intended to destroy Christianity. In addition to his many protests to government and party leaders, he also tried to convince other church leaders of the futility of concessions. Although he was in contact with resistance circle, however, he does not seem to have played a major part within them. Nor did he look forward to Germany's defeat by the Allies."

118. *DBWE-8*, 373. Bonhoeffer writes, "Barth was the first theologian—to his great and lasting credit—to begin the critique of religion, but he then put in its place a positivist doctrine of revelation that says, in effect, 'Like it or lump it.' Whether it's the virgin birth, the Trinity, or anything else, all are equally significant and necessary parts of the whole, which must be swallowed whole or not at all. That's not biblical ... The positivism of revelation is too easygoing, since in the end it sets up a law of faith and tears up so what is—through Christ becoming flesh!—a gift for us. Now the church stands in the place of religions—that in itself is biblical—but the world is left to its own devices, as it were, to rely on itself. That is the error."

119. *DBWE-8*, 362.

priori of mankind," can no longer be taken for granted.[120] He accepts this situation and begins to formulate a Christianity without religion.

Bonhoeffer's critique of religion has two primary targets, religion as metaphysics and religion as inwardness. His difficulty with metaphysics is its failure to help religion construct an adequate notion of the God-world relationship. Bonhoeffer writes,

> Religious people speak of God at a point where human knowledge is at an end (or sometimes when they're too lazy to think further), or when human strength fails. Actually it's a *deus ex machina* that they're always bringing on the scene, either to appear to solve insoluble problems or to provide strength when human powers fail, thus always exploiting human weakness or human limitations. Inevitably that lasts only until human beings become powerful enough to push the boundaries a bit further and God is no longer needed as a deus ex machina. To me, talking about human boundaries has become a dubious proposition anyhow. (Is even death still really a boundary, since people hardly fear it anymore, or sin, since people hardly comprehend it?) It always seems to me that we leave room for God out of anxiety.[121]

Relegating God to the boundaries, thinking of God as an entity taking up space, and thinking of God as simply a provider of answers about the physical world all have especially dangerous ramifications in a "world come of age," a world which "God is being increasingly pushed out of."[122] Theology responds by either fighting against the adulthood of the world or by assigning a specialized area of life as its province.[123] Ultimately, metaphysically-informed notions of religion have not effectively an-

---

120. Ibid., 362–63. Bonhoeffer writes, "'Christianity' has always been a form (perhaps the true form) of 'religion.' Yet if it becomes obvious one day that this 'a priori' doesn't exist, that it has been a historically conditioned and transient form of human expression, then people will become radically religionless—and I think that is already more or less the case (why, for example, doesn't this war provoke a 'religious' reaction like all the previous ones?)."

121. Ibid., 366. See also ibid., 405–6. In a May 1944 letter, Bonhoeffer expressed similar sentiment concerning positing God as a fill-in or stop-gap God. He writes, "Weizsäcker's book on the *Weltbild der Physik* continues to preoccupy me a great deal. It has again brought home to me quite clearly that we shouldn't think of God as the stopgap for the incompleteness of our knowledge, because then—as is objectively inevitable—when the boundaries of knowledge are being pushed ever. God too is pushed further away and thus is ever on the retreat."

122. Ibid., 450.

123. Ibid.

Phase 4: Church as World

swered the challenges presented by the world's coming of age. Their responses represent an establishment of two-sphered thinking by either pitting religion against a modernizing world or by giving it a special space just beyond our knowledge, a space which becomes smaller and smaller as our knowledge develops.

Religion as inwardness also reasserts two-sphered thinking. Bonhoeffer points to inwardness or individuality as one place where religion tried to reestablish itself in the face of the world coming of age.[124] This concentration on inwardness has, though, given rise to a series of ecclesial and theological difficulties. The inner person has been designated as the sole location of sin and the province of pastoral workers. There is clerical "prying into the sins of others in order to catch them out . . . as if you couldn't know a fine house until you had found cobwebs in the remotest cellar."[125] Bonhoeffer concludes, "From a theological viewpoint the error is twofold: first, thinking one can only address people as sinners after having spied out their weaknesses and meanness; second, thinking that the essential nature of a person consists of his innermost, intimate depths, and calling this his 'inner life.' And precisely in these most secret human places are to be the domain of God!"[126] Bonhoeffer also equates religion-as-inwardness with pietism. Pietism is the Protestantism's "final attempt to maintain Protestant Christianity as a religion."[127] In another letter he expressed his concern with "escapism in the guised of piety."[128] Religion-as-inwardness reasserts two-sphered thinking by making faith a province of the individual or an exclusive community unrelated to the outside world.

Bonhoeffer's answer to both religion's tendency towards bifurcating reality with metaphysics and to the otherworldly escapism resulting from the tendency to inwardness is "this-worldly" transcendence, a notion of God's relationship to the world wherein God is encountered only in the world. After describing the results of understanding religion as metaphysics (trying to reserve some space for God), Bonhoeffer writes,

> I'd like to speak of God not on the boundaries but in the center, not in weakness but in strength, thus not in death and guilt but

124. Ibid., 455.
125. Ibid., 456.
126. Ibid.
127. Ibid., 500.
128. Ibid., 367.

in human life and human goodness. When I reach my limits, it seems to me better not to say anything and to leave what can't be solved unsolved. Belief in the resurrection is not the "solution" to the problem of death. God's "beyond" is not what is beyond our cognition! Epistemological transcendence has nothing to do with God's transcendence. God is the beyond in the midst of our lives. The church stands not at the point where human powers fail, at the boundaries, but in the center of the village.[129]

Bonhoeffer writes in answer to the tendency to posit God as the stopgap for the incompleteness of our knowledge,

> We should find God in what we know, not in what we don't know; God wants to be grasped by us not in unsolved questions but in those that have been solved. This is true of the relation between God and scientific knowledge, but it is also true of the universal human questions about death, suffering, and guilt. Today, even for these questions, there are human answers that can completely disregard God. Human beings cope with these questions practically without God and have done so throughout the ages, and it is simply not true that only Christianity would have a solution to them. As for the idea of a "solution," we would have to say that Christian answers are just as uncompelling (or just as compelling) as other possible solutions. Here too, God is not a stopgap. We must recognize God not only where we reach the limits of our possibilities, God wants to be recognized in the midst of our lives, in life and not only in dying, in health and in strength and not only in dying, in health and strength and not only in suffering, in action and not only in sin. The ground for this lies in the revelation of God in Jesus Christ. God is the center of life and doesn't just "turn up" when we have unsolved problems to be solved.[130]

A profound worldliness is essentially Bonhoeffer's response to the tendency to otherworldly pietism associated with religion and understood as inwardness or individuality.

> Isn't God's righteousness and kingdom on earth the center of everything, And isn't Rom 3.24ff. the culmination of the view that God alone is righteous, rather than an individualistic doctrine of salvation? What matters is not the beyond but this world, how it is created and preserved, is given laws, reconciled and renewed.

129. Ibid., 366–67.
130. *DBWE-8*, 406–7.

Phase 4: Church as World

What is beyond this world is meant, in the gospel, to be there for this world—not in the anthropocentric sense of liberal, mystic pietistic ethical theology, but in the biblical sense of the creation and the incarnation, crucifixion, and resurrection of Jesus Christ.[131]

Bonhoeffer also responds to the tendency of inwardness, individuality, or piety to shove Christianity into an internal place separated from any relation to the outside world. He writes, "What I am driving at is that God should not be smuggled in somewhere, in the very last, secret place that is left. Instead, one must simply recognize that the world and humankind has come of age. One must not find fault with people in their worldliness but rather confront them with God where they are the strongest."[132] The Christian has no place to go but the fullness of the reality of the world. He or she confronts the real world as it is as a whole person.

Bonhoeffer's denial of religion as metaphysics and inwardness and his radical acceptance of the world or worldliness do have ramifications for Christian conduct. Bonhoeffer writes,

> Unlike believers in the redemption myths, Christians do not have an ultimate escape route out of their earthly tasks and difficulties into eternity. Like Christ ("My God . . . why have you forsaken me?"), they have to drink the cup of earthly life to the last drop, and only when they do this is the Crucified and Risen One with them, and they are crucified and resurrected with Christ. This-worldliness must not be abolished ahead of its time; on this, NT and OT are united. Redemption myths arise from the human experience of boundaries. But Christ takes hold of human beings in the midst of their lives.[133]

Faith, because of the reconciliation of two-sphered reality, can no longer mean retreating into pietism or assigning God a special place in the world. Bonhoeffer argues "that one only learns to have faith by living in the full this-worldliness of life."[134]

Finally, Bonhoeffer's notion of transcendence as an answer to religion as metaphysics and inwardness also has an explicitly Christological

131. Ibid., 373.
132. Ibid., 457.
133. Ibid., 448.
134. Ibid., 486.

thrust with distinct ramifications for action in the world. Persons experience transcendence in their participation in Jesus Christ specifically as one who acts on behalf of others. Bonhoeffer writes,

> Who is God? Not primarily a general belief in God's omnipotence, and so on. That is not a genuine experience of God but just a prolongation of a piece of the world. Encounter with Jesus Christ. Experience that here there is a reversal of all human existence, in the very fact that Jesus only "is there for others." Jesus's "being-for-others" is the experience of transcendence! Only through this liberation from self, through this "being-for-others" unto death, do omnipotence, omniscience, and omnipresence come into being. Faith is participating in this being of Jesus. (Becoming human [*Menschwerdung*], cross, resurrection). Our relationship to God is no "religious" relationship to some highest, most powerful, and best being imaginable—that is no genuine transcendence. Instead, our relationship to God is a new life in "being there for others," through participation in the being of Jesus. The transcendent is not the infinite, unattainable tasks, but the neighbor within reach in any given situation. God in human form! Not, as in oriental religions in animal forms as the monstrous, the chaotic, the remote, the terrifying, but also not in the conceptual forms of the absolute, the metaphysical, the infinite, and so on, either, nor again the Greek God—human form of the "God-human form [*Gott-Menschgestalt*] of the human being in itself." But rather "the human being for others"! therefore the Crucified One. The human being living out of the transcendent.[135]

Bonhoeffer both establishes the radical this-worldliness of transcendence and echoes his teaching on deputyship from *Ethics*. Authentic transcendence is only available within the context of serving the human other in relationship.

"Religionless Christianity," "this-worldly transcendence," and other ideas from the *Letters* posit a disavowal of two-sphered thinking even stronger than the one in *Ethics*. It is not surprising, then, that Bonhoeffer's explicit treatment of the church-world relationship finds him erasing the difference between them. In his notes describing a tripartite 100-page book he intended to write ("Outline for a Book"), Bonhoeffer explicitly critiques the Confessing Church as counter-world. In the first part, "Taking Stock of Christianity," he writes, "Generally in the Confessing Church: Standing up for the 'cause' of the church, and

135. Ibid., 501.

so on, but little personal faith in Christ. 'Jesus' disappears from view. Sociologically: no impact on the broader masses; a matter for the lower and upper-middle classes. Heavily burdened by difficult, traditional ideas. Decisive: Church defending itself. No risk taking for others."[136] In his second part, "What Is Christian faith, Really?" he continues, "Barth and the Confessing Church have encouraged people to entrench themselves again and again behind the 'faith of the Church' rather than asking and stating honestly what they really believe. This is why even in the Confessing Church the breezes are blowing less than freely."[137]

Bonhoeffer's answer to this entrenched, defensive and counter-worldly (phase 3) church is one that has broken the barriers between itself and the world. In the third part of the outline, "Conclusions," he writes,

> The church is church only when it is there for others. As a first step it must give away all its property to those in need. The clergy must live solely on the free-will offerings of the congregations and perhaps be engaged in some secular vocation [*Beruf*]. The church must participate in the worldly tasks of life in the community—not dominating but helping and serving. It must tell men of every calling [*Beruf*] what a life if Christ is, what it means "to be there for others." In particular, our church will have to confront the vices of hubris, the worship of power, envy and illusionism as the roots of all evil. It will have to speak of moderation, authenticity, trust, faithfulness, steadfastness, patience, discipline, humility, modesty and contentment. It will have to see that it does not underestimate the significance of the human "example" (which has its origin in the humanity of Jesus and is so important in Paul's writings!); the church's word gains weight and power not through concepts but by example. (I will write in more detail later about "example" in the NT—we have almost entirely lost track of this thought). Further: revision of the question of "confession" (Apostolikum); revision of apologetics; revision of preparation for and practice of ministry.[138]

Bonhoeffer's thinking on the church as participating fully in the secular realm for the benefit of others is consistent with his Christology wherein Jesus is the man for others. It is also consistent with his above-treated

---

136. Ibid., 500.
137. Ibid., 502.
138. Ibid., 503–4.

notion of this-worldly transcendence. Jesus is the "man for others" and transcendence is experienced in the community of persons.

Beyond his radical suggestion that the clergy might blend in with the larger population, Bonhoeffer is not explicit about what ramifications this Christology has for the boundaries between the church and the world. He does, however, realize that his thinking forces the question about the structure of the church in a religionless world come of age. He writes, "How do we go about being 'religionless-worldly' Christians, how can we be ἐκ-κλησία, those who are called out, without understanding ourselves religiously as privileged, but instead seeing ourselves as belonging wholly to the world? Christ would no longer then be the object of religion, but something else entirely, truly lord of the world. But what does that mean? In a religionless situation, what do ritual [*Kultus*] and prayer mean?"[139] In another letter he acknowledges Bethge's "question of whether the church has any 'ground' left to stand on, or whether it is losing it altogether."[140] In yet another letter Bonhoeffer asks, "What does a church, a congregation, a sermon, a liturgy, a Christian life mean in a religionless world?"[141] His premature death cut short any exhaustive treatment of what the church might actually look like given his radical embrace of secularity in the letters. A church with traditional markings and boundaries seems unnecessary given a worldview where Christ is declared Lord over the entire world, where standard formulations of God and religion are superfluous, and where action taken for another in the secular realm is just as much a mark of being part of Christ's community as action taken within any defined church boundaries.

Church-World Relationship and Political Thinking

Bonhoeffer did not make political matters or political involvement the explicit focus of his prison letters. The revolutionary aspect of his thinking is his radical disavowal of two-sphered thinking (more radical than that same disavowal in *Ethics*) and the attendant complete embrace of worldliness. "Religionless Christianity" means a Christian existence in the world unfettered by a religion which drives believers into either of the two spheres. Religion is not the problem. The problem is believers

---

139. Ibid., 364.
140. Ibid., 431.
141. Ibid., 364.

Phase 4: Church as World 319

for whom that word is either an excuse to immerse themselves uncritically into the secular sphere or to retreat from the secular sphere into some otherworldly sphere. Furthermore, the "world come of age" is not a world that has advanced to a place where Christ has become irrelevant. Christ is the one who restores the two spheres in middle of reality, the one who shows us that we are to be "for others." If the "world come of age" is a world that no longer needs a misunderstood conception of religion, it needs Christ all the more in order to center it as His reality.

Indeed, Bonhoeffer suggests that church members, and even the clergy, might engage in secular callings. Action in the world in a variety of contexts, including military involvement, would be consistent with this position. His disavowal of religion as metaphysics and inwardness and its implications for holding to a two-sphered reality has effectively cut off the possibility of any escapism. His equating being a Christian with being responsible for the other, echoing his notion of deputyship from *Ethics*, also makes the believer responsible for acting on behalf of anyone who is in need. It is not surprising, then, that in a November 18, 1943, letter to Bethge, Bonhoeffer writes of military conscription, "Might it be arranged, in the case of my not being sentenced but released and drafted, for me to come to your region? That would indeed be marvelous."[142] Bonhoeffer does not appear to have any problems with being called up to the military. Rasmussen, in fact, points out that the Bonhoeffer who took a stance for conscientious objection earlier in his career was now "willing to join Hitler's troops."[143]

FORMS OF POLITICAL INVOLVEMENT

Bonhoeffer's thinking on the church-world relationship and his activity are intimately connected in this period of his life. *Ethics*, as has been noted, has even been read by some as a program of political resistance.[144] Bonhoeffer wrote *Ethics* in several different locations. His movements

---

142. Ibid.,183. Rasmussen, in his translation of this passage, renders "region" as "regiment."

143 Ibid., 114. Rasmussen notes, "Yet it is worth pointing out that the man who seriously considered taking a stand for conscientious objection in 1939 now was willing to join Hitler's troops."

144. See, for example, *ATS*, 301–27. See also, Green, "Bonhoeffer's Christian Ethics in Resistance to Tyranny and Genocide." See also, *RR*. Rasmussen's thesis is that "Dietrich Bonhoeffer's resistance activity was his Christology enacted with utter seriousness" (15). This claim encompasses the Christological themes in the *Ethics*.

and activities are somewhat difficult to place in an entirely accurate time line due to his frequent travels, secretive activities, and guarded letters. What follows is a basic outline of Bonhoeffer's forms of political action. The political resistance to Hitler had been growing since 1937. Bonhoeffer made his initial contact with the resistance during the collective pastorates in February 1938.[145] He traveled to New York in June 1939. He was conflicted about going to America in the first place. Once in America, Bonhoeffer was haunted by the question of whether he should stay. Bonhoeffer's New York connections, including Henry Leiper, the Executive Secretary of the Federal Council of Churches, presented him with four options for activity in America, most of which stipulated that there could be no returns to Germany. Longing for information about Germany and homesick, Bonhoeffer had to inform a disappointed Leiper that he would be returning to Germany. Bonhoeffer's dramatic June 20, 1939 decision, made alone perhaps in the middle of Times Square or in the guest room at Union Theological Seminary, would seal his fate.[146] Consistent with the thinking in *Ethics* which he would write shortly, Bonhoeffer realized he must engage in the worldly in service or in solidarity with his neighbor in need. Bonhoeffer could no longer justify any type of escape or withdrawal. He was back in Berlin on July 27, 1939.[147]

The Collective Pastorates in Pomerania were not shut down by the Gestapo until March 1940.[148] Bonhoeffer was still involved there from August 1939 until the end. He enjoyed the community life but was always interested in what was happening in Berlin. He was no longer intimately involved in the church struggle or in the ecumenical sphere where frantic attempts were being made to work for peace.[149] Bonhoeffer could no longer work in the ecumenical sphere if Hitler was to be recognized as a legitimate leader. He "had already taken his stand on the one

---

145. *TF*, 533.

146. *DB*, 650–55. Bethge writes, "When the summer school at Union Seminary began, Professor John McNeill, the specialist on Calvin, occupied the 'prophets' chamber. He was surprised by the amount of illegible sheets of paper left by his unknown predecessor, and at the quantities of cigarettes he had smoked. McNeill thought he must be either a very hard worker or very disorderly. Only later did he realize who had lived there before him and had made the most difficult of all decisions in that room" (655).

147. Ibid., 662.

148. *TF*, 534.

149. *DB*, 668.

Phase 4: Church as World

condition of peace that could not be discussed in any church body inside Germany—the removal of Hitler."[150] During the first winter of the war Hitler's aggressive plans for Holland and Belgium and stories about S.S. behavior in Poland provided hope for a coup.[151] The conspirators' activity came in two phases and Bonhoeffer was involved in a small capacity (he was present during planning sessions). The first phase included Dohnanyi distributing the "chronicle of shame" to sympathetic generals.[152] Oster and Dohnanyi also contacted the pope through Munich lawyer Dr. Josef Müller. The pope informed the Allied countries that the German resistance was serious.[153] The second phase saw Canaris assign Müller to the German Military Intelligence so that his negotiations with Rome could not be detected by the Gestapo.[154] Hitler's military and diplomatic successes (the fall of France, for example) began to convince the resistance that takeover within the context of the military leadership would not work.[155]

Bonhoeffer's activities as a churchperson lessened significantly. Moreover, any involvement in that realm took on an overtly political character.[156] Bonhoeffer, for instance, used his political connections to help Confessing Church members avoid military conscription.[157] Bonhoeffer himself accepted Oster and Dohnanyi's political help in avoiding active military duty. They had him declared "officially indispensable" so he could, though drafted, remain in his civilian occupation.[158] Bonhoeffer was by this time well connected with the Military Intelligence Office and

---

150. Ibid., 670.

151. Ibid., 671.

152. Ibid., 672. The "chronicle of shame" consisted of security reports and S.S. films of Nazi atrocities in Poland.

153. Ibid., 672-73.

154. Ibid., 673-75. Great Britain was prepared to agree to an armistice before Hitler's next planned attack and when Hitler was actually removed from power. Müller was given the code name "X" and his negotiations were entitled the "X-report." Bonhoeffer was at the meeting where the conspirators turned the "X-report" into a memorandum to give to certain generals before Hitler's military offensive. Brauchitsch, an important military person, was not convinced by the report and considered it treasonous. The attempted coup failed.

155. Ibid., 682.

156. Ibid., 690.

157. Ibid., 690-91.

158. Ibid., 700-701.

members of the political resistance. He continued in limited church duties between February and August 1940, traveling to East Prussia three times where he preached in place of pastors who had been sent off to the war. Bonhoeffer ran into trouble during his second journey where Confessing Church students printed up flyers announcing his visit. The Gestapo showed up and ordered the meeting to disband. Bonhoeffer contacted Canaris, Oster, and Dohnanyi and they assured him that the Military Intelligence Office could ensure him unhindered travel in the East (on the grounds his travels were information-gathering missions).[159] Bonhoeffer could not, however, avoid controversy. He was called back to his official residence in Schlawe where he was told that his right to preach or make public statements had been revoked due to "subversive activity." Bonhoeffer was also required to report any movements to the police. He immediately lodged a complaint with the Reich Central Security Office.[160]

Bonhoeffer and his colleagues were not sure about his future activity. Oster and Dohnanyi came up with the idea of having Bonhoeffer actually work for the Nazis as a civilian member of the Munich Military Intelligence Office or *Abwehr*.[161] The *Abwehr*, loosely translated as counter-intelligence, was a group of senior military personnel with civilian advisors in many areas. The organization was headed by Admiral Canaris and his deputy Oster and was charged mainly with espionage or gathering information and getting it to the proper authorities. Agents in the *Abwehr* were in many ways above the Gestapo and S. S. These agents, if suspected of any wrongdoing, could be released back into the hands of Canaris and Oster by request.[162] Bonhoeffer, after some deliberation, decided to join the *Abwehr* in January 1941. This event marks his official entry into the conspiracy. His aunt, Countess Kalckreuth, who lived in Munich, allowed him to register as living in her house in order to meet the residency requirement. On January 31 Bonhoeffer was informed by the secret state police that he no longer had to report his travels to the authorities. He actually took up residence in a monastery in Ettal, where he worked on *Ethics*.[163]

159. Ibid., 696–98.
160. Ibid., 699.
161. Ibid., 700.
162. Robertson, *The Shame and the Sacrifice*, 197.
163. *DB*, 701–2.

Phase 4: Church as World 323

The next phase of the German resistance movement, from late 1940 until Bonhoeffer's arrest in April 1943, included his actual complicity in plots against Hitler. Bonhoeffer's first act was to travel to Switzerland in order to restore communications with the churches, provide signs of new resistance activity, and to explore ideas about peace aims.[164] He left for Switzerland in February 1941 with the goal of reestablishing contact with Geneva and his past contacts with the ecumenical movement. His talk of a viable resistance in Germany was looked upon with great suspicion by most, except for Willem Visser t' Hooft. Visser t' Hooft passed on Bonhoeffer's assessment of the German situation to Bishop Bell and other ecumenical leaders.[165] Bonhoeffer returned to Germany on March 24, 1941, to find that his right to publish had been revoked in connection with the previous revocation of preaching rights. He and his fellow conspirators had nevertheless become optimistic again about overthrowing Hitler due to his radical "commissar order" given in preparation for the attack on Russia. The order stated that Russian military and civilian commissars were to be killed immediately without trial. This order demanded behavior that was clearly illegal. Furthermore, the regular army was expected to follow a procedure once handled only by the S. S. The bizarre order raised hopes that the military command would stop Hitler. Oster and Dohnanyi drafted a memorandum emphasizing the outlandishness of the order and Rudolf Hess, Hitler's representative, even traveled to England in hopes of negotiating a peace treaty before the Russian offensive began. Hitler's military success once again quieted the potential opposition. The conspirators, however, remained optimistic.[166]

Bonhoeffer made his second trip to Switzerland in September 1941. Bonhoeffer's primary objective was to enter the discussion about possibilities for peace with Western Christian groups in the wake of Hitler's demise (which Bonhoeffer thought was coming soon). There was hope that the British government would acknowledge the resistance groups or even a post-Hitler alternative government in Germany as somehow distinct from Hitler's regime. Bonhoeffer was spurred on in this vision by Bishop Bell's book, *Christianity and World Order*. Bell argued that Germany and National Socialism are not the same thing. Churchill,

---

164. *DB*, 727.
165. Ibid., 730.
166. Ibid., 733.

however, demanded that a post-Hitler government would have to "surrender unconditionally" like the current one.[167]

Churches in Great Britain held public demonstrations and the *Times* newspaper printed statements calling for reasonable and just post-Hitler peace aims, including revisions of the Treaty of Versailles and respect for the needs of national minorities. Bishop Bell also spoke publicly on the need for a "just and honorable peace."[168] William Paton's controversial book, *The Church and the New Order*, which extended the discussion of post-Hitler peace aims, became the occasion of Bonhoeffer's next significant political activity. He issued a memorandum treating the topics in Paton's book. The memo was prepared in English by Visser t' Hooft and circulated to the Christian intelligentsia in London. Bonhoeffer was essentially trying to lay the foundations for the upcoming coup attempt by arguing against any demand for unilateral disarming of Germany. He saw that demand as a psychological blow to the conspirators who wanted the Allies to take their post-Hitler provisional government seriously. He even wanted the Allies to suspend military operations during the revolt and warned that the new government would not be liberal in the western sense.[169] Visser t'Hooft sent the Bonhoeffer memorandum to Archdeacon Hugh Martin in hopes that it would find its way into the hands of British government officials. He even requested a specific answer to the statement. Bonhoeffer actually decided to stay until late September for a response that never came.[170] Unfortunately for Bonhoeffer and his colleagues, leaders in London did not understand the aim of the letter. They, moreover, probably did not invest much authority in the names Bonhoeffer and Visser t' Hooft. In the end, the influential people could not be convinced there was a viable German opposition. Bonhoeffer's expectation that his political voice might be heard was unreasonable, especially since he presented little evidence that there actually was significant opposition in Germany.[171]

Bonhoeffer returned to Germany in October 1941 and was faced with the reality of yellow stars and the deportation of Jews. Bonhoeffer reacted immediately. He collected all of the facts he could about the

167. Ibid., 736–37.
168. Ibid., 739.
169. Ibid., 740.
170. Ibid., 741.
171. Ibid., 741–43.

Phase 4: Church as World 325

deportations and passed his report onto Dohnanyi, Beck, and Oster in hopes that the military would intervene or hasten its plans for an outright revolt against Hitler.[172] Bonhoeffer also got involved in a brave action initiated by the *Abwehr*. Canaris gave orders to save a group of Jews in a campaign called "Operation 7." The project, wherein Canaris made the group of Jews into *Abwehr* members to be sent to Switzerland, lasted over a year in length and involved Dohnanyi extensively. Bonhoeffer handled the initial consultation with Wilhelm Rott who asked if there might be any way to save Charlotte Friedenthal, a colleague of his in the Confessing Church forced to wear the yellow star. The operation was successful.[173]

Bonhoeffer's next form of involvement followed upon the bad news of Field Marshal Walter von Brauchitsch's resignation. Brauchitsch, one of Hitler's commanders, had become willing to cooperate with the resistance. With the addition of Brauchitsch, things looked good for a coup to be initiated in the high command. In mid-December, however, Hitler dismissed Brauchitsch and declared himself the commander in chief of the army. The conspirators were devastated as the army high command could no longer be the locus of a coup. The conspirators changed the sequence of events. Now Hitler must be assassinated first. Bonhoeffer accepted this course of action as necessary and went on an important mission to Sweden in late May 1942.[174] He was to give details, including names, about upcoming coup attempts and to try to assure the British government that the post-Hitler government would be peaceful. Finally, he was to express his wish that the British would not attack Germany in the unsettled period after the assassination. Bonhoeffer's main vehicle for passing on information on the coup and requests for British governmental acknowledgment of the resistance was Bishop Bell.[175] Bonhoeffer met with Bell in June 1942 and gave him a list of names of the conspirators and more detailed plans of action. They also set up secret codes and possible locations for future meetings. Bell, like he had

---

172. Ibid., 745–46. Bethge writes, "H. G. Adler later described these papers [Bonhoeffer's reports] as the first documentary evidence known to him of any action by the German conspiracy movement in connection with the deportation policy" (746).

173. Ibid., 747–49. The directive was titled "Operation 7" because there were seven Jews involved.

174. Ibid., 750–51.

175. Ibid., 757–60.

in earlier years, strived to "gain a hearing for the unexpected concerns of the German conspirators" and to promote a post-Hitler world order where the Germans would not be subject to Versailles-like stipulations.[176] Bell worked hard to make Bonhoeffer's message heard. He met with English Foreign Secretary Anthony Eden on June 18, cabinet member Sir Stafford Cripps on July 13 and even American ambassador John Gilbert Winant on July 30. There was some interest but overall these meetings could not convince the Allies that there was a legitimate resistance. Bell did not relent. He continued to push Bonhoeffer's position. Bell even addressed Parliament on March 10, 1943, and got the impression that the House looked favorably upon his position.[177]

Bonhoeffer, meanwhile, had undertaken a journey to Italy in June 1942 where he and Dohnanyi hoped to hear some reply from London. Bonhoeffer did not hear from Bell by July 10; Dohnanyi, however, received the negative telegram that Bell sent to Visser t' Hooft. Bell's last letter from Bonhoeffer (August 28) indicated that Bonhoeffer had not yet heard the news from London and, in general, the resistance was beginning to panic because Hitler's recent military successes in Russia and Africa meant a coup would be harder to undertake. The resistance nevertheless continued work and continued to grow and diversify.[178] Bonhoeffer worked on a document outlining church-state relations in the post-Hitler Germany. The written draft, "Ending the Church Struggle," gave the Confessing Church sole church leadership and included a speech to be proclaimed from the pulpits. The speech described the need for the churches strongly to confess their guilt.[179] Bonhoeffer also worked on the "Freiburg Memorandum," a document produced by a group of economists, legal scholars, and philosophers that laid out an extensive vision of the future legal, educational, and church system as well as foreign policy.[180]

The final development led to Bonhoeffer's eventual arrest. In October 1942, Dohnanyi was informed by a friend and fellow conspirator at the Reich Central Security Office that he and Bonhoeffer had been

---

176. Ibid., 763.
177. Ibid., 763–68.
178. Ibid., 771.
179. Ibid., 772.
180. Ibid., 775–76. Scholarship suggests that parts of *Ethics* were written while working on the memo.

Phase 4: Church as World

named in legal proceedings against Munich Consul Schmidhuber. The Reich Central Security Office tried to use a currency irregularity in the *Abwehr* in an attempt to destroy it. Specifically, a customs officer in Prague detected a currency irregularity by a man working for Schmidhuber. Schmidhuber was interrogated and his answers regarding "Operation 7," and the currency transactions on behalf of the Jews in the operation, implicated Bonhoeffer and Dohnanyi. Dohnanyi's phones were tapped and Bonhoeffer's travels and military exemption were scrutinized. Canaris, Oster, and others tried to deflect the scrutiny and cover for Bonhoeffer. They argued for the necessity of Bonhoeffer's international travel and for him as an indispensable civilian. Oster even overrode a request for Bonhoeffer to report for military duty. The clamps were tightening. It became a race between assassination and arrest.[181]

Bonhoeffer's travels were over by early 1943. Hitler's continued military successes made an attempt on his life more urgent than ever. The conspirators managed to load a special English explosive, delivered by Dohnanyi, onto Hitler's flight to East Prussia in early March. The explosive did not ignite. A few weeks later on March 21 Hitler was to tour an arsenal during the "Heroes' Remembrance Day" celebration. Major von Gersdorff, an officer in the Military Intelligence Office, planned to put explosives in his coat to kill Hitler (and himself). The explosion never happened.[182] Meanwhile, the Gestapo was closing in on Bonhoeffer and Dohnanyi. Two weeks later, on April 5, Bonhoeffer, Hans von Dohnanyi, Christine Dohnanyi (Hans' wife), and Josef Müller were arrested.[183] Bonhoeffer spent the rest of his life in the custody of the Nazis.

Bonhoeffer's church-world relationship and political activity are clearly linked during the writing of *Ethics*. Bonhoeffer had effectively, with his forceful correction of two-sphered thinking, challenged the distinction between acting in the world as a secular person and acting in the world as a churchperson or Christian. His embrace of a unified reality allowed him to support traditional moral norms in everyday living or situations and ultimately go past traditional moral norms in extreme situations.

Though designating himself as a representative of the Confessing Church in his dealings with the ecumenical community, Bonhoeffer

181. Ibid., 780–84.
182. Ibid., 779.
183. Ibid., 780.

was not really acting as a representative of the church. He was using his ecumenical contacts as a way to get messages to the British government about the existence of a legitimate political resistance movement. His mention of peace aims, moreover, should not be read as any manifestation of pacifism. Bonhoeffer was motivated strictly by practical politics and political expediency—he wanted to make sure the Allied powers considered the potential post-Hitler (provisional) government one which was not aggressive. Accordingly, there is absolutely no mention of pacifism in *Ethics* as a possible response to the problem of war. Bonhoeffer's actions were almost entirely geared toward the practical and the political. He could no longer withstand the churches' silence and even active complicity in Hitler's policies against the Jews; so he immediately jumped into action with "Operation 7." In addition, while most of the churches remained silent and passive in the face of Hitler's unreasonable aggression in war and the terror of his totalitarian state, Bonhoeffer decided that assassination was a legitimate course of action and made international trips in support of the conspiracy. This anti-state action was for him an expression of solidarity with his fellow Germans inside and outside of the churches. It was a course of action for the benefit of those in the realm of the church and those in the realm of the world.

As noted above, even with the radical breakdown between the church and the world (and the accompanying political action in the world), Bonhoeffer still held to at least a formal distinction between them in some places in *Ethics*. There is, accordingly, some evidence that he still thought in terms of action as a church member and action as a secular person. Bethge, noting Bonhoeffer's September 1941 remark, describes his thinking on the possibility of violent action, "if it ever fell to him to carry out the deed, he was prepared to do so, but [for] that he must first resign, formally and officially from his church." Bethge continues, "The church could not shield him and he had no wish to claim its protection. It was a theoretical statement of course, since Bonhoeffer knew nothing of guns or explosives."[184] It is clear, however, that Bonhoeffer accepted direct political action against the state as acceptable for a Christian. In his next set of writings it becomes questionable if the church can retain any distinction from the world whatsoever.

---

184. Ibid., 751–52.

Phase 4: Church as World

Bonhoeffer's explicitly political activity did not end with his imprisonment. The arrests of Bonhoeffer and others did not stop the resistance movement. Bonhoeffer was obviously unable to travel on behalf of the resistance. He was held in Tegel prison from April 5, 1943 to the end of September 1944, where he was interrogated by War Court Officer Roeder concerning his resistance activities.[185] Bonhoeffer had no experience in being interrogated. He was helped tremendously by the agreement amongst the conspirators to push the responsibility for the *Abwehr*'s workings onto Canaris, Oster, and Dohnanyi. Bonhoeffer was thus able to answer questions without incriminating contradictions. He also became somewhat of a star prisoner because of his connection to the city command in Berlin. He received gifts, books, and visits from family and friends. His communications with them through an elaborate coding system, transmitted via the books, allowed him to get information about resistance activities and about the status of the Nazi investigation of the *Abwehr*.[186] This information helped him to protect fellow conspirators in the interrogations. Bonhoeffer also made several notes and wrote post-interview letters to Roeder clarifying things said during interrogations. These writings reveal the extent to which Bonhoeffer concealed the truth in order to protect the conspiracy.[187]

Roeder's interrogations focused on Bonhoeffer's military exemption, his work in "Operation 7," his journeys, and the exemption from military service for Confessing Church members. With the help of information about the Dohnanyi investigations, Canaris's successful cover-ups and clever argumentation, Bonhoeffer was able to avoid the initial charge of high treason and treason against his country and the specific charges concerning his journeys and "Operation 7." Roeder's interrogation of Bonhoeffer ended in late July with notice that he would be charged only with participating in an antimilitary act, his own military exemption, and helping a Confessing Church member get a military exemption.[188] Bonhoeffer's hopes of being released from prison were dashed, though, with the failed coup attempt of July 20, 1944. It was the turning point in the resistance and in the fates of Bonhoeffer and his fellow conspirators. Colonel Count Claus von Stauffenberg had become

---

185. Ibid., 799.
186. Ibid., 812.
187. Ibid., 813–14.
188. Ibid., 822.

hostile to Hitler in response to the Nazi horrors. The Gestapo began to close in on the *Abwehr* so the conspirators would have to act soon. Stauffenberg, promoted at the beginning of July 1944 and thus able to attend Hitler's military conferences, was able to smuggle a bomb in a suitcase into Hitler's East Prussian headquarters on July 20. Stauffenberg left the bomb next to Hitler and excused himself from the meeting to make a phone call. Believing the blast was effective, Stauffenberg traveled to Berlin and set the takeover in motion (the conspirators actually took over general command in several places and arrested Nazi officers). Hitler, however, was shielded by a large oak table and only lost hearing and received burns. Hitler's headquarters, through the Ministry of Propaganda, was able to broadcast a warning against obeying the conspirators. Hitler's retribution was enormous. More than 5,000 persons were executed in retaliation.[189]

Bonhoeffer was certain that his life would now be ended. Canaris was arrested on July 23. The Gestapo, moreover, found incriminating evidence known as the "Zossen Files" on September 22. Bonhoeffer was transported from Tegel to the underground prison of the Reich Central Security Office on Prinz-Albrecht-Strasse on October 8.[190] He was interrogated repeatedly in light of the "Zossen Files" which included notes for two different plans for a coup, a record of discussions with the British government by way of the Vatican, diary excerpts from Canaris treating the resistance movement and front-line visits for the purpose of the winning over generals and, finally, correspondence concerning Bonhoeffer's resistance activities.[191]

Bonhoeffer's case was prosecuted separately by Walter Huppenkothen, a Gestapo lawyer from the Rhineland. Confidential reports of the interrogations (conducted between October 1944 and January 1945) were sent to Hitler, Himmler, and others. There are no existing copies of the reports. There is, in fact, only one existing official document concerning the investigation.[192] The only published document dealing with the interrogations indicates that Bonhoeffer was able to explain away his trips and meetings with Bishop Bell by reiterating his responses from the initial interrogations. In short, Bonhoeffer was able to hide the real rea-

---

189. See *HNG*, 262–4, for a description of the assassination attempt.
190. *DB*, 828.
191. Ibid., 897.
192. Ibid., 900.

Phase 4: Church as World

sons for the journeys to Sweden until the very end. However, Dohnanyi indicated in a March 8, 1945, letter that the Gestapo knew absolutely everything. In other words, at least one member of the conspiracy betrayed the others.[193] In any case, it is clear that Bonhoeffer "had not yet given up trying to save the situation . . . when he was able to deny facts he gave them a slanted meaning or introduced other facts that obscured or complicated the issue."[194]

Bonhoeffer was moved to Buchenwald in early February due to Allied bomb raids. There is some confusion over the reason the twenty prisoners were split up into two groups. Bethge speculates that some of the prisoners may have been considered useful for prisoner exchanges with the Allies. In any case, Bonhoeffer was handcuffed, taken to Buchenwald, and cut off entirely from his family.[195] Bonhoeffer was moved again from Buchenwald to Flossenbürg on April 3 (there were stops in Regensburg and Schöberg). Hitler ordered Bonhoeffer's death on April 5. Bonhoeffer was hanged on April 9 in the morning. His last words were, "This is the end—for me the beginning of life."[196] Hitler committed suicide twenty-one days later.[197]

It is true that Bonhoeffer's political activity during his writing of the letters was somewhat limited given that he was in the custody of the Nazis. It would, however, be incorrect to argue that he was entirely politically inactive. Bonhoeffer remained, in both series of interrogations (Tegel and Prinz-Albrecht-Strasse), unwilling to abandon his fellow conspirators. He continued to either conceal, mislead, or tell half-truths in order to protect the continuing conspiracy. Even after knowledge of the failed plot, where hopes of further successful conspiratorial activity were radically diminished, Bonhoeffer continued to protect his fellow conspirators. Bonhoeffer's actions along these lines, as well as being a continued manifestation of acting in a secular capacity in the world, were consistent with his Christological theme of being for others. A better example of an active manifestation of his thinking where Christ is the "man for others" was Bonhoeffer's remarkable ability to soothe

---

193. Ibid., 905–6. See ibid., 900–907, for a list of the sources of information about the interrogations.
194. *DB*, 907.
195. *DB*, 916.
196. *DB*, 927.
197. *HNG*, 229.

the pains and fears of his fellow inmates. Many of them clung to him during Allied air raids because "being close to Bonhoeffer gave them a welcome feeling of safety."[198] Bonhoeffer's calm and cool demeanor during crises made him a popular inmate with prisoners and guards. His warmth and congeniality earned him the respect and friendship of both prison guards and prisoners. Some prison guards allowed him special privileges, smuggled his letters and writings out of the prison and asked him for advice and counsel. One guard even left a bouquet of birthday flowers in his cell.[199] The prisoners, for their part, always wanted to be around Bonhoeffer and, notably, requested for him to conduct services the morning of their deaths.[200]

There are a few seeming inconsistencies in Bonhoeffer during this period of his writing. Bonhoeffer indicated in 1943 that he would be willing to serve in the military if he were "called up." It seems strange that a person who so valiantly fought against Hitler would be willing to serve in his army. Bonhoeffer did, though, argue both for the explicit possibility of military service as an acceptable behavior and for the implicit possibility of resistance in extreme situations in *Ethics*. In addition, his letter to Bethge about his willingness to serve in the military may have been made in expectation that the war would soon be over.[201] The analysis of *Ethics* also showed that he thought of war and resistance or even tyrannicide similarly, ethics *in extremis*. A brief letter to a friend, furthermore, is not a detailed excursus on the legitimacy of military service. Finally, and most importantly, both military service and antistate political behavior are consistent with a church-world vision that does not allow withdrawal from secular duty. That being said, the above-noted mention of conscientious objection does look like a withdrawal. It is only consistent with the church-world vision if the decision for conscientious objection is an explicitly political one, one that stands as an outward protest against war and not as an apolitical withdrawal from the world. It is difficult to determine the nature of the statement as the evidence is somewhat scarce and undeveloped.

198. Ibid., 847.
199. Ibid., 848.
200. Ibid., 926–27.
201. *RR*, 114.

Phase 4: Church as World 333

THE NATURE OF THE CHANGE

Bonhoeffer either pitted the church against the world in phase 3 or implied a necessary withdrawal. Being part of the church placed one into a sphere where any engagement with the worldly could not presuppose any shared reality between church and world. The motivation in instances where there was engagement in the political realm was purely to show how alien the churchly sphere was in relation to the worldly sphere. It was not an indication of the legitimacy of the world's structures. The motivation for pacifism, an instance where there would be conflict with secular authority, was strict adherence to the Sermon on the Mount and the clinging to the exclusive Christ-community to the point of withdrawal. Bonhoeffer's phase-3 pacifism was not a political one designed for either protest or for the purpose of societal change. Suffering and rejection by the world accompanied this passive activity or inactivity. True Christians willingly accept suffering and rejection in knowledge that the churchly sphere is already redeemed. The Christ-community was to abide strictly and faithfully to the directives of the Sermon on the Mount, waiting patiently and meekly until God ushers in God's kingdom.

Indeed, Bonhoeffer is clear that this church, while only accidentally political, does not disappear into total withdrawal. The church, rather, is a visible entity comprising those attached in total obedience to Christ and thereby marked off from the outside world. Bonhoeffer's phase-3 essay on the boundaries of church union, for example, with its claim that those not part of the Confessing Church have cut themselves off from salvation, makes perhaps the most extreme argument for the church as a visible and exclusive organization cordoned off from the larger world. Bonhoeffer also argues in several places in *Discipleship* that the Christ-community calls its disciples to separate from the larger community. Bonhoeffer's actual behavior in the world was, finally, consistent with his church-world thinking during this phase. He separated himself from the active Confessing Church in Germany with stays in London and in the illegal seminaries. Bonhoeffer did not respond to any of the political happenings around him. He was concerned mostly with the purity of the church and the nature of its confession. His commitment to the exclusivity and purity of the church alienated him from the Confessing church and forced him to withdraw from involvement in the ecumenical realm.

The move into phase 4 marks a dramatic change to a church-world vision wherein the difference between the two realms is initially softened (in *Ethics*) and arguably nullified (in *Letters and Papers from Prison*). Bonhoeffer argues explicitly in *Ethics* against two-sphered thinking. He writes, for instance, that "There are not two realities, but only one reality, and that is God's reality revealed in Christ in the reality of the world. Partaking in Christ, we stand at the same time in the reality of God and in the reality of the world."[202] Bonhoeffer's phase-3 adherence to Christ, on the other hand, was the occasion for separation from the world. The church member, while mostly passively obedient to government directives, was essentially indifferent to the structures of the world while waiting for the coming Kingdom. Phase 4 indicates an entirely different dynamic. The government is a mandate, one of the ways in which the reality of Christ actually structures the world. Partaking in the state is participating in Christ in the world.

There is no place to withdraw from normal governmental duties in phase 4. War, and even conspiratorial activity in extreme cases, can be responsible duty in accordance with the structure of reality in Christ. There is no mention of pacifism in *Ethics* or the *Letters and Papers from Prison*. In addition, Bonhoeffer's mention of the Sermon on the Mount in *Ethics* eases its sharp demands by removing its literal interpretation.[203] Bonhoeffer's whole framework in *Ethics* whereby action in the world is responsible if in accordance to reality does not lend itself to designating any particular text or any particular principles at all (except, of course, for the general principle of acting in accord with reality) as normative for ethical action. In short, while Bonhoeffer was close to absolute pacifism in phase 3, his phase-4 understanding of the world as the only legitimate sphere of operations for the church, and the state as a legitimate manifestation of Christ's reality in the world, does not allow him any form of pacifism.

Bonhoeffer is concerned in his phase-3 writings with the church and the church only. He was only involved with church people and church activities. In phase 4, his primary contact was with persons in secular roles (military personnel, the other conspirators, his fiancée, his family, and other prisoners). His resistance activity introduced him to a variety of people who acted in the world in a secular capacity. Bonhoeffer's in-

202. DBWE-6, 58.
203. Ibid., 359–60.

Phase 4: Church as World

volvement with them allowed him to exercise "the freedom to encounter men of every background, rank and conviction . . . cheerfully, imaginatively, and without doctrinaire exclusiveness."[204] His involvement with them and the other "unchurched masses" in prison surely helped move his thought along toward worldliness.[205] His phase-4 activity in the ecumenical realm and the Confessing Church was marginal at best. Much of his contact with the church, at least with the ecumenical movement, was politically motivated. He was, in fact, concerned that his contact with the ecumenical community in the capacity of conspirator would endanger their safety.[206]

Bonhoeffer was, indeed, radically involved in the world in phase 4. He entered the *Abwehr*, established contacts with fellow conspirators, traveled in hopes of informing the Allies that a legitimate resistance existed, and even helped to try to get the Allied governments to agree to a cease fire during the set-up of a new post-Hitler government. Bonhoeffer also participated in the drafting of a constitution for a post-Hitler Germany, including plans for governmental structure. Finally, while not actually expected to assassinate Hitler, Bonhoeffer was present during planning sessions and certainly authorized and supported the use of deadly force against the dictator. Ultimately, Bonhoeffer's phase-4 worldly political involvement has absolutely nothing in common with his phase-3 involvement. His move was truly a move from the self-enclosed and self-concerned church against the world to a radical embrace of the worldly. Bonhoeffer conceived of, and acted upon, obedience to the Lord in phase 3 as if the call to obedience was made available only in the church and had relevance only for the churchly sphere. In phase 4, since all reality has a "Christocratic" structure, obedience to the Lord can happen in responsible action anywhere, anyplace, and at anytime for

---

204. Phillips, *Christ for Us*, 131.

205. Godsey, *The Theology of Dietrich Bonhoeffer*, 263. Godsey writes, "One could point to many factors in Bonhoeffer's life during his last years that must have made deep impressions upon his mind and directed his thoughts toward 'worldliness.' One factor is his involvement in the resistance movement, where he came into contact with completely 'secular' men who were willing to suffer and even die for their fellow men. Another is his disappointment with the Confessing Church, which in later years worried too much about its own existence and thus neglected its responsibilities in and for the world. A third factor is the raw reality of prison life, where he was daily in contact with men who belonged to the 'unchurched masses' but for whom Christ died."

206. *DB*, 702.

any human being, church member or not. The location of obedience to the Lord was the church in phase 3. In phase 4 the location for obedience to the Lord is the world.

Another consideration in analyzing the nature of the change from phase 3 to phase 4 is Bonhoeffer's relationship with the Two Kingdoms doctrine. Bonhoeffer's phase-3 thought was outside of the proper framework of the doctrine. It posited no common reality, space, or overlapping area of concern between the church and the world. There was thus no justification for anything other than accidental involvement in the world. Phase 4, on the other hand, where Bonhoeffer places the Christian fully in the world as he does and thereby makes the Christian available for full engagement in the political, would seem to fit perfectly into the Two Kingdoms format. As noted above, there are parts of *Ethics* wherein Bonhoeffer supports behavior that would be acceptable in both more conservative and more liberal interpretations of the Two Kingdoms doctrine.

Bonhoeffer's later phase-4 thinking, however, makes possible behavior (tyrannicide), which falls outside Two Kingdoms thinking. The overlap between the world and the church is responsible for the similarities between his phase 4 and his phase-1 and -2 adherence to the doctrine. In both of these earlier phases some form of political involvement (either pro-state or criticism of the state) is acceptable. Yet, the later, phase-4 thinking goes beyond phases one and two by releasing the tension between the church and the world. The mark of this release is the possibility of direct political action against the state (where the form of action in the world is not affected by the fact that one is a Christian or a church member) in both thinking and action. This is an option not typically associated with most interpretations of the Two Kingdoms doctrine.

Almost all Bonhoeffer scholars recognize a change occurring in 1939. According to his three-part scheme, Bethge writes,

> The first change, around 1931–32, was when Bonhoeffer the theologian consciously grasped the fact that he was a Christian. At the beginning of 1939 Bonhoeffer the theologian and Christian was entering fully into his contemporary world, his place, and his time—into a world his bourgeois class had helped to bring about rather than prevent. He accepted the burden of that collective responsibility, and began to identify himself with those who

Phase 4: Church as World 337

were prepared to acknowledge their guilt and to begin shaping something new for the future—instead of merely protesting on ideological grounds, as the church had done up to that point. In 1939 the theologian and Christian became a man for his times ... In 1932 he found his calling, in 1939 his destiny ... In 1932 Bonhoeffer moved into the community of Christians which was confined to the group within the church that protested publicly with him. Nineteen thirty-three led him into an even more restricted circle of kindred spirits ... The year 1932 had opened up the ecumenical movement to Bonhoeffer ... In 1939, when he could have saved himself within that ecumenical movement, he shut himself out of it ... The possibility of "life together" ended forever in the spring of 1940 and, eventually, the theology of discipleship needed revision. Its context had been shattered. Ecclesiology as a priority receded. The earthly, bourgeois, and national future demanded responsibility.[207]

John Phillips, for his part, describes the same change.

> [Nineteen-thirty-seven] saw the premature end of the *Bruderhaus* experiment following a Gestapo ban; 1942 found Bonhoeffer in the midst of the "worldly sector." During the intervening years, his theological outlook appears to have done a complete about-face. This movement is perceptible in his writings and can be followed in the pages of the *Ethics*, the writing of which began in 1940 and continued until after Bonhoeffer's arrest in 1943. Here one finds at least four approaches to the problem of Christian ethics, each moving farther away from the exclusiveness which characterized Bonhoeffer's church struggle theology and further in the direction of the open worldliness of the prison letters.[208]

There is evidence of his own recognition of a decision for an alteration in addition to scholarly assessment of Bonhoeffer's change. There is, for instance, the now famous Bonhoeffer letter to Niebuhr written while in America describing the justification for returning to Germany in 1939. Bonhoeffer had already made contact with the conspiracy at the end of phase 3 and knew of its workings before he left for America. He informed Niebuhr that Christians in Germany would have to choose between "willing the defeat of their nation in order that Christian civilization may survive" and "willing the victory of their nation and thereby

---

207. *DB*, 678.
208. Phillips, *Christ for Us*, 128–29.

destroying our civilization."[209] Bonhoeffer chose to act towards the defeat of his nation. Bonhoeffer also anticipated the concepts of solidarity, responsibility for others, and taking on guilt which would appear in his *Ethics*. There is another important quote with implications for assessing a change in the church-world dynamic in addition to this testimony of a decision for a changed form of political involvement. Bonhoeffer wrote in a July 21, 1944 letter to Bethge,

> In the last few years I have come to know and understand more and more the profound this-worldliness of Christianity . . . I remember a conversation that I had thirteen years ago in America with a young French pastor. We had simply asked ourselves what we really wanted to do with our lives. And he said, I want to be saint (—and I think it's possible that he did become one). This impressed me very much the time. Nevertheless, I disagreed with him, saying something like: I want to learn to have faith. For a long time I did not understand the depth of this antithesis. I thought I myself could learn to have faith by trying to something like a saintly life. I suppose I wrote *Discipleship* as the end of this path. Today I clearly see the dangers of that book, though I still stand by it. Later on I discovered, and am still discovering right up to this day, that one only learns to have faith by living in the full this-worldliness of life. If one has completely renounced making something of oneself—whether it be a saint or a converted sinner or a church leader (a so-called priestly figure!), a just or unjust person, a sick or a healthy person—then one throws oneself completely into the arms of God, and this is what I call this-worldliness: living fully in the midst of life's tasks, questions, successes and failures, experiences and perplexities.[210]

Bonhoeffer does not state explicitly what he feels is the danger of *Discipleship*. From the perspective of the church-world relationship/political involvement dyad, the danger is not doing anything practical or tangible in the political realm in the face of an obvious evil. Bonhoeffer's sentences before the reference to *Discipleship* wherein he speaks of trying to be a saint and his statements after, where he indicates how he is learning to embrace the world fully, indicate acknowledgment of a significant change. Finally, there are statements from his prison letters wherein he

209. *TF*, 479–80.
210. *DBWE-8*, 485–86.

Phase 4: Church as World

expresses surprise at his own theological development, particularly his ideas about religionless Christianity and the world come of age.[211]

All of the foregoing evidence warrants the judgment that the change from phase 3 to phase 4 represents a fairly obvious and well-documented break in his conception of the church-world relationship and in its accompanying form of political involvement. Bonhoeffer became conscious of the inability of various forms of theology and behavior to really confront evil. The Confessing Church was not consistent in its positions. The majority of the leadership of the ecumenical churches, for their part, failed to provide effective help in resistance, at least on a strictly theological basis. Bonhoeffer's concrete love of Germany and its people overrode his desire to remain pure in the way he understood purity in phase 3.[212] He ultimately decided to abandon pacifism and the two-sphered thinking that made church membership a prescription for world-avoiding passivity.

Finally, there is some question or scholarly disagreement about the exact time of the break. The question does not center around whether there was a difference in his theology or in his form of involvement between *Discipleship* and *Ethics*. The concern is over another possible change between *Ethics* and some of the more radical later prison letters.[213] Hanfried Müller and Rainer Mayer, for example, posit a significant dis-

---

211. Ibid., 362. Bonhoeffer writes in an April 30, 1944, letter to Bethge, "What might surprise and perhaps even worry you would be my theological thoughts and where they are leading, and here is where I really miss you very much. I don't know anyone else with whom I can talk about them and arrive at some clarity. What keeps bothering me incessantly is the question, what is Christianity, or who is Christ actually for us today? The age when we could tell people that with words—whether theological or with pious words—is past, as is the age of inwardness and of conscience, and that means the time of religion in general. We are moving toward a completely religionless age."

212. Kuhns, *In Pursuit of Dietrich Bonhoeffer*, 230–31.

213. *DB*, 859. Bethge writes, "Such observations later raised the question as to where the essential change in Bonhoeffer's development occurred. Many placed the change before *Ethics*, others (for example, R. Gregor Smith, Hanfried Müller, J. A. T. Robinson, and H. J. Schultz) between *Ethics* and the 1944 letters from prison. They saw the real progress as having been made after the new start of April 1944, and described what had gone before more or less as a preparatory phase, if not indeed an orthodoxy that to some extent followed the 'wrong tracks.' Others, including Karl Barth, also viewed April 1944 as a major turning point; but for them the worthwhile reading was what had gone on before, mainly *Discipleship*, while they considered the theology of *Letters and Papers from Prison* immature and not worth passing on."

continuity between *Ethics* and the *Letters*.²¹⁴ Other scholars, Gerhard Ebeling for example, held continuity between *Ethics* and the *Letters and Papers from Prison*.²¹⁵ From the church-world perspective developed in this dissertation there is no question that a break occurred between *Discipleship* and *Ethics*. There are, however, parts of *Ethics* wherein Bonhoeffer reiterates themes from phase 1 and phase 2. In the *Ethics*, for instance, Bonhoeffer still argues for the church as having a physical presence apart from the outside world. In the *Letters*, however, Bonhoeffer raises the possibility that the church might blend in fully with the larger world. In this vision, clergy would take on secular roles and the church might sell all of its property.

Bonhoeffer's assertion of the unity of the church and world in Christ in *Ethics*, while not as severe as it is in the *Letters*, is starker and more explicit than his expression of that unity in phases one and two. Compared to *Discipleship* with its two-sphered thinking, the *Ethics* and the *Letters* are certainly linked. More specifically, questions about how the physical church might look in the world are natural given Bonhoeffer's *Ethics* vision where Christ's lordship breaks away from its ecclesiological shackles and extends over the whole of reality. It is in this sense that the church-world relationship in the *Letters* appears as the logical outcome of the movement begun in the *Ethics*.

---

214. *ADOB*, 42. Hopper writes, "Hanfried Müller, though not denying continuity and development in Bonhoeffer's thought, speaks of 'qualitative leaps' in his theological development and identifies a final 'leap' in Bonhoeffer's movement beyond the thought pattern of *Ethics* to those of the *Letters and Papers from Prison*. And another interpreter, Rainer Mayer . . . speaks of a collapse of Bonhoeffer's 'system of Christological ontology' set forth in *Ethics* as a basis for the transition to the thought patterns of the 'world come of age' in the prison letters."

215. *ADOB*, 41.

7

Conclusion

INTRODUCTION

THE PRECEDING CHAPTERS PRESENT a Bonhoeffer whose unique and tumultuous life found him responding to political, ecclesial, and personal events in four distinct phases marked by four distinct understandings of the church-world relationship. These four church-world visions are accompanied by, and consistent with, four distinct forms of political involvement. In phase 1, Bonhoeffer adheres to a typically Lutheran vision of the church-world relationship where church and world exist in the same historical and practical sphere. This church-world vision yields a church-state relationship where both are distinct in role and mission but do not present any actionable conflicts for each other. That is, Christians are not impeded from specifically pro-state political activity and the state should not prevent the church from proclaiming the gospel. Church and state have non-interfering roles. This church-state vision is (rightly) associated with political conformity to the state on the part of church members. Consistent with this adherence to a typically conservative version of the Lutheran Two Kingdoms doctrine, Bonhoeffer did not protest against the state and was willing to serve in a military organization. Furthermore, he was not a pacifist. Pacifism was considered an irresponsible withdrawal from duties to the neighbor and state in the Lutheran mindset.

Phase 2 saw the beginnings of the church struggle, where the *Deutsche Christen* and the Nazi Party in general overstepped the limits prescribed by the Lutheran Two Kingdoms doctrine (the accepted stipulation that the state should not interfere with the operation of the church and vice versa). The influences from his first American visit, including a spiritual awakening of sorts characterized by a commitment to the church and the scriptures, became manifest. Specifically, Bonhoeffer's unique adaptation of Barth and others, where the concentration on the purity and uniqueness of the church's message to the world combined with the concern for worldliness lingering from phase 1, yielded a vision of the church and world in a heightened tension. Bonhoeffer was thus able to highlight the church's ability to criticize the state from the perspective of the gospel. The beginnings of Bonhoeffer's tendencies toward some form of pacifism reflect the new theological vision resulting from his first American visit. His brush with pacifist ideas and his broadening notion of the church as a collection of persons not bound by national boundaries, attributable to his friendship with Jean Lasserre and his being outside of Germany respectively, allowed him to envision the church as a world-wide collection of persons with a message and mission for peace. Finally, his conversion to the Bible had the Sermon on the Mount as its central focus, and thus formed the content of the Word the church is supposed to offer to the world (in *Sanctorum Communio* from phase 1, this focus was not defined so sharply). Bonhoeffer did not, though, advocate for an anti-worldly pacifism associated with Protestant sectarianism or the historic peace churches.

Bonhoeffer's actions in phase 2 were consistent with his changed thought. Instead of passively accepting the negative intrusions into the church from the political sphere, he became involved in the world in the form of the ecumenical peace movement and the beginnings of the church struggle (*Kirchenkampf*) against the *Deutsche Christen*. His involvement with the ecumenical church, wherein he spoke out on behalf of world-wide church-based peace movements, was a clear manifestation of his understanding of a church whose boundaries were not circumscribed by nationality. His speaking out on behalf of the Jews, moreover, was the clear manifestation of his understanding of a church whose purity of Word and operation were not to be compromised by the outside world. Specifically, the church was not to be compromised by a state that was interfering in church policy. Yet, the move from phase 1 to phase 2 represents somewhat of a qualified break. His thinking on the church-world relationship is clearly different than its counterpart in phase 1. In addition, his attendant forms of political involvement and political thinking were also different. However, because he conceived the church and the world as distinct entities (albeit more polarized than in the first phase) in the same reality, it is difficult to call the movement from phase 1 to 2 an outright break. It is in this sense (the fact of a shared reality or sphere) that Bonhoeffer remained in the spirit of the Lutheran Two Kingdoms doctrine. The heightened tension between the church and world did, though, make his thinking consistent with a more liberal interpretation of the doctrine where the church can raise a protest voice. There are, however, a few stark changes that arguably move him beyond even liberal interpretations of the doctrine. The move to any form of pacifism is one. The suggestion of the possibility of direct political action against the state is another.

Bonhoeffer's entry into phase 3 represents a break from phase 2 to a church against world or church apart from world vision. He became dissatisfied with both the ecumenical movement and the Confessing church and withdrew into church activity in London. He also headed up two illegal seminaries whose operation was monastery-like, replete with communal living and intense study of the Sermon on the Mount. Bonhoeffer embraced a more profound and intense form of pacifism compared to his earlier work. His Fanø "peace speech," for example, saw him arguing for the most extreme form of pacifism (non-response even in the event of an aggressive war against one's nation). His *Discipleship*, which represents the pinnacle of his literal interpretation of the Sermon on the Mount, encouraged nonviolence. Even more, though, his thinking took on a decidedly world-avoiding and apolitical character. Bonhoeffer approached a sectarian vision of the church set against a hostile outside world. He even argued at one point that whoever did not belong to the Confessing church was cut off from salvation.

Bonhoeffer's actions were consistent with his church-world thinking. While still somewhat involved in the church struggle, he did so from locations outside of the center of the controversy. He was involved solely in the churchly sphere, but did not raise a public protest voice against Nazi abuses therein with the same intensity that he did in phase 3. Bonhoeffer did not publicly protest against Nazi abuses against various segments of the population outside of the church either. His changed relationship to the Lutheran Two Kingdoms doctrine across phases is another way to highlight the nature of the discontinuity in the thought-action dyad between phases two and three. He essentially releases the tensions in phases one and two by placing the church and world (and the church and state) into separate spheres, a "two-sphered" reality that he quite explicitly and self-consciously addresses and even corrects in his last phase. It thus becomes acceptable for the Christian to withdraw into the church, concentrate on its purity, and abstain from certain secular duties. When the Christian does submit to government rule or engage in secular roles, it is only to indicate how far the churchly sphere is from the secular sphere. In this sense, on the surface it can appear as if the church is making a political point in its withdrawal (some form of active resistance), and is therefore politically concerned or involved. A look at Bonhoeffer's church-world thinking here dictates otherwise. The secular or political behavior is not motivated by politics or an attempt to achieve any contrived political ends or goals. It is, rather, the patient submission to suffering in the wait for God's instatement of God's Kingdom.

The move from phase 3 to phase 4 represents perhaps the sharpest of the discontinuities in the thought-action dyad. Bonhoeffer, now fully dissatisfied with the ecumenical movement and the Confessing church, abandoned them almost entirely and entered fully into the secular realm with secular people. His church-world thinking from all three previous phases simply did not provide the practical provisions for confronting the absolute evil of Hitler and his regime. Bonhoeffer releases the tension between the church and the world in the exact opposite direction in comparison with the release in phase 3; he gets close to collapsing their difference. The ethical guidelines applicable in delineating action as a Christian or church member and action as a secular person become compromised. In phases one and two, action in the world (either pro-state or voicing criticisms of the state and even the remote possibility of direct action against the state on behalf of the church) was acceptable. Yet, the fact that the action was taken specifically as a church member imposed certain restrictions. The break in form of action accompanying the break in the church-world relationship from the earlier phases to the final one is stark. Bonhoeffer moved from seclusion in the church to direct political involvement in the world.

The differences between the phases also reveal themselves in light of an insight by Koch noted in earlier chapters. Koch writes, "What one sees in Bonhoeffer's thought is a struggle between his own sense of call and his Lutheran theological heritage. While the possibility of resistance is raised in 'Die Kirche von der Judenfrage,' one finds quite traditional views of church-state relations in *Nachfolge* and *Ethics*."[1] There is noth-

---

1. Koch, "The Theological Responses of Karl Barth and Dietrich Bonhoeffer," iv.

ing traditional about Bonhoeffer's phase-three pacifism (*Nachfolge*) or his phase-four (implicit) approval of tyrannicide (in *Ethics* and in "Ten Years After"). Koch is nevertheless generally correct about the struggle between Bonhoeffer's sense of duty to his nation as prescribed by traditional Lutheran standards and his desire to do what was needed to confront the terror of the Third Reich. He tracked Germany's World War I military conquests as a child. Bonhoeffer was willing to serve in a military organization in phase 1, a conservative one (his father was a member) traditionally supportive of monarchical governmental structures. He was clearly patriotic. His lecture in Barcelona (from phase 1) reiterated the thinking then in vogue that nations or *Volk* are like persons who might expand and grow according to God's will and the laws of strong and weak. Aggressive wars might be necessary for that expansion and growth.

In phase 2, though, it became difficult for Bonhoeffer's love of Germany to manifest in the same way. His identification of the church as both a bearer of an authoritative message of peace and an international community irrespective of national boundaries stretched his patriotism to the limits. He even suggested the possibility of direct political action against the state on behalf of the church. It is testimony to his attachment to his Lutheran heritage, though, that he did not recommend direct political action against the state at the time he wrote about its possibility. He did not, moreover, actually undertake any direct anti-state political action in phase 2. There is evidence, too, that Bonhoeffer was concerned about the survivability of his nation as a specifically Christian nation. His writings in phase 2 included a vision of the church and state linked in such a way that if one did not function according to its proper nature, the other one would collapse and vice versa. That is, even in the boldest vision of church-state relations, where he suggests the possibility of direct political action for the church, he still espouses a position associated with German Lutheran support of monarchical governments rather than a position associated with liberal democracies.[2]

2. See Willmer, "Costly Discipleship," 173–89. Willmer writes, "He [Bonhoeffer] opposed one discipleship to another. His way was different from Hitler's because Jesus Christ was, in Bonhoeffer's exposition and practice, evidently a quite different Lord. But it was a battle between Lords—not between an authoritarian conception of society and a liberal democratic one. Thus for many who in the last fifty years have most read Bonhoeffer, there is much to disturb and embarrass," 188. See also Hauerwas, *Performing the Faith*, 55. Hauerwas writes, "Those tempted to so criticize Bonhoeffer,

The struggle between Bonhoeffer's Lutheran heritage and his own calling becomes very clear in his thinking and behavior in phase 3. His own call to pacifism was directly at odds with his obligations to the state as dictated by traditional Lutheranism. Bonhoeffer's thinking and behavior in phase 4, including the decisions to enter the conspiracy and to plot tyrannicide, represents another significant challenge to his Lutheran heritage. His actions went beyond anything acceptable in his tradition. They were, however, strangely patriotic in the sense that Bonhoeffer thought his nation's defeat would be necessary for its ultimate survival as a Christian nation.[3]

Given this brief summary of my findings and argumentation, I will address some of the larger structural or methodological concerns raised in the introductory chapter. Specifically, I will show how, at least in an initial brief way, the church-world relationship provides a more effective and comprehensive framework for understanding Bonhoeffer's changes in political behavior than do the frameworks of Christology and Ethics. I will also show how the specific use of the church-world dynamic in the Theological Categories in Context Approach highlights the strengths and minimizes the weaknesses of the two other approaches to the problem of Bonhoeffer's changing forms of political involvement. Finally, I will comment on what Bonhoeffer's claim of "straight-line" continuity looks like in light of my way of understanding the changes in his political thinking and behavior in the most comprehensive manner.

CHRISTOLOGY AND ETHICS

I argued in the introductory chapter and throughout the text that changes in the church-world relationship are indicative of changes in Bonhoeffer's political thinking and behavior, that changes in this category are most sensitive to changes in thinking on war and peace and his political behavior. I argued further that the church-world dynamic was better suited for this form of analysis than either Christology or Ethics,

---

of course, have to give some account for the political character of his life. For example, they might suggest that Bonhoeffer's life was more political than his theology or even (as I suggested in the first chapter) that Bonhoeffer's theology is particularly well-suited for totalitarian contexts but fails to provide an adequate account of how Christians should live in democratic societies."

3. *TF*, 479–80. Bonhoeffer writes, "Christians in Germany will face the terrible alternative of either willing the defeat of their nation in order that Christian civilization may survive, or willing the victory of their nation and thereby destroying our civilization."

two other categories connected to his thinking on political matters and behavior in the world. I will in this section provide more extensive and detailed argumentation for my claims.

Christology

The connection between Bonhoeffer's Christology and his political involvement is exemplified mostly by Rasmussen's *Reality and Resistance* described in my first chapter. Rasmussen states clearly and plainly, "The thesis of this study is that Dietrich Bonhoeffer's resistance activity was his Christology enacted with utter seriousness. Bonhoeffer's resistance was the existential playing out of christological themes. Changes and shifts in his Christology were at the same time changes and shifts in the character of his resistance."[4] What follows is not a comprehensive attempt to refute Rasmussen's thesis or to even grapple with Rasmussen's text page by page. It is an attempt to take Rasmussen's thesis as a jumping off point for examining the relative merits of Christology and the church-world relationship as theological categories useful for understanding Bonhoeffer's changing forms of political involvement.

Rasmussen does not break Bonhoeffer's Christology off into phases. I will do so for the sake of comparison with the church-world relationship. Bonhoeffer's first phase Christology is a Christo-ecclesiology. The defining phrase for his vision of the church is "Christ existing as church community."[5] The church is a community of persons whom Christ confronts as the divine Thou in individual relations.[6] Bonhoeffer's Christology in this phase thus has commonality with his phase-4 notion where Christ is the "man for others." There is a sense of "ethical" or "social" transcendence in these phases (where God is encountered in proper relation with others).[7] The difference between the two phases is the locus of Christ's presence. Bonhoeffer never explicitly rules out the possibility that Christ is present outside of the church in phase 1. Also, in order for the Lutheran Two Kingdoms doctrine to operate in phase 1, there must be a sense in which Christ is present as both church and state. Bonhoeffer is not explicit about this and the implication in *Sanctorum*

---

4. *RR*, 15.

5. *SC-E*, 121.

6. *SC-E*, 54–55.

7. Bethge, "The Challenge of Dietrich Bonhoeffer's Life and Theology," in Smith, *World Come of Age*, 34.

Communio, at least, is that Christ existing as community refers only to the interactions between persons within the context of the church itself.

In phase 2, the scope of Christ's availability or presence to reality is explicitly broadened. The Christology, in some sense, begins to break away from its containment in ecclesiological theory and extend outward to become one of the ways in which God structures reality as a whole.[8] In his 1933 Christology lectures, for instance, he writes,

> Christ is present to us in the forms both of Church and State. But he is this only for us, who receive him as Word and Sacrament and Church; for us, who since the cross must see the state in the light of Christ. The state is God's 'rule with his left hand' (Luther, W.A. 36, 385, 6–9; 52, 26, 20–6). So long as Christ was on earth, he was the kingdom of God. When he was crucified the kingdom broke up into one ruled by God's right hand and one ruled by his left hand. Now, it can only be recognized in a twofold form, as Church and as State. But the complete Christ is present in his Church. And this Church is the hidden centre of the state. The state need not know that the Church is this centre, but in fact it lives from this centre and has no effective existence without it.[9]

Bonhoeffer does state that Christ is fully present in the Church and that only those who receive him as word, sacrament and church recognize him as state. He nevertheless broadens Christ's presence to the world from his phase Christo-ecclesiology by arguing that Christ is actually present as state.

The other prevailing Christological theme in Bonhoeffer's phase 2 is that of Christ as giver of God's distinctive commandment to the world. Bonhoeffer writes,

> Hence, neither the Biblical law as such nor the so-called orders of creation as such are for us the divine commandment which we perceive today. The commandment cannot stem from anywhere but the origin of promise and fulfilment, from Christ. From Christ alone must we know what we should do. But not from him as the preaching prophet of the Sermon on the Mount, but from him as the one who gives us life and forgiveness, as the

---

8. Phillips, *Christ for Us*, 75–76. Phillips writes, "In the course of these lectures [the 1933 lectures on Christology], Bonhoeffer freed his Christology from the limitations of his ecclesiology and provided a basis for a conception of revelation quite different from that of his two early dissertations."

9. Bonhoeffer, *Christ the Center*, 63–64.

one who has fulfilled the commandment of God in our place, as the one who brings and promises the new world. We can only perceive the commandment where the law is fulfilled, where the new world of the new order of God is established. Thus we are directed completely toward Christ.[10]

This direction toward Christ covers all of the orders of reality contained in fallen creation. Bonhoeffer writes, "It is not as though we now knew all at once from Jesus Christ what features we should regard as orders of creation and what not, but that we know that *all* the orders of the world only exist in that they are directed toward Christ."[11] His thinking here is the basis of his shift from orders of creation to orders of preservation. The church offers Christ's command to the world in order to preserve the world's orders for the continued proclamation of the gospel. This means that any order that does not allow for the continued proclamation of the gospel can and should be dismantled.

Bonhoeffer's Christology in phase 3 represents a move away from his phase-2 Christology in that Christ's call for direct obedience places a barrier between the Christian and all structures of reality. There is no longer any immediate relationship between the Christian and any segment of reality, including the state and familial relations. Bonhoeffer writes,

> Jesus' call itself already breaks the ties with naturally given surroundings in which a person lives. It is not the disciple who breaks them; Christ himself broke them as soon as he called. Christ has untied the person's immediate connections with the world and bound the person immediately to himself. No one can follow Christ without recognizing that that break is already complete . . . He wants to be the medium; everything should happen only through him. He stands not only between me and God, he also stands between me and the world.[12]

This call to have Christ as mediator does not only have ramifications for individual Christians. The call to obedience to Christ forms an entire church-community that is "called out of the world." Bonhoeffer continues,

---

10. Bonhoeffer, "A Theological Basis for the World Alliance," 105.
11. Ibid.
12. *Discipleship*, 93.

> All who belong to the body of Christ have been freed from and called out of the world. They must become visible to the world not only through the communal bond evident in the church-community's order and worship, but also through the new communal life among brothers and sisters in Christ . . . Christians will renounce all community with the world, for they serve the community of the body of Jesus Christ. Being part of this community, Christians cannot remain hidden from the world. They have been called out of the world and follow Christ.[13]

The other significant component to Bonhoeffer's phase-3 *Discipleship* Christology is his insistence on the demands of the Sermon on the Mount. The call to discipleship, or to direct obedience to Christ, takes definite form in obedience to the "way" of the Sermon on the Mount.[14] That is, Bonhoeffer designates this particular set of biblical directives as that which should govern both individual Christian lives and the structure and operation of the church-community as a whole. Direct or literal obedience to the strict demands of the Sermon on the Mount necessarily places the Christian and the church into a sphere whose functioning and standards are radically different than those of the outside world.

Bonhoeffer's Christology in phase 4 represents another change or development. In *Ethics* he returns to a theme reminiscent of his

---

13. Ibid., 236–37. See also, ibid., 253. Bonhoeffer writes, "The 'Ekklesia' of Christ, the community of disciples, is no longer subject to the rule of this world. True, it still lives in the midst of the world. But it already has been made into one body. It is a territory with an authority of its own, a space set apart. It is the holy church (Eph. 5:27), the church-community of saints (1 Cor. 14:34). Its members are the saints called by God (Rom. 1:7), sanctified in Jesus Christ (1 Cor. 1:2), chosen and set apart before the foundation of the world (Eph. 1:4). The goal of their call to follow Jesus Christ, indeed, of their being chosen before the foundation of the world, was that they be holy and blameless (Eph. 1:4)."

14. Willmer, "Costly Discipleship," 180–81. Willmer writes, "As true discipleship begins with a break from the world as a set of attempted direct relations, so it always realises and embodies the break within its primary direct response to the Lord. Giving up a direct relation with the world is a fundamental breach with normality and that breach is always present, though it may be concealed within the positive features of discipleship. The way of the disciple outlined in the Sermon on the Mount, which provides the central text for *The Cost of Discipleship*, points first to the 'extraordinariness' of the Christian life (Matthew 5), then to its 'hiddenness' (Matthew 6): both go to make up the 'separation' of the disciple community (Matthew 7). Extraordinariness and hiddenness are two modes of participative response to the Lord as well as two ways in which, within the disciple's obedience, the breach with the world is worked out."

Conclusion

Christology in phase 2 wherein Christ is the structure of reality. Bonhoeffer writes,

> In Jesus Christ the reality of God entered into the reality of this world. The place where the questions about the reality of God and about the reality of the world are answered at the same time is characterized solely by the name: Jesus Christ. God and the world are enclosed in this name. In Christ all things exist (Col. 1:17). From now on we cannot speak rightly of either God or the world without speaking of Jesus Christ. All concepts of reality that ignore Jesus Christ are abstractions.[15]

Christ's dominion extends over all of reality. It is not confined only to the church and the human interactions therein.[16]

The other significant component to Bonhoeffer's phase-4 Christology is prominent in *The Letters and Papers from Prison* and consistent with a concept from the *Ethics* and even some earlier works. In the *Letters*, Bonhoeffer portrays Christ as the man for others. In his "Outline for a Book" he writes,

> Encounter with Jesus Christ. Experience that here there is a reversal of all human existence, in the very fact that Jesus only "is there for others." Jesus's "being-for-others" is the experience of transcendence! Only through this liberation from self, through this "being-for-others" unto death, do omnipotence, omniscience, and omnipresence come into being. Faith is participating in this being of Jesus. (Becoming human [*Menschwerdung*], cross, resurrection). Our relationship to God is no "religious" relationship to some highest, most powerful, and best being imaginable—that is no genuine transcendence. Instead, our relationship to God is a new life in "being there for others," through participation in the being of Jesus. The transcendent is not the infinite, unattainable tasks, but the neighbor within reach in any given situation. God in human form! Not, as in oriental religions in animal forms as the monstrous, the chaotic, the remote, the terrifying, but also not in the conceptual forms of the absolute, the metaphysical,

---

15. DBWE-6, 54.

16. Moltmann and Weissbach, *Two Studies in the Theology of Bonhoeffer*, 121. Weissbach writes, "As has been pointed out above, there is nothing for Bonhoeffer, at any rate in *Ethics*, which is not subject to the *regnum Christi*. It cannot be accidental that it is in 1940 that he uses Ephesians 1:10 for the first time, and that the term 'genuine worldliness' appears. In the doctrine of the mandates, the church is coordinated with secular institutions."

the infinite, and so on, either, nor again the Greek God—human form of the "God-human form [Gott-Menschgestalt] of the human being in itself." But rather "the human being for others"![17]

Jesus as the "man for others" is consistent with Bonhoeffer's notions of Responsibility, Deputyship and taking on guilt from the *Ethics*. Bonhoeffer writes, "Vicarious representative action and therefore responsibility is possible only in completely devoting one's own life to another person."[18] He writes in another place, "Precisely because and when it is responsible, because and when it is exclusively concerned about the other human being, because and when it springs from the selfless love for the real human brother or sister—it cannot seek to withdraw from the community of human guilt."[19] Christians are to act in responsible deputyship toward their fellow persons. They must, furthermore, be willing to take on guilt in their actions.

There are two important issues to examine in terms of evaluating Christology as an effective mechanism for gauging Bonhoeffer's changes in his forms of political involvement. The first involves the question of continuity and discontinuity in his Christology. The second issue involves precisely how Bonhoeffer's Christology relates to his political positions in each phase of his development.

As many commentators have argued, Bonhoeffer's Christology appears to be relatively consistent or continuous, with some shifts or developments throughout his career.[20] Bonhoeffer's early Christology concerns itself with proper human relationality in the church. Church members should treat each other in community as if Christ were confronting them as the divine Thou in and through the human Thou. Bonhoeffer thus more than hints in *Sanctorum Communio* at his late stage Christology in the *Letters* where Jesus is the man for others and true experience of transcendence means service to Christ as neighbor or fellow person. Bonhoeffer's idea that the church is the new humanity in Christ hints that the whole human community might be included in the community governed by these types of relations. He does not, however, make it explicit that the whole of human community (including social or

17. *DBWE-8*, 501.
18. *DBWE-6*, 259.
19. *DBWE-6*, 275.
20. See *ADOB*, 80–95, for a summary discussion of the scholarly appreciation of Bonhoeffer's Christology.

Conclusion

political communal structures) are or should be Christ-centered or characterized by certain types of relations. In phase 2, however, Bonhoeffer begins to take this church-centered Christology and broaden it to include communities outside of the explicit church community. He argues, for instance, that both the church and the state are manifestations of Christ in the world.

Bonhoeffer's Christology develops from phase 1 to phase 2 in terms of a broadening context for Christ's Lordship over reality. What remains consistent across these phases is the idea that Christ is the concrete reality manifesting in a certain type of human relationality in the church or in the world. Another consistency between the phase-1 and phase-2 Christology is the idea that Christ, through the church, is the bearer or guarantor of an authentic Word and sacrament to the world. Bonhoeffer is not very specific about the content of the Word in phase 1. In phase 2 Bonhoeffer begins to suggest that for that "today" it is a word of peace. He even begins to mention the Sermon on the Mount as a central component of Christ's Word.

Discipleship significantly challenges any attempts to establish a fundamental continuity in Christology. It is clear that the response to Christ's Word or call creates a church-community apart from the larger civil community. The human interactions in this community have a different character than those of the larger secular world or community. The interactions in the church are supposed to mirror the absolute love of Christ for others as described in the Sermon on the Mount. There nevertheless remains a continuity in that Christians are to be conformed to Christ. Bonhoeffer writes,

> To be conformed to the image of Jesus Christ is not an ideal of realizing some kind of similarity with Christ which we are asked to attain. It is not we who change ourselves into the image of God. Rather, it is the very image of God, the form of Christ, which seeks to take shape within us (Gal. 4:19). It is Christ's own form which seeks to manifest in us. Christ does not cease working in us until he has changed us into Christ's own image. Our goal is to be shaped into the entire form of the incarnate, the crucified and the risen one.[21]

---

21. *Discipleship*, 284–85.

There is also continuity in that Christ offers an authoritative Word to the world.

The move from phase 3 to phase 4 seems to represent another radical change in Christology. Christ's form becomes relevant again or applicable again to structures in the world outside of the church. Even with this shift back to earlier phases, there remains the fundamental Christological continuity. Rasmussen writes, "In both books (*The Cost of Discipleship* and *Ethics*), the ethics of formation sounds a clear tone."[22] That is, in both phases, the Christian must be conformed to Christ. The only discernible difference or change is the lack of attention given to the content of Christ's message in Bonhoeffer's later stage theology.

There is, then, a basic structural continuity throughout the four phases along two different lines. Bonhoeffer is concerned throughout his career with the fact that reality has a Christocentric structure. This structure requires conformation on the part of the Christian and manifests in a certain type of human interrelatedness in community. The other theme is the idea that Christ offers an authoritative Word to the world through the church. Another way of articulating Bonhoeffer's career-long consistent Christology is through the question, "Who is Christ for us today?"[23] In phase 1, Christ is present in the church calling humanity to a new form of interrelatedness. In phase 2, Christ is the hidden center of all reality; he is hidden center of the church and the state. Christ is also one who calls for work toward international peace. In phase 3, Christ is the one who calls Christians to conform to Him in the church. Bonhoeffer assigns explicit guidelines for this conformation, strict obedience to Christ or clinging to Christ in terms of literal adherence to the directives of the Sermon on the Mount. In phase 4, Christ is "the man for others." Conformation to Christ means serving any other human being in any context.

If there is this basic structural continuity in Christology, then why isn't there a basic continuity in political action? The answer is simple. Bonhoeffer's Christology is able to accommodate a variety of political positions in each phase. The phase-1 Christo-ecclesiology, where the

---

22. *RR*, 28.

23. Ibid., 23. See also Pangritz, "'Who Is Jesus Christ, for Us, Today?'" 134–53. Pangritz writes, "It has become customary to regard Christology as the centre of Bonhoeffer's thought. And indeed, the question 'Who is Jesus Christ?' forms the cantus firmus of Bonhoeffer's theological development from the beginning to the end," 134.

"Church is Christ existing as community," can accommodate even conflicting political positions. One could argue that varieties of pacifism and just war thinking could be consistent with conforming to Christ as church community. This is true in phase 1 especially since Bonhoeffer does not really designate anything specific as Christ's authoritative Word to the community or the world. The only discernible moral norm is treating the other in church community as if he or she were the divine Thou confronting in the form of the human thou. Pacifism, or refusal to do harm to others, would seem to be consistent with this Christo-communal vision. Defending one's fellow church member from aggressive attack by an enemy would also seem consistent with this vision. The issue that determines political positions is not simply *that* Christ exists as community, but *how* that church-community sits, resides in, or interacts with the world outside of it. That is, does this vision of the new humanity in Christ that takes form in the church set that church-community apart from the outside world? Does membership in this Christ-community prevent one from fulfilling obligations to the outside civil community? These are questions that Bonhoeffer's Christology from phase 1 does not really answer in a way that excludes certain forms of behavior.

It would seem that a clear answer could be given in phase 2. Bonhoeffer extends his Christological vision of reality to cover both the church and the state. Obligations to the state, such as participating in defensive wars, would thus seem legitimate according to this Christology. Bonhoeffer, though, begins to designate the Sermon on the Mount as Christ's authoritative message to the world. Christ's message to the world is a Word of peace. There seems, thus, to be conflicting Christologies in phase 2. The first one would seem to support action in the world for the sake of the maintenance of the state as one of God's ways of ruling in the world (participation in war, for example). The other one calls for peace and unity irrespective of national or state boundaries.

Phase 3 would seem to be the only phase where Bonhoeffer's Christology commands a single type of political activity (or allows only one type of political thinking). He clearly presents a vision where adherence to Christ calls one into a type of community governed by demands and characterized by relationships that are radically different than those in the world outside of the church. Because strict adherence to the Sermon on the Mount is a requirement for membership, being part of this Christ-community disallows participation in war. Even here, though, the Christological format or structure itself (the fact that Christians are to be conformed to the Christocentric reality or respond to God's Word in Christ) cannot account for the pacifism. Rather, the political position (pacifism) depends largely on whether or not what Bonhoeffer designates as the central component of Christ's Word is something that forces a believer into the world or out of it. In phase 3, conforming to Christ means becoming part of a church-community that has a relationship to the outside world of a certain character. It is the character of this relationship that determines the political position.

Phase 4 would seem to be another phase where the Christology is a good indicator of political positions. Bonhoeffer moves away from a call to cling to Christ according to the demands of the Sermon on the Mount. Following Christ entails being "the man for others" in any and every possible context. Christians are to be conformed to the "incarnate, crucified and risen Christ." Again, this is a Christological theme taken almost directly from *Discipleship*.[24] Bonhoeffer argues for a position that is (arguably) a just war position in *Ethics*. So the very same Christology of conformation seems to be able to accommodate both pacifist and just war positions. A Christology where Jesus is the "man for others" also suffers from the same weakness in terms of determining political positions. That is, it seems that such a Christology would be able to accommodate either pacifist or just war positions. One might even argue that Bonhoeffer's participation in tyrannicide was a manifestation of this Christology where Jesus is the man for others. In this case, eliminating Hitler would be the expression of solidarity with the suffering others in his nation.

Ultimately, Bonhoeffer's relatively consistent Christological vision in itself cannot be a reliable indicator of the form of political involvement in any or each of the four phases, even with the nuances in each phase. The deciding factor in each phase is whether or not the conformation to Christ is one that forces the Christian out of the world and disallows participation in its structures or places him or her fully into the world and therefore allows participation in its structures. Furthermore, the political positions seem to depend on whether what Bonhoeffer designates as the central component of Christ's authoritative Word is one that

---

24. See Kelly and Godsey, "Editors' Introduction to the English Edition," 1–33. See especially pp. 19–21, where Kelly and Godsey argue for continuity between *Discipleship*, *Ethics*, and even the *Letters* in terms of the Christology of conformation.

Conclusion

forces the Christian out of the world (and disallows participation in its structures), or places him or her fully into the world (and therefore allows participation in its structures).

Ethics

An examination of Bonhoeffer's *Ethics* also provides evidence that the church-world relationship is a more effective means by which to gauge the changes in his political thinking and behavior. Bonhoeffer holds fairly consistently to something close to a situation ethics throughout his career. His career-long ethical stance was, more specifically, like the one he laid out in his Barcelona ethic from phase 1. Christians should do God's will in response to a confrontation with Jesus Christ in any and every given situation. There are really no eternally fixed or eternally valid norms to be applied uncritically irrespective of situation.[25] Christian behavior is in a sense beyond the concepts of good and evil. The point of departure for ethical action is doing God's will in a given situation rather than human constructions of what might be good action and what might be evil action.[26]

Bonhoeffer's ethical stances, like any ethical stances reliant on a more situational type ethics, are somewhat unpredictable as they depend on a dialectic between two poles. One pole consists of whatever is determined to be the compelling component about any given situation. The other pole is whatever is determined to be the content of God's will. In the above-noted Barcelona ethic, for example, Bonhoeffer designates war as God's call to participate in the history-making growth of a nation or people. Moreover, he designates the responsibility to other persons in one's nation (one's own *Volk*) as the deciding component in the situation in which Christians respond to God's will. That is, one should partake in war for the sake of one's own neighbor or *Volk*.[27] As compared to ethical systems reliant on more stable devices like eternal principles or natural law and others, one gets the general impression that both the content of God's will and also the texture of the concrete reality in which God's will is to be followed are somewhat arbitrary.

---

25. *TF*, 348–49.
26. *TF*, 349.
27. *RR*, 96–98.

My point is clearer in light of his thinking in phase 2. Bonhoeffer reasserts the spirit of the situation ethics from phase 1 when he rejects the Biblical Law or the Sermon on the Mount as the "absolute norm for our action."[28] He argues explicitly, like he did in the Barcelona ethic, that "the Sermon on the Mount cannot become the letter of the law to us."[29] Yet, he does indicate that the church has the authority to make authoritative interpretations of the Word of God having implications for specific ethical action in the world for Christians for any given present. In his Czechoslovakian address, Christ's command for that present was a command for international peace, a condition necessary for continued revelation. So the thing that accounts for the beginnings of his pacifism is not a difference in the general ethical framework (an interpretation of God's Word or command for a given present remains). It is, rather, whatever Bonhoeffer proposes as either the authoritative Word or command of God and the texture of the situation to which that Word speaks. This dynamic begs the further question of what factors might influence how Bonhoeffer determines either the content of the Word or the nature of the situation.

In phase 3, Bonhoeffer designates the Sermon on the Mount as the component of God's call or the Word of God that enters into any given present. Bonhoeffer arguably deviates from his career-long position that biblical directives, including specifically the ones in the Sermon on the Mount, cannot provide laws. That position, as he argues in a few places, would nullify the absolute freedom effected by Christ. With his call for strict obedience in discipleship to the Sermon on the Mount, Bonhoeffer implies that its directives are law-like. He is, however, consistent in that he never states definitively that this close following of the Sermon on the Mount is something that might be applicable to all times and places. In phase 4, Bonhoeffer argues that ethical action is action that corresponds to the Christocratic structure of reality. Bonhoeffer does provide ethical principles (he does not support the right to revolution for citizens of a state, for instance). In the end, though, those principles are flexible as evidenced by his implicit approval of tyrannicide. In some situations (some given "presents") the Christian is called to act in free responsibility in deputyship for the sake of others, even if that means going against standard Christian ethical directives.

28. Bonhoeffer, "A Theological Basis for the World Alliance," 104.
29. Ibid.

Conclusion

It is true that Bonhoeffer's ethical positions on war and peace do change phase by phase. It would seem, then, that Ethics would be as effective a means by which to trace Bonhoeffer's political thinking and involvement as the church-world relationship, Christology, or any other theological category. My foregoing brief analysis of both his ethical framework and the way he manipulates it in the four phases strongly suggests that the framework itself cannot be responsible for his changing positions. It is, again, what he designates as the Word or how he conceptualizes the situation (into which the Word is spoken) that determines the variations in his ethical positions. The other implication is that there are other factors that determine his choices on the message and the situation or how they relate to each other.

My argument for the superiority of the church-world category over Ethics presumes that the way Bonhoeffer views the relationship between the church and the world actually determines his choices on either the content of the Word or that of the situation in his ethical framework. In phase 1, for example, Bonhoeffer does not see the world as something that presents an insurmountable obstacle to the church's stated mission of offering the Word or the sacrament. The world or culture, while not wholly welcoming or receptive, is still potentially receptive. The church should thus continue to try to fulfill its role in preaching and offering the Word to the world. So while there might be some tension between the church and the world, there is no reason for the church to withdraw from the world or expect its members to do so. The church does not comprise a group of persons who, in their acceptance of the Word, have made themselves aliens amidst a hopelessly lost world. Church and world reside squarely in sin-ridden history with specific roles. With the church-world relationship so defined, there are no barriers to engagement in the political realm on the part of church members. More specifically, this church-world relationship influences both poles of the ethical framework. The situation in which ethical decisions are made is a world whose political matters are dictated by God's will for nations in sin-ridden history. The state is to make history according to God's will. Church members, fully part of both church and world in the same sin-ridden historical situation, freely participate in the world by helping the state make history. Bonhoeffer does not really define the content of the church's Word to the world in phase 1. Its authoritative message cannot thus interfere with full engagement in the political for the Christian.

In phase 1 the relationship between Bonhoeffer's church-world vision and the two poles in his ethical framework is somewhat indirect. In phase 2 Bonhoeffer's definition of both the situation and the Word is more clearly connected to his changed notion of the church-world relationship and, ultimately, his political positions. The church in phase 2 is a group of persons who define themselves against the world in terms of their acceptance of the peace command and the Sermon on the Mount. Bonhoeffer designates the Word as the peace command. He also begins to envision the world (or the situation into which the Word is offered) more negatively. The potential conflict between the Word so designated and the world so envisioned raises the possibility that the church and church members would take ethical (or political) positions that are counter-state. These ethical or political positions do not, however, call for extreme behavior. The world and its structures are not entirely negative and the peace command does not call for a radical withdrawal from the world or state.

In phase 3, Bonhoeffer's articulation of the Sermon on the Mount as the church's authoritative message is one that calls for strict obedience. This strict obedience pulls the Christian away from any activity in the political realm that might reaffirm it as legitimate or redeemable. The world and its structures are counter to Christ's message and aims. The Church and its members define themselves strictly against the world and act accordingly. Bonhoeffer's ethics are defined strictly by the dictates of the church and its strict adherence to the call of Christ. It is, therefore, likely that Bonhoeffer's ethical positions will have little in common with worldly dictates. Nonparticipation in war provides one example of an ethical position that follows directly upon Bonhoeffer's church-world vision in phase 3. The Christian's strict adherence to the Sermon on the Mount makes it impossible for him or her to participate in any activity not otherwise prohibited for the Christian (except in the case of unjust wars).

Bonhoeffer's vision in phase 4 includes a church whose boundaries with the world are hard to determine. He embraces worldliness or secularity to such an extent that it becomes hard to distinguish ethical directives that are proper to the church (i.e., that are distinctively church-derived) from ethical directives proper to the world. Bonhoeffer's phase-four ethical vision is similar to his phase-1 vision in that the content of the Word is not as explicit as the nature of the situation in which the

Conclusion

ethical operates. Specifically, the Christian's behavior is to conform to the Christocratic structure of reality.

GENERAL THINKING ON THE CHURCH-WORLD RELATIONSHIP AND POSITIONS ON WAR AND PEACE

As I have demonstrated in my treatment of the phases throughout this text, there are ways in which the church-world relationship is connected to political positions that are particular to Bonhoeffer's theology. In addition, there is scholarly support outside of Bonhoeffer's writings or Bonhoeffer studies for the connection between the church-world relationship and positions on war and peace.

The church's or individual theologian's stances toward war and peace have not been uniform throughout church history. There have been three basic positions (pacifism, just war, and the crusade or aggressive war for religious reasons). The early church was, with some exceptions, a pacifist church. Constantine's rise to power effectively ended the church's early pacifist phase and introduced the context for just war thinking. The third position, the Crusade, "a holy war fought under the auspices of the church or of some inspired religious leader . . . on behalf of an ideal, the Christian faith," arose in the high Middle Ages.[30] The remaining history of church engagement with government policy on war and peace is some version of these three basic positions. The Anabaptists, for example, were "absolute pacifists"; any form of violence was considered contrary to the gospel.[31] Other traditions' stances are generally more nuanced and fluid, leaving open the possibility for legitimate debate and varied positions amongst theologians, church members, and church leaders. For example, although the Roman Catholic Magisterium has since the fifth century traditionally adhered to some version of just war theory, it currently supports a provision for non-participation for those who find war against their individual consciences.[32]

---

30. Bainton, *Christian Attitudes*, 14.

31. Ibid., 152–57. There is, however, some scholarly debate about the "extremes" in the pacifist positions among Anabaptists in different historical periods. See, for example, Durnbaugh, "The Brethren and Non-Resistance," 125–44; and Stayer, "Anabaptists and the Sword Revisited," 111–24.

32. Doyle, *The Church Emerging from Vatican II*, 319–20. Doyle affirms the Roman Catholic Magisterium's traditional acceptance of some form of Just War thinking. Referring to *Gaudium et Spes* he also notes that pacifism ("those persons who reject violence and killing under any circumstances") is a legitimate option for Catholics.

The varied positions on war and peace are all framed by theological concerns. Early Church pacifism was influenced by eschatology,[33] a sense of God's ultimate justice,[34] and the fear of idolatry.[35] Other theological underpinnings include an understanding of the radical demands of Christ's call to love (any form of killing is simply irreconcilable with love)[36] and a rejection of the aggressive God in parts of the Hebrew Scriptures.[37] Theological concerns underpin just war thinking also. Ambrose's contribution to just war thinking, for example, was influenced by his idea that "defense of the empire coincided in his mind with the defense of the faith."[38] In addition, Augustine's just war thinking was in part influenced by his less optimistic view of the human person and the inability to attain perfection and thus peace.[39] Finally, the Crusades were undertaken in part out of concerns for "vindicating the rights of

---

He writes, "official Catholic teaching holds that individuals may decide for themselves whether they interpret pacifism or Just-War Theory as the more authentic path of following Christ." Doyle also notes, however, that the church cannot prevent governments from engaging in war when the just war criteria are met.

33. Bainton, *Christian Attitudes*, 75–76, 81. Notwithstanding some debate by historians, Tertullian, for example, represents an early-church pacifism based on eschatology. The expected imminent overthrow of the present political order rendered any current fighting for the existing order unnecessary.

34. Ibid., 76. This theological underpinning is related to eschatology. Suffering and the ravages of war are acceptable as the persecuted would be vindicated in the next life.

35. See Geoffrey F. Nuttall's first chapter, "The Fear of Idolatry," in his *Christian Pacifism in History*, 1–14, for a detailed discussion of the relationship between idolatry and pacifism in the early church. Nuttall speaks of the Christian refusal to take part in war as just one manifestation of a broader theological concern—the fact that the world is condemned and evil. Christians are called out of the world and should avoid participation in any of its structures. The issue of idolatry arises from one aspect of that fallen world—the mandatory military ceremonies and rituals involving worship of pagan deities. See also Bainton, *Christian Attitudes*, 73–74. Bainton affirms, "Some modern interpreters assert that the primary reason (to repudiate the participation in warfare) was the danger of idolatry in military service. The danger was real. The cult of the deified emperor was particularly prevalent in the camps. Officers were called upon to sacrifice; privates participated at least by their attendance." Bainton, however, does offer some evidence that weakens this argument.

36. Bainton, *Christian Attitudes*, 77–78.

37. Ibid., 82. This was Marcion's theological justification for pacifism.

38. Ibid., 90.

39. Ibid., 91–92.

Conclusion

religion under a jurisdiction" and out of concern for the souls of heretics and those they might lead astray.[40]

The foregoing presents just a few major examples of several possible theological categories supporting each of the three church stances toward war and peace. These theological concerns fall into basically two categories: 1) a vision of God[41] or God's will for people as manifest in either Jesus Christ (and Christ's love) or in the sustained presence of a church and 2) a vision of the human person, including his or her sinfulness and potential to achieve perfection (or to create a perfect society).[42] These categories are of limited use, however, because of their constancy throughout the history of Christian thinking and the fact that opposing positions arise from these theological mainstays. As regards the first category, most Christian theologians would agree that a just God somehow simultaneously transcends the world and is immanent therein, has a loving concern for created reality, is involved in history, and wills the continued presence of a church with an authoritative message. Most Christian theologians would also agree that a vision of Jesus as warmonger is inconsistent with the gospel. Along the same lines, most would agree that Christ's healing and loving nature is somehow normative for Christian conduct in the world. As regards the second category, most Christian theologians understand human beings to be compromised, limited, or otherwise affected by sin to the extent that personal or corporate church or societal perfection is humanly unattainable. Yet, again, three relatively discrete historical theological responses to war and peace result from these relatively consistent theological positions. These two major theological categories are clearly important foundations, and certainly related to the category world,[43] but simply not the exclusive or

---

40. Ibid., 111–16.

41. See Dombrowski, *Christian Pacifism*, 115–31. Dombrowski explores the relationship between the theological category of God and pacifism. He writes, "I agree with Stanley Hauerwas when he says that Christian pacifism is unintelligible apart from the theological convictions that support it. As I argued in Chapter Four, art has an important effect on how one will view Christian Pacifism, but an even greater effect is produced by the abstract categories one uses (implicitly or explicitly) to talk about God. Hence in this chapter I will try to get clear on why an inadequate conception of God tends to play into the hands of the just war theorist (or war is hell theorist), whereas a more rationally defensible and consistent conception of God lends itself to pacifism" (115–16).

42. Bainton, *Christian Attitudes*, 14–15.

43. Ibid., 15. Bainton, in fact, links up the anthropology with "world." He writes,

decisive ones in determining any particular church position on war and peace.

The relationship between the church and world can explain more clearly and directly the three different stances. That is, the varying theological stances any given church or theological system has taken toward the world in the different historical phases more directly or decisively determines the three positions on war and peace. Bainton writes,

> These three attitudes [pacifism, just war and crusade] were not rooted in different views of God and only to a degree in different views of man, because all Christians recognized the depravity of man. The question was how to treat his depravity and the problem came to be an aspect of the relationship between the church and the world. Pacifism has commonly despaired of the world and dissociated itself either from society altogether, or from political life, and especially from war. The advocates of the just war theory have taken the position that evil can be restrained by the coercive power of the state. The Church should support the state in this endeavor and individual Christians as citizens should fight under the auspices of the state. The crusade belongs to a theocratic view that the Church, even though it be a minority, should impose its will upon a recalcitrant world. Pacifism is thus often associated with withdrawal, the just war with qualified participation, and the crusade with dominance of the Church over the world.[44]

Bonhoeffer's support of pacifism is consistent with Bainton's framework. His phase-3 pacifism is connected to the idea the world outside the church is in a hopeless condition, the church should neither engage with it nor try to change it for the better.[45] Rather, the church should be concerned only with itself and its own purity. Bonhoeffer's adherence to the just war position, on the other hand, clearly presupposes that the state has a legitimate role in making sure both church and the state can continue to function properly. Here, the Church and the world have similar aims and must share the same space in a cooperative effort.

H. Richard Niebuhr's *Christ and Culture* provides further scholarship outside of Bonhoeffer or Bonhoeffer studies supporting the idea of a connection between the church-world relationship and political posi-

---

"The question was how to treat his [human] depravity and the problem came to be an aspect of the relationship of the Church and the world."

44. Ibid., 14–15.

45. *Discipleship*, 246–47.

tions. His chapter on "Christ Against Culture" is the most helpful as it shares similar themes with Bonhoeffer's position in phase 3. The Christ against Culture position "uncompromisingly affirms the sole authority of Christ over the Christian and resolutely rejects culture's claims to loyalty."[46] Niebuhr writes,

> The succinct statement of the positive meaning of Christianity is, however, accompanied by an equally emphatic negation. The counterpoint of loyalty to Christ and the brothers is the rejection of cultural society; a clear line of separation is drawn between the brotherhood of the children of God and the world . . . the word "world" evidently means for the writer of this letter the whole society outside the church, in which, however, the believers live . . . The world appears as a realm under the power of evil; it is the region of darkness, into which the citizens of the kingdom of light must not enter.[47]

Niebuhr connects withdrawal from political life and especially nonparticipation in the military with the "Christ Against Culture" position.[48] In these ways Bonhoeffer's pacifism from phase 3 is consistent with Niebuhr's typology.

Another feature of Niebuhr's typology consistent with Bonhoeffer's vision from phase 3 is the leaning toward legalism where Christ becomes the giver of the new law. He writes,

> Opponents of the exclusive type frequently accuse its representatives of legalism . . . or of so emphasizing the character of Christianity as a new law for a select community that they forget its gospel is to all men. This much is true, that they all insist on the exhibition of Christian faith in daily conduct. How can a follower of Jesus Christ know that he is a disciple if his conduct in love of the brothers, in self-denial, in modesty, in nonresistance, and in voluntary poverty does not distinguish him from other men? The emphasis on conduct may lead to the definition of precise rules, concern for conformity to such rules.[49]

The "select community" in the case of Bonhoeffer's phase-3 vision is the church-community that follows the directives of the Sermon on the

---

46. Niebuhr, *Christ and Culture*, 45.
47. Ibid., 47–48.
48. Ibid., 65–76.
49. Ibid., 80–81.

Mount obediently as if they were laws. Niebuhr connects this position with monasticism and Protestant sectarianism.[50] Bainton's description of the Anabaptists also echoes Bonhoeffer's stance in phase 3. Bainton writes,

> His kingdom [Christ's] they held to be based upon the Sermon on the Mount and his injunctions to be literally obeyed, not only with regard to war but also with regard to the oath. Here, then, is a New Testament legalism. Obedience, discipleship, and the imitation of Christ are the recurrent words in the Anabaptist confessions. They suggest something more than individual behavior and stand in the context of a program for the Church, which must itself first be restored to the purity of the apostolic time, when Christianity was persecuted rather than supported by the state. The great fall in the history of the Church came with Constantine when the two kingdoms were fused and the sword of the empire intimidated the heretics. The restitution of the Christianity of the golden age was the object of the Anabaptists' endeavor, and to this end adherents were expected to embark upon missionary tours for the conversion of the heathen Christians, whether Catholic or Protestant. The gathering of the pure Church would be the prelude to the coming of the Lord to establish his kingdom upon earth. Thus they held hope for society, but only through the conversion of individuals and the intervention of Christ.[51]

The only significant differences from Bonhoeffer's vision in phase 3 are the notion that Christians might go on missionary tours for the purpose of conversions and the suggestion that gathering the faithful together might have some positive effects for society at large. The adherence to the Sermon on the Mount, the leaning toward a New Testament legalism, the ideas of obedience and discipleship, and the notion that the coming of Lord's kingdom is imminent are all arguably characteristic of Bonhoeffer's *Discipleship* vision.

The final piece of scholarship outside of Bonhoeffer or Bonhoeffer studies which supports the thesis of a relationship between church-world thinking and political postures comes from discussions of sects and sectarianism. Geoffrey Nuttall's description of a form of mediaeval pacifism could describe Bonhoeffer's position as well. He writes, "The outstanding characteristic of these medieval pacifists, as at the outset we observed to

---

50. Ibid., 67.
51. Bainton, *Christian Attitudes*, 154–55.

be true generally of the sect-movement in which they take their place, is their return to the Bible; within the Bible to the New Testament; and within the New Testament to the Sermon on the Mount."[52] Bonhoeffer's *Discipleship* vision, with its concentration on the Sermon on the Mount, certainly meets this qualification of sects as Nuttall describes them.

The most famous scholarship on sects is found in Ernst Troeltsch's *The Social Teaching of the Christian Churches*. Troeltsch's thinking helps illuminate Bonhoeffer's church-world thinking and political positions in phases other than the third. He distinguishes the "Church-type" from the "Sect-type." He writes,

> The Church is that type of organization which is overwhelmingly conservative, which to a certain extent accepts the secular order, and dominates the masses; in principle, therefore, it is universal, i.e. it desires to cover the whole life of humanity. The sects, on the other hand, are comparatively small; they aspire after personal inward perfection, and they aim at a direct personal fellowship between the members of each group. From the very beginning, therefore, they are forced to organize into small groups, and to renounce the idea of dominating the world. Their attitude towards the world, the State and Society may be indifferent, tolerant or hostile, since they have no desire to control and incorporate these forms of social life; on the contrary, they tend to avoid them.[53]

Bonhoeffer's vision in phase 1 is clearly along the lines of Troeltsch's Church-type. The church desires positive interaction with the larger world. Bonhoeffer speaks of the possibility of a conservative-sounding *Volkskirche*, one into which all members of a nation are born. All persons are part of a church whether they are aware of it or not. There are obviously no barriers to participation in duties to the state. Bonhoeffer's vision of the church-world relationship in phase 3 fits the Sect-type. In his particular vision, the church is either tolerant or indifferent to the outside world rather than outwardly hostile.

Troeltsch's continued description of the Sect-type resonates with Bonhoeffer's phase-3 church. Troeltsch writes,

> It [the sect] is, however, naturally a somewhat limited form of fellowship, and the expenditure of so much effort in the mainte-

---

52. Nuttall, *Christian Pacifism in History*, 27.
53. Troeltsch, *The Social Teaching of the Christian Churches*, 1:331.

nance and exercise of this particular kind of fellowship produces a certain indifference towards other forms of fellowship which are based upon secular interests; on the other hand, all secular interests are drawn into the narrow framework of the sect and tested by its standards, in so far as the sect is able to assimilate these interests at all. Whatever cannot be related to the group of interests controlled by the sect, and by the Scriptural ideal, is rejected and avoided. The sect, therefore, does not educate nations in the mass, but it gathers a select group of the elect, and places it in sharp opposition to the world. In so far as the sect-type maintains Christian universalism at all, like the Gospel, the only form it knows is that of eschatology; this is the reason why it always finally revives the eschatology of the Bible . . . Since the sect-type is rooted in the teaching of Jesus, its asceticism also is that of primitive Christianity and of the Sermon on the Mount, not that of the Church and of the contemplative life; it is narrower and more scrupulous than that of Jesus, but, literally understood, it is still the continuation of the attitude of Jesus toward the world.[54]

Bonhoeffer's vision in phase 3 accords with Troeltsch's description in a few ways. First, there is Bonhoeffer's indifference to those secular activities or realms of secular concern that cannot be incorporated into the church's aims. There is also the gathering of persons who stand in opposition to the world. In addition, Bonhoeffer's vision in phase 3 concerns persons outside of the church only inasmuch as they will eventually be part of the restoration at the end of the world. Finally, the asceticism associated with Bonhoeffer's church in phase 3 is one associated with a strict adherence to the Sermon on the Mount. It is not the asceticism associated with a Church-type that emphasizes "mortification of the senses in order to further the higher religious life" or a "heroic special achievement of a special class, restricted by its nature to particular instances."[55] Rather, the sect-type asceticism, like Bonhoeffer's, is "simple detachment from the world, the reduction of worldly pleasure to a minimum, and the highest possible development of fellowship in love."[56]

---

54. Ibid., 339–40.
55. Ibid., 340.
56. Ibid.

THE TWO APPROACHES

Another part of my thesis is that use of the church-world relationship in the Theological Categories in Context Approach both maximizes the strengths and minimizes the weaknesses of the Definition of Pacifism Approach and the particular ways others have used the Theological Categories in Context Approach. I will now address that claim more extensively.

Definition of Pacifism Approach

To summarize briefly from my first chapter, those using the Definition of Pacifism Approach choose a definition of pacifism and judge whether Bonhoeffer's thinking and activity remained consistent therewith throughout his career. There are three problems associated with this method: 1) there are several definitions of pacifism; 2) the only way Bonhoeffer can appear to be consistent is if one uses a definition of pacifism broad enough to encompass tyrannicide and 3) the Definition of Pacifism Approach tends to concentrate solely on the most famous shift in 1939. My development and use of the Theological Categories in Context Approach addresses these concerns. It also maximizes the strength of the Definition Approach.

In terms of the first problem, my approach does not call one to choose any given definition of pacifism divorced from Bonhoeffer's life. Rather, I determine the exact form of pacifism or any other position on politics to which Bonhoeffer adheres in terms of several different conditioning factors, including primarily his understanding of the church-world relationship. Other factors include his relationship with the church, his relationship with the political situation in Germany, the German church situation, etc. The focus thus shifts from judging Bonhoeffer by means of an objective measure to examining the nature of his changes in relation to the varied and complex contexts that helped produce them.

The second weakness in the Definition of Pacifism Approach is the concern with whether or not the chosen definition allows for the judgment that Bonhoeffer's outward actions demonstrate continuity throughout his life. Bonhoeffer can appear two ways depending on the chosen definition. He looks entirely fragmented and discontinuous if one chooses a definition of pacifism on the absolute or principled pacifist end of the spectrum, one where any form of killing in any situation is unacceptable. If one chooses a definition of pacifism characterized by a vague and general desire for peace among nations and therefore allows for removing a tyrant if he or she stands in the way of this peace, then he appears continuous. There may indeed be a definition of pacifism that allows for tyrannicide. My approach, however, bypasses these concerns altogether because it does not concentrate on establishing a single definition in the first place. Rather, as just noted, it allows for a more thorough analysis and a more informed judgment concerning what type of pacifist Bonhoeffer actually was in any given phase or time in his life. The answer to the question of Bonhoeffer's continuity or discontinuity is given in an analysis of how he changes from one phase to the next. It favors this rather than judgments made from an ahistorical standpoint detached from the development in the life of a real man who was responding to a complicated set of real circumstances.

My method combats the third weakness (concentrating only on the shift in 1939 in the end stages of his life) by casting Bonhoeffer's shifts and changes against the backdrop of the development of his whole life. Later developments in his thinking and behavior look different when seen in the context of a developing theologian responding to his political and personal situation. His thinking and behavior in phase 4, for example, represent something of a return to the thinking and behavior in phase 1 and phase 2 because they place the Christian back into the world in a way that allows for action for the sake of the world's structures. His thinking and behavior in phase 4 ultimately transcends his phase-1 and phase-2 thinking and behavior. Nevertheless, looking at the relationship between thought and behavior throughout Bonhoeffer's whole life allows for a fuller, a more well-informed and thus a more balanced judgment on the nature of his changes.

Even with the weaknesses, the Definition Approach does offer a methodological benefit. It is concerned with judging changes in Bonhoeffer's political positions. As stated in the thesis, this work attempts to understand the changes in Bonhoeffer's political positions in the most comprehensive manner and with respect to the broadest range of information. It is, then, important to determine or to define the exact nature of Bonhoeffer's pacifism (provide definitions) in each phase in order to make a judgment about his shifts or changes. Because my approach takes into account several factors that condition his political thinking and conduct, it provides for a fuller appreciation of his pacifism in each phase. Judgments of continuity and discontinuity are thus more nuanced and more accurate. Ultimately, my analysis does lend itself to a judgment of discontinuity in political positions. The way the church-world relationship informs his political thinking in the final phase, for example, rules out the possibility of a phase-3 type pacifism in that phase. This represents an obvious break from his position in phase 3.

Theological Categories in Context Approach

The Theological Categories in Context Approach involves connecting a theological category in Bonhoeffer's thinking with his activity and then gauging overall continuity or discontinuity in this thought-action dyad. It also includes a comprehensive analysis of how the elements in his personal, political, and ecclesial situation inform the specific elements of his thought and action and affect how he changed in his thinking or behavior. The only weakness of this method concerns the efficacy of the chosen theological category might be in terms of gauging the changes in his political thinking and involvement. I have demonstrated at length throughout the text how the church-world relationship is an effective category. I have argued above how this category is more effective than Christology and Ethics.

The strengths of this method are many. One of the significant strengths is the way it allows several possible influences to speak or present themselves in terms of painting a full picture of Bonhoeffer. The method is phenomenological in the sense that it allows the relevant determinants in Bonhoeffer's theology and action to simply present themselves without being judged by any particular standard outside of his thought and action. The church-world hermeneutic does not actually constitute Bonhoeffer's thinking or action in any given phase, does not stand as an external measuring stick, and does not falsely force Bonhoeffer into four phases. Four different church-world visions and four different forms of political involvement appear throughout my presentation of the historical phenomena. The church-world interpretative device is adequate to the historical phenomena.

In addition, this method is eminently historical and contextual in that it seeks to understand Bonhoeffer's thinking and action only within the context in which they developed. Some Bonhoeffer scholars designate one phase of his life and thinking, set it as the standard, and then appreciate the other phases in terms of how they are either similar to or different from the thinking in that phase. This way of approach is subject to a type of criticism similar to one that could be leveled against the Definition of Pacifism Approach; it takes one moment from Bonhoeffer's life and uses it as a standard for judging the whole of Bonhoeffer's life. My approach instead allows one to judge the thinking or action in any current phase only in terms of how it looks from the perspective of the phase preceding it or backwards from the phase proceeding it. The judging standard thus comes from within the flow or development itself rather than from outside of the development. Bonhoeffer's pacifism in phase 3, for example, is judged only in terms of how it differs from his pacifism in phase 2 rather than from the perspective of an arbitrary definition of pacifism from outside his thinking altogether. Bonhoeffer's political involvement in phase 4 is judged only in terms of how it differs from his pacifism in phase 3. In this way the development of Bonhoeffer's life dictates the method rather than the method dictating how one can view his development.

STRAIGHT-LINE CONTINUITY CLAIM

A final consideration is the extent to which seeing Bonhoeffer's thought-action dyad in terms of four distinct phases, with a qualified break and two more pronounced discontinuities, makes his life and thought appear entirely fragmented, broken, or inconsistent. It may appear to some who are concerned with establishing continuity that I have established four entirely different Bonhoeffers. Bonhoeffer's claim of explicit "straight-line" continuity highlights the difficulty. The quote from Bonhoeffer's April 11, 1944 letter to Bethge from Tegel Prison in the 1972 "New Greatly Enlarged Edition" of the *Letters* reads,

> I heard someone say yesterday that the last years had been completely wasted as far as he was concerned. I'm very glad that I have never yet had that feeling, even for a moment. Nor have I ever regretted my decision in the summer of 1939, for I'm firmly convinced—however strange it may seem—that my life has followed a straight and unbroken course, at any rate in its outward conduct. It has been an uninterrupted enrichment of experience, for which I can only be thankful. If I were to end my life here in these conditions, that would have a meaning I think I could

understand; on the other hand, everything might be a thorough preparation for a new start and a new task when peace comes.[57]

Bethge places a footnote after the phrase "my decision in the summer of 1939," indicating that the decision refers to his choice to return home from the USA.[58] Thus, Bethge suggests that Bonhoeffer did not mean specifically his decision to help the conspirators assassinate Hitler. Nevertheless, as I noted in my introductory chapter, Bonhoeffer does assert continuity in outward conduct in reflecting upon an entire life in 1944, a life which obviously included movement from pacifist statements to helping in the conspiracy.

Quite simply stated, an honest appraisal of the facts concerning Bonhoeffer's outward conduct does not allow for the judgment that it followed a straight and unbroken course. One could point to the more general fact that Bonhoeffer was not active in the explicitly political sphere until his last phase as evidence for discontinuity even without noting the specific difference between leading seminarians in meditations on a literal interpretation on Sermon on the Mount in two monastery-like seminaries and contributing to planning sessions for an assassination attempt. The only way to avoid the implication that Bonhoeffer's statement is a plainly inaccurate assessment of his conduct is to somehow interpret it or take it to have meaning beyond the literal. I have argued throughout this work, for example, that Bonhoeffer's outward conduct was in fact consistent with his thinking throughout his career. There was in this very nuanced sense continuity in Bonhoeffer's outward conduct. Another way to legitimize Bonhoeffer's claim would be to emphasize the general continuity in his Christology or his Ethics. Specifically, as noted, there were his consistent notions of responding to Christ's call or being conformed to Christ in any given present. One could argue that Bonhoeffer's outward conduct was continuous in the sense that his particular actions were consistently the response to Christ's call or a conformation to Christ. That is, Bonhoeffer's outward conduct in each phase, although objectively different in each phase, was in each and every instance his particular way of responding to Christ's call.

As discussed above, if scholars take his statement literally they either make Bonhoeffer look like someone with an inaccurate self-percep-

---

57. *LPP*, 272.
58. Ibid., 363. The footnote reads, "To return home from the USA, see *DB*, 557ff."

tion or they broaden the definition of pacifism to the point where it loses its meaning (where it can include tyrannicide). These are two implications I have tried to avoid. Bonhoeffer's claim of "straight and unbroken" continuity simply must be taken as one piece and one type of evidence in addition to many others helpful in terms of judging discontinuities and continuities in his political involvement.

CONCLUSION

An analysis of his changing positions on the church-world relationship highlighting discontinuities should not be the occasion for a negative assessment of Bonhoeffer from the perspective of those who need to see continuity. His ability to undergo or exhibit significant change should have the very opposite effect. This ability shows a person and theologian who, in a thought-action dyad sensitive to his political and life contexts, stood out from contemporaries even if from our historical perspective he seemed to fail at points. It is true that Bonhoeffer's first phase was noteworthy only in his theology. His second-phase thinking, however, saw an interesting change to a church-world relationship which allowed him to criticize the church's and the state's policies on the Jews, even suggesting at one point that direct political action against the state was a possibility. While the majority of German theologians, church persons, and Christians, and even some of his own colleagues, were abiding by a theology wherein the church embraced wholeheartedly the negative aspects of the world as its own, Bonhoeffer was standing up for the rights of Jewish persons and calling for peace.

Bonhoeffer's phase-3 church-world vision supported action that, while arguably apolitical, sounded a brave call to a greater purity for the church and outright pacifism in the face of the world's warmongering. While the majority of German theologians, church persons, and Christians, and even some of his own colleagues, persisted in thinking and behavior that did not challenge war, Bonhoeffer was meditating on the Sermon on the Mount and training pastors for the church struggle. His phase-4 thinking saw a church-world vision that allowed him to enter the political realm for the purpose of confronting evil in the world. While the majority of German theologians, church persons and Christians, and even some of his colleagues, were abiding by a theology that allowed them to engage in the secular sphere only in an uncritical way, Bonhoeffer engaged fully in the secular realm without any restrictions or qualifications. While the majority of German theologians and church persons were adhering to a tainted gospel and remaining inactive in the face of the merciless slaughter of millions of Jews, outright aggressive war, and war crimes committed against conquered nations, Bonhoeffer was negotiating with the British and heading towards the hangman's pole.

Bonhoeffer was, indeed, in phases two through four, ahead of both his contemporaries and his colleagues. The discontinuities in his understanding of the church-world relationship are especially effective in highlighting his unique contribution to theology, the church struggle, and the political struggle against Hitler. Bonhoeffer's greatness lies in the fact that his thought was malleable and that his actions were consistent with his thought. His later life challenges those theologians, religious, or church members who hide comfortably in the detached home that a two-sphered reality builds for them. The reconciled reality of God's and our world was for Bonhoeffer worth preserving even at the risk of betraying the norms given by the Sermon on the Mount or those given in any interpretation of Luther's Two Kingdoms doctrine. For Dietrich Bonhoeffer, the consistency between his actions and his thought lends validity to both and thus defines him as an exemplary thinker and person.

Bibliography

PRIMARY SOURCES

Bonhoeffer, Dietrich. *Act and Being: Transcendental Philosophy and Ontology in Systematic Theology.* Edited by Wayne Whitson Floyd, Jr. Translated by H. Martin Rumscheidt. Dietrich Bonhoeffer Works (DBWE) 2. Minneapolis: Fortress, 1996.

———. "After Ten Years." Translated by Barbara and Martin Rumscheidt. Supplementary material translated by Douglas W. Stott. DBWE 8. Minneapolis: Fortress, 2009.

———. *Barcelona, Berlin, New York: 1928–1931.* Edited by Clifford J. Green. Translated by Douglass W. Stott. DBWE 10. Minneapolis: Fortress, 2008.

———. *Berlin: 1932–1933.* Edited by Larry L. Rasmussen. Translated by Isabel Best and David Higgins. Supplementary material translated by Douglas W. Stott. DBWE 12. Minneapolis: Fortress, 2009.

———. *Christ the Center.* Translated by Edwin H. Robertson. San Francisco: Harper & Row, 1978.

———. *Conspiracy and Imprisonment: 1940–1945.* Edited by Mark S. Brocker. Translated by Lisa E. Dahill. Supplementary material translated by Douglas W. Stott. DBWE 16. Minneapolis: Fortress, 2006.

———. *The Cost of Discipleship.* Translated by R. H. Fuller. New York: Macmillan, 1961.

———. *Creation and Fall: A Theological Exposition of Genesis 1–3.* Edited by John W. de Gruchy. Translated by Douglas S. Bax. DBWE 3. Minneapolis: Fortress, 1997.

———. *Dietrich Bonhoeffer Werke.* 17 vols. Munich: Kaiser, 1986–1999.

———. *Dietrich Bonhoeffer: Witness to Jesus Christ.* Edited by John W. deGruchy. The Making of Modern Theology: Nineteenth- and Twentieth-Century Texts. Minneapolis: Fortress, 1991.

———. *Discipleship.* Edited by Geffrey B. Kelly and John D. Godsey. Translated by Barbara Green and Reinhard Krauss. DBWE 4. Minneapolis: Fortress, 2001.

———. *Ethics.* Edited by Eberhard Bethge. Translated by Neville Horton Smith. New York: Macmillan, 1964.

———. *Ethics.* Edited by Clifford J. Green. Translated by Reinhard Krauss et al. DBWE 6. Minneapolis: Fortress, 2005.

———. *Fiction from Tegel Prison.* Edited by Clifford J. Green. Translated by Nancy Lukens. DBWE 7. Minneapolis: Fortress, 2000.

———. *Gesammelte Schriften.* 4 vols. Munich: Kaiser, 1958–1961.

———. *Gesammelte Schriften.* Vol. 1. Edited by Eberhard Bethge. Munich: Kaiser, 1965

———. *I Loved This People.* Translated by Keith R. Crim. Richmond: John Knox, 1964.

———. *Letters and Papers from Prison.* Edited by Eberhard Bethge. Translated by Reginald Fuller et al. Enlarged ed. New York: Macmillan, 1971.

———. *Letters and Papers from Prison*. Edited by John W. de Gruchy. Translated by Isabel Best et al. Supplementary material translated by Douglas W. Stott. DBWE 8. Minneapolis: Fortress, 2009.

———. *Life Together/Prayerbook of the Bible*. Edited by Geffrey B. Kelly. Translated by Daniel W. Bloesch and James H. Burtness. DBWE 5. Minneapolis: Fortress, 1996.

———. *Life Together*. Translated by John W. Doberstein. San Francisco: Harper & Row, 1954.

———. *London:1933–1935*. Edited by Keith Clements. Translated by Isabel Best. Supplementary material translated by Douglas W, Stott. DBWE 13. Minneapolis: Fortress, 2007.

———. *The Martyred Christian: 160 Readings*. Edited by Joan Winmill Brown. New York: Collier, 1983.

———. *Meditating on the Word*. Edited and Translated by David McI. Gracie. Cambridge, MA: Cowley, 1986.

———. *No Rusty Swords: Letters, Lectures and Notes 1928–1936*. Edited by Edwin H. Robertson. Translated by Edwin H. Robertson and John Bowden. New York: Harper & Row, 1965.

———. *Preface to Bonhoeffer: The Man and Two of his Shorter Writings*. Translated by John D. Godsey. Philadelphia: Fortress, 1965.

———. *Sanctorum Communio: A Theological Study of the Sociology of the Church*. Edited by Clifford J. Green. Translated by Reinhard Krauss and Nancy Lukens. DBWE 1. Minneapolis: Fortress, 1998.

———. *A Testament to Freedom: The Essential Writings of Dietrich Bonhoeffer*. Edited by Geoffrey B. Kelly and F. Burton Nelson. Rev ed. San Francisco: HarperSanFrancisco, 1995.

———. "A Theological Basis for the World Alliance." In *Dietrich Bonhoeffer: Witness to Jesus Christ*, edited by John W. de Gruchy, 98–110. The Making of Modern Theology: Nineteenth- and Twentieth-Century Texts. Minneapolis: Fortress, 1991.

———. *True Patriotism: Letters, Lectures and Notes 1939–1945*. Edited by Edwin H. Robertson. Translated by Edwin H. Robertson and John Bowden. New York: Harper & Row, 1973.

———. *The Way to Freedom: Letters, Lectures and Notes 1935–1939*. Edited by Edwin H. Robertson. Translated by Edwin H. Robertson and John Bowden. New York: Harper & Row, 1966.

———. *The Young Bonhoeffer: 1918–1927*. Edited by Paul Duane Matheny et al. Translated by Mary C. Nebelsick with the assistance of Douglas W. Stott. DBWE 9. Minneapolis: Fortress, 2003.

SECONDARY SOURCES

Althaus, Paul. *The Ethics of Martin Luther*. Translated with a foreword by Robert C. Schultz. Philadelphia: Fortress, 1972.

Altizer, Thomas J. J., and William Hamilton. *Radical Theology and the Death of God*. New York: Bobbs-Merrill, 1966.

Aveling, Harry G. "Dietrich Bonhoeffer's Christology." *Colloquium* 16 (1983) 23–30.

Bailey, Charles E. "*Gott Mit Uns*: Germany's Protestant Theologians in the First World War." PhD diss., University of Virginia, 1978.

Bibliography

Bailey, J. Martin and Douglass Gilbert. *The Steps of Bonhoeffer: A Pictorial Album*. New York: Macmillan, 1969.
Bainton, Roland H. *Christian Attitudes toward War and Peace: A Historical Survey and Critical Re-evaluation*. New York: Abingdon, 1960.
Bax, Douglas S. "From Constantine to Calvin: The Doctrine of the Just War." In *Theology & Violence: The South African Debate*, edited by Charles Villa-Vicencio, 147–71. Grand Rapids: Eerdmans, 1988.
Bergen, Doris L. *Twisted Cross: The German Christian Movement in the Third Reich*. Chapel Hill: University of North Carolina Press, 1996.
Bethge, Eberhard. *Bonhoeffer: Exile and Martyr*. Edited with an essay by John W. de Gruchy. New York: Seabury, 1974.
———. "Bonhoeffer's Pacifism." *Newsletter of the International Bonhoeffer Society for Archive and Research, English Language Section* 12 (1978) 6–7.
———. "The Challenge of Bonhoeffer's Life and Theology." In *World Come of Age: A Symposium on Dietrich Bonhoeffer*, edited by Ronald Gregor Smith, 22–92.
———. *Dietrich Bonhoeffer: A Biography*. Translated and revised by Victoria J. Barnett. Minneapolis: Fortress, 2000.
———. *Dietrich Bonhoeffer: Man of Vision—Man of Courage*. Edited by Edwin Robertson. Translated by Frank Clarke et al. New York: Harper & Row, 1970.
———. "Dietrich Bonhoeffers Weg vom 'Pazifismus' zur Vershwörung." In *Frieden das unumgängliche Wagnis*, 119–36. Internationales Bonhoeffer Forum 5. Munich: Kaiser, 1982.
———. *Friendship and Resistance: Essays on Dietrich Bonhoeffer*. Grand Rapids: Eerdmans, 1995.
Borg, Daniel R. *The Old Prussian Church and the Weimar Republic: A Study in Political Adjustment, 1917–1927*. Hanover, NH: University Press of New England, 1984.
Bosanquet, Mary. *The Life and Death of Dietrich Bonhoeffer*. Harper Colophon Books. New York: Harper & Row, 1973.
Bowden, John, and James Richmond, editors. *A Reader in Contemporary Theology*. London: SCM, 1967.
Brock, Brian. "Pacifism and Tyrannicide: Bonhoeffer's Christian Peace Ethic." *Studies in Christian Ethics* 18/3 (2005) 7–29.
Brown, Dale. *Biblical Pacifism: A Peace Church Perspective*. Elgin, IL: Brethren, 1986.
———. "Bonhoeffer and Pacifism." *Bulletin of the Peace Studies Institute* 11 (1981) 32–43.
Burtness, James H. *Shaping the Future: The Ethics of Bonhoeffer*. Philadelphia: Fortress, 1985.
Butler, Gerald A. "Karl Barth and Political Theology." PhD diss., Duke University, 1973.
Cameron, Euan. *The European Reformation*. Oxford: Clarendon, 1991.
Chapman, G. Clarke. "What Would Bonhoeffer Say to Christian Peacemakers Today?" In *Theology, Politics, and Peace*, edited by Theodore Runyon, 167–75. Maryknoll, NY: Orbis, 1989.
Chiba, Shin, et al., editors. *Christian Ethics in Ecumenical Context: Theology, Culture, and Politics in Dialogue*. Grand Rapids: Eerdmans, 1995.
Clements, Keith. "Ecumenical Witness for Peace." In *The Cambridge Companion to Dietrich Bonhoeffer*, edited by John W. de Gruchy, 154–72. Cambridge Companions to Religion. Cambridge: Cambridge University Press, 1999.

———. "Worldliness or Unworldliness? The Issue between Bonhoeffer and Bultmann as Seen by Ronald Gregor Smith." *Scottish Journal of Theology* 34 (1981) 531–49.
Cochrane, Arthur C. *The Church's Confession under Hitler*. Philadelphia: Westminster, 1962.
Conway, J. S. *The Nazi Persecution of the Churches 1933–45*. New York: Basic Books, 1968.
Cornwell, John. *Hitler's Pope: The Secret History of Pius XII*. New York: Viking, 1999.
Cox, Harvey. "Using and Misusing Bonhoeffer." *Christianity and Crisis* 24 (1964) 195–99.
Craig, Gordon A. *Germany: 1866–1945*. Oxford History of Modern Europe. Oxford: Clarendon, 1980.
Dahill, Lisa E. *Reading from the Underside of Selfhood: Bonhoeffer and Spiritual Formation*. With a foreword by Martin Rumscheidt. Princeton Theological Monograph Series 95. Eugene, OR: Pickwick Publications, 2009.
Davis, Dena. "Gandhi and Bonhoeffer." *Bulletin of the Peace Studies Institute* 11 (1981) 44–49.
Day, Thomas I. *Dietrich Bonhoeffer on Christian Community and Common Sense*. Toronto Studies in Theology 11. Bonhoeffer Series 2. New York: Mellen, 1982.
De Gruchy, John W. *Bonhoeffer and South Africa*. Grand Rapids: Eerdmans, 1984.
———, editor. *The Cambridge Companion to Dietrich Bonhoeffer*. Cambridge Companions to Religion. Cambridge: Cambridge University Press, 1999.
———. *Christianity and Democracy: A Theology for a Just World Order*. Cambridge Studies in Ideology and Religion. Cambridge: Cambridge University Press, 1995.
———. "The Reception of Bonhoeffer's Theology." In *The Cambridge Companion to Dietrich Bonhoeffer*, edited by John W. de Gruchy, 93–109. Cambridge Companions to Religion. Cambridge: Cambridge University Press, 1999.
Deutsch, Harold C. *The Conspiracy against Hitler in the Twilight War*. Minneapolis: University of Minnesota Press, 1968.
Dietrich, Donald. "Catholic Resistance to Biological and Racist Eugenics in the Third Reich." In *Germans against Nazism*, edited by Francis R. Nicosia and Lawrence D. Stokes, 137–55. New York: Berg, distributed by St. Martin's, 1990.
Dombrowski, Daniel A. *Christian Pacifism*. Ethics and Action. Philadelphia: Temple University Press, 1991.
Douglass, J. Robert. "Dietrich Bonhoeffer: The Violent Pacifist." *Ashland Theological Journal* 27 (1995) 41–53.
Doyle, Dennis M. *The Church Emerging from Vatican II: A Popular Approach to Contemporary Catholicism*. Mystic, CT: Twenty-Third, 1992.
Dramm, Sabine. *Dietrich Bonhoeffer and the Resistance*. Translated by Margaret Kohl. Minneapolis: Fortress, 2009.
Duchrow, Ulrich, and Dorothea Millwood, editors. *Lutheran Churches—Salt or Mirror of Society?—Case Studies on the Theory and Practice of the Two Kingdoms Doctrine*. Geneva: Lutheran World Federation Department of Studies, 1977.
Dulles, Allen Welsh. *Germany's Underground: The Anti-Nazi Resistance*. New York: DaCapo, 2000.
Dulles, Avery. *The Dimensions of the Church: A Postconciliar Reflection*. Woodstock Papers: Occasional Essays for Theology 8. Westminster, MD: Newman, 1967.
———. *Models of the Church*. Expanded edition. Garden City, NY: Image, 1987.
Dumas, André. *Dietrich Bonhoeffer: Theologian of Reality*. Translated by Robert McAfee Brown. New York: Macmillan, 1968.

———. "Religion and Reality in the Work of Dietrich Bonhoeffer." In *A Bonhoeffer Legacy: Essays in Understanding*, edited by A. J. Klaussen, 258–67. Grand Rapids: Eerdmans, 1981.

Durnbaugh, Donald F. "The Brethren and Non-Resistance." In *The Pacifist Impulse in Historical Perspective*, edited by Harvey L. Dyck, 125–44. Toronto: University of Toronto Press, 1996.

Dyck, Harvey L., editor. *The Pacifist Impulse in Historical Perspective*. Toronto: University of Toronto Press, 1996.

Eldridge, Stephen W. "Ideological Incompatibility: The Forced Fusion of Nazism and Its Impact on Anti-Semitism in the Third Reich." *International Social Science Review* 81:3/4 (2006) 151–65.

Eley, Geoff, editor. *Society, Culture, and the State in Germany 1870–1930*. Social History, Popular Culture, and Politics in Germany. Ann Arbor: University of Michigan Press, 1997.

Ericksen, Robert P. "A Radical Minority: Resistance in the German Protestant Church." In *Germans against Nazism: Essays in Honour of Peter Hoffmann*, edited by Francis R. Nicosia and Lawrence D. Stokes, 115–33. New York: Berg, distributed by St. Martin's, 1990.

———. *Theologians under Hitler: Gerhard Kittel, Paul Althaus, and Emmanuel Hirsch*. New Haven: Yale University Press, 1985.

Ericksen, Robert P., and Susannah Heschel, editors. *Betrayal: German Churches and the Holocaust*. Minneapolis: Fortress, 1999.

Feil, Ernst. "Dietrich Bonhoeffer's Understanding of the World." In *A Bonhoeffer Legacy: Essays in Understanding*, edited by A.J. Klaussen, 237–55. Grand Rapids: Eerdmans, 1981.

———. *The Theology of Dietrich Bonhoeffer*. Translated by Martin Rumscheidt. Philadelphia: Fortress, 1985.

Feige, Franz G. M. "Responses of German Protestant Theology to National Socialism: Background, Typology and Evaluation." PhD diss., Drew University, 1988.

Fortin, Ernest L. *Classical Christianity and the Political Order: Reflections of the Theologico-Political Order*. Edited by J. Brian Benestad. Ernest Fortin Collected Essays 2. Lanham, MD: Rowman & Littlefield 1996.

Floyd, Wayne Whitson, Jr. "Bonhoeffer's Literary Legacy." In *The Cambridge Companion to Dietrich Bonhoeffer*, edited by John W. de Gruchy, 71–92. Cambridge Companions to Religion. Cambridge: Cambridge University Press, 1999.

Gellately, Robert. *Backing Hitler: Consent and Coercion in Nazi Germany*. Oxford: Oxford University Press, 2002.

Glenthøj, Jørgen. "Dietrich Bonhoeffer's Way between Resistance and Submission." In *A Bonhoeffer Legacy: Essays in Understanding*, edited by A. J. Klassen, 170–77. Grand Rapids: Eerdmans, 1981.

———. "Dietrich Bonhoeffers Weg vom Pazifismus zum politischen Widerstand." In *Dietrich Bonhoeffer heute*, edited by Rainer Mayer and Peter Zimmerling, 41–57. ABCteam 490. Geissen: Brunnen, 1992.

Godsey, John D. *The Theology of Dietrich Bonhoeffer*. Philadelphia: Westminster, 1960.

Godsey, John D., and Geffrey Kelly. *Ethical Responsibility: Bonhoeffer's Legacy to the Churches*. Toronto Studies in Theology 6. Lewiston, NY: Mellen, 1981.

Goldberg, Michael. "Bonhoeffer and the Limits of Jewish-Christian Dialogue." *Books and Religion* 14 (1986) 3–4.

Gould, William Blair. *The Worldly Christian: Bonhoeffer on Discipleship*. Philadelphia: Fortress, 1967.
Green, Clifford J. *Bonhoeffer: A Theology of Socialty*. Rev. ed. Grand Rapids: Eerdmans, 1999.
———. "Bonhoeffer's Christian Ethics in Resistance to Tyranny and Genocide." Paper delivered at the Conference called *Bonhoeffer's Dilemma: The Ethics of Violence*, at Pennsylvania State University, October 28–31, 1999.
———. "Bonhoeffer's 'Non-Religious Christianity' as Public Theology." *Dialog* 26 (1985) 275–81.
———. "Pacifism and Tyrannicide: Bonhoeffer's Christian Peace Ethic." *Studies in Christian Ethics* 18/3 (2005) 31–47.
———. "Sociality and Church in Bonhoeffer's 1933 Christology." *Scottish Journal of Theology* 21 (1968) 416–34.
Hamilton, Kenneth. *Life in One's Stride: A Short Study in Dietrich Bonhoeffer*. Grand Rapids: Eerdmans, 1968.
Hamilton, William Hughes. "Bonhoeffer's Christology and Ethic United." *Christianity in Crisis* 24 (1964) 195–99.
Harnack, Adolf von. *What Is Christianity?* Translated by Thomas Baily Saunders. Fortress Texts in Modern Theology. Philadelphia: Fortress, 1986.
Hartwell, Herbert. *The Theology of Karl Barth: An Introduction*. Philadelphia: Westminster, 1964.
Hauerwas, Stanley. *Performing the Faith: Bonhoeffer and the Practice of Nonviolence*. Grand Rapids: Brazos, 2004.
Hauerwas, Stanley et al., editors. *The Wisdom of the Cross: Essays in Honor of John Howard Yoder*. Grand Rapids: Eerdmans, 1999.
Haynes, Stephen R. *The Bonhoeffer Legacy: Post-Holocaust Perspectives*. Minneapolis: Fortress, 2006.
———. *The Bonhoeffer Phenomenon: Portraits of a Protestant Saint*. Minneapolis: Fortress, 2004.
Heimbucher, Martin. *Christusfriede-Weltfrieden: Dietrich Bonhoeffers kirchlicher und politischer Kampf gegen den Krieg Hitlers und seine theologische Begründung*. Munich: Kaiser, 1997.
Heschel, Susannah. *The Aryan Jesus: Christian Theologians and the Bible in Nazi Germany*. Princeton: Princeton University Press, 2008.
Heuser, Stefan. "The Cost of Citizenship: Disciple and Citizen in Bonhoeffer's Political Ethics." *Studies in Christian Ethics* 18/3 (2005) 49–69.
Hinnebusch, Paul. *Secular Holiness: Spirituality for Contemporary Man*. Denville, NJ: Dimension, 1971.
Helmreich, Ernst Christian. *The German Churches under Hitler: Background, Struggle, and Epilogue*. Detroit: Wayne State University Press, 1979.
Heuser, Stefan. "The Cost of Citizenship: Disciple and Citizen in Bonhoeffer's Political Ethics." *Studies in Christian Ethics* 18/3 (2005) 49–69.
Hoover, A. J. "God and Germany in the Great War: The View of the Protestant Pastors." *Canadian Review of Studies in Nationalism* 14 (1987) 65–81.
———. *The Gospel of Nationalism: German Patriotic Preaching from Napoleon to Versailles*. Stuttgart: Steiner, 1986.
Hopper, David H. *A Dissent on Bonhoeffer*. Philadelphia: Westminster, 1975.

Hordern, Richard P. "Lutheran Theology and the Witness of Peace." *Word & World* 6 (1986) 133–60.
Hunsinger, George. *Disruptive Grace: Studies in the Theology of Karl Barth.* Grand Rapids: Eerdmans, 2000.
———, editor and translator. *Karl Barth and Radical Politics.* Philadelphia: Westminster, 1976.
Jehle, Herbert. "Dietrich Bonhoeffer on War and Peace." In *A Bonhoeffer Legacy: Essays in Understanding*, edited by A. J. Klassen, 362–66. Grand Rapids: Eerdmans, 1981.
Jenkins, Julian. "War Theology, 1914 and Germany's *Sonderweg*: Luther's Heirs and Protestantism." *Journal of Religious History* 15 (1989) 292–310.
Kaltenborn, Carl-Jürgen. "Adolf von Harnack and Bonhoeffer." In *A Bonhoeffer Legacy: Essays in Understanding*, edited by A. J. Klassen, 48–57. Grand Rapids: Eerdmans, 1981.
Kaplan, Marion A. *Between Dignity and Despair: Jewish Life in Nazi Germany.* Studies in Jewish History. New York: Oxford University Press, 1998.
Kelly, Geffrey B. "Bonhoeffer's Theology of History and Revelation" in *A Bonhoeffer Legacy: Essays in Understanding*, edited by J. A. Klassen, 89–130. Grand Rapids: Eerdmans, 1981.
———. "Interview with Jean Lasserre." *Union Seminary Quarterly Review* 27 (1972) 149–60.
———. *Liberating Faith: Bonhoeffer's Message for Today.* Minneapolis: Augsburg, 1984.
Kelly, Geffrey B., and John D. Godsey. "Editors' Introduction to the English Edition." In *Discipleship*, by Dietrich Bonhoeffer, edited by Geffrey B. Kelly and John D. Godsey, 1–33. Translated by Barbara Green and Reinhard Krauss. DBWE 4. Minneapolis: Fortress, 2001.
Kelly, Geffrey B., and F. Burton Nelson. *The Cost of Moral Leadership: The Spirituality of Dietrich Bonhoeffer.* Grand Rapids, Eerdmans, 2003.
Kershaw, Ian. *Hitler: 1889–1936: Hubris.* New York: Norton, 1998.
Klan, J. S. "Luther's Resistance Teaching and the German Church Struggle under Hitler." *Journal of Religious History* 14 (1987) 432–43.
Klassen, A. J., editor. *A Bonhoeffer Legacy: Essays in Understanding.* Grand Rapids: Eerdmans, 1981.
Koch, Robert F. "The Theological Responses of Karl Barth and Dietrich Bonhoeffer to Church-State Relations in Germany, 1933–1945." PhD diss., Northwestern University, 1988.
Kraft, Kenneth, editor. *Inner Peace, World Peace: Essays on Buddhism and Nonviolence.* SUNY Series on Buddhist Studies. Albany: State University of New York Press, 1992.
Kuhns, William. *In Pursuit of Dietrich Bonhoeffer.* Dayton: Pflaum, 1967.
Laney, James T. "An Examination of Bonhoeffer's Ethical Contextualism." In *A Bonhoeffer Legacy: Essays in Understanding*, edited by A. J. Klassen, 294–313. Grand Rapids: Eerdmans, 1981.
Lindt, Andreas. "Dietrich Bonhoeffer und der Weg vom christlichen Glauben zum politischen Handeln." *Reformatio* 16 (1967) 251–57.
Lovin, Robin W. *Christian Faith and Public Choices: The Social Ethics of Barth, Brunner and Bonhoeffer.* Philadelphia: Fortress, 1984.
Marsh, Charles. *Reclaiming Dietrich Bonhoeffer: The Promise of His Theology.* New York: Oxford University Press, 1994.

Marty, Martin E., editor. *The Place of Bonhoeffer: Problems and Possibilities in His Thought*. New York: Association Press, 1962.

Matheson, Peter, editor. *The Third Reich and the Christian Churches*. Edinburgh T. & T. Clark, 1981.

McKim, Donald K., editor. *How Karl Barth Changed My Mind*. Grand Rapids: Eerdmans, 1986.

Metaxas, Eric. *Bonhoeffer: Pastor, Martyr, Prophet, Spy; A Righteous Gentile vs. The Third Reich*. Nashville: Nelson, 2010.

Miller, William Robert. *Nonviolence: A Christian Interpretation*. New York: Schocken, 1964.

Mohaupt, Lutz. "Zwischen Pazifismus und Verschworung: Gerechtigkeit und Schult im Denken Dietrich Bonhoeffers." *Luther* 57 (1986) 127–43.

Molnar, Thomas. *Politics and the State: The Catholic View*. Chicago: Franciscan Herald, 1980

Moltmann, Jürgen, and Jürgen Weissbach. *Two Studies in the Theology of Bonhoeffer*. New York: Scribner, 1967.

Morton, Thomas. *Faith and Violence: Christian Teaching and Christian Practice*. Notre Dame: University of Notre Dame Press, 1968.

Moses, John A. "Bonhoeffer's Germany: The Political Context." In *The Cambridge Companion to Dietrich Bonhoeffer*, edited by John W. de Gruchy, 3–21. Cambridge Companions to Religion. Cambridge: Cambridge University Press, 1999.

———. "The British and German Churches and the Perception of War, 1908–1914." *War & Society* 5 (1987) 23–44.

———. "Dietrich Bonhoeffer's Repudiation of Protestant German War Theology." *Journal of Religious History* 30 (2006) 354–70.

Müller, Hanfried. *Von der Kirche zur Welt: Ein Betrag zu der Beziehung des Wortes Gottes auf die Societas in Dietrich Bonhoeffers theologischen Entwicklung*. Leipzig: Koehler & Amelang, 1961.

Nation, Mark Thiessen. "Discipleship in a World Full of Nazis: Dietrich Bonhoeffer's Polyphonic Pacifism as Social Ethics." In *The Wisdom of the Cross: Essays in Honor of John Howard Yoder*, edited by Stanley Hauerwas, et al., 249–77. Grand Rapids: Eerdmans, 1999.

———. "The First Word Christians Have to Say about Violence Is 'Church': On Bonhoeffer, Baptists and Becoming a Peace Church." In *Faithfulness and Fortitude: In Conversation with the Theological Ethics of Stanley Hauerwas*, edited by Stanley Hauerwas, et al., 83–115. Edinburgh: T. & T. Clark, 2000.

———. "Pacifist and Enemy of the State: Bonhoeffer's 'Straight and Unbroken Course' from Costly Discipleship to Conspiracy." *Journal of Theology for Southern Africa* 77 (1991) 61–77.

Nelson, F. Burton. "The Relationship of Jean Lasserre to Dietrich Bonhoeffer's Peace Concerns in the Struggle of Church and Culture." *Union Seminary Quarterly Review* 40 (1985) 71–84.

Nicosia, Francis R., and Lawrence D. Stokes, editors. *Germans against Nazism: Essays in Honour of Peter Hoffmann*. New York: Berg, distributed by St. Martin's, 1990.

Niebuhr, H. Richard. *Christ and Culture*. New York: HarperCollins, 1951.

Nuttall, Geoffrey F. *Christian Pacifism in History*. Oxford: Blackwell, 1958.

Oberman, Heiko A. *Luther: Man between God and the Devil*. Translated by Eileen Walliser-Schwarzbart. New York: Image, 1992.

Bibliography

Ott, Heinrich. *Reality and Faith: The Theological Legacy of Dietrich Bonhoeffer.* Philadelphia: Fortress, 1972.
Palmer, Russell W. "Christology of Dietrich Bonhoeffer." *Evangelical Quarterly* 49 (1977) 132-40.
Pangritz, Andreas. *Karl Barth in the Theology of Dietrich Bonhoeffer.* Translated by Barbara and Martin Rumscheidt. Grand Rapids: Eerdmans, 2000.
―――. "'Who Is Jesus Christ, for Us, Today?'" In *The Cambridge Companion to Dietrich Bonhoeffer*, edited by John W. de Gruchy, 154-72. Cambridge Companions to Religion. Cambridge: Cambridge University Press, 1999.
Peachy, Paul, editor. *Peace, Politics, and the People of God.* Philadelphia: Fortress, 1986.
Peters, Tiemo Rainer. *Die Präsenz des Politischen in der Theologie Dietrich Bonhoeffers: Eine historische Untersuchung in systematischer Absicht.* Gesellschaft und Theologie Abteilung Systematische Beiträge 18. Munich: Kaiser, 1976.
―――. "Orders and Interventions: Political Ethics in the Theology of Dietrich Bonhoeffer." *A Bonhoeffer Legacy: Essays in Understanding*, edited by A. J. Klassen, 314-29. Grand Rapids: Eerdmans, 1981.
Pfeifer, Hans. "Editor's Afterword to the German Edition." In *The Young Bonhoeffer: 1918-1927*, edited by Paul Duane Matheny et al., 563-78. Translated by Mary C. Nebelsick with the assistance of Douglass W. Stott. DBWE 9. Minneapolis: Fortress, 2003.
Phillips, John A. *Christ for Us in the Theology of Dietrich Bonhoeffer.* New York: Harper & Row, 1967.
Plant, Stephen. "The Sacrament of Reality: Dietrich Bonhoeffer on Ethics for Christian Citizens." *Studies in Christian Ethics* 18/3 (2005) 71-87.
Pongatz, Walter. "Suggestions for a Public Theology: Dietrich Bonhoeffer's Work as a Stimulus for a Public Theology." PhD diss., Drew University, 1991.
Power, Michael. *Religion in the Reich.* London: Longmans, Green and Co., 1939.
Rasmussen, Larry L. "Bonhoeffer, Gandhi and Resistance." In *Reflections on Bonhoeffer: Essays in Honor of F. Burton Nelson*, edited by F. Burton Nelson and Geffrey Kelly, 50-55. Chicago: Covenant, 1999.
―――. "The Ethics of Responsible Action." In *The Cambridge Companion to Dietrich Bonhoeffer*, edited by John W. de Gruchy, 206-25. Cambridge Companions to Religion. Cambridge: Cambridge University Press, 1999.
―――. *Dietrich Bonhoeffer: Reality and Resistance.* Louisville: Westminster John Knox, 2005.
Rasmussen, Larry L., with Renate Bethge. *Dietrich Bonhoeffer: His Significance for North Americans.* Minneapolis: Fortress, 1990.
Reist, Benjamin A. *The Promise of Bonhoeffer.* The Promise of Theology. Philadelphia: Lippincott, 1969.
Reynolds, Terrence. *The Coherence of Life without God before God: The Problem of Earthly Desires in the Later Theology of Dietrich Bonhoeffer.* Lanham, MD: University Press of America, 1989.
Roberts, J. Deotis. *Bonhoeffer and King: Speaking Truth to Power.* Louisville: Westminster John Knox, 2005.
Robertson, E. H. *Christians against Hitler.* London: SCM, 1962
Robertson, Edwin. *The Shame and the Sacrifice: The Life and Martyrdom of Dietrich Bonhoeffer.* New York: Macmillan, 1988.
Robinson, John A. T. *Honest to God.* Philadelphia: Westminster, 1963.

———. *The Human Face of God.* Philadelphia: Westminster, 1973.
Rognon, Frédéric. "Pacifism et Tyrannicide chez Jean Lasserre et Dietrich Bonhoeffer: Première Partie: L'Établissement des faits Historiques." *Etudes Théologiques & Religieuses* 80:1 (2005) 1–23.
———. "Pacifism et Tyrannicide chez Jean Lasserre et Dietrich Bonhoeffer: Seconde Partie: L'Interprétation des Incidences Théologiques." *Etudes Théologiques & Religieuses* 80/2 (2005) 159–76.
Rosenbaum, Stanley N. "Dietrich Bonhoeffer: A Jewish View." *Journal of Ecumenical Studies* 18 (1981) 301–7.
Rothfels, Hans. *The German Opposition to Hitler: An Appraisal.* Translated by Lawrence Wilson. New revised edition. Foundation for Foreign Affairs Series 6. Chicago: Regnery, 1962.
Rumscheidt, Martin. "The Formation of Bonhoeffer's Theology." In *The Cambridge Companion to Dietrich Bonhoeffer,* edited by John W. de Gruchy, 50–70. Cambridge Companions to Religion. Cambridge: Cambridge University Press, 1999.
Runia, Klass. "Bonhoeffer and His Political Stance." *Themelios* 8 (1972) 3–9.
Runyon, Theodore, editor. *Theology, Politics and Peace.* Maryknoll, NY: Orbis, 1989.
Rupp, George. *Culture-Protestantism: German Liberal Theology at the Turn of the Twentieth Century.* AAR Studies in Religion 15. Missoula, MT: Scholars, 1977.
Scharffenorth, Ersnt-Albert. "Bonhoeffers Pazifismus." In *Schopferische Nachgfolge,* edited by Cristofer Frey et al., 363–87. Texte und Materialien der Forschungsstätte der Evangelischen Studiengemeinschaft A 5. Heidelberg: Forschungstätte d. Evang. Studiengemeinschaft, 1978.
Schoelles, Patricia Ann. "Discipleship and Social Ethics: A Study in Light of the Works of Dietrich Bonhoeffer and Johann B. Metz." PhD diss., University of Notre Dame, 1984.
Shin, Chiba. "Christianity on the Even of Postmodernity: Karl Barth and Dietrich Bonhoeffer." In *Christian Ethics in Ecumenical Context: Theology, Culture, and Politics in Dialogue,* edited by Shin Chiba et al., 167–204. Grand Rapids: Eerdmans, 1995.
Shirer, William L. *The Rise and Fall of the Third Reich: A History of Nazi Germany.* New York: Simon & Schuster, 1960.
Smith, Ronald Gregor, editor. *World Come of Age: A Symposium on Dietrich Bonhoeffer.* London: Collins, 1967.
Soelle, Dorothee. *Political Theology.* Translated by John Shelley. Philadelphia: Fortress, 1974.
Soosten, Joachim von. "Editor's Afterword to the German Edition." In *Sanctorum Communio: A Theological Study of the Sociology of the Church.* Edited by Clifford J. Green. Translated by Reinhard Krauss and Nancy Lukens. DBWE 1. Minneapolis: Fortress, 1998.
Spielvogel, Jackson J. *Hitler and Nazi Germany: A History.* Englewood Cliffs, NJ: Prentice Hall, 1988.
Stassen, Glen Harold. "Healing the Rift between the Sermon on the Mount and Christian Ethics." *Studies in Christian Ethics* 18/3 (2005) 89–105.
Stayer, James M. "Anabaptists and the Sword Revisited: The Trend from Radicalism to Apoliticism." In *The Pacifist Impulse in Historical Perspective,* edited by Harvey L. Dyck, 111–24. Toronto: University of Toronto Press, 1996.

Steigmann-Gall, Richard. *The Holy Reich: Nazi Conceptions of Christianity, 1919-1945.* Cambridge: Cambridge University Press, 2003.
Sutherland, Stewart R. "Ethics and Transcendence in Bonhoeffer." *Scottish Journal of Theology* 30 (1977) 543-54.
Taylor, Michael J., editor. *The Sacred and the Secular.* Englewood Cliffs, NJ: Prentice-Hall, 1968.
Thils, Gustave. *A "Non-Religious" Christianity?* Staten Island, NY: Alba House, 1970.
Tödt, Heinz Eduard. *Authentic Faith: Bonhoeffer's Theological Ethics in Context.* Edited by Glen Harold Stassen. Translated by David Stassen and Ilse Tödt. Grand Rapids: Eerdmans, 1993.
———. "Dietrich Bonhoeffer's Decisions in the Crisis Years 1929-33." *Studies in Christian Ethics* 18/3 (2005) 107-23.
Troeltsch, Ernst. *The Social Teaching of the Christian Churches.* 2 vols. Translated by Olive Wyon. New York: Harper & Row, 1960.
Vorkink Peter, editor. *Bonhoeffer in a World Come of Age.* Philadelphia: Fortress, 1968.
Walker, Hamish. "The Incarnation and Crucifixion in Bonhoeffer's *Cost of Discipleship*." *Scottish Journal of Theology* 21 (1968) 407-15.
Weikhart, Richard. *The Myth of Dietrich Bonhoeffer: Is His Theology Evangelical?* San Francisco: International Scholars, 1997.
Welch, Claude. *Protestant Thought in the Nineteenth Century*, 2 vols. New Haven: Yale University Press, 1972.
Wilcken, John. "Bonhoeffer: Church in Conflict." *Heythrop Journal* 10 (1969) 162-79.
———. "The Ecclesiology of *Ethics* and the Prison Writings." In *A Bonhoeffer Legacy: Essays in Understanding*, edited by A. J. Klassen, 195-203. Grand Rapids: Eerdmans, 1981.
Williamson, René de Visme. *Politics and Protestant Theology: An Interpretation of Tillich, Barth, Bonhoeffer, and Brunner.* Baton Rouge: Louisiana State University Press, 1976.
Willmer, Haddon. "Costly Discipleship." In *The Cambridge Companion to Dietrich Bonhoeffer*, edited by John W. de Gruchy, 176-89. Cambridge Companions to Religion. Cambridge: Cambridge University Press, 1999.
Wilson, John E. *Introduction to Modern Theology: Trajectories in the German Tradition* Louisville: Westminster John Knox, 2007.
Wind, Renate. *Dietrich Bonhoeffer: A Spoke in the Wheel.* Translated by John Bowden. Grand Rapids: Eerdmans, 1992.
Wink, Walter. "Toying with Violence." *Witness* 77 (1994) 6.
Woelfel, James W. *Bonhoeffer's Theology: Classical and Revolutionary.* Nashville: Abingdon, 1970.
Wogaman, J. Philip. *Christian Perspectives on Politics.* Revised and expanded ed. Louisville: Westminster John Knox, 2000.
Wright, J. R. C. *"Above Parties": The Political Attitudes of the German Protestant Church Leadership 1918-1933.* Oxford Historical Monographs. Oxford: Oxford University Press, 1974.
Wüstenberg, Ralf K. *A Theology of Life: Dietrich Bonhoeffer's Religionless Christianity.* Translated by Doug Stott. Grand Rapids: Eerdmans, 1998.
Yoder, John H. *Karl Barth and the Problem of War.* Studies in Christian Ethics. Nashville: Abingdon, 1970.

———. *Nevertheless: The Varieties and Shortcomings of Religious Pacifism.* Rev. ed. Scottdale, PA: Herald, 1992.

———. *The Pacifism of Karl Barth.* Washington DC: The Church Peace Mission, 1964.

———. *The Politics of Jesus.* 2nd ed. Grand Rapids: Eerdmans, 1994.

Zabel, James A. *Nazism and the Pastors.* AAR Dissertation Series 14. Missoula, MT: Scholars, 1976.

Zerner, Ruth. "Church, State and the 'Jewish Question.'" In *The Cambridge Companion to Dietrich Bonhoeffer*, edited by John W. de Gruchy, 190–205. Cambridge Companions to Religion. Cambridge: Cambridge University Press, 1999.

———. "Dietrich Bonhoeffer's American Experiences: People, Letters and Papers from Union Seminary." *Union Seminary Quarterly Review* 31 (1976) 261–82.

———. "Dietrich Bonhoeffer's Views on the State and History." In *A Bonhoeffer Legacy: Essays in Understanding*, edited by A. J. Klassen, 131–57. Grand Rapids: Eerdmans, 1981.

Zimmermann, Wolf-Dieter, and Ronald GregorSmith, editors. *I Knew Dietrich Bonhoeffer.* Translated by Käthe Gregor Smith. London: Collins, 1966.

Index

Abwehr, 2, 322, 325, 327, 329, 330, 335
Abyssinian Baptist Church, 140, 146
Act and Being (Bonhoeffer), 116, 119–32, 135, 136
Adam, 86, 87, 87n39, 87n41, 88, 88n42, 97n72, 125n171, 126, 126n175, 127n176, 128, 135
Africa, 55, 55n51, 76, 326
African-Americans, 39, 145, 146, 146n29, 151
"After Ten Years" (Bonhoeffer), 299, 303, 304
Althaus, Paul, x, xii, 78n4, 154n52, 168n117, 240n132, 245n245
Ambrose, St., 362
America, 1n2, 3n13, 32, 132, 138, 140, 140n2, 142, 145, 146, 146n29, 147, 149–52, 155, 161, 171, 198, 198n234, 206, 206n239, 257, 259, 260, 272, 281, 320, 337, 338
Ammundsen, Bishop Valdeman, 217, 217n34, 267
Anabaptists, 78n4, 91, 245n154, 255n189, 361, 361n31, 366
Aquinas, Thomas, 99, 99n81
Aryan Clauses, 1n3, 137, 139, 155, 181, 190–92, 195, 196, 210n5, 211, 262
asceticism, 25, 368
Asmussen, Paster Hans, 234
Augustine, St., 362
Auschwitz, 284

Baillie, John, 140, 147, 150n46
Bainton, Roland H., 16n47, 255n189, 361n30, 362n33, 362nn35–36, 363nn42–43, 364, 366, 366n51
Barcelona, 76, 104, 105, 105n92, 105n96, 106–8, 108n107, 109, 116, 116n132, 118, 118n141, 119, 120, 125, 128, 134, 134n188, 135, 136n193, 140n5, 145, 149, 152n48, 157, 159, 165, 166, 200, 202, 219, 220, 288, 301, 345, 357, 358
Barmen Declaration, 1n3, 71, 71n128, 139, 228n85
Barmen Snyod, 1n3, 71, 71n128, 139, 208, 212, 213, 213n17, 216, 217, 224, 228, 228n85, 231n97, 232, 234, 259, 268, 270, 271, 279
Barth, Karl, x, xi, 7, 7n18, 8n21, 10, 34n83, 39, 42n1, 56, 56n53, 58,n67, 79n6, 80, 80n10, 82, 82n18, 94, 118n140, 123, 129, 143n17, 146, 147, 161, 161n77, 172n128, 179, 188n196, 189n202, 190n208, 191, 192n215, 213, 234, 265, 274n252, 277, 311, 311n118, 317, 339n213, 342, 344n1; Bonhoeffer's criticism of in *Act and Being*, 124, 124n167, 129; influence on Bonhoeffer, 71–73; letter to Bonhoeffer, 266n233, 278

Beck, Colonel-General Ludwig, 261, 325
Bell, Dr. George K. A., Bishop of Chichester, 212n16, 216, 217n34, 218n37, 260, 262, 263, 263n221, 265, 323–26, 330
Berlin, 45, 48, 53, 58, 68n119, 139, 161–63, 163n90, 189, 190, 193, 210, 214, 216, 217n34, 225n72, 258n199, 262, 263, 263n221, 282, 310, 320, 329, 330; Bonhoeffer studies/teaches in, 5n15, 38, 55–56, 56n53, 76, 80, 80n11, 81n15, 82, 114, 119, 134, 136n193, 140n5, 147n35, 155, 176n152, 179, 180n165, 277, 278
Bethge, Eberhard, 3n13, 4n15, 8n21, 9, 10, 10nn24–25, 14, 17, 17n49, 19n50, 44, 48, 50, 50n30, 51, 74, 74n136, 106, 109, 118, 120, 130, 131, 131n184, 132, 140n5, 145n27, 155n56, 198, 206n239, 214, 260, 261, 270, 282, 309, 318, 319, 328, 331, 332, 336, 338, 372, 373
Bethge, Renate (Schleicher), 49, 52n38
Bismarck, Otto von, 42, 43, 43n2, 46, 48, 48, 48n22, 57
Black Reichswehr (Black Corps), 53
Bodelschwingh, Friedrich von, 189, 191, 193, 217n34
Bonhoeffer, Dietrich; continuity and discontinuity in thought or action, 6–11, 197–206, 272–78, 333–40, 372–75; conversion, 51, 136, 197–199, 342; death (hanging), 2, 331; death of brother (Walter), 50–51; family experience with war, 50–51; family experience with church, 51–52; friendship with Albert F. Fisher (Frank), 137, 145–46; friendship with Jean Lasserre, 2n8, 19n52, 32, 137, 143–46, 151, 160n74, 264, 342; friendship with the Lehmann family, 146; interrrogation, 329–31; reason for studying theology, 52; self-designation as pacifist, 1, 1n2
Bonhoeffer, Friedrich (grandfather), 43n3, 45
Bonhoeffer, Julie Tafel (grandmother), 43n3, 45, 45n10
Bonhoeffer, Karl (father), 43n3, 45, 46, 48, 50
Bonhoeffer, Karl-Friedrich (brother), 48, 49, 50, 52n40
Bonhoeffer, Klaus (brother), 48, 52n40
Bonhoeffer Legacy: Post-Holocaust Perspectives, The (Haynes), 38
Bonhoeffer Phenomenon: Portraits of a Protestant Saint, The (Haynes), 74
Bonhoeffer, Walter (brother), 50, 51
Borg, Daniel R., 47n20, 60, 60n76, 60n79, 61, 61n82, 62n85, 63n91, 63n94, 63n96, 64n98, 68n113, 68n115, 68nn118–19, 70n124, 156n60
Brauchitsch, Walter von, 321n154, 325
Brown Synod, 190
Brüning, Heinrich (Reich Chancellor), 153, 153n49, 163n90, 120
Buchenwald, 331

Calvin, John, 65n103, 234, 253, 320n146

Index

Canaris, Admiral Walter-Wilhelm, 261, 321, 322, 325, 327, 329, 330
Catechism (Bonhoeffer and Hildebrandt), 155–60
Charlottenburg, 161
"cheap grace," 237, 238, 238n123, 239, 240, 241
Christ and Culture (Niebuhr, H. Richard), 364–66
"Christ and Peace" (Bonhoeffer), 17
Christendom, 148, 175, 219, 277
Christo-Ecclesiology, 130n130, 347, 348, 354
Christology, 8n22, 11, 21, 22, 22n64, 23, 23n59, 24, 25, 27, 28, 28n79, 30, 35, 36, 36n84, 39, 40, 97n72, 129, 130, 152n48, 167, 251n176, 297, 301, 309n111, 317, 318, 319n144, 346, 359, 371, 373; as indicator of Bonhoeffer's forms of political thinking and involvement, 347–57; lectures on, 194, mediator, 241, 242, 298, 349
"The Church and the Peoples of the World" (Bonhoeffer), 217–22
church-state relationship, xiii, 31, 32, 42n1, 60, 62–70, 71, 73, 75–79, 79n6, 80, 93, 93n64, 95, 96, 98, 98n77, 99, 100–104, 106, 128, 133, 136, 138, 139, 142n13, 158–60, 168, 170–72, 175–77, 182n173, 183, 184, 184nn185–86, 185, 186, 186n194, 187, 188, 193–97, 199, 200, 202–7, 212, 213, 213n17, 217n36, 226nn75–77, 228–30, 255n189, 257, 257n193, 259, 261, 267, 268, 270, 272, 273, 274n252, 275, 276, 281, 282, 285n16, 286, 298–300, 308, 309, 326, 334, 336, 341–48, 353–55, 359, 360, 364, 366, 367, 374
church-world relationship, xii, xiii, 4–6, 30–38, 75, 77–80, 106, 109, 133, 136, 139, 147, 192, 196, 199–206, 208, 209, 218, 249, 266, 273–76, 276n253, 280–82, 288, 289, 311, 316, 327, 332–34, 338–44, 346, 347, 357, 359, 360, 369, 371, 374, 375; and political thinking in *Act and Being*, 128–32; and political thinking in the *Catechism*, 158–60; and political thinking in "Die Kirche vor der Judenfrage," 186–88; and political thinking in *Discipleship*, 250–56; and political thinking in *Ethics*, 298–309; and general thinking on and positions on war and peace, 361–68; and political thinking in *Grundfragen einer christlichen Ethik*, 117–19; and political thinking in *Letters and Papers from Prison*, 318–19; and political thinking in "On God's Message of Love to Germany and the Community of Nations," 150–52; and political thinking in *Sanctorum Communio*, 93–104; and political thinking in "The Church and the Peoples of the World," 222; and political thinking in "The Question of the Boundaries of the Church and Church Union," 235–37; and political thinking in "The Theological Basis for the World Alliance," 170–72; and political thinking in "Thy Kingdom Come," 176–77

Church Struggle (*Kirchenkampf*), 34, 66n108, 71n128, 72n129, 131n183, 154, 164, 193n216, 195, 197, 204, 206, 209, 214, 224, 225, 234, 261, 263n221, 265, 265n232, 267, 274, 276, 279, 320, 326, 341–43, 374, 375
Church-Type (Troeltsch), 367, 368
Communist Party (KPD), 46, 47, 53, 141, 153, 162, 172, 178, 188, 209, 223n55, 310
Confessing Church (*Bekennende Kirche*), 1, 5n15, 20n54, 34, 70n126, 128n180, 137, 163, 208, 209, 212, 213, 213n18, 214, 216–18, 218n37, 224, 227, 228, 228n85, 229, 229n87, 230, 231, 231nn96–97, 232–34, 234n111, 235, 257, 257n193, 258, 259, 259n201, 260, 264, 265n232, 266–71, 273, 274, 278n258, 279, 281, 285, 287, 310, 316, 317, 321, 322, 325–27, 329, 333, 335, 335n205, 339, 343, 344
conscience, 42n1, 87, 87n39, 87n41, 102n87, 103, 106, 114, 115, 118, 119, 127, 127n176, 158, 239, 286n21, 288n27, 305, 307, 339n211, 361
conscientious objection, 15, 65, 78, 158, 201, 264, 267, 268, 303, 306, 307, 319n143, 332
Constantine, 65n103, 361, 366
continuity claim (straight and unbroken), 3, 4, 4n14, 12–15, 17, 21, 24–27, 35, 40, 372–74
cor curvum in se, 123, 126n175
Cox, Harvey, 7

Creation and Fall: A Theological Exposition of Genesis 1–3 (Bonhoeffer), 73n136, 179, 179nn162–63
Crusades, the, 361, 362, 364

Dahlem, 190, 193
Dahelm Synod, 224, 224n68, 231n97, 232, 233, 259, 268, 270, 271, 279
Dahelmites, 229, 230
Dawes, Charles, 81
Dawes Plan, 81, 120, 140
Day, Thomas, 116n132, 118, 118n141, 131, 131n184, 136n193
death of God theology, 8, 9, 40
Decree for the Protection of People and State, 178–79
Democratic Party (DDP), 46, 48
deputyship, 300, 300n80, 308, 309n111, 316, 319, 352, 358
"Die Kirche vor der Judenfrage" (Bonhoeffer), 1n3, 42n1, 79n6, 182–88, 344
Diels, Rudolf, 194
Diestal, Superintendent Max, 161
Dietrich Bonhoeffer: Reality and Resistance (Rasmussen), 22, 347
Discipleship (Bonhoeffer), 3, 3n12, 5, 10, 13, 14, 17, 17n49, 24, 40, 219, 237–56, 264n225, 270–76, 276n253, 277, 293, 309n111, 333, 338, 339, 339n213, 340, 343, 350, 350n14, 353, 354, 356, 366, 367
Dohnanyi, Hans von, 187n194, 260, 260n210, 321–23, 325–27, 329, 331
Dramm, Sabine, 2n5
Duchrow, Ulrich, 62, 62n86, 64, 65, 65n100

Duensing, Pastor Friedrich, 234
Dumas, André, 8, 8n22, 10n24, 10n26, 11, 11n27, 22n64
duty, 31, 103, 116, 214, 254, 258n196, 259, 285n13, 288n27, 289, 299, 305, 321, 327, 332, 334, 345

Ebeling, Gerhard, 340
Ecclesiology, 23, 55n51, 82, 94, 95n66, 97n72, 100n85, 126, 130, 130n183, 135, 266, 271, 337, 347, 348, 348n8, 354
Ecumenical Movement, 212n16, 214, 218, 262, 280, 339; Bonhoeffer's participation in, 20n52, 32, 34, 74n136, 128n180, 137–39, 144, 144n23, 145n27, 150, 152, 153–55, 160–72, 179, 191, 192, 198n234, 203, 204, 206, 208, 209, 216, 217, 217n36, 218n37, 259, 260, 263, 266–68, 271, 273, 274, 276, 278n258, 279, 281, 320, 323, 327, 328, 333, 335, 337, 342–44
Eidem, Erling, 269
Einsatzgruppen, 284
elections; church, 139, 162, 173, 173n132, 189, 193, 194, 228, 257; state, 46, 81, 139, 141, 141n7, 142n16, 143, 153, 172, 173, 173n132, 177, 178, 180
Enabling Act (Law for the Removal of the Distress of People and Reich), 181
Engelke, Dr. Fritz, 285
England (Britain),74n136, 224, 227, 229, 257, 259, 260, 265, 265n232, 278, 323, 283, 321n154, 324
enthusiasts (enthusiasm), 50, 79n5, 160n73, 231n96, 237, 240, 240n132, 245, 245n154, 246, 291, 297
Ericksen, Robet P., x, xn2, xi, xii, 55, 55n52, 70n126, 154n52
Eschatology, 90, 92, 99n80, 176, 177, 206n240, 214, 276n253, 362, 362nn33–34, 368
ethics, 22, 22n62, 23, 24, 28, 29, 29n80, 30, 35–37, 39, 42n1, 61n82, 71, 84, 109, 109n111, 110, 115n131, 116, 117, 118n140, 134n189, 147n32, 149, 165, 171, 219, 237n119, 280, 299, 299n76, 300n80, 304n95, 332, 357–61; of everyday life, 21; of tyrannicide, 303–6; *in extremis*, 21, 332; situation, 13, 13n32, 171
Ethics (Bonhoeffer), xiii, 10, 21, 29n80, 39, 42n1, 79n6, 280, 282–98, 302, 303, 305–9, 309n111, 316, 318–20, 322, 236n180, 327, 328, 332, 334, 336–39, 339n213, 340, 340n214, 344, 345, 350, 351, 351n16, 352, 354, 356, 356n24
Evangelical Youth of Germany, 210
extra ecclesiam nulla salus, 233, 234, 234n112

Faith Movement of German Christians (*Deutsche Glaubensbewegung*), 73n136, 79n5, 154, 162
Fanø (conference), 2, 2n10, 5, 217–22, 244, 263, 264, 266–68, 274, 343
Feil, Ernst, 8, 8n22, 22n64, 23n59, 106, 108, 108n107
Final Solution (Holocaust), 282, 284
Finkenwalde, 1n1, 198n231, 198n234, 227, 227n79, 231, 237, 237n119, 256, 259, 267, 268, 270, 271, 274

Index

Fisher, Albert F., 137, 145, 146, 146n28
Forest Hill, 209
France, 44, 48n22, 81, 143n17, 224, 227, 257, 283, 321
Freiwilligkeitkirche, 90
Friedenthal, Charlotte, 325
Friedrich III, Kaiser Wilhelm Nikolaus Karl, 43n3, 44

Gandhi, Mohandas K., 19n51, 215, 215n27, 216; Bonhoeffer's plans to visit, 2, 3n11, 13, 17, 140n5, 265, 265n233, 278
Gauleiter, 173, 181, 225
German Christians (*Deutsche Christen*), 137, 154, 162, 163, 173, 188–90, 190n207, 191, 192n215, 193–97, 203, 204, 208, 210, 210n5, 213, 213n18, 217, 242, 258, 263, 273, 285, 286, 341, 342; Bonhoeffer's resistance to, 139, 191, 194–97, 203, 204, 217, 242, 273, 342
German Christian League, 162
German Faith Movement, 225n72
German National Peoples' Party (DNVP), 47
German People's Party (DVP), 46, 48, 81
Gestapo, 139, 193, 194, 196, 197, 211, 213, 223, 224, 227, 229n90, 230, 230n93, 231, 256, 270, 274, 282, 285, 304n95, 320, 321, 322, 327, 330, 331, 337
Gleichshaltung, 177, 181, 182, 188, 209
Godsey, John, 5n15, 8, 8n22, 9n23, 23n64, 52n40, 237n119, 251n175, 335n205, 356n24
Gollwitzer, Helmut, 234, 236
Göring, Herman, 178, 211

Green, Clifford, 10n25, 21, 21nn57–58, 22, 22n62, 27n75, 28, 29nn80–81, 39, 39n87, 80n7, 83n21, 85nn32–33, 86n37, 87n40, 97n72, 99n81, 104n90, 121n153, 125n172, 128n180, 130n182, 131, 131n186, 136n192, 197n230, 198, 199n235, 299n76, 300n78, 303, 304n95, 306n107, 319n144
Groos, Karl, 52
Grundfragen einer christlichen Ethik, (Bonhoeffer), 109–19

Hamilton, William, 8, 8n20
Harlem, 32, 38, 137, 140, 146, 151, 161, 203
Harnack, Adolf von, 55, 56, 71, 80, 179n163
Hase, Clara von (Countess Kalckreuth), 43n3, 44
Hase, Karl-Alfred von, 43n3, 44, 45, 45n8
Hase, Karl August von, 44
Hedgehogs (*Igel*), 46, 48, 53, 53n42, 54, 54n45
Hegel, Georg Wilhelm Friedrich, 57, 57n61, 59, 71, 78, 83n22, 89, 99, 100n85, 101–3, 114, 117, 132, 133, 199
Heidegger, Martin, 123
Heltmüller, Wilhelm, 52
Henriod, Henry Louis, 217n34, 269
Hess, Rudolph, 323
Heydrich, Reinhard, 285
Hildebrandt, Franz, 155, 156n58, 191, 192n214, 193, 237, 261
Himmler, Heinrich (SS leader), 223, 223n55, 223n60, 226n74, 230, 230n93, 270, 330
Hindenburg, Paul von, 48, 48n22, 81, 153, 177, 178, 182, 189, 210, 211, 263

Hirsch, Emanuel, x, xii, 152n52, 169n117, 193
history, 24, 31, 32n82, 42n1, 57, 57n61, 58n61, 66, 71, 73, 77, 78, 85, 86n38
Hitler, Adolf, ix, ixn1, x, xn3, xi, xii, 1, 1n3, 2, 13, 17, 18n49, 19n51, 24, 34, 42n1, 46, 46n13, 47, 47n20, 48, 48nn21–22, 53, 55n52, 66n108, 70, 70n126, 71n128, 72, 72n128, 72n129, 73, 74n136, 79n5, 79n6, 103, 132, 139, 141n9, 142, 142nn12–13, 144n23, 153, 153n49, 154, 154n54, 163, 188, 189, 190, 190n207, 192, 192n214, 196, 197, 211n10, 212n11, 213, 213n18, 214, 222, 222n54, 224n62, 225, 225n70, 257, 257n192, 258, 258n196, 259, 261, 261n213, 264, 267, 270, 277, 280–84, 284n11, 285, 285n13, 285n16, 309, 310, 319, 319n143, 320, 321, 321n154, 323–28, 330–32, 335, 344, 345n2, 356, 373, 375; as divine, 73, 103; relationship with the churches, 41, 42, 154, 163, 173, 188–92, 196, 197, 211, 213, 214, 225, 226, 228, 229, 258, 259, 264, 270, 277, 281, 285–87, 320; resistance to, 20, 256, 261, 288, 304, 305, 320, 321; rise of, 43, 43n2, 46, 48n22, 53, 70, 70n126, 141, 153, 153n49, 162, 172, 177–82, 206, 208–10, 221–23, 227, 257, 267, 270, 282–84, 309, 310
Hitler Youth, 211
Hitler-Papen Government, 177
Holl, Karl, 80

Holy Spirit, 84n31, 88, 88n45, 89, 89n50, 90, 92, 94, 98, 112, 114n128, 117, 150, 250
Hordern, Richard P., 62, 62nn85–87, 63n90, 63n93, 63n95, 64, 64n97, 64n99, 65n102, 78n4
Horn, Maria, 51
Hossenfelder, Joachim, 162, 182, 189, 210
Huppenkothen, Walter, 330
Husserl, Edmund, 123

idealism, 83, 83n22, 83n25, 84, 84n26, 95n65, 122, 122n157
internationalism, 60, 78, 79n5, 143, 144, 144n23, 148, 155, 161, 162, 163n87, 218, 219
Italy, 74n136, 224, 326

Jacobi, Pastor Gerhard, 192, 194, 198
Jäger, August, 189, 190n207, 193, 212, 216, 224, 225, 228, 267
Jesus Christ, 5n15, 8n22, 24, 25, 58, 74n136, 89, 107, 109n109, 110, 111, 111n114, 131n184, 134n188, 148, 154n52, 159n73, 160n73, 179n163, 198, 215n27, 217n36, 231, 237n119, 238, 239, 239n131, 240, 240n135, 241, 242, 244, 245, 245n154, 246, 247, 247n162, 253, 295n59, 297, 298, 315–18, 345n2, 349, 350, 350n13, 351–53, 354n23, 356, 357, 363, 365, 368; and worldliness, 243, 288–94, 295n56, 298, 301, 314, 350, 351; as "man for others," 129, 130, 130n182, 316–18, 331, 347, 351, 352, 354, 356; as order of preservation, 167, 169, 175

Jews, 39, 47n20, 60, 62, 141, 154n52, 155, 162, 163nn87–88, 179n163, 184, 184nn185–86, 186, 186nn193–94, 187n194, 192n214, 196, 205, 222, 223n55, 223n60, 258, 258n199, 261, 283; Bonhoeffer's actions on behalf of, 38, 49n28, 137, 155, 183, 274, 276, 325, 325n173, 327, 342, 374; persecution of, ix, 45, 181–83, 258, 273, 282, 284, 286, 286n16, 286n21, 287, 287n23, 324, 328, 375
Just War Theory, 18, 26, 28, 34, 36–38, 65, 281, 300, 303, 303n92, 307, 355, 356, 360, 361, 361n32, 362, 362n32, 363n41, 364
justification, 92, 98, 104, 239, 296

Kaftan, Julius, 68n119
Kaiserreich, 42, 46, 47
Kalckreuth, Count Stanislaus (great grandfather), 43n3, 44
Kant, Immanuel, 57n61, 83n22, 121, 122
Kelly, Geffrey B., 29n80, 43n4, 45n8, 49n28, 95n66, 101, 101n86, 102, 105n96, 128n180, 129n181, 143n17, 144n22, 144n24, 145n27, 146n29, 147n36, 156n60, 227n227, 237n119, 251n175, 356n24
Kerrl, Hans, 226, 226n77, 228, 229, 229n87, 230, 231, 231n97, 233, 257, 257n193, 268, 270, 279, 285, 286
Kierkegaard, Søren, 10n26, 71
killing, xii, 18, 22n62, 114, 287, 303, 303n92, 306n107, 309, 361n32, 362, 370
Kittel, Gerhard, x, xii, 154n52

Kleist, Major Ludwig von, 259, 260
Koch, Robert F., 42n1, 73n134, 79n6, 133n187, 172n128, 188n196, 189n202, 190n208, 192n215, 197, 274n252, 344, 345
Kollectivperson, 77, 86, 97n72, 110, 128n180, 132n186, 199, 200
Krause, Reinhold, 210, 210n5
Kristallnacht, 258, 271, 274
Kuhns, William, 19, 19nn51–52, 20, 20n53, 27, 198

Landeskirchen, 67, 162, 182
Lasserre, Jean, 2n8, 19n52, 32, 137, 143, 143n17, 144, 144n24, 145, 145n27, 151, 160n74, 264, 342
Law for the Restoration and Protection of Civil Servants, 181
League of Nations, 81, 192, 192n214, 223, 224n63, 277
Lebensraum, 228, 247, 284
Leffler, Siegfried, 154n52
Lehmann, Marion, 146
Lehman, Paul, 1n2, 14, 146
Leiper, Henry Smith, 260, 320
Lenz, Max, 57
Letters and Papers from Prison (Bonhoeffer), 3n13, 7, 34, 280, 309–19, 334, 339n213, 340, 340n214, 351
Leuthauser, Julius, 154n52
Life Together (Bonhoeffer), 10
London, 262, 263n221, 264, 265, 265n232, 269, 273, 274, 276, 324, 326; Bonhoeffer's sermons from, 216, 261, 266; Bonhoeffer's stay in, 34, 191, 192n214, 195, 207–9, 214, 222–26, 237, 264, 267, 274, 277, 278, 333, 343
Lubbe, Marinus van der, 178

Luther, Martin, 63n90, 63n93, 63n95, 68, 72n129, 73, 95n66, 96n68, 123, 133n187, 155, 156, 156n60, 161, 200, 203, 213n18, 234, 238, 239, 245n154, 248, 253, 282, 347, 348; and conscientious objection/pacifism, 65, 65n100, 65nn102–3, 78, 78nn3–4, 79, 79nn5–6; and the two kingdoms doctrine, 30–32, 62, 64, 64nn97–99, 66, 66n108, 101, 133, 136, 170, 188, 272, 274, 274n252, 293, 293n49, 308, 375; on the Jews, 186, 186n193
Lutheran church(es), 67, 234
Lutheranism, 15, 30–32, 42n1, 51, 64, 64n98, 65n102, 66n108, 67, 73, 75–78, 79nn5–6, 96n68, 123, 133, 133n187, 134n189, 135, 144, 155, 158, 159, 161, 171, 175, 176, 188, 189, 197, 203, 213n18, 231, 234, 240n132, 245, 245n154, 261, 267, 282, 291, 301, 341, 344–46
Lyman, Eugene, 140

Magisterium, Roman Catholic, 361, 361n32
mandates, 295, 295n59, 296n59, 297, 300, 300n80, 307, 308, 351n16
Marcks, Erich, 57
Marsh, Charles, 36, 36n84
Marxism, 46, 100n85, 162, 163n87
Mayer, Rainer, 339, 340n214
Menn, Pastor Wilhelm, 216
military conscription, 259, 260, 272, 319, 321
Minthe, Eckhard, 7, 11
Moltmann, Jürgen, 8, 8n22, 351n16

monastery, 78n4, 208, 209, 226, 238, 248, 266, 276, 282n5, 286, 322, 343, 373
monasticism, 96, 227n79, 238, 238n124, 239, 248, 366
Müller, Hanfried, 8, 8n22, 280n1, 339, 339n213, 340n214
Müller, Ludwig (Reich bishop), 182, 188–91, 191n211, 193, 210, 211, 211n7, 212, 212n12, 212n16, 216, 224–26, 226n77, 228, 230, 261–63, 267, 285
murder, 19n51, 54n48, 103, 112, 114, 115, 119, 153n49, 280, 286n21, 310n116, 311n117

National Socialist German Workers' Party (NSDAP) (Nazi), 48, 141, ix, x, xi, 32–34, 45, 48n22, 49, 56, 59, 59n72, 61n80, 72, 73, 73n134, 74n136, 75, 128n180, 137, 139, 141, 141n7, 142, 142nn13–14, 142n16, 143, 153, 154, 154nn52–53, 155, 157, 162, 164, 172, 173, 177–82, 187n194, 189, 190, 190n207, 196, 206–8, 210n5, 211n7, 212, 213, 213n18, 217, 223, 223n55, 223n60, 224n62, 225, 225n72, 226nn74–75, 226n77, 227, 229, 230, 230nn92–93, 231, 251n175, 257n193, 258, 260, 263, 271, 278, 280, 284–86, 286n21, 287, 288, 307, 311n117, 321n152, 322, 327, 329–31, 341, 343
nationalism, x, 31n82, 41, 44, 45, 49, 60, 65, 68, 74n136, 78, 79n5, 102, 104n90, 118, 119n142, 121, 132, 138, 139, 142, 142n13, 143, 144,

nationalism (cont.)
144n23, 145, 145n27, 148,
149, 151, 154n52, 156,
160n74, 162, 200, 218, 219,
228, 284
natural law, 298, 357
necessità, 302
neo-Rankeans, 57
New Testament, 110, 112, 114n128,
234n112, 255n189, 366, 367
Niebuhr, H. Richard, 364–66
Niebuhr, Reinhold, 3n11, 140, 146,
147n32, 150n46, 260, 278,
281, 337
Niemöller, Martin, 163, 190, 192,
192n214, 195, 211, 211n10,
212n12, 213n18, 228,
228n85, 229, 229n87, 231,
257, 261, 270, 277
Nietzsche, Friedrich, 31n82, 110,
111, 114, 116n132
Night of the Long Knives (Blood
purge), 210, 210n3, 215, 223
non-violence, 18n49, 39
Nuttall, Geoffrey F., 16n47, 362n35,
366, 367

Oeynhausen Synod, 229, 231
Old Prussian Union (church),
47n20, 61n82, 67, 68, 189
Old Testament, 109n109, 154n52,
179, 179n163, 210n5, 262
"On God's Message of Love
to Germany and the
Community of Nations"
(Bonhoeffer), 147–52
"Operation 7," 325, 325n173,
327–29
orders of creation, 61, 61nn81–82,
69, 73n136, 78, 100, 100n83,
102, 118n140, 138, 154n52,
156, 156n60, 164, 164n91,
166, 167, 167n105, 168, 171,
180, 188, 195, 202, 203, 218,
348–49

orders of preservation, 138, 167–69,
171, 175, 180, 183, 188, 202,
203, 349
Oster, General Major Hans, 261,
321–23, 325, 327, 329
otherworldliness, 173, 174, 248
Ott, Heinrich, 8, 8n22
Oxford Conference, 268, 269

pacifism, 1nn1–2, 2n9, 3, 3nn12–
13, 4, 5, 11, 12, 14n41, 15,
15n45, 16, 16nn46–48, 17,
17n49, 18–20, 20nn53–54,
21, 22n63, 24–28, 28n78, 29,
29n80, 35–40, 50n30, 50n32,
51, 55n50, 65, 71n128, 78,
78n4, 79, 79n5, 103, 104,
109, 117, 119, 137, 139, 140,
140n5, 144, 144n22, 149,
149n43, 155, 160nn73–75,
161, 162, 163n87, 169, 171,
198, 203, 207, 222, 231n96,
246, 251n176, 267, 276,
278, 300, 302n89, 303n92,
328, 333, 334, 339, 341–43,
345, 346, 355, 356, 358, 361,
361n32, 362, 362nn32–33,
362n35, 363n41, 364–66,
369–72, 374; absolute, 2n10,
12, 12n31, 13, 33, 34, 200,
205, 209, 218, 221, 266,
334, apolitical (world-withdrawn), 33, 160, 205, 209,
264, 266, 307, 342; humanist,
168; provisional, militant,
struggle, political, or worldly,
14, 32, 33, 138, 151, 151n47,
160, 171–73, 276
Papen, Franz von, 163n90, 172, 177,
178
Pastors' Emergency League
(*Pfarrernotbund*), 139, 163,
190, 192, 192n214, 195, 208,
210, 211, 212n12, 261
Paton, William, 324

Index

Paul's Letter to Philemon, 252
peace, 1, 2nn8–9, 3, 14–16, 20n52, 21, 22n62, 26, 31, 32, 39, 47n20, 50n30, 57n61, 60, 65n103, 76, 79n5, 81, 103, 128n180, 132, 140, 143, 143n17, 144, 145, 145n27, 148, 149, 149nn42–43, 150–52, 153n49, 155, 156, 156n57, 156n60, 157–59, 159n73, 160, 160n74, 160n75, 161, 162, 168, 168n117, 169, 171, 172, 192, 200, 201, 207, 209, 215n26, 219–22, 224, 244, 255, 266, 267, 268, 272–74, 303, 306n107, 320, 321, 323, 324, 328, 342, 343, 345, 346, 353–55, 358–64, 370, 373, 374
penultimate (and ultimate), 180, 296, 297, 297n68, 298, 307
Pfeiefer, Hans, 49
Phillips, John, 7n18, 11n28, 23n59, 58n63, 76n1, 89n50, 130n183, 251n176, 335n204, 337, 337n208, 348n8
pietism, 66n108, 91, 313–15
Point 24 (Article 24), 141, 163, 163n88, 181
Poland, 223, 223n62, 257, 257n92, 282–85, 321, 321n152
post-Kantian idealism, 122
private virtuousness, 288, 288n27, 289, 305
Provisional Church Administration, 265
Prussian Synod, 228, 310
Przywara, Erich, 123

"The Question of the Boundaries of the Church and Church Union" (Bonhoeffer), 231–37

Ranke, Leopold von, 57, 57n61

Rasmussen, Larry, 1n2, 2n10, 11n28, 12, 13, 13n35, 14, 14n41, 15, 15n45, 22, 22n63, 23–25, 27, 28nn78–79, 115n131, 118, 118n140, 149n43, 151n47, 152n48, 200, 201, 289nn31–32, 299n76, 300n80, 302n89, 303, 303n92, 304n98, 309n111, 319, 319nn142–143, 347, 354
Reformation (Protestant), 62, 68, 72n128, 79n5, 183, 190, 191, 195, 240n132, 245, 292
Reformed Church, 67, 189
Reich Church, 163, 182, 189, 217, 218n37, 232, 234n112, 259, 262, 264, 266, 268, 269, 269n244, 271, 273, 279, 286
Reinhardt, Max, 80n11
religion, 7, 58, 59, 71, 82, 174, 181, 183, 290, 311, 311n118; as inwardness, 312, 313, 315, 319; as metaphysics, 312, 315, 319
"religionless Christianity," 8, 311, 312n120, 316, 318, 339, 339n211
Rentenmark, 81
revelation, 2n9, 7, 8n22, 57, 57n61, 58, 58n61, 61n82, 71, 72n129, 73n134, 73n136, 91, 95n66, 103n88, 121, 121n154, 122, 123, 123n165, 124, 124n165, 125, 125n169, 125n171, 126, 127, 127n177, 128, 128n180, 129, 129n181, 130n183, 131, 131n184, 132, 135, 166, 166n102, 167, 169, 206n240, 213n17, 234n112, 292, 293, 311, 311n118, 314, 348n8, 358
Reynolds, Terrence, 198, 199n235
Ritschl, Albrecht, 58

Roeder, Manfred, 329
Röhm, Ernst, 210
Roman Catholic Center Party, 43, 46, 47
Roman Catholic Church, 67, 92n61, 142, 236
Rome, 55, 55n51, 76, 130n183, 321
Rommel, Erwin, 283, 284
Rössler, Helmut, 147, 147n37, 148
Rott, Paster Wilhelm, 325

Sack, Dr. Karl, 261
Sanctorum Communio (Bonhoeffer), 80–104, 117, 126, 128, 129, 130n182, 131, 135, 342, 347–48, 352
Sasse, Hermann, 163n88, 234n113
Scheler, Max, 86n35, 123
Schlatter, Adolf, 52
Schleicher, Kurt von (General and Chancellor), 177
Schönfeld, Pastor Hans, 218, 263, 268, 269
Schmidhuber, Adolf Wilhelm, 327
Schutzstaffeln (SS), 223
sect (sectarianism), 33, 77, 91, 92, 92nn60–61, 93, 95–97, 97n72, 102, 102n87, 104, 112, 131, 131n186, 135, 159, 165, 205, 207, 209, 213n18, 234–36, 251, 255, 255n187, 273, 282, 289, 342, 343, 366, 367
Sect-type (Troeltsch), 367, 368
secular/secularity, 7, 34, 52, 59, 63, 64, 64n98, 68, 152, 173, 174, 174n138, 175, 238, 239, 246–49, 252, 254, 255, 255n189, 256, 272, 275, 280n1, 281, 292, 295, 297, 308, 309, 309n111, 311, 317–19, 327, 328, 331–34, 335n205, 340, 344, 351n16, 353, 360, 367, 368, 374

Seeberg, Reinhold, 56–62, 66, 71, 102, 103, 103n88, 121, 132, 133; as Bonhoeffer's dissertation mentor, 80, 89n50, 199
Sein, Herberto, 2n8, 145
Sermons; Barcelona, 105n96, 106–9, 116, 119, 134n188, 155; London, 216, 261, 266
Sermon on the Mount (*Bergpredigt*), 20n52, 32, 39, 77, 110, 112–14, 117, 134n189, 138, 144, 160, 166, 166n102, 198, 201, 202, 202n238, 203, 207, 216, 227n79, 237, 237n119, 247, 247n162, 255, 255n189, 272, 273, 275, 276, 278n258, 298, 333, 334, 342, 343, 348, 350, 353–56, 358, 360, 365, 368, 373–75; Bonhoeffer designates as central Gospel message, 32, 166, 201, 202, 272, 274, 350, 355, 356, 358, 360, Gandhi and, 3n11; in *Discipleship*, 243–45, 274, 350n14, 366, 367; Luther/Lutheran interpretation, 159, 159n73, 160n73, 245n154
sin, 31, 63, 74n136, 77, 89, 91, 92, 95, 95n66, 96, 98, 99, 101, 103, 104, 106–8, 115–17, 119, 127n176, 135, 136, 148, 156, 156n60, 157, 160n73, 165, 166, 166n101, 167, 167n105, 168, 176, 177, 179n163, 186n93, 199, 200, 215n27, 238, 245, 250, 296, 298, 306, 312–14, 338, 359, 363; as communal, 86n37, 87nn39–41, 88, 88n42
Social Democrat Party (SPD), 42, 46, 48, 81, 120, 140

Social Teaching of the Christian Churches, The (Troeltsch), 64n98, 367–8
Stab in the back theory, 47n20
Stählin, Wilhelm, 164n91
state, xii, 31, 32, 42n1 55–57, 59, 60, 61n83, 62, 71, 71n128, 72, 72n129, 73, 74n136, 75–79, 79n6, 80, 93, 93n64, 98, 98n77, 99, 99n81, 100, 100n85, 101–4, 106, 128, 132, 133, 133n87, 134–36, 138, 139, 141, 142n13, 154n52, 157–60, 162, 165, 168, 170–72, 175–77, 179–82, 182n173, 183, 184, 184nn185–86, 185, 185n186, 185n189, 186–89, 193–97, 199–207, 212, 213, 213n17, 217n36, 226n75, 226n77, 228, 229, 229n90, 230, 231, 245n154, 255n189, 257, 259, 267–74, 274n252, 275, 276, 281, 282, 285n16, 286, 298, 299, 299n76, 300, 302, 303, 308, 309, 310n116, 326, 328, 332, 334, 336, 341–49, 353–55, 358–60, 364, 366, 367, 374
statecraft (*Staatskunst*), 301, 302
status confessionis, 191
status quo, 13, 30–32, 42, 42n1, 43, 43n3, 44, 45, 49, 75, 78, 133, 134, 136, 203, 296, 301
Stauffenberg, Claus von, 329, 330
Stellvertretung, 300
Stöhr, Hermann, 260n206
Strasser, Gregor, 173
Stresemann, Gustav, 46, 81, 120, 135, 135n191, 140
Stuckart, Wilhelm, 226
Sturmabteilung (SA), 53, 141, 210
Sutz, Erwin, 227n79, 237
Sweden (Bonheffer's travel to), 268, 269, 269n244, 270, 325, 331

Tegel, 3, 197, 329, 330, 331, 372
"The Theological Basis for the World Alliance" (Bonhoeffer), 164–72, 202n238, 349n10, 358n28
Third Reich, 49n28, 73, 178, 345; and the Christian churches, 141n10, 154n54, 162, 163n88, 210n3, 284n11, 287; rise of, 43, 43n2, 48n22, 73, 208, 210n3, 284n11; surrender, 310
Thomism, 123
Thüringen German Christians, 154n52, 162
"Thy Kingdom Come" (Bonhoeffer), 172–77
Tillich, Paul, x, xi, 7, 154n54
Tödt, Heinz Eduard, 39, 39n86
transcendentalism, 122, 122n158
transcendence; ethical, 94, 107, 130n182; social tramscendence, 94, 347; this worldly, 31, 85, 94, 107, 129, 313, 316, 318
Troeltsch, Ernst, 56n53, 64n98, 80, 80n10, 92, 92nn60–61, 255, 255n189, 367, 367n53, 368
Tübingen (Bonheffer's experience at), 52, 52n40, 53, 55, 55n50, 76, 82n18, 134
Two Kingdoms (realms or regiments) Doctrine, 30, 101, 183, 187, 205, 207, 274, 275, 281, 291–93, 298, 308, 309, 336, 343, 347, 375; and Luther, 62, 293, 293n49; and pacifism, 33, 34; and the Weimar Republic, 65–66; and tyrannicide, 34; and war theology, 66; Bonhoeffer's adherence to, 31–34, 71, 79, 101, 133, 134, 138, 170, 175, 183, 184, 187, 188, 196,

Two Kingdoms, Bonhoeffer's adherence to (*cont.*)
203–7, 272, 274, 275, 281, 282, 298, 299, 308, 309, 336, 341, 343, 347, 375; conservative interpretations, 31, 64, 70, 78, 79, 133, 134, 175, 184, 203, 272, 283, 299, 336, 341; liberal interpretations, 32, 63–65, 71, 138, 170, 188, 196, 204, 206, 272, 336, 343
two-sphered thinking, 25, 33, 102, 252–56, 273, 275, 281, 289, 291–93, 297, 307, 313, 315, 316, 318, 319, 327, 334, 339, 340, 343, 375
tyrannicide, xiii, 16n48, 17, 18, 22, 24–29, 34, 36, 39, 40, 281, 336, 369, 370, 374; Bonhoeffer's involvement in, 3, 3n13, 4, 5, 11, 16, 20–22, 24, 29n80, 37, 346, 356; Bonhoeffer's justification for, 299–309, 332, 345, 356, 358

Ulms Rifle Troops, 53
ultima ratio, 302, 302n89, 303n92, 304, 304n98
Union Theological Seminary, 1n2, 19n52, 32, 137, 140, 140n3, 143, 143n17, 145, 146, 146n31, 147, 161, 320, 320n146
United Prussian Church (Old Prussian Union), 67, 68, 189
United States, 3n13, 34, 74n136, 143n17, 186n194, 260, 283

Versailles Treaty, 53, 60, 81, 120, 222n54, 224, 224n63, 227, 257n192, 270, 324, 326
vicarious representative action (responsibility), 21, 102n87, 300, 301, 306n107, 352

visible church/invisible church, 90, 95, 95nn66–67, 96n68, 135, 148, 231–35, 247–49, 251, 273, 275, 308, 333, 350
Visser t' Hooft, Willem, 323, 324, 326
Voelker, 115
Völker, 114
Volk, 57, 59–61, 75, 78, 99, 102, 103, 103n88, 113–17, 119n142, 145, 152n48, 164n91, 200, 218, 345, 357
Volkgeist, 57, 59
Volkisch, 78, 104n90, 119n142, 138, 139, 223n55
Volkskirche, 68, 69, 90, 96, 104, 104n90, 133, 200, 236, 265n232, 367
Volkspartie, 135, 135n191,
Volkstheologie, 118n140
voluntary church, 68, 69, 90, 91, 95, 96, 96n68, 102, 104, 236, 245

Wall Street crash, 120, 140
war, ix, 2n9, 12, 14–16, 26, 31, 34, 35, 38, 42, 52, 57, 59, 60, 62, 63, 65, 65n103, 71, 75, 78, 79n5, 93, 103, 103n88, 104, 109, 112–16, 118, 119, 119n142, 121, 132–34, 134n189, 135, 138, 143, 145, 145n27, 149, 149nn41–42, 151, 155, 156, 156n57, 157–59, 160n73, 165, 166, 167n104, 169, 169n119, 171, 172, 192, 192n214, 200, 201, 203, 218–22, 224, 227, 228, 245, 245n154, 254, 255, 255n189, 257, 264, 264n225, 267, 274, 275, 281–88, 300–302, 302n89, 303, 303n92, 304, 304n98, 307–10, 311n117, 312n120, 321, 322, 328, 332, 334, 343,

war (cont.)
    345, 346, 355, 357, 359, 360,
    361–68, 374, 375
War Theology (*Kriegstheologie*), x,
    59, 59n68, 61, 61n82, 102,
    114
Ward, Harry F., 147, 161
Webber, Charles C., 147, 147n35
Weber, Karl "Max," 80, 92, 92n60,
    92n61, 102n87
Wedemeyer, Maria von, 307
Weikart, Richard, 13n32, 31n82
Weimar Republic, 30, 41, 46–48,
    48n22, 49, 53, 55n49, 56, 60,
    80, 105, 120, 132–34, 142n14,
    177, 181; fall of, 43n2, 47,
    48n22, 52, 120, 140, status of
    the churches in, 62–70
Weissbach, Jürgen, 351n16
Weissler, Dr., 230
Weizsäcker, Carl Friedrich von,
    312n121
Werner, Dr., 257 258n196
"What is the Church?"
    (Bonhoeffer), 176, 176n152,
    206n241
Wilm, Werner, 154
Wieneke, Dr. Friedrich, 162
Wilhelm, Kaiser II, 43n3, 44, 45,
    45n8, 71
Wilhemine Empire, 42, 47, 57n61
Word and Sacrament, 77, 93, 133,
    203, 231, 348, 353
Word of God, 58, 59, 72, 72n129,
    74n136, 92, 92nn60–61, 98,
    124, 136n193, 139, 147, 179,
    213n17, 228, 233, 358

World Alliance for Promoting
    International Friendship,
    2n9, 137, 155, 160, 160n75,
    161, 164n92, 168, 179, 180,
    217n34
"world come of age," xii, 7, 8, 9n23,
    251n175, 312, 318, 319, 339,
    340n214
World War I, 46, 50, 50n30, 64n98,
    224n62, 345
worldliness, 60, 135, 165, 166,
    174, 175, 207, 251, 292, 293,
    293n49, 311, 314, 315, 318,
    335, 335n205, 337, 342,
    351n16, 360
Wurm, Bishop, 212, 287, 287n23,
    310, 310n117

Yoder, John Howard, 16, 16n46,
    71n128
Young Plan, The, 120, 140
Young Reformers Movement, 139,
    192, 192n215, 193, 193n216,
    208
"The Younger Generation's Altered
    View of the Concept of
    Führer" (Bonhoeffer radio
    address), 1n3, 180

Zerner, Ruth, 56nn54–56, 60n75,
    61n83, 62n84, 98n77,
    100n85, 133n187, 184n185,
    186n194
Zöllner, Wilhelm, 228
"Zossen Files," 330